A Gift of Tongues

A Gift of Tongues

Critical Challenges in Contemporary American Poetry

Edited by

Marie Harris and Kathleen Aguero

The University of Georgia Press
Athens and London

© 1987 by the University of Georgia Press
Athens, Georgia 30602
"Documentaries and Declamadores" © 1987 by Martín Espada
"The Influence of Anxiety" © 1985 by Annette Kolodny
"Caste, Class, and Canon" © 1987 by Paul Lauter

Designed by Kathi L. Dailey
Set in 11 on 13 Mergenthaler Electra with Antique Olive
The paper in this book meets the guidelines for permanence and
durability of the Committee on Production Guidelines for Book
Longevity of the Council on Library Resources.

Printed in the United States of America

91 90 89 88 87   5 4 3 2 1

Library of Congress Cataloging in Publication Data

A Gift of tongues.

  Bibliography: p.
  1. American poetry—20th century—History and criticism.
  2. American poetry—Minority authors—History and criticism.
  3. Canon (Literature) I. Harris, Marie. II. Aguero, Kathleen.
PS153.M56G54 1987   811'.5'09920693   87-1042
ISBN 0-8203-0952-4 (alk. paper)
ISBN 0-8203-0953-2 (pbk.: alk. paper)

British Library Cataloging in Publication Data available.

To all the editors who have brought the work of important and neglected poets into print.

May they flourish!

Contents

 **Preface**

It is the poet's gift to communicate across boundaries created by class and culture. The American poet speaks in a voice that incorporates and echoes, perhaps more than in any other country, many languages and traditions, resulting in an extraordinarily various literature. A *Gift of Tongues* has been compiled to celebrate and evaluate this diversity. The contemporary canon, as defined in anthologies and reflected in critical works, does not, unfortunately, accurately portray this variety. Collections of poetry with titles that suggest they contain the work of our important poets offer disappointingly few surprises: the poets are of similar backgrounds and usually draw upon the shared assumptions of the dominant culture. Likewise, critical volumes attend to these same poets, while those outside the dominant culture are relegated to "special" status and effectively denied the support and challenge serious criticism provides.

We must begin to break down the boundaries that divide our literature as artificially as any map, to introduce to a wider audience some of the poets who have been ignored, and to propose that a new canon be developed that more fairly represents the range and cross-referential nature of American poetry.

Critical responses are learned. We understand those experiences which are familiar to us; we value subject matter and forms that we have been taught to value. The process of enlarging the scope of what is currently considered to be American poetry involves the use of new critical tools to work with a far larger body of work than has yet been acknowledged. We have been taught to hear a narrow band of voices; we can learn to hear many more.

It is not our purpose further to divide American poets into categories. Yet, ironically, it may be that only by drawing attention to poets who have been perceived as falling into this or that category can they be recognized as authentic claimants to a place in a real American canon.

In collecting essays for this book, we have undertaken a task that is far from completed. While these essays grow from many literary and political viewpoints, we are aware that there are traditions not represented here. This collection, therefore, must be seen as a beginning, an example of the kind of criticism needed to challenge the student of poetry—within and outside of the university—to explore further. All the voices that have contributed to the shape of our language, all the traditions that have enriched our poetry must be attended to in order that an integration can be achieved.

The tone and style of the essays are diverse, as is consistent with a poetry and criticism often developed outside academia. Our authors chose their own subject matter within the guidelines of the book. Some discuss problems within the existing canon, some write overviews of particular groups of writers, others focus on specific poets. These last are intended to serve as examples of the kind of detailed consideration necessary to acquaint readers with "uncanonized" poets and are not meant to promote one writer to the exclusion of others.

The work of the poets discussed here is available to the interested reader, but much of it is difficult to locate, consigned as it has been to small publications. We have tried, with the help of our critics, to include sufficient information to make possible the acquisition of the work. We are also planning a companion poetry anthology that will make available in a single volume poetry that has been ignored or underrepresented in anthologies of American poetry.

If it is true that the poet speaks to everyone, it is essential that the listener not hear selectively, responding only to the familiar voice, the expected message. Poets have a gift of tongues. It is our responsibility and delight to hear them when they speak.

Marie Harris
Kathleen Aguero

 # Acknowledgments

We editors would like to extend our thanks and appreciation to our authors, who stood by this project throughout its labyrinthine course toward publication; to Charter Weeks and Richard Hoffman, who encouraged us to keep going; to Houston Baker, who pointed the way to this book's final destination; to the anonymous reader of all the versions of this book, who provided invaluable criticism and insight; to Annette Kolodny and Joseph Bruchac for their advice; and to Karen Orchard, for her commitment to our project.

The editors and publisher gratefully acknowledge these poets and publishers for permission to reprint the material listed.

Lucille Clifton, "what the mirror said," from *Two-Headed Woman*, published by the University of Massachusetts Press. By permission of the author.

Lucha Corpi, "Como la semilla en espera/Like the seed that waits," from *Palabras de Mediodia/Noon Words*, translated by Catherine Rodriguez-Nieto, published by El Fuego de Aztlan Publications. By permission of the author.

Margarita Cota-Cárdenas, "Soliloquio Travieso," from *Noches despertando en conciencias*, published by Scorpion Press. By permission of the author.

Lance Henson, "comanche ghost dance an impression" and "at chadwick's bar and grill," from *Selected Poems*. By permission of the publisher, the Greenfield Review Press.

Robert Peters, "Ann at twilight, Ann / at dawn," from *The Gift To Be Simple: A Garland for Ann Lee*. By permission of the author and the publisher, Liveright Publishing Corporation. Copyright 1973, 1974, 1975 by Robert Peters.

Wendy Rose, "Walking on the Prayerstick," from *Lost Copper*. By permission of the author and publisher, Malki Museum Press.

Steve Abbott and Rudy Kikel's essay, "In Search of a Muse: The Politics of Gay Poetry," originally appeared in *The Advocate*. Reprinted by permission of Liberation Publications, Inc.

P. J. Laska's essay, "Poetry at the Periphery," appeared in different forms in both *The Arts Journal* and *Hyperion*.

George Ella Lyon's essay, "Contemporary Appalachian Poetry: Sources and Directions," appeared in a slightly different form in *The Kentucky Review*.

Raymond Patterson's essay, "What's Happening in Black Poetry?" appeared in a slightly different form in *The Poetry Review*, published by the Poetry Society of America.

Carmen Tafolla's essay, "Chicano Literature: Beyond Beginnings," was based on a briefer commentary with the same title in *Southern Exposure*.

A Gift of Tongues

The Bones of This Body Say, Dance

Self-Empowerment in Contemporary Poetry by Women of Color

We Were Never Meant to Survive: Resistance to Violence

Anger, resistance, and transformation, sexuality, self-knowledge, and joy, language, memory, and history: all these are crucial aspects of the theme of self-empowerment in the poetry of North American women of color.

Third World feminists have begun to devote their primary creative energies to conversations with each other. The economic, social, and political conditions of their lives appear in their poems as challenges to the institutions of white male privilege. Although Margaret Atwood and others have observed that all women have been colonized under patriarchy, the term "colonization" is often a *metaphor* for white women's experience.[1] It is a historical *reality* for most black women, whose ancestors were slaves and who may themselves have witnessed or been survivors of incidents of racial violence. For Native Americans and Asian Americans, "colonization" refers to the experience of living on reservations or in internment camps; for Latina women, to the economic and cultural exploitation of Latin America by the United States.

For Third World women, the journey to power and selfhood necessarily begins with an unflinching examination of these aspects of racism. The journey to transcendence, to self-celebration, begins with

1

anger at cultural, economic, physical, and psychic violence. Resistance to violence, the determination—even in the face of death—to not be a victim empowers the poetry of Third World women writers. Poems which reflect direct violence against people of color are often appropriately direct in their fury. In June Jordan's "Poem about Police Violence," for instance, the poet demands:

> tell me something
> what you think would happen if
> everytime they kill a black boy
> then we kill a cop
> everytime they kill a black man
> then we kill a cop
>
> you think the accident rate would lower
> subsequently?[2]

In Safiya Henderson's defiant poem "harlem/soweto," the poet denies the separation of the Afro-American struggle against racist oppression from the courage of South African freedom fighters like Winnie and Nelson Mandela, whose spirits remain unbroken in the face of the overwhelming viciousness and violence of Botha's white South African regime. The poem ends with a brilliant sequence of images in which the unity of the spirit world and the natural world empower the unity of a resistance in which possessing one and not many tongues (metaphorically, being of one mind, speaking the same language) acquires a wonderfully visceral actual meaning:

> we are woven
> inseparable as sky
> with one sun
>> one moon
>> one tongue
>> rolled to spit
>> in one
>> eye . . .[3]

Resistance takes many forms. Audre Lorde's "Power" warns that power is not the simple possession of the means of violence. She refuses to accept a vision of power or revolution in which oppressed people turn the tables on their oppressors.[4] In her essay "Uses of the

Erotic: The Erotic as Power," Lorde suggests that power is not a *thing*, a quantity, but an inner source enabling the deepest feeling.[5] Real power—not that fraudulent concoction that passes for power in a racist, sexist, classist society—is not power over other's lives but power over one's own life. Unlike a kind of power that is rooted in physical force, political domination, and economic subjugation, Lorde insists that power resides in individual awareness and integrity; it is claimed by the individual and is something that can be neither bestowed nor wrested away. In claiming that one's "power rises / . . . from the same source / as [one's] pain," Lorde is suggesting in "For Each of You" that real power requires profound self-knowledge, and the process of acquiring such knowledge inevitably causes pain.[6] In this conception, power is a means to individual transformation. Like the Reverend Dr. Martin Luther King or Mahatma Gandhi, Lorde insists that the use of this power *is* the revolution and will engender the muscular, cohesive vision that makes social revolution possible.

Gwendolyn Brooks' "The Boy Died in My Alley" also explores violence by focusing on the issue of individual transformation. In the poem, the literal cause of the violent death of a black boy whose blood, whose body "ornaments [the poet's] alley," remains unmentioned. Indeed, no possible cause is ever speculated about, encouraging the reader to consider the multiple ways in which young black men in this country mysteriously end up dead: deaths that are alcohol or drug related, products of gang warfare, a robbery gone awry, police violence, suicide—all of these are secondary causes to racism, poverty, powerlessness, and despair. The poet acknowledges a sorrowful and determined responsibility for the death of the boy, and in so doing teaches each of us the tragic consequences of "knowledgeable unknowing," of ever failing to act against oppression and violence:

> I never saw his face at all.
> I never saw his futurefall.
> But I have known this Boy.
>
> I have always heard him deal with death.
> I have always heard the shout, the volley.
> I have closed my heart-ears late and early.
> And I have killed him ever.[7]

Brooks insists upon accountability, not self-indulgent guilt; it is that accountability, as well as Brooks' compassion, which transforms the waste of a young man's life into not only the hope for a different world but a call to action.

Lucille Clifton's "Miss Rosie," a poem about an impoverished, mentally confused older black woman reduced in the eyes of the world to bag-lady status, pivots on a similar theme of accountability and commitment. Like the boy who died in the alley, Miss Rosie, a "wet brown bag of a woman / who used to be the best looking gal in Georgia," is a castoff of society, discarded like yesterday's garbage, a parallel made explicit in the poem. This terrible disregard of the value of a human life ignites in the speaker of the poem a fierce and determined resistance fueled by compassion. The refrain "when I watch you," which in its first two usages sets the stage for images of destruction and human waste, is used a third time in the poem but with a twist; the final lines of the poem are an affirmation and a vow, a promise never to stand by and watch the destruction but to stand up and fight against it. With dignity and with love, the speaker announces:

> when I watch you
>
> .   .   .   .   .   .
>
> I stand up
> through your destruction
> I stand up.[8]

In another Clifton poem, "For de Lawd," we see how the capacity to not only survive but aspire, to be "contrary and self-affirming across continents and generations" (what critic Chinosole has referred to in black women as "matrilineal diaspora," the "strength and beauty [black women] pass on as friends and lovers from foremothers to mothers and daughters"), is an important source for Clifton's resistance.[9] A tradition of resistance to oppression, a legacy of will and respect for possibilities, can elicit from characters or individuals a willingness to hold on to what is difficult. The speaker in this poem, like the speaker in many other poems by Clifton, and by June Jordan, Audre Lorde, Alice Walker, and other black feminist writers as well, acknowledges the importance of that historical tradition and names herself part of it. In the face of generations of racial violence, the speaker in the poem refuses to be paralyzed by grief. She draws upon the resolute tenacity and strength of generations of black women across the diaspora, declaring simply:

> . . . I got a long memory
> and I come from a line
> of black and going on women.[10]

Sometimes survival itself in the context of racial violence is sufficient cause for celebration. In "Anchorage," Native American poet Joy Harjo draws a portrait of a woman on a park bench who could be Miss Rosie's sister:

> . . . someone's Athabascan
> grandmother, folded up, smelling like 200 years
> of blood and piss, her eyes closed against some
> unimagined darkness, where she is buried in an ache
> in which nothing makes
>   sense.[11]

Like Clifton, Harjo names the cast-aside of society as family, "claim[s] her / as our own history . . . know[s] that our dreams / don't end here." The poem recounts the improbable, actual story of another survival, Henry's:

> And I think of the 6th Avenue jail, of mostly Native
> and Black men, where Henry told about being shot at
> eight times outside a liquor store in L.A., but when
> the car sped away he was surprised he was alive,
> no bullet holes, man, and eight cartridges strewn
> on the sidewalk
>   all around him.

> Everyone laughed at the impossibility of it,
> but also the truth. Because who would believe
> the fantastic and terrible story of all of our survival
> those who were never meant
>   to survive?[12]

The poem, dedicated to Audre Lorde, echoes in its final lines Lorde's "A Litany for Survival," which ends with an affirmation to move beyond fear and silence into language and action:

> . . . when we are silent
> we are still afraid.

So it is better to speak
remembering
we were never meant to survive. [13]

Incidents such as the 1979 savage murders of thirteen black women
in the Roxbury section of Boston and, more recently, the murder of
twenty-seven black children in Atlanta have inspired poems of anguish
and resistance. The poetic images are as visceral and devastating as the
actual events they describe. Poems such as Jayne Cortez's "Rape,"
Donna Allegra's "A Rape Poem for Men," or Audre Lorde's "Need"
often do not suggest any semblance of conventional poetic diction and
syntax, as if the nightmare being named demands an immediate, unmediated description. These poems derive tremendous impact from
their escalating cadences. As readers are caught up in the increasing
momentum of the poem, they experience viscerally (through breath,
while reading silently or aloud) the horror of the situation, as in the
final lines of Ntozake Shange's "with no immediate cause":

> . . . "there is some concern
> that alleged battered women
> might start to murder their
> husbands & lovers with no
> immediate cause"
> i spit up   i vomit   i am screaming
> we all have immediate cause
> every 3 minutes
> every 5 minutes
>
> every 10 minutes
> every day
> women's bodies are found
> in alleys & bedrooms / at the top of the stairs
> before i ride the subway / buy a paper / drink
> coffee / i must know /
> have you hurt a woman today
> did you beat a woman today
> throw a child across a room
>   are the lil girl's panties
>   in yr pocket
> did you hurt a woman today
>
> i have to ask these obscene questions

the authorities require me to
establish immediate cause

every three minutes
every five minutes
every ten minutes
every day.[14]

In her repeating lines about time (every three minutes, every five minutes), Shange forces the reader to experience *frequency*, not as statistical, but as minute-to-minute time, life being eradicated *while you are reading*, every day.

Ntozake Shange's choreopoem *For Colored Girls Who Have Considered Suicide / When the Rainbow Is Enuf*, like Alice Walker's novel, *The Color Purple*, has unleashed a tidal wave of controversy in the black community for exposing the sexism and violence of some black men. Historically, black male violence, in fact and myth, has been used by whites to foster racist assumptions about black men rather than to demonstrate the pervasiveness, across cultural boundaries, of misogyny. Thus, until very recently, it has been a matter of survival for black women to gloss over their anger and despair.

Audre Lorde has written eloquently on the necessity of black women breaking silence about violence within the black community:

> . . . In this country, black women traditionally have had
> compassion for everybody else except ourselves. We cared for
> whites because we had to for pay or survival; we cared for our
> children and our fathers and our brothers and our lovers. We
> need to also learn to care for ourselves. Our history and
> popular culture, as well as our personal lives, are full of tales of
> black women who had "compassion for misguided black men."
> Our scarred, broken, battered and dead daughters and sisters
> are a mute testament to that.[15]

Poems in which women refuse to be victimized by men are not only affirming and necessary for women's lives but for men's lives as well. As critic Barbara Smith has insisted:

> Acknowledging the sexism of Black men does not mean that we
> become "man-haters" or necessarily eliminate them from our
> lives. What it does mean is that we must struggle for a different
> basis of interaction with them. *That if we care about them and*

*ourselves we will not permit ourselves to be degraded or manipu-
lated.*[16] (Italics mine)

In poetry by Native American women, the refusal to be victimized
and exploited often presents itself in metaphors whose contexts are
historical and in which the desecration of the land is experienced both
as a profoundly personal, spiritual assault and as a metaphor for the
violent, urban, technological, compulsively contemporary death
culture in which petrochemical products and other poisons replace
wool and wood and all that is natural, a theme of Paula Gunn Allen's
"Wool Season, 1973." In Allen's "Riding the Thunder," the history of
the betrayal and genocide of Native Americans rides the poet's shoul-
ders. Time past and time present merge: "noon, history, night are
/ stars, are fixed and counted nails / on the doors of hope, the dying
bloody dream."[17] In the midst of this horror, not only of violence but
of the obliteration of all things sacred, Allen turns to poetry as medita-
tion, as prayer, as solace. Her poems suggest a sense of timelessness, of
belonging to an ancient tribal past, of being what all poets once were:
shamans,   healers,   prophets,   translators,   and   transformers   of
consciousness.

A spiritual heritage of reverence for the smallest living things, the
"tiny desert flower / micro beetle bug" inspires Terri Meyette's "Celebration 1982."[18] Ironically titled, given the poem's subject matter (the
strip-mining of land, the poisoning of water with radioactive waste,
and especially the U.S. government policy of using sacred Shoshone
and Paiute Indian land in the Nevada desert for bombing practice),
"Celebration 1982" nevertheless *is* a celebration. Meyette celebrates
Native American traditional values of reverence "for all of life," and
she celebrates as well the writing of the poem, which is itself an act of
protest against genocidal U.S. government policies and nuclear
madness.

In an untitled poem, Lydia Yellowbird remembers the destruction
of her gentle, peace-loving people because the white settlers were
unable to see them as fully human.

When you came
    you found a people
    with red skin
      they were one
      with all living things

But you did not see this
                beauty
        instead you saw them
            as animals, primitive
                    savage
Because you had lost this
                whole
In the progress of your civilization
            look now what
                    your knowledge
                has made them

You ask me to plow the ground. Shall I take a
knife and tear my mother's breast? Then when I
die she will not take me to her bosom to rest.

You ask me to dig for stone. Shall I dig under
her skin for bones? Then when I die I cannot
enter her body to be born again.[19]

The last two stanzas of the poem are a direct echo of the writings of
Smohalla, of the Columbian Basin Tribes, who voiced Indian objections to European attitudes in the mid 1800s.[20]

In "Long Division: A Tribal History," Wendy Rose recounts the
slow death of her people, who are "bought and divided" by the white
colonists.[21] After the destruction of ritual and the magic of song and
shamanic healing, all that remains for the poet is the wilderness within
her and the wilderness outside. She becomes a legendary figure, the
women who "suckle[s] coyotes and grieve[s]."

                . . . we die in granite scaffolding
        on the shape of the Sierras and lay down with lips open
        thrusting songs on the world. Who are we

        and do we still live? Our shamans sleep
        saying no. So outside of eternity we struggle
        til our blood has spread off our bodies and
        frayed the sunset edges; it's our blood that

        gives you those southwestern skies.[22]

She refers sarcastically to tourists and white settlers who enthuse about
beautiful Southwest sunsets with no awareness of the politics of white
claims on that land.

Rose travels geographically and temporally to Wounded Knee, whose massacre is reenacted every time a tourist buys an artifact, a piece of Indian history, unmindful of its human cost. In "I expected my skin and my blood to ripen," the poet becomes the Indian woman who fought in battle only to be stripped bare by the white victors, her clothing sold as curios. She laments the transformation of magic, of shamanic or tribal power, into science and curatorship:

> My feet were frozen to the leather,
> pried apart, left behind—bits of flesh
> on the moccasins, bits of papery deerhide
> on the bones
>
> . . . . . .
>
> My leggings were taken like in a rape
> and shriveled to the size of stick figures
> like they had never felt
> the push of my strong woman's body
> walking in the hills.
> It was my own baby whose cradleboard I held.
> Would've put her in my mouth
> like a snake
> if I could, would've turned her
> into a bush or old rock
> if there'd been enough magic
> to work such changes. Not enough magic
> even to stop the bullets.
> Not enough magic
> to stop the scientists.
> Not enough magic
> to stop the collectors.[23]

While agents of the U.S. government no longer deliberately hand out smallpox-infested blankets to American Indian people, they have replaced that form of attempted genocide with another almost as evil: spiritual annihilation. As Beth Brandt, editor of A *Gathering of Spirit*, a special issue of *Sinister Wisdom* devoted to Native American women's writing, has written, "they take our children to remove the inside of them. Our power. . . They steal our food, our sacred rattle, the stories, our names."[24]

Anger is often spoken of in poems by women of color as an empowering force or a catalyst for movements from racism to resistance and transcendence. As Native American poet Chrystos explores the metaphor:

> My sacred beliefs have been made pencils, names of
>   cities, gas stations
> My knee is wounded so badly that I limp constantly
> Anger is my crutch
> I hold myself upright with it
> My knee is wounded
> see
> How I Am Still Walking.[25]

"I Walk in the History of My People" alludes to the massacre of the Sioux people at Wounded Knee and the continuing assaults on Native Americans by the U.S. government and by U.S. citizens. "Crutch," "limp," "wounded"—these words are not often found in poems which also speak of dignity, of not crawling, of walking "upright." Chrystos' poem includes both realizations; it neither romanticizes nor denies but affirms rightful anger and its place in transformation.

Cherríe Moraga's "The Welder" pivots on a similar theme. In this poem, anger is also seen as engendering social change; Moraga "understand[s] the capacity of heat / to change the shape of things."[26] The anger in this poem speaks specifically to radical people of color and feminists who want a sense of unity against oppression so desperately that individuals' different needs and visions, dissent and anger within radical movements are often suppressed. Although Moraga includes herself in the "we" who "plead to each other" . . . "we all come from the same rock / we all come from the same rock," she also insists on acknowledging our differences and on the necessity of anger for forming real bonds, not superficial agreements:

> Yes, fusion *is* possible
> but only if things get hot enough—
> all else is temporary adhesion,
> patching up.[27]

In the final lines of the poem, Moraga herself becomes the welder, she who refuses to smooth things over:

> I am the welder
> I am taking the power
> into my own hands.[28]

Audre Lorde has also written about her desire to heal through her poems, to encourage the profusion of voices within every woman. She alludes to the dialogue among these voices in the title of her 1976 book, *Between Our Selves*.[29] Before our fractured and embattled communities can begin this dialogue, Lorde recognizes that individuals must experience and accept chaos and dissent for and within themselves. In "Outside," a poem from this volume, Lorde celebrates this process as a source of healing: "for most of all I am / blessed within my selves / who are come to make our shattered faces / whole."[30]

In her poem "Epilog," Wendy Rose borrows from Hopi legend to describe her shared political determination in solidarity with other contemporary Native American women writers Leslie Silko, Paula Gunn Allen, and Joy Harjo; the poem speaks to the complexities of change and the power within poets and all people of color to transcend extreme obstacles. The Hopi way is to convert obstacles into sources of strength, and this she promises to do:

> Drop a kernel of corn on a rock
> and say a prayer. It will shoot up
> proud and green, tassel out,
> pull the next crop from the thunderheads.
> That's the Hopi way.
> If the corn doesn't grow
> you eat the rocks,
> drink the clouds
> on the distant plains.
>
> Silko and Allen and Harjo and me:
> our teeth are hard
> from the rocks we eat.[31]

In "A Tribute to Rosa Parks," Alice Walker describes her hopes for all of humanity: our potential for courage, dignity, and love.

> The Cubans have created a word that they call each other in recognition of their common struggle against oppression and their common goal of realizing a common dream. The word is "compañera." It means Sister, it means Comrade, it means Companion, it means Friend. It means we are together. It means we are one.
> I wish we had a word like that. A word that praises the

> splendor of our ordinary dignity and courage—and not our bio-
> logical or religious destinations. A word that reminds us, when-
> ever we use it, that we are together, not separate, and that the
> courage and dignity that is possible for one of us is possible for
> us all.[32]

In individual acts of self-love and self-empowerment, in acts of compassion and unity, in poems that reflect anguish, outrage, and despair as well as the determination to "survive confirmed," the poets discussed here are proving that Alice Walker's vision is not only dream but possibility.

In their unflinching gaze into much that is nightmare in American culture, many of these are not comforting poems. But because they imagine what Adrienne Rich has called "the possibilities of truth be-tween us," they are poems which chart a new, essential geography, one whose terrain we ignore only at our own peril.

This is Not Romance/Private Fictions: Redefining the Language, Redefining the Culture

Given not only the poet's traditional relationship to lan-guage but also the relationship of silence and invisibility to power-lessness, it is not surprising that finding one's voice has been such a compelling issue in contemporary feminist poetry generally and es-pecially in poetry written by women of color. Having been denied the right to speak her truths in a language and form that accurately reflect her, the Third World woman writer must inevitably seek a language in which these truths are undiminished. The woman writer in this culture—whether Afro-American, Chicana, Asian American, Native American, or white—has written in a language determined by pa-triarchy as well as racism and thus has a double urgency to redefine that language, to claim a language and form unfettered by those twin forces of the dominant culture.

In the preface to *Passion: New Poems, 1977–1980*, June Jordan es-tablishes a relationship among "Black and Third World poets . . . [generally and] those feminist poets who are evidently intent upon speaking with a maximal number and diversity of other American lives." She calls these writers, who range from Pablo Neruda and Victor Hernandez Cruz to Jessica Hagedorn and Margaret Walker, "poets of The New World," and suggests that there is a unifying thread of linguistic interconnectedness among them:

> In the poetry of The New World, you meet with a reverence for the material world that begins with a reverence for human life, an intellectual trust in sensuality as a means of knowledge and of unity, an easily deciphered system of reference, aspiration to a believable, collective voice and, consequently, emphatic preference for broadly accessible language and/or "spoken" use of language.[33]

Those who must forge a literature out of generations of contempt and denial bring to that literature an explosive energy, courage and will, a visionary anger. Perhaps this is when the most incisive literature is made, when celebration is the Janus face of struggle, when a passionate energy soars through the language.

In poems that are as compelling for their ethical vision as for their language, women of color dare to imagine a changed world. And if imagining a changed world will not cause it to come into being, we know the consequences of failing to imagine it.

The very act of putting pen to paper, of giving voice to one's own ideas and dreams, is especially precious in the context of Afro-American poetry, for it is a metaphor for the claiming of one's cultural, spiritual, and emotional existence—one's very right to be. In "In Search of Our Mothers' Gardens," Alice Walker asks her readers to consider the context in which black women have created, against all odds, throughout their history, in this country:

> How was the creativity of the Black woman kept alive, year after year and century after century, when for most of the years Black people have been in America, it was a punishable crime for a Black person to read or write? And the freedom to paint, to sculpt, to expand the mind with action, did not exist. Consider, if you can bear to imagine it, what might have been the result if singing, too, had been forbidden by law. Listen to the voices of Bessie Smith, Billie Holiday, Nina Simone, Roberta Flack, and Aretha Franklin, among others, and imagine those voices muzzled for life.[34]

A poet who to my mind is more lyrical in her fiction than in her poetry, Alice Walker provides in the early pages of her novel *Meridian* what may be the most terrifying and metaphysically accurate paradigm in all of Afro-American literature for the black woman writer whose language has been stolen from her. Louvinie, a slave woman, literally loses her tongue as punishment for the one creative act allowed her: storytelling. Her ghost story, told upon request to the Saxon plantation children, inadvertently frightens the youngest child to death. As a result,

> Louvinie's tongue was clipped out at the root. Choking on blood, she saw her tongue ground under the heel of Master Saxon. Mutely, she pleaded for it, because she knew the curse of her native land: Without one's tongue in one's mouth or in a special spot of one's own choosing, the singer in one's soul was lost forever to grunt and snort through eternity like a pig.[35]

Like Alice Walker, poet Sherley Anne Williams borrows from the slave narrative tradition to emphasize that for the Afro-American woman writer finding a means of articulation is still not only precious but hard-won. A central experience of the narrator of Williams' stunning collection of poems, *Some One Sweet Angel Chile*, is the claiming of self as text, the act of telling one's own story. It is central also to the narrator of a number of Williams' earlier poems, as indeed it emerges as a formal device whose implications are as much thematic as a question of poetics in the work of many Afro-American and other Third World poets. But in the historical context of antebellum slavery and the early period of Reconstruction, the setting for many of Williams' poems, the courage and the power of speech take on much deeper levels of meaning. Consider these lines from "I Sing This Song for Our Mothers," in which Williams takes on the persona of a newly freed black man who announces quietly, surely:

> I was a man full growed
> when the otha folks freedom come, had
> a wife and sons o' my own
> and wa'n't nary-a-one o' us
> eva belongst to no one but us selves.[36]

Odessa's son, the narrator in this poem, knows that through his own resistance and love and through the love and kinship of family and friends he belongs to himself in the deepest sense.

"I Sing This Song for Our Mothers" shifts narrators from Odessa's son to Odessa, following his admonition to black people to carry on the story of freedom by telling it "to yo daughters most especial / cause this where our line come from." Forced to live in a world in which speech and naming are forbidden, even the right to name her own children, Odessa paradoxically claims the power of naming, of living in a world of self-authored meanings and perceptions:

> I say yo name
> Now and that be love. I say
> yo daddy name and that be
> how I know free. I say Harker
> name and that be how I
> keep loved and keep free. . .[37]

In this and other poems from *The Peacock Poems* and *Some One Sweet Angel Chile*, Sherley Anne Williams has sought out the slave narrative as a structural and thematic device for exploring the black woman's quest for freedom, selfhood, and language. The poem contains an actual account of an escape from slavery into freedom as well as a number of traditional slave narrative elements: first-person narrative without the filtering consciousness of an amanuensis; the story of recognition of, resistance to, and the gaining of freedom from oppression; and the chronicling of the social fabric of the community through a chronicling of the life of an individual. Most of all, it celebrates the richness, acuity, energy, and vision of black folk dialect. Here Williams pays homage not only to the first authentically Afro-American genre, but to Zora Neale Hurston's *Their Eyes Were Watching God*, a book whose spirit and language are echoed in this and other poems by Williams.[38]

The self-affirming spirit of Odessa resurfaces in Williams' most recent volume of poetry, *Some One Sweet Angel Chile*, in which Williams again borrows from the slave narrative tradition to create a compelling social and psychological context for the courage and determination of the women who inhabit these poems. The book opens with a series of epistolary poems written in the persona of Hannah, a New

England black woman, who comes to the South as a teacher after the Civil War. Despite Hannah's quiet restraint and dignity, she embodies the spirit of resistance and rebellion. When Miss Esther, the head teacher, is dismayed that Hannah insists on leaving the Big House where the teachers now live to spend time in the old slave quarters among the students and other freedmen, not just for an occasional prayer meeting but to partake in conversation, music, and a shared history, Hannah goes anyway, and recounts:

> It is a stalemate:
> she will not give her permission;
> I go and ask no one's consent. [39]

Despite her respect for Miss Esther, Hannah recognizes the symbolic power of all the ways in which her people have been divided from one another. Paradoxically, in quietly going her own way Hannah is also affirming her solidarity with her community by choosing to resist the unconscious demarcations of power and status which Miss Esther would unwittingly perpetuate.

In another wonderfully understated poem, Hannah refuses the implications of her slave name, Patience, and "answer[s] roughly / some harmless question, My name is Hannah. Hannah. There is / no Patience to it."[40]

The middle section of this collection, exhuberant, boisterous, and sexy, skips sixty years to the 1930s to celebrate a similar spirit of rebelliousness in the persona of famed blues singer Bessie Smith. In these poems Bessie Smith, the "angel chile" in this book, the wild woman of the traditional blues song, is not mythologized but remembered for the ways in which her spirit brought courage, hope, and humor into the lives of others, one of whom comments:

> she touched me; and I
> knowed her. The rest is
> my own memories. [41]

In the final sequence of poems, we hear echoes of Hannah and Bessie in a profusion of contemporary voices. Although the poems in this section seem loosely autobiographical, the narrator of "WITNESS," the opening poem in this sequence, sternly warns us that she speaks not just for herself but for the generations which preceded her and the generations to come: "I give voice to the old stories. This is not romance, / private fictions. . ."[42]

The speaker in Kathy Elaine Anderson's "Keep a Weathered Eye Lifting" also reaches across continents and generations to name herself one of the three defiant, captured Africans on a slave ship bound for America, who "leaped with crazy laughter to / the waiting sharks, sang as they went under." The poem summons the spirit of this rebellion, the courage of Afro-American ancestors, as an apparition and actual hurricane, a wind that fills the sails of ships, a wished-for beacon in a storm-tossed night, a song whose siren call will give its listeners no peace until they acknowledge its compelling beauty and take a similar journey to freedom:

> Listen,
> as they chant stories of lost Griots,
> your language will fall away
> and ours will settle in your mouth.[43]

Mari Evans adopts a strategy similar to Williams and Anderson, that of borrowing slave narrative elements in order to affirm and celebrate not only her own selfhood but the earlier generations of black women whose resistance to slavery, racism, and oppression is indelibly a part of her own struggle and her own empowering. Evans' "The 7:25 Trolley" is not about the demeaning conditions of poverty (although it certainly exposes them) but rather about the determination of black women to transcend their lives' circumstances, to not simply endure:

> ain't got time for a bite to eat
> I'll have to catch my trolley at the end of the block
> and if I take
> my coffee
> there
> she looks at the cup and she looks at the clock
>   (Sure hope I don't miss my car . . .)
> . . . .
> I may scrub floors
> but
> I don't
> get on my knees . . .
> and someday
> I won't go at all
>   (Sure hope I don't miss my car . . .)[44]

Evans here uses repetition and line breaks to illuminate an alternating awareness of self in racist society and as dignified transcender. She inserts the line "(Sure hope I don't miss my car . . .)" a number of times in dialogue with a growing awareness on the part of the persona that she someday "won't go at all" to scrub floors. The double awareness of the persona here seems to flash quickly back and forth between realities, creating a tension that moves toward transcendence with the last phrases. Evans exploits the use of short, broken lines to emphasize this aspect of the inner dialogue: "I don't / get on my knees. . . ." The echo is to slavery: the order "get on your knees" is a familiar one in the master-slave situation. The woman in the poem is refusing slavery, but the line is cut in such a way as to deliberately highlight the fact that in former times she *had* to get on her knees. And in fact she still does get on her knees to scrub floors, physically, but the psychic meaning of the kneeling is explicitly refuted.

Refusing to kneel to the dominant culture by refusing to speak in what has been called "the oppressor's language" takes on additional layers of difficulty in American poets whose native language is not English. Metaphors of speech and of translating between languages and cultures surface with exceptional vigor in the writing of Asian American and Chicana poets, who not only write out of a multicultural identity but a multilingual one as well. In *The Third Woman*, feminist critic Dexter Fisher speaks of "translating oneself into understandable terms" as "a major preoccupation" of most of the Asian American women poets included in her anthology. This preoccupation is "symbolized by the literal problem of speaking another language—again the dilemma of being caught between speech and demon silence."[45] The paradox here, of course, is that in "translating oneself into understandable terms" the North American woman of color whose native tongue is not English runs the risk of being increasingly understandable to the Anglo world while becoming increasingly alienated from her own identity.

Such poets may turn to childhood images to clarify the learning and the feelings in these experiences. Diana Chang has written in "Allegory" of the tension between her historical culture and the one in which she now lives; she writes of being the child who is "misplaced / and found again."[46] In "How a Girl Got Her Chinese Name," Nellie Wong reflects on her childhood feelings of blessedness and security when her family and teachers give her two Chinese names, Nah Lei (meaning "where," "which place") and Lai Oy (meaning "beautiful love"). Through this naming she is able to discover an ethnic heritage which had been erased by the demands to assimilate. Wong is restored to a child's sense of omnipotence: "between these names / I never knew I would ever get lost."[47]

The relationship between language and assimilation is also the subject of Tina Koyama's "Next," about a visit to the dentist's office. The poet, whose tongue is literally invaded by the dentist's apparatus, is struck silent as well by the invasiveness of his attitudes and the attitudes of the Anglo world he represents. His questions, pleasantries about the poet's "dog, / undergraduate education, the muffler on [her] car," evade any attempt at real knowledge or understanding. His race, gender, occupation, and class privilege encourage him—and empower him—to formulate not only the questions he poses in his attempts to define her but the answers as well:

> . . . He knows my life can be answered with a nod,
> knows the stoney surface of my tooth
> and the narrow parabola of my jaw
> better than his own hand. He fears
> extraction will be necessary, taps with his mirror
>
> deep cracks that even promises won't fill. Here,
> decisions come in the shape of pliers. I nod,
> swallowing old questions with a numbing tongue.[48]

The poet's "numb[ed]" tongue is robbed of speech by more than novocaine; if the dentist (and the world he represents) has his way, the promised "extraction" will be the forcible separation of the poet from her culture as well as the forcible separation of the molar from her mouth.

The title poem of Fay Chiang's *In the City of Contradictions* affirms in Asian American poets a belief in the essential and necessary power of a nonassimilated mother tongue. Those who shape the world through their own "songs, dreams and dances, / . . . myths, legends, symbols" will make survival in the city of contradictions—metaphor for all of U.S. culture—possible. The poem ends with these affirming words:

> but we with our spirit, our love, our sinew
> we are among the survivors
>
> spread the news.[49]

Sometimes the paralyzing pressure to assimilate comes from within the family. Part of the grief-stricken, charged connection between black mothers and daughters is the heritage of colorism that black mothers often have been forced to pass on to their daughters in the name of their children's survival. In "Prologue," Audre Lorde exclaims:

> . . . When I was a child
> whatever my mother thought would mean survival
> made her try to beat me whiter every day
> and even now the color of her bleached ambition
> still forks throughout my words
> but I survived
> and didn't I survive confirmed . . . [50]

In "Pathways: From Mother to Mother" she adds, "wherever [my mother] wore ivory / I wear pain."[51] The black mother who is clothed in survival clothes—white in "Prologue" and ivory in "Pathways"— wraps her daughter in the same bleached binding rags that she herself has been forced to wear. Audre Lorde's "Outside," Nellie Wong's "When I Was Growing Up," June Jordan's "Poem about My Rights," and Gloria Anzaldúa's autobiographical essay "La Prieta" all focus on Third World parents' attempts to convince their daughters to straighten their hair or teeth and stay out of the sun, or are about obsessions over white skin and cleanliness.[52]

In "Lullabye," Janice Mirikitani examines her mother's apparent acquiescence to the imprisonment of Japanese Americans at Manzanar and Tule Lake during World War II and to the racial hatred that permitted the United States to target the Japanese for atomic destruction at Hiroshima and Nagasaki. The poet concludes that she will remain orphaned, "parentless," until her mother's political consciousness is born. But Mirikitani plays with the Japanese attitude of resigned acceptance: "shikata ga nai / it can't be / helped."[53] She interposes her own "waiting, / waiting" with the patience and waiting of her mother to make it clear that she is not just waiting but *willing* her mother to be born, to be free.

The poetry of women of color is more focused on themes of healing, bonding, and nurturing between Third World mothers and daughters than on rupture and anger. There has been a healing between mothers and daughters, and that healing has been an essential source for Third

World women poets "hearing themselves forth from silence," of returning to deeper sources.[54] In a letter to Barbara Smith, Cherríe Moraga writes of this process:

> I went to a concert where Ntozake Shange was reading. There,
> everything exploded for me. She was speaking a language that I
> knew—in the deepest parts of me—existed, and that I had ig-
> nored in my own feminist studies and even in my own writing.
> What Ntozake caught in me is the realization that in my devel-
> opment as a poet, I have, in many ways, denied the voice of my
> brown mother—the brown in me. I have acclimated to the
> sound of a white language which, as my father represents it,
> does not speak to the emotions in my poems—emotions which
> stem from the love of my mother.
>
> The reading was agitating. Made me uncomfortable. Threw me
> into a week-long terror of how deeply I was affected. I felt that I
> had to start all over again. That I turned only to the perceptions
> of white middle-class women to speak for me and all women. I
> am shocked by my own ignorance.
>
> Sitting in that auditorium chair was the first time I had realized
> to the core of me that for years I had disowned the language I
> knew best—ignored the words and rhythms that were the closest
> to me. The sounds of my mother and aunts gossiping—half in
> English, half in Spanish—while drinking cerveza in the kitchen.
> And the hands—I had cut off the hands in my poems. But not
> in conversation; still the hands could not be kept down. Still
> they insisted on moving.[55]

In "For the Color of My Mother," Moraga writes of returning to the
words and rhythms closest to her; the "white girl" who "[goes] brown to
the blood color of [her] mother" speaks for both of them when she
returns to the tongue they share.[56] Moraga describes the mutilation of
the spirit that accompanies the mutilation of one's own speech. Aurora
Levins Morales writes of a similar mutilation of her mother: "the fear
of racist violence that clipped her tongue of all its open vowels, into
crisp, imitation British."[57] In Moraga's poem, her mother is forced to
speak a different kind of English but also a language of subservience, of
"yes," of "stoop" and "carry." Both mother and daughter have been
mutilated: the mouth that is not allowed to speak its own language
becomes a wound, a gaping hole, a gash, central images in the poem.

I am a white girl gone brown to the blood color of my mother
speaking for her through the unnamed part of the mouth
the wide-arched muzzle of brown women

At two
my upper lip split open
clear to the tip of my nose
it spilled forth a cry that would not yield
that travelled down six floors of hospital
where doctors wound me into white bandages
only the screaming mouth exposed

the gash sewn back into a snarl
would last for years

I am a white girl gone brown to the blood color of my mother
speaking for her

at five, her mouth
pressed into a seam
a fine blue child's line drawn across her face
her mouth, pressed into mouthing english
mouthing yes yes yes
mouthing stoop lift carry
(sweating wet sighs into the field
her red bandana comes loose from under the huge brimmed hat
moving across her upper lip) . . . [58]

The ragged gash of the daughter's mouth is contrasted to "the fine blue child's line" of her mother's mouth, which becomes increasingly distorted. Even at five years of age, the mother's mouth is "pressed" into colonized service, literally in stoop labor, metaphorically in having to begin to adopt the language of yes, of oppression. In the stanzas that follow, the thin line widens to become the lipstick-smeared mouth of a fourteen-year-old, pushed into a sexuality she is not yet ready for; finally, at forty-five, her mother's mouth literally stretches into a bleeding ulcer.

The poem explores multiple injuries and multiple healings. The poet suffers both literal and metaphoric wounding. Her scream of outrage and pain, "spill[ing] forth a cry that would not yield," is simultaneously literal and metaphoric, like the white bandages in which she is swathed, which cover her brownness. She is robbed of her mother's tongue and also of her mother.

The wound of the daughter becomes an emblem of defiance, its blood-red color a return to her mother's darkness. In the final lines of the poem, Moraga invokes shamanic power to cast a ritual circle in which women of color are rejoined through the reclaiming of their mothers.

> *I am a white girl gone brown to the blood color of my mother*
> *speaking for her*
>
> as it should be
> dark women come to me
>   sitting in circles
> I pass through their hands
> the head of my mother
> painted in clay colors
>
> touching each carved feature
>   swollen eyes and mouth
> they understand the explosion the splitting
> open   contained within the fixed expression
>
> they cradle her silence
>   nodding to me. [59]

Moraga names herself a priestess, a healer. Through compassion for her mother and an understanding of her mother's enforced silence, "the splitting / open contained within the fixed expression," Moraga is restored to speech, as to her mother *"speaking for her* / as it should be." Moraga intends a double meaning: she is speaking for her mother, and this is as it should be—both as it ought to be (a future one wishes for, in which daughters and mothers share the same speech, the same vision) and as it is proper (a present now attained, at least for the speaker in the poem). The line enjambs forward as well as backward to read: "as it should be / dark women come to me." Again, a double meaning is implied: Moraga envisions a future in which she is a woman who brings women of color together, and this is fitting, proper, "as it should be." The poet offers the healing wisdom of this poem, an explosion out of silence into naming. It is a sacred offering, like the altar-sculpture of her mother, which is passed with reverence from hand to hand.

I Am / a Dark Temple Where Your True Spirit Rises: Resistance to Colorism

Like resistance to speechlessness, resistance to colorism (the mapping of Anglo standards of beauty onto people of color) empowers the vision and the poems of women of color.

In a poem of astonishing loveliness, Native American poet Wendy Rose apprehends, on the deepest level, the beauty of "Julia the Lion Woman," a sideshow freak, "the ugliest woman in the world." By extrapolation, Rose apprehends as well the beauty of all those destined by the racism, colorism, cruelty, and clouded vision of others to be invisible, unfully seen.

> . . . Beauty twisted within
> and pushed your pain against you
> to be nailed like a bronze wolf pelt
> on your bones.
> They called you the ugliest woman in the world,
> the woman with a face like a lion or
> an ape, the woman whose long fur swirled
> like a shawl around her
> in a land where even the wolves
> run naked.
> I call you
> the most beautiful she-wolf,
> the highest flying canary,
> the most ancient song,
> the most faithful magic.
> I call you
> my mother and my sister
> and my daughter and me.[60]

Healing and essential to both self and community, such a re-visioning in the lives of people of color is not to be taken lightly. Consider, for example, the degree to which destructive ideas about physical beauty shatter the community in Toni Morrison's novel *The Bluest Eye* and eventually succeed in driving Pecola Breedlove, one of its members, insane.

Lyric re-visioning is one of many forms of resistance to colorism. Others are more plainspoken, understated, but no less effective. In a

poem from Sherley Anne Williams' "Letters from a New England
Negro" sequence, set in the period immediately following the Eman-
cipation, a black school teacher confronted by white children taunting
"'Nigger!'" responds, unruffled (laughing, in fact), "'and / a free one,
too,'" thus indicating to the children as well as herself that the naming
of her blackness no longer has the power to hurt her.[61] And in her
series of poems on Bessie Smith, Sherley Anne Williams creates a
Bessie who refuses the terrible legacy of white racism: the belief that
lighter is better, is more beautiful; Bessie bewitches even those black
men who "bragged [they] didn't deal in coal" into her bed.[62]

As an antidote to colorism, novelist Maxine Hong Kingston, who
describes fear and alienation as "the white ghosts," and other Third
World writers have for some time used whiteness as a negative qualifier.
Lucha Corpi and Audre Lorde among others reverse the conventional
association of whiteness with goodness and purity. In the opening poem
of Corpi's bilingual volume *Palabras de Mediodia/ Noon Words*, whiteness becomes a metaphor for those things which hold the poem back
from flowering into creation, out of silence:

> Como la semilla en espera
> de la benevolente lluvia
> el verso sediento calla.
> Su quietud se desparrama
> en los adentros y me asusta.
> su sequedad mustia y blanca.

> Like the seed that waits
> for gentle rain
> my poem is silent in its thirst.
> Its quietude scatters
> inside me and I am frightened
> by its withered whiteness.[63]

Other recent poems speak more directly to black women's changing
consciousness about skin color. In "I Used to Think," Chirlane Mc-
Cray first describes herself through the distorted lens of an internalized
racist self-image: "A nappy-headed, no-haired / fat-lipped, / big-bot-
tomed Black girl," wanting to be pecan-colored instead of black. By the
end of the poem she is transformed, able to recognize her own ebony
beauty, "the woman in darkness / who flowers with loving."[64]

As Audre Lorde's poems shift from metaphors of earth brown to coal black, a fierce and articulate voice emerges. The title poem from *Coal*, written twenty years ago, invokes a powerful and joyous recognition of self and of the beauty of blackness:

> I am Black because I come from the earth's inside
> now take my word for jewel in the open light.[65]

In a kind of linguistic reclaiming, Lorde reverses the racist stereotypes connoting darkness with fear, hatred, and death; in many of her poems, she associates darkness with strength, integrity, beauty, vision, and magic. In "Black Mother Woman," Lorde announces,

>   look mother
> I am
> a dark temple where your true spirit rises
> beautiful and tough as a chestnut
> stanchion against your nightmares of weakness.[66]

In "For Each of You" she entreats all people of color to claim the majesty of their darkness, to tell their children

> you are the offspring of slaves
> and your mother was
> a princess
> in darkness.[67]

And in a poem from *The Black Unicorn*, "From the House of Yemanja," Lorde again imbues positive associations of blackness with the healing power of the motherbond.

> Mother I need your blackness now
> As the August earth needs rain.[68]

In these three poems Lorde speaks as a mother, a daughter, or as both at once. She calls on these female kinship ties for access to the redemptive love of her blackness. In this way she extends maternal/ familial love to all people of the earth. She implores all of us to "speak proudly to [our] children / Where ever [we] may find them."[69]

Perhaps more than any other poet, Lucille Clifton's poems trace the transformation in consciousness enabling black women to delight in their own physical beauty, to celebrate their skin color, their nappy hair, their sometimes ample hips. In a poem from the early 1960s,

Clifton glances backward to an earlier, more repressive time and remembers "The Way It Was" to be "a nice girl / not touching / trying
to be white."[70] But in Clifton's recent award-winning volume of poems
Two-Headed Woman, she describes not only a change in her own individual consciousness but a shift which has taken place among black
women in general. In "homage to my hips," Clifton sings of her big
hips that "Have never been enslaved / . . . that go where they want
to go / and . . . do what they want to do."

> these hips are mighty hips.
> these hips are magic hips.
> i have known them
> to put a spell on a man and
> spin him like a top![71]

In "homage to my hair," Clifton celebrates the nappiness of her hair as
a source of erotic pleasure both for herself and for black men:

> when i feel her jump up and dance
> i hear the music! my God
> i'm talking about my nappy hair!
> she is a challenge to your hand
> Black man
> she is as tasty on your tongue as good greens.[72]

This poem also reverses the conventional association of aging and
asexuality for women. Instead, Clifton suggests that as black women
become older, the essence of their racial consciousness increasingly
shines through their bodies as well as their spirits. The final lines of
"homage to my hair" conclude:

> the grayer she do get, good God,
> the Blacker she do be![73]

Finally, in "what the mirror said," Clifton carries the theme of self-
affirmation a step farther. While both "homage to my hips" and
"homage to my hair" pivot to some extent on black male recognition of
black female beauty, in "what the mirror said" Clifton articulates the
profound sense of self-acceptance, self-esteem, and self-love that ema-
nates from black women's newly evolved delight in their own physical
characteristics. The poem draws a parallel between the physical terrain

of the body—its "geography"—and the terrain of the psyche; knowledge and love of one leads to knowledge and love of the other.

> listen,
> you a wonder.
> you a city
> of a woman.
> you got a geography
> of your own.
> listen,
> somebody need a map
> to understand you.
> somebody need directions
> to move around you.
> listen,
> woman,
> you not a noplace
> anonymous
> girl;
> mister with his hands on you
> he got his hands on
> some
> damn
> body![74]

I Will Be Black Light as You Lie against Me: Joyous Sexuality

Poetry by women of color is rich with metaphors of sexuality, passion, and love. These poems often are rooted in the same experiences that give rise to other celebrations of tribal or revolutionary culture and affirmation. Sometimes sexual metaphors and images are used to describe feelings and encounters that belong to a wider definition of erotic than we usually employ; in other poems, sex itself is a theme for women of color as for almost all feminist poets. The fracturing and expanding of the conventional definitions of "sexual" are not surprising for a movement that has claimed, as Adrienne Rich states in "Tear Gas," that "the will to change begins in the body not in the mind / My politics is in my body."[75] Affirming one's sexuality in a culture that despises the erotic while glorifying the pornographic, as Audre Lorde and others have observed, is an unmistakably political act.[76]

Third World and white women must contend with different kinds of sexual repression. Aurora Levins Morales, a Puerto Rican and Jewish New York poet, describes one aspect of this repression in an article entitled, "'. . . And Even Fidel Can't Change That!'"

> . . . if I'm in a Latin [Salsa] scene I freeze. I can't make my hips fluid or keep my feet from tripping. It's the perversion of sexuality that frightens me. It's the way the women around me exude a sexiness that has nothing to do with the heart. Of course Latin women love as well as any other women . . . but while the chilliest Anglo-Saxon repression of sex pretends it simply doesn't exist, Latin repression says it's a filthy fact of life, use it for what it's worth . . . shake it in his face, wear it as a decoy. It's all over the floor and it's cold and savage. It's the hatred of the powerless, turned crooked.[77]

While the poems of Third World feminists (and white feminists as well) by no means conform to a single world view, they tend to depict a sexuality that reflects the capacity for joy and deep feeling. And as Audre Lorde has insisted:

> . . . once we begin to feel deeply all the aspects of our lives, we begin to demand from ourselves and from our lives' pursuits that they feel in accordance with that joy which we know ourselves to be capable of. Our erotic knowledge empowers us, becomes a lens through which we scrutinize all aspects of our existence, forcing ourselves to evaluate those aspects honestly in terms of their relative meaning within our lives. And this is a grave responsibility, projected from within each of us, not to settle for the convenient, the shoddy, the conventionally expected, nor the merely safe.[78]

Ntozake Shange's recent small press book *From okra to greens* is filled with vibrant expressions of sexuality, often playful but also acknowledging to the lover feelings so profound that there isn't a language "big enough / to say your name."[79] In "okra to greens / an aside on amsterdam avenue," the speaker literally transforms her lover into that heart-dish of black culture—mustard greens and collard greens—

and delightedly admits to having a "greens overdose."[80] These lines are
a sensual delight and a poetic delight, like the joyous eroticism of
Nikki Giovanni's "Beautiful Black Men" in their "fire red, lime green,
burnt orange / royal blue tight pants that hug / what I like to hug."[81]
But when examined contextually, they are all the more moving. For as
June Jordan has noted, "affirmation of Black values and lifestyle within
the American context is, indeed, an act of protest."[82]

The poet Ai insists, "I do not write about race, social comment,
etc., but about people, life, suffering, and am now trying to bring
about the transfiguration of men and women in my poetry."[83] In "Before You Leave," Ai assumes the persona of a woman who is powerfully
strong, not traditionally "feminine":

> I set the bowl of raw vegetables on
>   the table.
> You know I am ripe now.
> You can bite me, I won't bleed;
> just take off my kimono. Eat, then go
>   ahead, run.
> I won't miss you, but this one hour
> lift me by the buttocks
> and press me hard against your belly.
> Fill my tunnel with the howl
> you keep zipped in your pants
> and when it's over, don't worry, I'll
>   stand.
> I'm a mare. Every nail's head
>   in my hooves wears your face,
> but not even you, wolf, can bring me
>   down.[84]

And in "Twenty Year Marriage" she takes the persona of a woman who
compares her own body to a pickup truck and huskily informs her
husband that he should "hurry" because she has "nothing on under
[her] skirt":

> . . . get inside me, start the engine;
> you'll have the strength, the will to move.
> I'll push, you push, we'll tear each other in half.
> Come on, baby, lay me down on my back.
> Pretend you don't owe me a thing

> and maybe we'll roll out of here,
> leaving the past stacked up behind us;
> old newspapers nobody's ever got to read again.[85]

In this poem, sex becomes a passport for these two lovers to take leave of the past and make a fresh start together.

The determination to direct her own erotic energy also motivates the speaker in Asian American poet Cyn Zarco's "Saxophonetyx." Jubilantly acknowledging her erotic attraction toward a saxophone player, she nevertheless is determined not to be victimized by her own desire. Warned not to fall in love with musicians because they "take love / don't give love / 'cause they're saving it for the music," she envisions a surreal and fantastic solution to the problem at hand. To transform the saxophonist into a lover who can give love as well as receive it, she transforms herself—literally—into the music he's "savin it for":

> . . . when I slowly closed my eyes
> I saw his fingers wrap around my waist
> my spine turn into saxophone keys
> my mouth become his mouthpiece
> and there was nothing left in the room
> but mercy.[86]

Transformation, fantasy, and dream-vision are also crucial to Native American poet Linda Hogan's "Wall Songs," a poem of astonishingly lovely lyricism and enormous shamanistic power. The speaker in the poem names that fragile covering of the body, her skin, as "the real life / of love and sorrow," thus affirming sexuality and the physical apprehension of a beloved as crucial to the deepest levels of emotional understanding. The walls here are material and actual: roads which separate jungles, wire fences, ledges "embedded with green / and broken glass." In the face of the things which divide us (race, class, and sexual preference), in the face of danger and violence, "the singing of machetes," the speaker utters a prayer for healing, for the dissolution of boundaries—geographical, physical, and those of the heart. A priestess, a shaman, she claims the terrain of the body and the cartography of compassion, friendship, sexuality, and love as a force to transform divisions into bridges, to create a community, a world at peace:

> . . . Sometimes a lover
> and I turn our flesh to bridges

and the air between us disappears
like in the jungle
where I am from.
Tropical vines grow together, lovers,
over roadways men have slashed,
surviving
the sounds of those lost inside
and the singing of machetes.

May all walls be like those of the jungle,
filled with animals
singing into the ears of night.
Let them be
made of the mysteries further in
in the heart, joined with the lives of all,
all bridges of flesh,
all singing,
all covering the wounded land
showing again, again
that boundaries are all lies. [87]

The valuing of self as well as the refusal to be categorized by the tenets of traditional romantic love often characterize lesbian poetry by women of color. Some of the most extraordinary love poems by feminists of color celebrate love between women. Sometimes this love is explicitly sexual. But just as often it is embedded in what Mary Daly has called "radical female friendship."[88] These multiple meanings and expressions of love are mutually inclusive and perhaps equally valued. They testify to the richness of intimacy and affection which has surfaced from feminism for Third World and white women alike.

June Jordan's poetry reveals her belief that love is the central emotional force in her life and work. In a recent essay "Where Is the Love?" Jordan defines her life commitment to ending "those tyrannies, those corrosions of sacred possibility [of human love]."[89] In the title poem of *Things That I Do in the Dark*, Jordan explains her poems' urgency in lines which evoke the power of desire:

These poems
they are things that I do
in the dark
reaching for you

whoever you are
and
are you ready?[90]

Sexuality is not separate here from the passionate impulse that infuses her poems, the impulse to discover, in all of their complexities, both self and other, "whoever you are / whoever I may become."[91]

Paula Gunn Allen writes of a spiritual and psychic geography embedded in the New Mexico skies and the deserts of Cubero and Albuquerque. Her poems are sinewy and delicate, a poetry of the lacunae and mergings of double consciousness. Allen's love poems to women smell of persimmon, sweet orange, shiny pears, bitter seeds, but most of all they evoke rain, renewal, an end to spirit thirst.

Political as well as spiritual vision empowers the love poetry of lesbians of color. As black lesbian poet Cheryl Clarke suggests in "Lesbianism: An Act of Resistance":

> . . . If radical lesbian-feminism purports an anti-racist, anti-classist, anti-women-hating vision of bonding as mutual, reciprocal, as infinitely negotiable, as freedom from antiquated gender prescriptions and proscriptions, *then all people struggling to transform the character of relationships in this culture have something to learn from lesbians.* . . . The lesbian has decolonized her body. She has rejected a life of servitude implicit in Western, heterosexual relationships and has accepted the potential of mutuality in a lesbian relationship. . .[92]

Clarke's poem "Of Althea and Flaxie" celebrates a nearly thirty-year-long span in the life of a lesbian couple and suggests the way in which women's erotic autonomy empowered their ability to claim other forms of autonomy: of dress and work as well as of resistance to the established codes of such institutions as welfare, jail, even funeral homes. Part of the power of the poem is that it dares to celebrate an explicitly butch-femme relationship, but not the stereotypical one. Althea, "very dark / very butch," is a welder who wears suits and ties, but she also "love[s] to cook, sew, and drive a car."[93] Her lover, Flaxie, may wear tight dresses and high heels, but she also "love[s] to shoot, fish, [and] play poker"—not exactly the sort of hobbies usually ascribed to femme women.

> Althea was set up and went to jail
> for writing numbers in 1958.

> Flaxie visited her every week with gifts
> and hungered openly for her thru the bars
> and did not give a damn who knew she waited for a woman.
>
> When her mother died in 1965 in New Orleans
> Flaxie demanded that Althea walk beside her in the funeral
>   procession
> and did not care how many aunts and uncles knew she slept
>   with a woman.
>
> When she died in 1970
> Flaxie fought Althea's proper family not to have her laid out in
>   lace
> and dressed the body herself
> and did not care who knew she'd made her way with a
>   woman. [94]

The poem is one of the few examples in feminist writing that brings to the poetry a radical feminist analysis of butch-femme relationships, an analysis first begun in print by Joan Nestle, who a year prior to the publication of Clarke's poem wrote an essay called "Butch-Fem Relationships: Sexual Courage in the 1950's," in which she declared:

> Butch-fem relationships, as I experienced them, were complex
> erotic statements, not phony heterosexual replicas. They were
> filled with a deeply Lesbian language of stance, dress, gesture,
> loving, courage, and autonomy. [95]

Refusing the split between personal and political, refusing romance, which, as Judy Grahn has stated, "is so much / easier and so much less / than any of us deserve," Audre Lorde's love poems also insist on the primacy of self-empowering. [96] In "Meet," the relationship between love and power, between healing and revolution, is exquisitely revealed. "Meet" is a vow from one lover to another:

> Woman when we met on the solstice
> high over halfway between your world and mine
> rimmed with full moon and no more excuses
> your red hair burned my fingers as I spread you
> tasting your ruff down to sweetness
>
> . . . .
> I will be black light as you lie against me
> I will be heavy as August over your hair
> our rivers flow from the same sea

and I promise to leave you again
full of amazement and our illuminations

. . . .

you will be white fury in my navel
I will be sweeping night
Mawulisa foretells our bodies
as our hands touch and learn
from each others hurt.

. . . .

now you are my child and my mother
we have always been sisters in pain.

Come in the curve of the lion's bulging stomach
lie for a season out of the judging rain . . . [97]

These lovers are priestesses on the solstice night; they draw a ritual circle in which the changing season is celebrated. But their lovemaking is also an act of healing, a place where black and white women meet.

The title of the poem, "Meet," has several meanings, each of which is important here. A meet can be a contest, a challenge, and so the women challenge each other ("no more excuses") to their fullest power. To meet also means to face without avoidance as well as to be united, to concur. "Meet" can also mean proper—Lorde here claims that nothing in their loving is wrong. And finally, of course, "meet" is a verb, meaning to come together, to greet. In this final sense there is a deep, powerful, and proper meeting between the two women.

"Meet" also draws power from the tension produced by ambiguous line breaks, which permit the poem to reveal its meanings slowly. The conventional ideology of romance promotes the fear of abandonment by one's lover. When Lorde endstops a line "I promise to leave you again," she fills the poem with a subtle tension until we read the next line, "full of amazement and our illuminations." The pause between these two lines also encourages the reader to consider what it would be like for lovers to promise one another leavetakings, separations, and independence.

In the line "I will be black light as you lie against me," Lorde's body is a metaphor for beauty, blackness, and luminescence, all qualities engendered by the juxtaposition of these two psyches, two bodies, touching, adjacent. However, the word "you" can also refer to the world at large, not just a single lover. In this second reading, the world is filled with ignorance and cruelty as well as love, and the verb "to lie" means to utter a falsehood, not the resting of one body against another. The poet vows to resist the lies uttered against loving and the censure and denial of lesbian relationships: she will be transformed into oxymoronic black light, incadescent darkness.

This poem can be read at yet another level, which emphasizes the intertwining of sexuality with other aspects of female power. As critic Harriet Desmoines suggests, Lorde ". . . envision[s] the tentative beginnings of a common language between black women and white women, according to the prophecies of the Dahomeyan mother of the Vodu, 'high over halfway between your world and mine / rimmed with full moon and no more excuses. . .'"98 Lorde borrows from the legend of Mawulisa as a prophecy for the possibility of the deepest healing between "black light" and "white fury," a healing in which "hands touch and learn / from each others hurt."99 This is the revolutionary vision of love between women that Lorde offers in "Meet." It is a vision of integrity and certitude. The deepest meanings of power and empowerment have been restored to the readers of this fierce, astonishing poem which both questions and embraces the meanings of power.

Remember the Sky that You Were Born Under: African and Native American Memory, History, and Myth

History, myth, and legend, as well as individual and collective memory, infuse the present in the poetry of many women of color; metaphors of transcendence and community in the poetry of Third World women span continents as well as time frames. Although some black poets (like Nikki Giovanni, for example, in "They Clapped") have claimed that American blacks have romanticized Africa and their relationship to it, both ancient and present-day Africa remain crucial sources for poets like Donna Allegra, whose powerful identification with African culture gives rise to poems like "When People Ask":

When people ask who you are

. . . .

Say that you are Africa
who birthed the rainbow children

and that they who ask must also remember
the house of sisters

Africa—a spirit risen
not from the dead
but a life run underground
now swelling to the surface
in your children's dreams now awakened
Say that you are Africa come calling
Say it until the children of every house
can give the same answer
Say it so that there's never again
the question denying
Who you are
Say: You are Africa.[100]

The poem is an incantation and a vow; its cadence sweeps over the reader like the rising crescendo of voices calling out "Amen! Tell it brother," in a black Baptist church service, or the distant drumbeats heard above the African plains. Africa provides identity, affirmation, pride.

Perhaps more than any other contemporary Afro-American woman poet, Audre Lorde has unearthed in African myth and culture images which provide for what Harriet Desmoines has called "the recovery of essential knowledge."[101] In a review of *The Black Unicorn*, Desmoines observes that

> [Lorde] reaches back across an ocean and centuries of atrocity to the country of the Dahomeyan Amazons, a homeland rife with imagery, with magic, with legend, with female Power. . .
> *The Black Unicorn* connects black women with each other through the common imagery of their finest past, the Dahomeyan Amazons, witches, warrior queens of the southern continent, the first home of human culture.[102]

In "125th Street and Abomey," Lorde draws from the myth of Seboulisa, the "mother goddess with one breast," the strength to face the aftermath of a mastectomy as an Amazon warrior. In the final lines of the poem, Lorde entreats Seboulisa, the Abomeyan creator of the world, to gaze upon her own spirited courage as a tribute to the ancient myths. As the poet is a daughter to the old legends, so she will become mother to the new.

> see me now
> your severed daughter
> laughing our name into echo
> all the world shall remember.[103]

Lorde again uses a powerful double entendre: your *severed* daughter as the one separated from you but now returning home; and your daughter with the severed-off breast, like you physically, the same. She thus highlights this double experience of simultaneous belonging and expatriation, of difference and identification.

Lorde is a contemporary feminist speaking an American diction that draws from linguistic sources and images that are more often white and urban than black. But she is also an African whose sources are ancient, female, and black. The poet describes her alliances to cultures separated by time and geography as ammunition for impending battle:

> Bearing two drums on my head I speak
> whatever language is needed
> to sharpen the knives of my tongue.[104]

And in "A Woman Speaks," another poem from *The Black Unicorn*, Lorde again asserts her geographic and transtemporal bonds:

> I do not dwell
> within my birth nor my divinities
> who am ageless and half-grown
> and still seeking
> my sisters
> witches in Dahomey.[105]

For Lorde, ancient Africa is reality as well as metaphor. Like a shaman or a witch, she travels between the worlds, visiting past lives for the knowledge they contain. In "Harriet," she returns to a childhood friendship, one embedded in an ancient past and a tribal past before the pain of slavery taught black women to keep their distance, even from one another.

> I remember you Harriet
> before we were broken apart
> we dreamed the crossed swords
> of warrior queens
> while we avoided each other's eyes

and we learned to know lonely
as the earth learns to know dead
Harriet Harriet
what name shall we call our selves now
our mother is gone?[106]

In her poem "For James Baldwin," white poet Kay Boyle describes how the knowledge of African culture and history has transformed and revolutionized the lives of black Americans:

. . . Young blacks saw Africa emerging
And knew for the first time, you said,
That they were related to kings and
To princes. It could be seen
In the way they walked, tall as cypresses,
Strong as bridges across the thundering falls. [107]

In a similar vision of power and certitude, Mari Evans names herself the towering cypress tree in "I Am a Black Woman":

I
am a black woman
tall as a cypress
strong
beyond all definition still
defying place
and time
and circumstance
    assailed
        impervious
            indestructible
Look
    on me and be
renewed[108]

The "I" here stands alone and "tallest" in the poem, itself like a cypress tree in a concrete way.

In an untitled poem by Thulani Davis, first published more than a decade ago in *Third World Women*, the poet embraces her African heritage and telescopes the space and time between herself and her African parents:

I am Brown
I am a child of the third world
 my hair black n long
  my soul slavetraded n nappy
yellow brown-Safronia
in this world, illegitimate seed
mishap of the honkies goodtimes
but I recall the past
I remember the sea n my real home
my mother, a queen from the upper Nile
my father, a Congo boatman
I am Zulu
Xhosa / Masai
many rivers flow into my waters
I am from ages ago. [109]

In "Vive Noir," a joyous, defiant celebration of blackness, Mari Evans transforms herself into an Amazon who "turn[s] rivers / from their courses" and "level[s] mountains / at a word."[110]

Such poems are the bridges between contemporary black women and their powerful foremothers like the Queen of Sheba and Nefertiti. This heritage is particularly meaningful for black woman poets because it confers the sense of individual power and tribal authority which women held in ancient Africa. As the historian John Henrik Clarke has described the status of the Amazons of Dahomey and other African women:

> In ancient Afrika . . . [the African woman] often ruled society
> with unquestioning power. Many Afrikan women were great
> militarists, and on occasion led their armies into battle. The
> Afrikan had produced a civilization where men were secure
> enough to let women advance. . . [111]

The 1920s, too, provided an important source of empowering imagery for black women's poetry, primarily in the vital Afro-American blues tradition. Taking the blues somewhat at face value, that is, as an emblem of the grief and suffering of black people's lives and especially of black women's lives, poet Sonia Sanchez, in "For Our Lady," feistily announces to famed blues singer Billie Holiday that black women are refusing to hold onto sorrow any longer—there is a revolution to attend to!

> no mo.
> > blues/trains running on this track
> > they all been de/railed.
>
> am I blue?
> . . . no. i'm blk
> > and ready.[112]

But the traditional blues song, of course, is a far more complex evocation of pain than Sanchez implies. It was—and is—an expression of self-love and anger, of defiance (Ma Rainey's "Bo-Weevil Blues" and "Prove It on Me Blues," for example) as well as an act of self-solacing, the transformation of loneliness and vulnerability through acknowledging, even itemizing one's troubles (Ma Rainey's "Counting the Blues").[113] Sherley Anne Williams' Bessie Smith poems address the importance of the blues for encouraging black women not to be victims. In "I Want Aretha to Set This to Music," Williams implies that pain is not "the sum of all of [Bessie's] knowing":

> . . . I'll
> make book Bessie did
> more than just endure.[114]

She calls the misconception that "the blues ain't nothin / but some man on yo mind" a version only of "young woman Blues."[115] Williams' Bessie acknowledges and celebrates erotic joy ("it wouldn't be blues if I didn't trance / mens to my side"), but she also uses the blues to repudiate male violence, insisting that black women have no reason to tolerate being battered: "Don' no man jes beat on / me . . . / don' care who / right who wrong that's the time / he stop bein my man."[116]

Like ancient Africa and the Afro-American blues tradition for Afro-Americans, earlier historical periods of Native American culture provide images of vision and power for many American Indian writers. Poetry, like prayers, chants, the telling of dreams, folktales, tribal lore, or oral history, is an essential part of the spiritual and aesthetic survival of American Indian people. In a culture whose people are disappearing, art and survival are not mutually exclusive, for language is a way to pass on tradition, history, tribal memory, literally a way to insure the survival of the culture. For this reason, American Indian poetry often takes on a quality of urgency. In an oral tradition, language is both revered and woven into the fabric of everyday life. Like myth or folklore, legend or dream, poetry makes the unknowable intelligible. In Native American poetry, as in all these language art forms, access is provided to the mysterious and creative powers of the universe and thus to one's own inner power.

For Native American women poets, history also provides a source of female-based power, a psychological return to a period in their native culture in which women were often respected and revered. As Dexter Fisher has noted:

> The respect accorded women in the Creation Myths has been reflected historically in the position of women within tribal societies. Many tribes are matrilineal, passing both clan names and ownership of property through the female line. Navajos honor women in the construction of their traditional home, the hogan, which is built on four poles representing the four directions. Each pole is named after a female deity, so that the support of the home literally depends on the female. Before reservation life considerably changed traditional roles, women often held positions of importance in tribal government.[117]

Grandmother Spider is one such emblem of female power. Paula Gunn Allen's "Affirmation" is a prayer and acknowledgment to Creator-Figure Grandmother Spider, whose unseen gifts reside within the poet, and whose wisdom makes possible the poet's own. Through access to Grandmother Spider's tribal memory, the poet gathers essential knowledge, learns that

> small things count after all:
> each leaf a tale
> each journey retracing some ancient myth . . .
> the power of spider thoughts
> so small
> mount, thread by thread.[118]

Similarly, in "Skeleton of Winter," Joy Harjo responds as shaman to a season of barrenness, forgotten dreams, a time "almost too dark / for vision."[119] Through the transformational power of "Memory / the other-sight," a memory tribal as well as individual, a sensory and verbal knowledge, mythic as well as historic, both the poet's and the earth's power are returned to them. The poet insists on the possibility of memory as it is transfigured in language to give birth to life, to enable those who apprehend it to become one with the earth:

I am memory alive
                    not just a name
but an intricate part
of this web of motion,
meaning: earth, sky, stars circling
my heart

                    centrifugal. [120]

This sequence of memory to language to connection with the natural world is not fixed but circular. In Linda Hogan's "Potatoes," nature
is the catalyst to memory; in digging for potatoes, the poet and her
daughter reconnect with their reverence for the earth and thus with
their tribal culture, which instills in them that reverence:

In one day of digging the earth
there is communion
of things we remember
and forget.
We taste starch
turn to sugar in our mouths. [121]

Like Charlotte De Clue's "To the Spirit of Monahsetah," in which
the poet repeats as shamanic prescription the refrain "touch earth"
after each listing of possible spiritual or geographic displacement, or
Celie's observation of the oneness of the human and natural worlds in
The Color Purple (". . . that feeling of being part of everything, not
separate at all. I knew that if I cut a tree, my arm would bleed"), Linda
Hogan depicts a world in which "even the trees with their rings / have
kept track / of the crimes that live within / and against us," and oceans
are "tongues of water / . . . sing[ing] the earth open."[122] Hogan's "To
Light" celebrates the reclaiming of spirit-based memory and affinity
with the natural world as necessary and essential components not only
of Native American culture but of human speech, of poetry, of life:

noisy tongues that once were silenced,
all the oceans we contain
coming to light. [123]

Joy Harjo's "Remember," like Linda Hogan's "To Light," insists on
the importance not only of memory and affinity with the natural world
but of language as one crucial way in which memory is continued,

carried on. The poem is an incantation whose cadence is startlingly similar to Donna Allegra's "When People Ask." In Allegra's poem, Africa is the source of a people's identity and confirmation; in Harjo's poem, that source is the natural universe, "the star's stories," "the sun's birth at dawn," "the earth whose skin you are."[124] These memories, these precious stories of the earth's life, will be lost if they are not remembered through language. Thus, the poet prays that the reader will

> Remember that all is in motion, is growing, is you.
> Remember that language comes from this.
> Remember the dance that language is, that life is.
> Remember.[125]

The invocation to remember the stories passed on by ancestors culminates with the express admonition of the necessity of tradition for survival in Carol Lee Sanchez's "Corn Children," a poem which ends with the magical, nonlinear logic: "you must remember your ancestors so they / will remember you."[126]

In Joy Harjo's "Explosion," the imagined "violent birth of horses" becomes another kind of birth: the poet's explosion into language out of speechlessness.[127] Each has a wild, astonishing beauty to it, volcanic and galvanizing. The poet and the horses "bursting out of the crazy earth" are one, their unwillingness to be tamed, contained, hers. Their urgency, wisdom, and magic, hers as well. She sees the horses through an act of volition, a willingness to apprehend, to be alive to all that is. She knows that like the poem itself, and the vision of transformation, articulation, and power which it represents, the horses which she sees will be invisible to some. But she writes for those who, in reading her words, will be able to

> . . . see the horses with their hearts of sleeping volcanoes
> and . . . be rocked awake
> > past their bodies
>
> > to see who they have become.[128]

In another poem from *She Had Some Horses*, Harjo accesses the power of language to make sense out of an often brutally senseless world. In "Rain," a young man loses his life in a truck accident. What remains—for the poet and for the reader—is not the violence of his death but rather the poet's healing and transfiguring vision of "a light in the river / folding open and open / blood, heart and stones / shimmering like the Milky Way."[129] Through language, the scene of Bobby's death is recreated and given its meaning by the poet, not by the outside world.

Finding metaphors that reconcile spirit-based knowledge and perspectives with materialist or political ones is the task of a poet who stands at the center of two worlds and who must unify diverse and conflicting experience, a frequent theme of Paula Gunn Allen's work. Allen writes of the necessity for other reconciliations as well: ceremonial with industrial understandings, psychological with mechanical time, individual with group-shared understandings of public and private events. In her poem "The Blessing," individual memory becomes communal and provides access to shared experiences, perceptions, and understandings, to an ancestral past, to the world of tribal meanings. Memory restores us to ourselves, transforms the present material world to one far more expansive and empowered:

> The circles, however large their arcs,
> close at last,
> reminding us of what we've seen
> and why we come round again.
> And so memory, that
> undying arabesque,
> that blue and silver air of being
> we helpless ride
> forever circles the eternal pueblos
> of our lives, restores the ruined
> and faded kivas of our dreams.[130]

Wendy Rose, Paula Gunn Allen, Leslie Silko, Carol Lee Sanchez, Linda Hogan, and others have referred in their poems to the healing power of ritual, the transformative power of Native American shamanism for its poets. The poet and the Native American storyteller also perform similar roles within the culture: both relate the wisdom of the tribe and are part medicine-woman and part priestess. Harriet Desmoines describes the basis of Native American religion as a poet's vision, as a

> . . . spirit quest, which is essentially a search for balance, a
> dangerous journey undertaken alone, but with the blessings of

the tribe, toward wholeness, toward the moment when inner
and outer forces merge . . . the Native American healer-singer-
poet could draw on hundreds of years of unbroken tradition to
effect her cures. She was a woman equipped to deal with her
fate and the fate of those she cared for.[131]

In a poem of profound beauty, Wendy Rose's "Walking on the
Prayerstick" celebrates the spirit-based lives of Indian people, the
power of tradition and memory, the transformation of pain into song,
song into joy, self-love into radical healing:

> When we go to the fields
> we always sing; we walk
> each of us at different times
> on the world held
> like a feathered and fetished prayerstick.
> We map our lives this way: trace our lineage
> by the corn, find our words in the flute,
> touch the shapes that feed us with dry seed.
> We grow as shrines grow from human belief;
> we sing a penetration through our pottery bodies.
> Nothing is old
> about us yet;
> we are
> still waiting.
>
> > Imagine you float
> > to those white scar marks
> > on the granite where water
> > drains breaking open the rocks
> > below, turning to ice
> > and raining on in.
> > This is where
> > we first learned to sing
> > on ancient mornings
> > because our skin was
> > red sand, because our eyes
> > floated in flashflood water,
> > because our pain was made
> > of burdens bound in cornhusk,
> > because our joy flowed
> > over the land,

> because touching ourselves
> we touched everything.[132]

Linda Hogan reveals a similar legacy of strength, a similar commitment to the future, in "Watch Me," a transcendentally beautiful litany to survival and joy. The speaker, whose "heart never believed / the end of anything," summons the majesty of her own indomitable and compassionate spirit to offer words that are both a vow and a prayer.[133] For all the women of her mother's generation and of her own whose lives have been bent by sorrow, whose bones have been too burdened to dance, Hogan promises to "dance the story of life . . . / [of] all our lives."

In a voice both individual and collective, she speaks for the transformational, tenacious, and empowered vision of all the poets whose work is discussed here when she announces to the reader, and to the world:

> I am done with weeping.
> The bones of this body say, dance.[134]

Notes

1. Margaret Atwood, *Survival: A Thematic Guide to Canadian Literature* (Toronto: Anansi, 1972); Barbara Charlesworth Gelpi, "A Common Language: The American Woman Poet," in *Shakespeare's Sisters: Feminist Essays on Women Poets*, ed. Sandra M. Gilbert and Susan Gubar (Bloomington: Indiana University Press, 1979), pp. 269–279. See also these lines from Robin Morgan's "Monster" (New York: Vintage/Random House, 1972), pp. 81–86:

   > No colonized people so isolated one from the other
   > for so long as women.
   > None cramped with compassion for the oppressor
   > who breathes on the next pillow each night.
   > No people so old, who, having, we now discover, invented
   > agriculture, weaving, pottery, language, cooking
   > with fire, and healing medicine, must now invent a revolution
   > so total as to destroy maleness, femaleness, death.

2. June Jordan, "Poem about Police Violence," in *Passion: New Poems 1977–1980* (Boston: Beacon Press, 1980), pp. 34–35.
3. Safiya Henderson, "harlem/soweto," in *Confirmation: An Anthology of African*

American Women, ed. Amiri Baraka (Le Roi Jones) and Amina Baraka (New York: Quill, 1983), pp. 134–135.

4. Audre Lorde, "Power," in *The Black Unicorn* (New York: W. W. Norton, 1978), pp. 108–109.

5. Audre Lorde, "Uses of the Erotic: The Erotic as Power," in *Chrysalis* 9 (Fall 1979): 29–31.

6. Audre Lorde, "For Each of You," in *From a Land Where Other People Live* (Detroit: Broadside Press, 1973), pp. 7–8.

7. Gwendolyn Brooks, "The Boy Died in My Alley," in *To Disembark* (Chicago: Third World Press, 1981), pp. 49–53.

8. Lucille Clifton, "Miss Rosie," in *Good Times* (New York: Random House, 1969), p. 5.

9. Chinosole, "Audre Lorde and Matrilineal Diaspora: Moving History beyond Nightmare into Structures for the Future," unpublished paper, part of a forthcoming Ph.D. dissertation, the University of Oregon, 1986, p. 1.

10. Lucille Clifton, "For de Lawd," in *Good Times* (New York: Vintage Books, 1970), p. 18.

11. Joy Harjo, "Anchorage," in *She Had Some Horses* (New York: Thunder's Mouth Press, 1983), pp. 14–15.

12. Ibid.

13. Audre Lorde, "A Litany for Survival," in *The Black Unicorn* (New York: W. W. Norton and Co., 1978), pp. 31–32.

14. Ntozake Shange, "with no immediate cause," *Nappy Edges* (New York: St. Martin's Press, 1978), pp. 114–117.

15. Audre Lorde, "Feminism and Black Liberation: The Great American Disease," in *The Black Scholar* 10, no. 8/9 (May/June 1979): 17–18. See also her article "Scratching the Surface: Some Notes on Barriers to Women and Loving," in *The Black Scholar* 9, no. 7 (April 1978): 31–35: "Black women and black men who recognize that the development of their particular strengths and interests does not diminish the other, do not diffuse their energies fighting for control over each other. We focus our attentions against the real economic, political and social forces at the heart of this society which are ripping ourselves and our children and our worlds apart."

16. Barbara Smith, "Notes for Yet Another Paper on Black Feminism, or Will the Real Enemy Please Stand Up?" *Conditions: Five* (The Black Women's Issue, ed. Lorraine Bethel and Barbara Smith) 2, no. 2 (Autumn 1979): 124.

17. Paula Gunn Allen, "Riding the Thunder," in *Shadow Country* (Los Angeles: American Indian Studies Center, UCLA, 1982), pp. 31–33.

18. Terri Meyette, "Celebration 1982," in *A Gathering of Spirit*, ed. Beth Brant (North American Indian Women's Issue of *Sinister Wisdom*), nos. 22–23 (1983): 50.

19. Lydia Yellowbird, untitled poem, in *The Third Woman: Minority Women Writers of the United States*, ed. Dexter Fisher (Boston: Houghton Mifflin, 1980), p. 15.

20. Carolyn Merchant, *The Death of Nature: Women, Ecology, and the Scientific Revolution* (San Francisco: Harper and Row, 1980), p. 28.

21. Wendy Rose, "Long Division: A Tribal History," in *Lost Copper* (Banning, Calif.: Malki Museum Press, 1980), p. 10.

22. Ibid.

23. Wendy Rose, "I expected my skin and my blood to ripen," in *Lost Copper*, pp. 14–15.

24. Brant, *A Gathering of Spirit*, p. 95.

25. Chrystos, "I Walk in the History of My People," in *This Bridge Called My Back: Writings by Radical Women of Color*, ed. Cherríe Moraga and Gloria Anzaldúa (Watertown, Mass.: Persephone Press, 1981), p. 57.

26. Cherríe Moraga, "The Welder," in *This Bridge Called My Back*, pp. 219–220.

27. Ibid.

28. Ibid.

29. Audre Lorde, *Between Our Selves* (Point Reyes: Eidolon Editions, 1976). Also in *The Black Unicorn*, pp. 112–114.

30. Audre Lorde, "Outside," in *Between Our Selves*, pp. 18–20. The poem is reprinted in *The Black Unicorn*, pp. 61–62.

31. Wendy Rose, "Epilog," in *Lost Copper*, p. 129. While many Third World feminists write about themselves as powerful women, there are real obstacles and contradictions implicit in moving past romanticized stereotypes of Third World women's strength. Gloria Anzaldúa discusses this issue in an autobiographical essay entitled "La Prieta," in *This Bridge Called My Back*, p. 204:

> I am always surprised by the image that my white and non-Chicano friends have of me, surprised at how much they *do not* know me, at how I do not allow them to know me. They have substituted the negative picture the white culture has painted of my race with a highly romanticized, idealized image. "You're strong," my friends said, "a mountain of strength."
>
> Though the power may be real, the mythic qualities attached to it keep others from dealing with me as a person and rob me of my being able to act out my other selves. Having this "power" doesn't exempt me from being prey in the streets nor does it make my scrambling to survive, to feed myself, easier. To cope with hurt and control my fears, I grew a thick skin. Oh, the many names of power—pride, arrogance, control. I am not the frozen snow queen but a flesh and blood woman with perhaps too loving a heart, one easily hurt.
>
> *I'm not invincible, I tell you. My skin's as fragile as a baby's. I'm brittle bones and human, I tell you. I'm a broken arm.*
>
> *You're a razor's edge, you tell me. Shock them shitless. Be the holocaust. Be the black Kali. Spit in their eye and never cry. Oh broken angel, throw away your cast, mend your wing. Be not a rock but a razor's edge and burn with falling.*

32. Alice Walker, in *The Monthly* (Berkeley), July 1980, p. 43. Delivered to the

testimonial dinner to honor Rosa Parks, Septima Clark, and the Highlander School on May 1, 1980.

33. Jordan, *Passion*, p. xxiv.
34. Alice Walker, "In Search of Our Mothers' Gardens," in *In Search of Our Mothers' Gardens* (New York: Harcourt, Brace, Jovanovich, 1983), p. 234.
35. Alice Walker, *Meridian* (New York: Washington Square Press, 1977), p. 44.
36. Sherley Anne Williams (Shirley Williams), "I Sing This Song for Our Mothers," in *The Peacock Poems* (Middletown, Conn.: Wesleyan University Press, 1975), pp. 79–83.
37. Ibid.
38. Zora Neale Hurston was the first American novelist, black or white, to write an entire novel in black folk idiom and to do so without caricaturing, condescending, or apologizing for it. Hurston's impact on black language can be seen in a poet like June Jordan, who in *Civil Wars* makes an impassioned and eloquent plea for the survival of black English as a cultural and poetic necessity:

> . . . A young friend of mine went through some scarifying times, leaving her homeless. During this period of intense, relentless dread and abuse, she wrote poems, trying to cope. Here are two lines from her poetry: "What have life meanted to me" and, "You are forgotten you use to existed." There are no adequate, standard English translations possible for either expression of her spirit. They are intrinsically black language cries of extreme pain so telling that even the possibilities of meaning and existence have been formulated in a past tense that is empathic, severe. I deeply hope that more of us will want to learn and protect black language. If we lose our fluency in our language, we may irreversibly forsake elements of the spirit that have provided for our survival.

(June Jordan, "White English/Black English: The Politics of Translation," in *Civil Wars* [Boston: Beacon Press, 1981], pp. 72–73). For a fuller discussion of slave narrative as a genre, see Frances Smith Foster, *Witnessing Slavery: The Development of Antebellum Slave Narratives* (Westport, Conn.: Greenwood Press, 1980), p. 122. Darwin T. Turner, in *The Art of Slave Narrative* (Western Illinois University, 1982, p. 134) makes a similar claim for the structural relationship between slave narrative and more contemporary Afro-American work. For a fuller discussion of *Their Eyes Were Watching God* and the use of slave narrative as sources for Sherley Anne Williams, see Lynda Koolish, "Freedom, Selfhood and Language: The Slave Narrative in the Work of Zora Neale Hurston, Alice Walker and Sherley Anne Williams," a paper presented to the Afro-American Literature section of the Philological Association of the Pacific Coast, Santa Cruz, California, November 1985.
39. Sherley Anne Williams, untitled poem, dated February 7, 1868, in "Letters from a New England Negro" section of *Some One Sweet Angel Chile*, p. 32.
40. Ibid. (dated December 15, 1867), p. 25.

41. Sherley Anne Williams, "fragments," in *Some One Sweet Angel Chile*, p. 63.
42. Sherley Anne Williams, "WITNESS," in *Some One Sweet Angel Chile*, p. 69.
43. Kathy Elaine Anderson, "Keep a Weathered Eye Lifting," in *Sunbury* 10 (1981): 53–54.
44. Mari Evans, "The 7:25 Trolley," in *Sturdy Black Bridges: Visions of Black Women in Literature*, ed. Roseann P. Bell, Bettye J. Parker, and Beverly Guy-Sheftall (New York: Doubleday/Anchor, 1979), p. 338.
45. In *The Third Woman*, p. 439.
46. Diana Chang, "Allegory," in *The Third Woman*, p. 430.
47. Nellie Wong, "How a Girl Got Her Chinese Name," in *Dreams in Harrison Railroad Park* (Berkeley, Calif.: Kelsey St. Press, 1977), pp. 8–9.
48. Tina Koyama, "Next," in *Breaking Silence: An Anthology of Contemporary Asian-American Poetry*, ed. Joseph Bruchac (Greenfield Center, N.Y.: Greenfield Review Press, 1983), p. 119.
49. Fay Chiang, *In the City of Contradictions* (New York: Sunbury Press, 1979), p. vi.
50. Audre Lorde, "Prologue," in *From a Land Where Other People Live*, pp. 43–46.
51. Audre Lorde, "Pathways: From Mother to Mother," in *The Black Unicorn*, pp. 71–72.
52. Audre Lorde, "Outside" in *The Black Unicorn*, pp. 61–62. See also Nellie Wong, "When I Was Growing Up," in *This Bridge Called My Back*, pp. 7–8. Gloria Anzaldúa, "La Prieta," in *This Bridge Called My Back*, pp. 198–209.
53. Janice Mirikitani, "Lullabye," in *Third World Women* (San Francisco: Third World Communications, 1972), pp. 164–165.
54. Mary Daly, *Gyn/Ecology* (Boston: Beacon Press, 1978).
55. Cherríe Moraga, "La Güera," in *This Bridge Called My Back*, p. 31.
56. Cherríe Moraga, "For the Color of My Mother," in *This Bridge Called My Back*, pp. 12–13.
57. Aurora Levins Morales, "'. . . And Even Fidel Can't Change That!'" in *This Bridge Called My Back*, p. 53.
58. Cherríe Moraga, "For the Color of My Mother," in *This Bridge Called My Back*, pp. 12–13.
59. Ibid.
60. Wendy Rose, "Sideshow: Julia the Lion Woman/The Ugliest Woman in the World," in *A Gathering of Spirit*, pp. 88–89.
61. Sherley Anne Williams, untitled poem from "Letters from a New England Negro" section, dated November 24, 1867, in *Some One Sweet Angel Chile*, pp. 23–24.
62. Sherley Anne Williams, ". . . a rowboat out on the stormy seas . . . ," in *Some One Sweet Angel Chile*, p. 48.
63. Lucha Corpi, "Como la semilla en espera/Like the seed that waits," in *Palabras de Mediodia/Noon Words*, trans. Catherine Rodriguez-Nieto (Berkeley, Calif.: El Fuego de Aztlán Publications, 1980), pp. 2–3.
64. Chirlane McCray, "I Used to Think," in *Conditions: Five* 2, no. 2 (Autumn 1979): 29.

65. Audre Lorde, "Coal," in *Coal* (New York: W. W. Norton and Co., 1976), p. 6.
66. Audre Lorde, "Black Mother Woman," in *From a Land Where Other People Live*, p. 16.
67. Audre Lorde, "For Each of You," in *From a Land Where Other People Live*, pp. 7–8.
68. Audre Lorde, "From the House of Yemanja," in *The Black Unicorn*, pp. 6–7.
69. Audre Lorde, "For Each of You," in *From a Land Where Other People Live*, pp. 7–8.
70. Lucille Clifton, "The Way It Was," in *Good News about the Earth* (New York: Random House, 1972), p. 3.
71. Lucille Clifton, "homage to my hips," in *Two-Headed Woman* (Amherst: University of Massachusetts Press, 1980), p. 6.
72. Lucille Clifton, "homage to my hair," in *Two-Headed Woman*, p. 5.
73. Ibid.
74. Lucille Clifton, "what the mirror said," in *Two-Headed Woman*, p. 7.
75. Adrienne Rich, "Tear Gas," in *Poems Selected and New, 1950–1974* (New York: W. W. Norton, 1975), p. 140.
76. Audre Lorde, "Uses of the Erotic: The Erotic as Power," *Chrysalis* 9 (Fall 1979): 29–31. See also *Heresies: A Feminist Publication on Arts and Politics* 3, no. 4, and Laura Lederer, ed., *Take Back the Night: Women on Pornography* (New York: William Morrow, 1980) for articles on this subject.
77. Aurora Levins Morales, " '. . . And Even Fidel Can't Change That!' " in *This Bridge Called My Back*, p. 56.
78. Audre Lorde, "The Erotic as Power," *Chrysalis* 9 (Fall 1979): 30–31.
79. Ntozake Shange, "okra to greens/again! special delivery," in *From okra to greens* (St. Paul, Minn.: Coffee House Press, 1984), n.p.
80. Ntozake Shange, "okra to greens/an aside on amsterdam avenue," in *From okra to greens*, n.p.
81. Nikki Giovanni, "Beautiful Black Men," in *No More Masks! An Anthology of Poems by Women*, ed. Florence Howe and Ellen Bass (Garden City, N.Y.: Anchor/Doubleday, 1973), p. 304.
82. June Jordan, "Notes toward a Black Balancing of Love and Hatred (1974)," in *Civil Wars* (Boston: Beacon Press, 1981), p. 87.
83. Ai, quoted in *The Third Woman*, p. 543.
84. Ai, "Before You Leave," in *Cruelty* (Boston: Houghton-Mifflin, 1973), p. 45.
85. Ai, "Twenty Year Marriage," in *Cruelty*, p. 1.
86. Cyn Zarco, "Saxophonetyx," in *Breaking Silence: An Anthology of Asian-American Poetry*, p. 294.
87. Linda Hogan, "Wall Songs," in *Seeing through the Sun* (Amherst: University of Massachusetts Press, 1985), pp. 67–68.
88. Daly, *Gyn/Ecology*, p. 373.
89. June Jordan, "Where Is the Love?" in *In the Memory and Spirit of Frances, Zora, and Lorraine: Essays and Interviews on Black Women and Writing*, ed. Juliette Bowles (Washington, D.C.: Institute for the Arts and the Humanities, Howard University, 1979), p. 31.

90. June Jordan, "Things That I Do in the Dark," in *Things That I Do in the Dark* (New York: Random House, 1977), frontispoem.
91. Ibid.
92. Cheryl Clarke, "Lesbianism: An Act of Resistance," in *This Bridge Called My Back*, pp. 134, 128.
93. Cheryl Clarke, "Of Althea and Flaxie," in NARRATIVES: *Poems in the tradition of black women* (New York: Kitchen Table, Women of Color Press, 1982), pp. 15–16.
94. Ibid.
95. Joan Nestle, "Butch-Fem Relationships: Sexual Courage in the 1950's," in *Heresies* 12 (1981): 21.
96. Judy Grahn, untitled poem from the section *Confrontations with the Devil in the Form of Love*, in *The Work of a Common Woman* (Trumansburg, N.Y.: Crossing Press Feminist Series, 1980), pp. 157–158.
97. Audre Lorde, "Meet," in *The Black Unicorn*, pp. 33–34.
98. Harriet Desmoines, "Sweet Medicine: A Review of *The Black Unicorn*, by Audre Lorde," *Sinister Wisdom* 13 (Spring 1980): 60–61.
99. In "Woman," Lorde uses an equally powerful metaphor for the healing between black and white women; she dreams of a time when the "commonest rock / is moonstone and ebony opal. (*The Black Unicorn*, p. 82).
100. Donna Allegra, "When People Ask," in *Lesbian Poetry: An Anthology*, ed. Elly Bulkin and Joan Larkin (Watertown, Mass.: Persephone Press, 1981), pp. 257–259. The text of Giovanni's claim in "They Clapped" that American blacks found the freedom to be themselves when they returned to Africa only to discover that they had romanticized Africa and their relationship to it is as follows:

> . . . they shook their heads when they understood there was no
> difference between the french and the english and the
>   americans
> and the afro-americans or the tribe next door or the country
>   across the border
> they were exasperated when they heard sly and the family
>   stone
> in francophone africa and they finally smiled when little
>   boys
> who spoke no western tongue said "james brown" with
>   reverence
> they brought out their cameras and bought out africa's
>   drums
> when they finally realized they are strangers all over
> and love is only and always about the lover not the beloved
> they marveled at the beauty of the people and the richness
> of the land knowing they could never possess either
>
> they clapped when they took off
> for home despite the dead
> dream they saw a free future.

(Nikki Giovanni, "They Clapped," in *My House* [New York: William Morrow, 1972], pp. 51–52).

101. Harriet Desmoines, "Sweet Medicine," *Sinister Wisdom* 13 (Spring 1980): 61.
102. Ibid.
103. Audre Lorde, "125th Street and Abomey," in *The Black Unicorn*, p. 13.
104. Audre Lorde, "Dahomey," in *The Black Unicorn*, p. 11.
105. Audre Lorde, "A Woman Speaks," in *The Black Unicorn*, p. 4.
106. Audre Lorde, "Harriet," in *The Black Unicorn*, p. 21.
107. Kay Boyle, "For James Baldwin," in *No More Masks! An Anthology of Poems by Women*, pp. 81–82.
108. Mari Evans, "I Am a Black Woman," in *I Am a Black Woman*, pp. 11–12. I am reminded of the contrast between Mari Evans' towering cypress tree and Marge Piercy's dwarfed bonsai tree in "A Work of Artifice," in *To Be of Use* (New York: Doubleday, 1973), p. 3.
109. Thulani (Nkabinde) Davis, untitled poem, in *Third World Women*, p. 50.
110. Mari Evans, "Vive Noir!" in *I Am a Black Woman*, pp. 70–73.
111. John Henrik Clarke, "The Black Woman: A Figure in World History," *Essence* (May 1971): 28. I will refrain from commenting at length here on Clarke's sexism in assuming that women only advanced because men were secure enough to *allow* them to.
112. Sonia Sanchez, "For Our Lady," in *We a BaaddDD People* (Detroit: Broadside Press, 1970), p. 41.
113. For a discussion of the blues and these lyrics in particular, see Sandra Lieb, *Mother of the Blues: A Study of Ma Rainey* (Amherst: University of Massachusetts Press, 1981).
114. Sherley Anne Williams, "I Want Aretha to Set This to Music," in *Some One Sweet Angel Chile*, p. 53.
115. Sherley Anne Williams, "the blues ain't nothin," in *Some One Sweet Angel Chile*, p. 44.
116. Sherley Anne Williams, "port arthur," in *Some One Sweet Angel Chile*, pp. 41–42.
117. Dexter Fisher, *The Third Woman*, p. 11.
118. Paula Gunn Allen, "Affirmation," in *Coyote's Daylight Trip* (Albuquerque, N.M.: La Confluencia, 1978).
119. Joy Harjo, "Skeleton of Winter," in *She Had Some Horses*, pp. 30–31.
120. Ibid.
121. Linda Hogan, "Potatoes," in *Seeing through the Sun*, p. 51.
122. Charlotte De Clue, "To the Spirit of Monahsetah," in *A Gathering of Spirit*, pp. 42–44; Alice Walker, *The Color Purple* (New York: Harcourt, Brace, Jovanovich, 1982), p. 167; Linda Hogan, "To Light," in *Seeing through the Sun*, p. 35.
123. Ibid.
124. Joy Harjo, "Remember," in *She Had Some Horses*, p. 40.
125. Ibid.
126. Carol Lee Sanchez, "Corn Children," in *excerpts from A Mountain Climber's Handbook: Selected Poems, 1971–1984* (Santa Margarita, Calif.: Taurean Horn Press/Out West Limited, 1985), pp. 58–60.

127. Joy Harjo, "Explosion," in *She Had Some Horses*, pp. 68–69.
128. Ibid.
129. Joy Harjo, "Rain," in *She Had Some Horses*, p. 17.
130. Paula Gunn Allen, "The Blessing," in *Shadow Country*, pp. 9–10.
131. Harriet Desmoines, "Sweet Medicine," *Sinister Wisdom* 13 (Spring 1980): 59.
132. Wendy Rose, "Walking on the Prayerstick," in *Lost Copper*, p. 4.
133. Linda Hogan, "Watch Me," in *Seeing through the Sun*, p. 34.
134. Ibid.

Caste, Class, and Canon

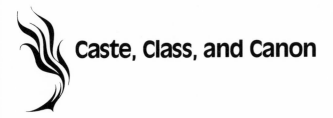

I want to consider two problems in this essay, problems which, as I shall try to show, are closely related, although they may not at first glimpse appear to be. One problem, as my title suggests, involves the "canon" of literature, that is, the works from the past that we continue to read, teach, and write about. I am less concerned here with describing the history or features of a canon or proposing alternatives to the canons we have inherited than in exploring some of the factors which have continued to shape it.[1] In particular, I want to consider how "class" and "caste," especially as they emerge in the work of literary analysis, shape canon. Examining the relationships of class, caste, and canon will, I believe, aid in understanding what we might mean by "feminist criticism," the second problem I wish to address. To frame that problem somewhat differently, how does—does?—the project of feminist criticism differ from others forms of literary analysis, and especially the formalisms rooted in the work of the New Critics? Can the question of the canon serve as a lens to help focus the project of feminist criticism?

I want to begin with an experience I had at the 1980 National Women's Studies Association convention during a session on the practice of feminist literary criticism. A group of young critics, all women, described to the audience how they met regularly at a library centrally located in their city, how they prepared and discussed various texts, and how they aided each other in developing their critical skills and range. They then handed out a poem and read it aloud, each one taking one section, and began discussing it by having each member of the group present a short statement about it. Then the audience was invited to join in the discussion. It seems like a reasonable process, and I am sure that—especially for those living in relatively isolated areas— it felt like the rushing of waterfalls in the desert. But as the session wore on I found myself getting more and more restive, indeed rather irritated.

I tried to trace my growing anger. It seemed to derive from the dynamic of the panel itself; it had, I thought, to do with the *form* of criticism, almost all close analysis of text. I found myself, reluctantly, painfully, being drawn back into the tortured style of graduate-school competition: "Can you top this?" As much macho as mind filled the room. Was this feminist criticism? I began to wonder: is the *form* of criticism value-free? Is critical technique simply a tool, like trigonometry? Well, is trigonometry value-free?

There was a second problem, the poem under consideration. As might be guessed, the poem was one from Adrienne Rich's *The Dream of a Common Language.* I want to be very clear about my comment here: I respect Adrienne Rich's poetry very much, and I particularly like that book. I think the poem that was under discussion quite a good poem indeed. But I remembered Deborah Hilty's questioning such a focus in a paper she prepared for a Midwest Modern Language Association conference. Why was it, she asked, that such panels always seem to take up poems by Adrienne Rich? Why not Judy Grahn or Susan Griffin? Or Vera Hall? Or Malvina Reynolds? Or Gwendolyn Brooks? Adrienne Rich, by the way, was among the first to ask precisely that question.

Those two questions—about the technique of criticism and the subject for analysis—led, in turn, to a third question: what connection existed between the selection of the poem and the kind of criticism, really the kind of response, being undertaken? Or, to put it another way, how is canon—that is, selection—related to, indeed a function of, critical technique? That is the fundamental question I want to consider here—the relationship of style in criticism to the canon of literature. But before I address that question specifically, I want simply to outline the nest of questions implicit in the central one:

—Can the canon significantly change if we retain essentially the same critical techniques and priorities?

—Where do the techniques of criticism come from? Do they fall from the sky? Or do they arise out of social practice? And if the latter, from what social practice?

—Out of what social practice, from what values, did close analysis of complex texts arise?

—Do we perpetuate those values in pursuing the critical practice derived from them?

—Does such critical practice effectively screen from our appreciation, even our scrutiny, other worlds of art?

—Are there other worlds of art out there whose nature, dynamics, values we fail to appreciate because we ask the wrong questions or don't know what questions to ask? Or maybe shouldn't simply be asking questions?

Such questions clearly enough reveal the drift of my argument. But to summarize it: I think the literary canon as we have known it is a product in significant measure of our training in a male, white, bourgeois cultural tradition, including in particular the formal techniques of literary analysis. And further, that other cultural traditions provide alternate views about the nature and function of art and of approaches to it. Indeed, if our concern is to change the canon "radically"—that is, at its roots—as distinct from grafting on to it a few odd branches, we must look at the full range of these alternate traditions. This argument holds, I believe, whether one is concerned with working-class art, the art of minority groups, or much of the art of women. For in significant ways all "marginalized" groups have experiences and traditions distinct from those of the dominant majority. In this paper I focus initially on working-class and black traditions, both for their inherent interest and also because they provide us with revealing perspectives on women's art as well as on feminist criticism.

Raymond Williams' distinction between "working-class" and "bourgeois" culture provides a useful starting point:

> . . . a culture is not only a body of intellectual and imaginative work; it is also and essentially a whole way of life. The basis of a distinction between bourgeois and working-class culture is only secondarily in the field of intellectual and imaginative work. . . . The crucial distinguishing element in English life since the Industrial Revolution is not language, not dress, not leisure—for these indeed will tend to uniformity. The crucial

distinction is between alternative ideas of the nature of social relationship.

"Bourgeois" is a significant term because it marks that version of social relationship which we usually call individualism: that is to say, an idea of society as a neutral area within which each individual is free to pursue his own development and his own advantage as a natural right. . . . [Both] this idea [of service] and the individualistic idea can be sharply contrasted with the idea that we properly associate with the working class: an idea which, whether it is called communism, socialism, or cooperation regards society neither as neutral nor as protective, but as the positive means for all kinds of development, including individual development.[2]

Writing from a British perspective, Williams perhaps underestimates the significance of works of imagination in defining "working-class culture": "It is not proletarian art, or council houses, or a particular use of languages; it is, rather, the basic collective idea, and the institutions, manners, habits of thought and intentions which proceed from this."[3] But his fundamental point is critical to understand: while broad areas of the culture are common to the working class and the bourgeoisie, there remains a "crucial distinction . . . between alternative ideas of the nature of social relationship." This distinction significantly explains differing "institutions, manners, habits of thought and intentions." Distinct cultures also help shape ideas about the nature of art, its functions, the processes of its creation, the nature of the artist and of the artist's social role.

There is nothing very mysterious about this: people whose experiences of the world significantly differ, whose material conditions of life, whose formal and informal training, whose traditions, sometimes even whose language differ, and especially people whose understanding of their own life-chances and opportunities, their "place" differs will think about things differently, will talk about things differently, will value at least some things differently, will express themselves *to* different people *in* different ways and *about* different experiences, at least in some measure.

But that is all very abstract. We need to be somewhat more specific about differences between working-class and bourgeois art and literature. Unfortunately, there are relatively few cultural, and particularly literary, analyses of working-class materials (at least in Western practice). Martha Vicinus' *The Industrial Muse*[4] is a unique full-length study but confined to Great Britain; Dan Tannacito examines the poetry of Colorado miners around the turn of this century;[5] an article of mine provides bibliographical and some theoretical approaches to working-class women's literature;[6] Lawrence Levine brilliantly explores the historical relationships between black culture and consciousness.[7] Even from this limited number of analyses certain features of working-class or "popular"[8] art emerge clearly. First, working-class art often is produced in group situations rather than in the privacy of a study (or garret) and it is similarly experienced in the hall, the church, the work-site, the quilting bee, the picket line. It thus emerges from the experiences of a particular group of people facing particular problems in a particular time. Much of it is therefore not conceived as timeless and transcendent; rather, it might be called "instrumental." As Tannacito puts it, "the value of the Colorado miners' poetry derived exclusively from the use made of the poems by their audience. The audience was an immediate one. The objective [in writing] was inseparable from those goals" toward which the workers' lives directed them. Vicinus points out that working-class artists, themselves persuaded of the power of literature to "influence people's behavior," aimed to "persuade readers to adopt particular beliefs." Some recommended the bourgeois values embodied in the culture of what they thought of as their "betters." Others, despairing of social and political change, devoted their work to reassuring readers that their lives, debased as they might have become, still had value and to providing at least some entertainment and consolation in an oppressive world. Many wrote to help change the status quo. Their work, Vicinus says, aimed "to arouse and focus social tension in order to channel it toward specific political actions." By "clarifying" or making vivid economic, social, and political relationships between working people and those who held power, they helped to "shape individual and class consciousness" and to "imbue a sense of class solidarity that encouraged working people to fight for social and political equality."

Tannacito provides a number of instances of the ways in which the miner poets tried to accomplish such goals. Poems of "praise," for example, explicitly tried to link heroic deeds of the past with the contemporary workers' community. Other poems sought to inspire specific forms of struggle, job actions, voting, boycotts. Miner poets, like working-class artists generally, wrote about the world they and their readers shared: the job, oppression by bosses, the militia and the scabs, a heritage of common struggle. They saw art not as a means for removing people from the world in which they lived—however desirable that might seem—nor as a device for producing "catharsis" or "stasis." Rather, art aimed to inspire consciousness about and actions within the world, to make living in that world more bearable, to extend experiences of that world, indeed to enlarge the world working people could experience. Thus, even as sophisticated an example of working-class fiction as Tillie Olsen's "Tell Me a Riddle" centrally concerns the problem of inspiring a new generation with the values, hopes, and images that directed the actions and aspirations of an earlier generation and that lie buried under the grit produced by forty years of daily life. Or consider how Morris Rosenfeld renders the experience of time-discipline in his work as a pants presser:

> The Clock in the workshop,—it rests not a moment;
> It points on, and ticks on: eternity—time;
> Once someone told me the clock had a meaning,—
> In pointing and ticking had reason and rhyme. . . .
> At times, when I listen, I hear the clock plainly;—
> The reason of old—the old meaning—is gone!
> The maddening pendulum urges me forward
> To labor and still labor on.
> The tick of the clock is the boss in his anger.
> The face of the clock has the eyes of the foe.
> The clock—I shudder—Dost hear how it draws me?
> It calls me "Machine" and it cries [to] me "Sew!"[9]

Rosenfeld is concerned to capture, and to mourn, the passing in a particular historical moment of an older, less time-disciplined order of work as well as the degradation of the worker to the status of machine. The poem gives names and pictures to the experiences that Rosenfeld and his fellow workers encountered in moving from the shtetl to the sweatshops of the new world.

Working-class art thus functions to focus consciousness and to develop ideology, but it can also play a variety of other roles. Songs were used, especially by black slaves and nominally free laborers, to set the pace of work in a group and, at the same time, to relieve the tension and pent-up feelings born of oppressive labor. Leaders lined out a rhythm for hoeing, chopping, lifting bales, rowing boats. At the same time, the songs spoke realistically about the shared labor, and more covertly, perhaps, about those exacting it.[10] Similarly, sorrow songs or spirituals served not only to express grief and to sustain hope in slavery, but they were also used as signals to prepare for escapes from it.[11] Similarly, during the Civil Rights movement of the 1950s and 1960s, what were originally church hymns underwent conversion to marching songs and sometimes means for triumphing over one's jailers.

Clearly, the conception of the functions of art are here very different from those propounded, say, by Aristotle, or Milton, or Coleridge—or formalist criticism, as I shall indicate in a moment. It is not, however, only conception or function which differs, but also form and technique and even the manner of creation of much working-class art. In characterizing the distinctive qualities of the song styles of black slaves, Levine emphasizes "its overriding antiphony, its group nature, its pervasive functionality, its improvisational character, its strong relationship in performance to dance and bodily movements and expression. . . ."[12] Some of these qualities are peculiar to styles derived from West African roots, but some are characteristic of other working-class cultures. New songs are often based upon old ones, and there is less concern with the unique qualities of art than with building variations upon tunes, themes, and texts well known in the community. For example, songs like "Hold the Fort" and "We Are Building a Strong Union," which began as gospel hymns, went through a series of metamorphoses in order to serve the needs of a diverse sequence of workers' organizations—in the case of the former, including the British transport workers, the Knights of Labor, and the Industrial Workers of the World. The Wobbly poet Joe Hill constructed some of his best-known songs as take-offs on Salvation Army hymns. The spiritual "Oh, Freedom" became one of the most popular songs of the Civil Rights movement; as the movement's militance increased, many singers changed the song's refrain from "Before I be a slave / I be buried in my grave / And go home to my Lord / And be free" to "Before . . . grave / And I'll fight for my right / To be free."

In many ways, working-class art, like other elements in working-class life, is highly traditional; certainly innovative form is not a primary consideration and "make it new" a slogan which would be viewed with some suspicion. Similarly, working-class poetry and song especially, but also tales and stories, are often built around repeated elements—refrains, formulae, commonly accepted assumptions about characters. Language, too, is often simpler, sometimes commonplace, certainly less "heightened" than that of "high culture" verse. Many of these characteristics are common to literary forms rooted in oral art, made necessary by the exigencies of memory and improvisation. Some may arise from the artist's desire to avoid a fancy vocabulary unfamiliar to the audience or esoteric images and allusions. Thus, a poem like Rosenfeld's carefully works with materials as familiar to his readers as gaberdine was to him.

In some respects as well these characteristics are derived from the communal character of the creation of certain working-class art forms. One old former slave describes the creation of a "spiritual" in a pre–Civil War religious meeting in these words:

> I'd jump up dar and den and hollar and shout and sing and pat, and dey would all cotch de words and I'd sing it to some old shout song I'd heard 'em sing from Africa, and dey'd all take it up and keep at it, and keep a-addin' to it, and den it would be a spiritual.[13]

In such situations, the individual creator is generally less significant than the group; or, rather, to the extent that individuals are creators, they shape a common stock to new group purposes without diminishing or expropriating that common stock. The song leader in church is not asked to provide new hymns (much less copyright old ones) and would be looked at with suspicion if she did so. She is asked to reinvigorate a hymn that is known, perhaps to add something especially appropriate for the occasion.[14] The jazz musician may be admired for a new melody, but probably more important—at least until recently— is the ability to ring variations on melodies the listeners know and follow. I am emphasizing here the "folk," communal elements of working-class art, in some degree at the expense of art produced by self-conscious individual working-class artists. I do so because an approach through people's culture helps to focus certain distinctive qualities of working-class art, certain "centers of gravity," not so easily seen if one concentrates on the productions of separate artists. Yet, obviously, a continuum exists between songs, poems, and tales which are, so to speak, common property and works created primarily by individual imaginations.

But what is critical here is precisely the relationship between individual and community. Levine, for example, directly connects the *form* of the spiritual with the underlying social reality of black slave life:

> Just as the process by which the spirituals were created allowed
> for simultaneous individual and communal creativity, so their
> very structure provided simultaneous outlets for individual and
> communal expression. The overriding antiphonal structure of
> the spirituals—the call and response pattern which Negroes
> brought with them from Africa and which was reinforced in
> America by the practice of lining out hymns—placed the indi-
> vidual in continual dialogue with his community, allowing him
> at one and the same time to preserve his voice as a distinct entity
> and to blend it with those of his fellows.[15]

I would carry the argument in a slightly different direction by suggesting that one center of gravity of working-class art is its high level of integration of creator and audience. Works often have their origin, as well as their being, in situations which do not absolutely distinguish active performer/artist from passive audience. Or when the distinction is relatively clearer, the artist's "product" is offered not primarily for its exchange value (money for that song or painting), but for its use in the lives of the people to whom it is directed. A moving example is provided by the Kentucky mountain songs sung at the funeral of "Jock" Yablonski and recorded with great majesty in the film *Harlan County, U.S.A.*

In a larger sense, all working-class art (perhaps all art)[16] must be explored precisely in terms of its use. Partly that is a function of marginality itself: the struggle for existence and dignity necessarily involves all available resources, including art. But partly, I think, this phenomenon is explained by the fundamental character of working-class culture, what Williams called "solidarity." It is not simply a slogan or an abstraction that happens to appeal to many people who work. It is, rather, a way of describing the culture of people who have been pushed together into workplaces and communities where survival and growth enforce interdependence. In this context, the work of the artist—while it may in some respects be expressive and private—remains overwhelmingly functional in his or her community. And an approach to it cannot strip it of this context without ripping away its substance.

My argument began from the premise that the conditions of life of working-class people have produced ideas about social relationships crucially distinct from those of the bourgeoisie. This distinction shaped differing institutions, manners, ideas about culture and art. In order to approach working-class culture, then, we must begin not with presuppositions about what literature is and is not, or what is valuable in it or not, but rather by asking in what forms, on what themes, in what circumstances, and to what ends do working people speak and sing and write and signify to each other. We must, in other words, discover the distinctive rules and measures of working-class art and thus the critical strategies and tools appropriate to them.

"Are you saying," someone might object, "that the rules and measures—the critical tools—we now possess are invalid, somehow biased or irrelevant?" Here, indeed, is the nub of the matter. For we do approach culture with certain presuppositions, frameworks, touchstones which we learn and which we learn to valorize. I have tried here to state as neutrally as I can certain of the qualities and origins of working-class art. I have not tried to lay a spiritual like "Roll, Jordan" or a poem like Rosenfeld's alongside, say, Donne's "A Valediction: forbidding mourning" in order to evaluate one in relation to another or all against some "universal" standard of measurement. For the central issue is not which is "better," but what we mean by "better." And I am sure it is clear by now that I believe such standards of judgment, which shape the canon, to be rooted in assumptions derived from class and caste about the techniques, qualities, and especially the functions of art.

I do not want to be misleading here: I do not believe that somewhere out there is a working-class poet, ignored through bourgeois prejudice, who actually wrote better metaphysical poems than Donne or more singular ones than Shelley. No more do I think that a factory organized along truly socialist lines will be more "efficient" and "productive" than a capitalist factory; capitalists often find means to do rather well what it is they want to do—in this case to squeeze as much profit from workers as they can. But that does not necessarily make for a humane, safe, creative, or socially responsible workplace. The goals are different; the values and thus the priorities different. On the other hand, it has been demonstrated that there are forgotten black and white women writers who wrote fiction as good in traditional terms as that of many of the white men with whom we are familiar. As Williams pointed out, there are vast shared areas of culture. My main point, however, is that if there probably are no working-class metaphysical poets, neither did Donne write verses for "Roll, Jordan." And if "Roll, Jordan" does not demonstrate the fine elaboration of complex language to be found in "A Valediction," it is also the fact that none of Donne's poems—not all of them together, I dare say—has served to sustain and inspire so many thousands of oppressed people. What, finally, is art about?

Mr. Allen Tate had an answer for us. "Good poetry," he writes in "Tension in Poetry," "is a unity of all the meanings from the furthest extremes of intension and extension . . . . the meaning of poetry is its 'tension,' the full organized body of all the extension and intension that we can find in it."[17] In the same essay he attacks Edna St. Vincent Millay's "Justice Denied in Massachusetts," a poem written in gloomy reaction to the execution of Sacco and Vanzetti.

> Let us abandon then our gardens and go home
> And sit in the sitting-room.
> Shall the larkspur blossom or the corn grow under this cloud?
> Sour to the fruitful seed
> Is the cold earth under this cloud,
> Fostering quack and weed, we have marched upon but cannot
>   conquer;
> We have bent the blades of our hoes against the stalks of them.
>
> Let us go home, and sit in the sitting-room.
> Not in our day
> Shall the cloud go over and the sun rise as before,
> Beneficent upon us
> Out of the glittering bay,
> And the warm winds be blown inward from the sea
> Moving the blades of corn
> With a peaceful sound.

"These lines," Tate claims, "are mass language: they arouse an affective state in one set of terms, and suddenly an object quite unrelated to those terms gets the benefit of it." The Millay poem, he continues,

> is no doubt still admired, by persons to whom it communicates certain feelings about social justice, by persons for whom the

lines are the occasion of feelings shared by them and the poet.
But if you do not share those feelings, as I happen not to share
them in the images of dessicated nature, the lines and even the
entire poem are impenetrably obscure.[18]

It once occurred to me that Tate might be using "obscure" in a Pick-
wickian sense, for whatever one might think of the Millay poem it
seems rather less obscure than Tate's critique. But then, from his point
of view, "communication in poetry" is a fallacy. The poet is "not responsible to society for a version of what it thinks it is or what it wants."
The poet is responsible to his conscience. And he (the pronoun remains Tate's) is responsible "for the virtue proper to him as poet, for his
special *arête*: for the mastery of a disciplined language which will not
shun the full report of reality conveyed to him by his awareness: he
must hold, in Yeats' great phrase, 'reality and justice in a single
thought.'"[19] Elsewhere Tate approvingly quotes I. A. Richards to the
effect that poetry is "complete knowledge": "The order of completeness
that it achieves in the great works of the imagination is not the order of
experimental completeness aimed at by the positivist sciences. . . .
For the completeness of *Hamlet* is not of the experimental order, but of
the experienced order; it is, in short, of the mythical order."[20]

Given this self-contained idea of poetry, it is not surprising that formalist critics like Tate should develop techniques emphasizing intense
analysis of a poem's language and its "tensions," or that they should
conceive the primary task of the "man of letters" as preserving "the
integrity, the purity, and the reality of language wherever and for whatever purpose it may be used." "He must," Tate goes on to explain,
approach this task "through the letter—the letter of the poem, the
letter of the politician's speech, the letter of the law; for the use of the
letter is in the long run our one indispensable test of the actuality of
our experience."[21] How different this conservative, monitory role from
that staked out for the American Scholar by Emerson. Besides, is it
really necessary to talk about the taste of rotting fruit to test its actuality? However that might be, Tate's ultimate vision of the "man of
letters" asserts an even weightier function: ". . . the duty of the man of
letters is to supervise the culture of language, to which the rest of
culture is subordinate, and to warn us when our language is ceasing to
forward the ends proper to man. The end of social man is communion
in time through love, which is beyond time."[22] The man of letters thus

stands a priest of language, linking society and culture with the transcendent.

But why devote such attention to these ideas, or once again pillory an often-abused guru of the New Criticism? Has not criticism passed beyond the exegetical stage? In theory, it has. In practice, however, and especially in the common practice of the classroom, the dominant mode of procedure remains exploring the "furthest extremes of intension and extension" we may find in a text. And the texts we prefer are, on the whole, those which invite such explication. One or another version of formalism remains, in short, the meat and potatoes of what men—and women—of letters stir up for our students and readers. And while Tate's ecclesiastical trappings may have been doffed as rather too quaint and burdensome, something of the incense lingers in the justifications for what we do. Thus, it seems to me important to ask what social and political values generate the forms of criticism and its jusifications we find in Tate and his fellows.

There is a second, perhaps more fundamental reason for examining Tate's ideas. He and his New Critical peers were the first generation to pose what became, and still is, the dominant paradigm of academic criticism. I want to suggest that, regardless of form, academic criticism in the past half-century has retained a common set of social and political roots and a consistent function. An image may help flesh this assertion. In *Invisible Man* Ellison pictures a statue of the "Founder," his hands holding the edges of a veil which covers the face of the black youth kneeling before him. The speaker of the book comments that it is never clear whether the Founder is lifting the veil from the boy's face or holding it ever more firmly in its place. That ambiguous image may stand for the academic critic; is he (I want to retain the overwhelmingly appropriate pronoun) offering enlightenment by lifting the veil or holding the student in a kind of darkness?

In feminist pedagogy a distinction has developed between two forms of teaching: one, which often involves the display of a specialized vocabulary, has the tendency to overwhelm students, paralyzing them before the erudition of the teacher; another, seen as developing from the equalitarian ideals of feminism, tries to legitimize the student's own responses to a text, to history, to experience as the starting points for analysis and thus understanding. To be sure, it has often been easy to overstate this distinction between—in crude shorthand—lecturer as authority and discussion leader as participant, to convert pedagogical tendencies into behavioral absolutes; indeed, to elevate difference in style into fiercely held educational principles. For all that rhetoric has burdened us with inflation of difference, the differences remain, more perhaps as foci or what I have called "centers of gravity" than as differences in kind. Analogous "centers of gravity" can, I think, be charted in criticism. Is the objective result of criticism to help readers formulate, understand, and develop their own responses? To open a text to a common reader? Or is it to make the reader feel excluded from the critical enterprise, sense his or her own responses to a work as essentially irrelevant to the process of its exploration? The latter result has, it seems to me, the concomitant effect—or, perhaps I should say, underlying motive—of confirming the position, the cultural power of the critic himself, even while, as was historically the case in the 1920s and 1930s, the real social authority of the class from which "men of letters" were drawn was being eroded. In fact, I want to argue, the major project of criticism as it developed from patriarchs like Tate was the confirmation of the authoritative position, at least with respect to culture, of the Man of Letters and his caste. And while the *forms* of criticism have changed—from New Criticism to Structuralism to Post-Structuralism—the *functions* of academic criticism seem to me to have remained constant, related primarily to the status, power, and careers of critics.[23]

There is, furthermore, an awful logic to the changes in form that derives precisely from the persistence of function. At the beginning, formal analysis did—as it still can—help illuminate texts. And as differing kind of analyses developed, these too added to the illumination, albeit with increasing marginality. But a law of diminishing returns necessarily begins to operate with the thirtieth explication of "A Valediction" or the eighteenth lick of ice-cream, and the eye of the beholder starts to shift from the qualities of the text to the qualities of the comment, from the poet to the critic; with the exhaustion of the ways of looking at a pigeon, we begin to observe the antics of the pigeon-watchers. And thus emerges a speculative criticism claiming equality with the literary texts (once the objects to be illuminated) and framed a language increasingly impenetrable to the common reader. The project of such criticism *is* its politics.

This is not to say that academic critics are by character and inclination conscious elitists; my point is not, in any case, characterological.

The very momentum, not to say corpulence, of academic criticism hides its political origins. But in sad fact, cultural institutions move in the directions established by their initial political impetus unless or until they are redirected by the intervention of a new political force—like the social and cultural movements of the 1960s and 1970s. Thus, to understand contemporary academic criticism we must examine its roots and its values as these appear in their rudimentary form.

These values emerge into severe profile from Tate's account of the limitations of Southern literature:

> But the abolition of slavery did not make for a distinctively Southern literature. We must seek the cause of our limitations elsewhere. It is worth remarking, for the sake of argument, that chattel slavery is not demonstrably a worse form of slavery than any other upon which an aristocracy may base its power and wealth. That *African* chattel slavery was the worst groundwork conceivable for the growth of a great culture of European pattern, is scarcely at this day arguable. . . . The distance between white master and black slave was unalterably greater than that between white master and white serf after the destruction of feudalism. The peasant *is* the soil. The negro slave was a barrier between the ruling class and the soil. If we look at aristocracies in Europe, say in eighteenth-century England, we find at least genuine social classes, each carrying on a different level of the common culture. But in the Old South, and under the worse form of slavery that afflicts both races today, genuine social classes do not exist. The enormous "difference" of the Negro doomed him from the beginning to an economic status purely: he has had much the same thinning influence upon the class above him as the anonymous city proletariat has had upon the culture of industrial capitalism. . . .
>
> The white man got nothing from the Negro, no profound image of himself in terms of the soil. . . . But the Negro, who has long been described as a responsibility, got everything from the white man. The history of French culture, I suppose, has been quite different. The high arts have been grafted upon the peasant stock. We could graft no new life upon the Negro; he was too different, too alien.[24]

It is not my intent to comment upon the less than genteel racism, the abysmal cultural chauvinism, or even the simple historical ignorance of this passage. But it does make amply clear the elitist soil in which Tate's formalist ideas of poetry and the "man of letters" are rooted. The New Criticism is the fruit—strange fruit—of such plants. But that metaphor is rather too easy. In plain fact, criticism which makes all-important the special languages that specially trained critics share with specially cultivated poets is finally a means for defending special privilege. It is a version of what Raymond Williams calls the "dominative" use of language.

Meridel LeSueur, who studied with Tate and others at the University of Minnesota, has a different way of drawing the connection between the politics and the critical style of these men of letters: "It was just like being bitten every morning by a black spider—paralysis set in. They taught the structure of the short story this way: you run around Robin Hood's barn, have two or three conclusions, and then come to a kind of paralysis. Ambiguity is a very seductive idea."[25] The paralysis of ambiguity in a world crying for change fits well with *Reactionary Essays on Poetry and Ideas.*

I am not suggesting that formalist critics are necessarily racists or political reactionaries in their personal outlooks or that every formalist move necessarily builds higher the bulwarks of bourgeois culture. But it seems to me natural to suspect a project with such roots and thus (returning at last to the nest of questions I raised many pages back) to propose that, indeed, critical tactics carry with them rather more ideological baggage than we might at first have suspected.

In the opening section of *Stealing the Language: The Emergence of Women's Poetry in America* (1986), Alicia Ostriker has analyzed how that ideology operated to marginalize women poets. She cites, among other documents, John Crowe Ransom's essay on Millay,[26] which nicely illustrates how the formalist aesthetic principles Ransom shared with Tate worked in practice. Ransom writes:

> Man distinguishes himself from woman by intellect, but he should keep it feminized. He knows he should not abandon sensibility and tenderness, though perhaps he has generally done so. . . . But the problem does not arise for a woman. Less pliant, safer as a biological organism, she remains fixed in her famous attitudes, and is indifferent to intellectuality. I mean, of course, comparatively indifferent; more so than a man. (P. 78)

Thus, from Ransom's point of view, Millay's is a lesser "vein of poetry," "spontaneous, straightforward in diction," with "transparently simple" structures and "immediate" effects (pp. 103–105). Indeed, a good deal of Ransom's essay is devoted to showing how, in effect, Millay's "excitingly womanlike" poems display little analyzable "intention" or "extension" and thus are not intellectually challenging. It seems to me clear how patriarchy and racism emerge into critical categories and a methodology that helped place the work of most white women and black writers behind the veil.

By this long and perhaps burdensome route we return to that room in Lawrence, Kansas, that panel on feminist criticism, and maybe even my growing anger. For I came to that panel with the ideas I've outlined. It seemed to me that while there are broad shared areas, the social experiences and the cultures of women and men diverge at significant points. I do not have ready terms, like "individualism" and "solidarity," to characterize the distinct organizing principles, but it seemed quite plain that significantly diverse experiences will produce significantly diverse cultural forms among men and women, just as among blacks and whites, working people and bourgeoisie. And that, therefore, the application to women's art of principles and standards derived almost exclusively from the study of men's art will tend to obscure, even hide, and certainly undervalue what women have created. Indeed, the application of critical standards and tactics derived from white, male—not to say racist and elitist—culture not only obscures female accomplishment, on the one side, but reinforces the validity of those critical standards and what they represent, on the other. Thus, I thought that panel's project was grafting Adrienne Rich's poem onto Allen Tate's stock—to borrow a Tate metaphor—rather than joining the dialogue in which *The Dream of a Common Language* and *The Common Woman* poems both participate. It is not that the panelists shared Tate's and Ransom's values; rather, in pursuing their techniques, the panel seemed to me to reinforce the structures of academic elitism.

I hope this will not be misconstrued into an odd shorthand report like "Lauter says there's a peculiar female sensibility and that criticism is male, so feminists should be doing something else, as yet unspecified." I do *not* know if there is such a thing as a female sensibility. "Sensibility" is a psychological category and is approachable, I think, only through individuals. I am talking not of sensibility but of *culture*, which is a social category. It cannot be used to predict individual behavior, but it is critical to understanding how we perceive, indeed what we look at, as well as how we conceive the structures of language we call works of art.

Formalist critics, I am suggesting, are trapped within their culture, restricted in what they look at and by who looks. Why? First, because they have derived much of their cultural data from a narrow base, largely art composed by white Western men (as Tate's comment on Southern culture reveals). They have not adequately considered art from outside that tradition, except, as it were, after the fact, after they had donned their theoretical spectacles. Also, these spectacles have been ground by the social and economic pressures which characteristically mold the residents of academe. For criticism is not solely a pure activity of mind, an expression of altruism directed toward revealing truth, or even the play of intellect upon the surfaces of language. It may upon occasion be these. It will also in some measure be an ideology constructed in order to insure and enhance the social and economic position of the critic and his class—even occasionally, now, "her" class. To put it another way, the connection we have seen of New Critical methodology with reactionary politics is no accident, nor is the obscurity, of, say *Diacritics*. An adequate theory of criticism can only be developed by fully considering the art produced by women, by working people, and by national minorities; further, such art needs to be understood in light of its own principles, not simply in terms and categories derived from so-called high culture or on the basis of the imperatives imposed by careerism or reigning institutional priorities.

Thus, the first task in the project of feminist criticism seems to me the recovery of lost works by women and the restoration of the value of disdained genres. In part a restorative literary history is required simply for the sake of intellectual honesty. But more important, as I have suggested, is the imperative for broadening the "text milieu" from which we derive critical and historical propositions. Now this task has considerably been advanced in the last decade, as witness, on the one hand, the publications of feminist and university presses and, on the other, the recent issuance of Gilbert and Gubar's *Norton Anthology of*

Literature by Women. But the work is by no means complete or, for a number of reasons, is it likely soon to be. For example, women writers of early and mid nineteenth-century America are known to most readers, even most academics, mainly secondhand, through such useful studies as Nina Baym's.[27] In fact, writers of substance like Caroline Kirkland, Lydia Maria Child, Alice Cary are seldom read, in part because their books have not been reissued for over a hundred years,[28] in part because they have not been given the legitimation of academic study even to the degree that someone as marginal as William Gilmore Simms has been. Most important, the modern outlook, and particularly modern criticism, has been out of sympathy with the sensibilities displayed in the work of such authors. I shall have more to say about that in a moment. Suffice it here to say it is unlikely that the deep obscurity in which women writers from Sherwood Bonner to Zitkala-Sa are hidden is peculiarly an American phenomenon; thus, I doubt whether we are close to the end of the process of rediscovery.

More certainly, even, we are far from establishing the distinctive qualities of the art of these and many better-known women writers. This seems to me the second major task of feminist criticism. Studies like Baym's, Barbara Christian's, Elaine Showalter's, and Sandra Gilbert's and Susan Gubar's[29] are only among some of the better-known works devoted to establishing thematic and formal connections among women writers. A parallel task is defining the distinctive thematic and formal characteristics of particular women writers. Elizabeth Ammons' examination of the structure of Jewett's *The Country of the Pointed Firs*[30] provides an especially useful example because it implicitly questions received norms about the structure of short fictions and suggests that Jewett used a distinct and perhaps gender-linked form.

There is, of course, a certain dialectic between the rediscovery of works and an adequate account of characteristics that link them to other texts. In reevaluating the writing of Caroline Kirkland, Judith Fetterley has suggested that *A New Home, Who'll Follow* is in essence a series of elaborated letters and that the letter form represented for women a literary halfway house between the privacy of correspondence and the public act of authorship, an act seen by many in the early nineteenth century as unseemly for women. That suggestion took on for me powerful implications as I recently reread Sarah Grimke's

Letters on the Equality of the Sexes and Lydia Maria Child's *Letters from New York,* thought about the letter form adopted by Margaret Fuller in the last years of her life, and finally focused (thanks particularly to one of my students, Ellen Louise Hart) on the implications of such precedents on the major form of Emily Dickinson's (self-)"publication"—letters:

> This is my letter to the World
> That never wrote to Me . . .

It would at this point claim too much to propose correspondence as constituting a fundamental model for many American nineteenth-century women of letters, but as we come to know more about these writers that may, indeed, be our conclusion. I pose this hypothesis as a minor illustration of how the dialectic between rediscovery and definition of characteristic themes and forms operates. It also leads us toward two additional objectives in the project of feminist criticism.

These I would describe as decentering male texts, on the one hand, and moving female texts from the margins of culture to the core. Decentering male texts (including phallocentric criticism) was in many respects the initial concern of the earliest feminist critics. It took two forms: study of the images of women, often absurd or vile, projected in widely respected work by male writers. Second, and in these days of theoretical sophistication too often condescended to, were works like Kate Millett's pioneering and courageous *Sexual Politics* (1970). It need hardly be said that the work of decentering phallocentric culture as it is expressed in language, syntax, form, and institutional configuration remains a major concern of current feminist criticism. Indeed, the major contribution of contemporary French feminist writing may be in this area. What is surprising, perhaps, is how persistent phallocentric historical models have remained despite the accumulated weight of contrary evidence.

A vivid illustration of how phallocentric literary history continues to obscure the work of women writers was provided by Leslie Fiedler in an essay called "Literature and Lucre" and features in the *New York Times Book Review* (May 31, 1981). Fiedler pictures the history of the novel in America as a struggle between "high Art and low," between "those writers among us who aspire to critical acclaim and an eternal place in libraries" and "the authors of 'best sellers.'" The former, "sophisticated novelists," include Charles Brockden Brown, Poe, Hawthorne, and Melville—all male, as Fiedler points out. The latter tradition, "a series of deeply moving though stylistically undistinguished fictions . . . begins with Susanna Rowson's *Charlotte Temple*, reaches a 19th-century high point with Harriet Beecher Stowe's *Uncle Tom's Cabin* and a 20th-century climax with Margaret Mitchell's *Gone with the Wind*."

This spurious battle of the sexes and the image of the failed artist which supposedly emerges from it can be sustained only by ignoring huge parts of American literary history. For example, Fiedler proclaims that "only in the last decade of this century did it become possible, first in fact, then in fiction, for a novelist highly regarded by critics (Norman Mailer is an example) to become wealthy long before his death." This is patrifocal history with a vengeance, since it altogether ignores Edith Wharton, Willa Cather, and Ellen Glasgow, not to speak of Stowe, E. D. E. N. Southworth (who was much praised by contemporary critics), Jewett, Mary Austin, and even William Dean Howells. Most of these women novelists, among others, were and still are "highly regarded by critics" and did very well from their writing. But more to the point, bringing them up altogether explodes the theory, or perhaps myth, Fiedler wishes to float, that in America writers have either been (until our generation) successful *or* artistic: "both primary and secondary literature in the United States, the novels and poems of which we are most proud and the critical autobiographical [*sic*] works written on them, reflect the myth of the 'serious' writer as an alienated male, condemned to neglect and poverty by a culture simultaneously commercialized and feminized." Since the women novelists don't fit this nice theory, "we" need to ignore them. And also ignore the fact that writers like Melville and Hawthorne indeed aspired to popularity and were enraged by what they took to be the failure of their audience to appreciate them.

Nor is it at all clear, as Fiedler makes out, that Stowe, for example, was not artistic as well as successful. On the contrary, recent studies have documented her artistry. In linking her to Rowson and Mitchell, Fiedler is trying to stigmatize her with the unstated labels, familiar from critics like Tate, of "sentimental" and "mass market." "Sentimental" and "mass" are terms, like "regional," "popular," "minor," which have been undergoing reexamination[31] since it became clear they were used to bury much of value on specious assumptions, like the proposition that the suppression of feelings, even tears, is a more legitimate basis for fiction than their display. [32] In short, the problem with Fiedler's theory is that it begins with a truncated set of data, examines them from a dazzlingly parochial angle of vision, and, not surprisingly, concludes by reinforcing the artistic centrality of the traditional male texts which have constituted the canon.

Moreover, the myth of the unappreciated artist itself requires a differing analysis. Myths constitute metaphorical ideologies. Here, the problem for American male writers is construed as the frailty of his audience. It might equally well be posed as the obstinate refusal of many male novelists to take that dominantly female audience seriously. In concluding her second series of stories entitled *Clovernook* (1853), Alice Cary deftly questions the motives of those who, as Fiedler puts it, aspire to "an eternal place in libraries":

> In our country, though all men are not "created equal," such is the influence of the sentiment of liberty and political equality, that:
> "All thoughts, all passions, all delights,
> Whatever stirs this mortal frame,"
> may with as much probability be supposed to affect conduct and expectation in the log cabin as in the marble mansion; and to illustrate this truth, to dispel that erroneous belief of the necessary baseness of the "common people" which the great masters in literature have in all ages labored to create, is a purpose and an object in our nationality to which the finest and highest genius may wisely be devoted; but which may be effected in a degree by writings as unpretending as these reminiscences of what occurred in and about the little village where I from childhood watched the pulsations of surrounding hearts. [33]

Cary's comment not only raises questions about the values of the literary "masters," but suggests the importance of an alternative standard embodied in the "unpretending . . . reminiscences" of her village which she—and, indeed, many American women writers—presents.

And that comment brings me to the last part of the project of feminist criticism upon which I wish to touch: the effort to move the work of women from the margins toward the center of culture. Here the work of criticism and of political action most fully converge. For in the first instance it was not the work of critics that refocused attention on

the distinctive concerns of women writers any more than black aesthet-
icians initially established the conditions for recognizing the traditions
of African-American composition. On the contrary, it was the movements for social, economic, and political change of the 1960s and
1970s that challenged long-held assumptions about what was significant as subject matter for literary art by challenging the assumptions
about what was significant for *people.* Meridel LeSueur once described
how her story "Annunciation," which deals with pregnancy, was
turned down by editors demanding conflict and action. That may
stand as a symbol of my point here: it will *not* be on the basis solely of
"literary" criteria that the days and works of women—any more than of
other marginalized groups—will be established at the center of cultural concern.

In California, the school system in cooperation with certain universities has launched an ambitious "literature project" designed to reinvigorate the teaching of English at the secondary level. Part of that
effort has involved the creation of model curricula, including what are
called "core" and "extended" readings. One model thematic unit is
titled "Journey to Personal Fulfillment." The "core" readings are these:
Dickens, *Great Expectations*; Twain, *Huckleberry Finn* and *Life on the
Mississippi*; Shaw, *Pygmalion*; Cather, "Paul's Case"; Kafka, "The
Hunger Artist"; Auden, "The Unknown Citizen"; Eliot, "The Hollow
Men"; and Whitman, "The Ox-Tamer." These selections suggest that
an old canard still lives: "Choose works that interest the boys; the girls
will read anything." That reflection is reinforced by considering that
among the "extended readings" are *Jane Eyre*, *Wuthering Heights*, E.
B. Browning's *Sonnets from the Portuguese*, the autobiographies of
Mme. Curie and Helen Keller, and Alice Walker's "African Images."
Further, one might wonder, in a state in which Latinos, Asian Americans, American Indians, and blacks will shortly constitute a majority,
whether all of these works together constitute any adequate portrait of
journeys to "personal fulfillment." I do not cite this instance to mock
the very concerned people working in this important project. On the
contrary, I think we need to admire and support their efforts even as we
criticize them. But it will not be critical practice alone that will shift
what is perceived and treated as "core." To be sure, as literary people
we need to reexamine hierarchies of taste as expressed in subject matter, genre, language, and imagery as well as in conceptions of literary

function and audience.[34] Still, there is little more that can be done to establish the *literary* equality of the work of the Brontës and Twain. It will be our work as political people—rather, as citizens of real communities—that will be critical to achieving the axial transformation to which we aspire. Revolution is not, finally, in and of the word alone.

Nor should this come as a surprise. It is a commonplace of scholarship informed by a working-class perspective—often honored, I must admit, in the breach—that the point is not to describe the world but to change it. So it must be, I think, with feminist criticism: it cannot be neutral, simply analytic, formal. It needs always to be asking how its project is changing the world, reconstructing history as well as consciousness, so that the accomplishments of women can be fully valued and, more important, so that the lives of women and men can more fully be lived.

Notes

1. I have examined the history of the American literary canon in "Race and Gender in the Shaping of the American Literary Canon: A Case Study from the Twenties," *Feminist Studies* 9 (Fall 1983): 435–463, and have posed some alternative frameworks to the existing canon in the introduction to *Reconstructing American Literature* (Old Westbury: Feminist Press, 1983), pp. xi–xxv.
2. Raymond Williams, *Culture and Society, 1780–1950* (New York: Harper Torchbooks, 1966), pp. 325–326.
3. Ibid., p. 327.
4. Martha Vicinus, *The Industrial Muse* (New York: Barnes and Noble, 1974), see especially pp. 1–3.
5. Dan Tannacito, "Poetry of the Colorado Miners: 1903–1906," *Radical Teacher* 15 (March 1980): 1–8. Appended to Tannacito's article is a small anthology of miners' poetry.
6. Paul Lauter, "Working-Class Women's Literature—An Introduction to Study," *Women in Print, I,* ed. Ellen Messer-Davidow and Joan Hartman (New York: Modern Language Association, 1982), pp. 109–134.
7. Lawrence Levine, *Black Culture and Black Consciousness: Afro-American Folk Thought from Slavery to Freedom* (New York: Oxford University Press, 1977).
8. I am distinguishing between "working-class," "folk," or "popular" (peoples') culture and what Dwight MacDonald characterized as "mass culture." Popular culture, what people who share class (or ethnicity and race) produce in communicating with one another, can be separated from what is produced as a commodity, generally at the lowest common denominator, for consumption by

masses of people. To be sure, the distinction is not always clear-cut, but it is worth seeking.

9. Quoted by Herbert G. Gutman, *Work, Culture, and Society in Industrializing America* (New York: Knopf, 1976), pp. 23–24, from Melech Epstein, *Jewish Labor in the United States* (New York, 1950), pp. 290–291.

10. See John W. Blassingame, *The Slave Community* (New York: Oxford, 1972), pp. 49–59.

11. See Levine, *Black Culture and Black Consciousness*, pp. 30–31.

12. Ibid., p. 6.

13. Jeanette R. Murphy, "The Survival of African Music in America," *Popular Science Monthly* 55 (September 1899): 662; quoted by Blassingame, *The Slave Community*, pp. 27–28.

14. See "The Burning Struggle: The Civil Rights Movement," an interview with Bernice Johnson Reagon, *Radical America* 12 (November–December 1978): 18–20.

15. Levine, *Black Culture and Black Consciousness*, p. 33; cf. p. 207.

16. The usual distinctions between "poetry" and "propaganda," or between "fine arts" and "crafts" hinge on the issue of function. Modern critics have, in one form or another, generally assumed that "poetry is its own excuse for being" and that a poem should "not mean, but be." This is not the place to argue such claims. I don't find them particularly convincing, though it is obvious enough that art can have differing functions in different cultures. Let it suffice here to assert that viewing working-class culture from the standpoint of such assumptions will fatally mislead the critic.

17. Allen Tate, "Tension in Poetry," in *Essays of Four Decades* (Chicago: Swallow Press, 1968), pp. 64, 65.

18. Ibid., p. 58.

19. "To Whom Is the Poet Responsible?" in *Essays of Four Decades*, p. 27.

20. "Literature as Knowledge," in *Essays of Four Decades*, p. 104.

21. "The Man of Letters in the Modern World," in *Essays of Four Decades*, p. 14.

22. Ibid., p. 16.

23. In rereading this, it seems to me that I have made it sound like all academic critics are centers of independent power. Clearly, people in academe respond to institutional priorities, corporate definitions of appropriate career tracks. Indeed, most teachers and literary scholars are the victims of established modes of performance rather than their creators. It is not my intention to blame the victims but rather to make clear the source of that victimization.

24. Allen Tate, *Reactionary Essays on Poetry and Ideas* (Freeport, N.Y.: Books for Libraries, 1968), pp. 154–157.

25. The comment was quoted in a press release connected with the publication of her collection *Ripening* (Old Westbury, N.Y.: Feminist Press, 1982).

26. "The Poet as Woman," *The World's Body* (New York: Scribner's, 1938).

27. *Women's Fiction: A Guide to Novels by and about Women in America, 1820–1870* (Ithaca: Cornell University Press, 1978).

28. Steps toward changing the absolute unavailability of texts were taken when Indiana University Press issued Judith Fetterley's collection of early and mid-nineteenth-century American women writers and Rutgers University Press began to issue its series of reprints of the work of writers like Child, Susan Warner, and Cary. But these are only beginning steps. To illustrate the problem: none of the work of Catherine Maria Sedgewick, considered in her day the equal of Cooper and Irving, is easily available. Little of Child, Fanny Fern, or Sarah Josepha Hale is accessible. Only one work by Rebecca Harding Davis is available, "Life in the Iron Mills," first restored in an edition from the Feminist Press and now enshrined in the Norton anthology of American literature. Only within the last two years have two works by Elizabeth Stuart Phelps become available: *The Silent Partner* (Feminist Press) and *The Story of Avis* (Rutgers). Even some of H. B. Stowe's texts are unavailable in paperback. Nor is there any edition of the work of the most widely published black woman writer of the nineteenth century, Frances Ellen Watkins Harper.

29. Barbara Christian, *Black Women Novelists: The Development of a Tradition, 1892–1976* (Westport, Conn.: Greenwood Press, 1980); Elaine Showalter, *A Literature of Their Own: British Women Novelists from Brontë to Lessing* (Princeton: Princeton University Press, 1977); Sandra M. Gilbert and Susan Gubar, *The Madwoman in the Attic: The Woman Writer and the Nineteenth-Century Literary Imagination* (New Haven: Yale University Press, 1979).

30. "Going in Circles: The Female Geography of Jewett's *Country of the Pointed Firs*," *Studies in the Literary Imagination* 16 (Fall 1983); especially 85–89.

31. See, for example, Jane Tompkins, "Sentimental Power," *Glyph* (1981).

32. See, for example, Baym, *Women's Fiction*, pp. 25, 144.

33. Alice Cary, *Clovernook, or Recollections of Our Neighborhood in the West, Second Series* (New York: Redfield, 1853), pp. 363–64.

34. I have taken some steps in this area in a paper entitled "The Literatures of America—A Comparative Discipline," prepared for a Soviet-American conference on minority literatures in the United States, University of Pennsylvania, July 1985.

From the Bottom Up:
Three Radicals of the Thirties

Those of us who came to maturity in the sixties would do well to remember the thirties. From a certain perspective, the two decades are not so far apart. In fact, they overlap. Nor is it only that the differences between the Old Left and the New, in hindsight, seem more apparent than real. In both periods the separate worlds of art and politics interlocked. Briefly, the classic alienation of intellectuals from the masses of ordinary people was dissipated; boundaries between high culture and low seemed dissolved; those who thought and those who acted were one and the same; those who created culture and those who made history were one. For makers of poetry it was a time when poetry meant politics. And whether they were artists or not, people who lived through the experience were afterward profoundly marked by it.

When we think of the poetry of the thirties, we are apt to think of Auden, Spender, and Day Lewis. They were English, and as poets they have not been neglected.[1] I have omitted discussion of them here. Turning to the American scene, it is apparent that the signal works and names of the decade are clustered in areas that are also beyond the scope of this essay. The thirties were rich in reportage,[2] polemic, and criticism—Agnes Smedley, Josephine Herbst, Meridel LeSueur, and Dorothy Thompson gave first-hand reports from the various fronts, Joseph North, Mike Gold, and Granville Hicks argued current issues, and Edmund Wilson, Kenneth Burke, and V. F. Calverton played the role of engagé critic. As an extension of many of the same concerns, much of the literature of the period, especially that which is remembered now, takes the form of fiction or drama. In the short story, there were Tillie Olsen, Tess Slesinger, and Dorothy Parker. In the novel, John Dos Passos, James T. Farrell, and Jack Conroy. In drama, Lillian Hellman and Clifford Odets and the Group Theatre.[3]

Who, then were the American poets of the thirties, and why are they so little thought of now? If they were writing proletarian poetry, poetry "from the bottom up," what was it and how has it survived the years? In a time when literature and politics met, what was the result, and were the aims of each so irreconcilable that one extinguished the other?

First and always, when speaking of proletarian poetry or art we must keep in mind what Big Bill Haywood said to the members of Mabel Dodge's salon (as described in Max Eastman's novel *Venture* [1927]):

> "Not only is art impossible to such a man [a Pittsburgh steel-worker]," he said, "but life is impossible. He does not live. He just works. He does the work that enables you to live. He does the work that enables you to enjoy art, and to make it, and to have a nice meeting like this and talk it over. . .
>
> "The only problem, then, about proletarian art," he continued, "is how to make it possible, how to make life possible to the proletariat. In solving that problem we should be glad of your understanding, but we don't ask your help. We are going to solve it at your expense. Since you have got life, and we have got nothing but work, we are going to take our share of life away from you, and put you to work.
>
> "I suppose you will want to know what my ideal of proletarian art is," he continued, "what I think it will be like, when a revolution brings it into existence. I think it will be very much kindlier than your art. There will be a social spirit in it. Not so much boasting about personality. Artists won't be so egotistical. The highest ideal of an artist will be to write a song which the workers sing, to compose a drama which great throngs of workers can perform out of doors. When we stop fighting each other—for wages of existence on one side, and for unnecessary luxury on the other—then perhaps we shall all become human beings and surprise ourselves with the beautiful things we do and make on the earth. Then perhaps there will be civilization and civilized art. But there is no use putting up pretenses now. The

important thing . . . is that our side, the workers, should fight without mercy and win. There is no hope for humanity anywhere else."[4]

In other words, there is a great silence where proletarian art, art created by the common people, ought to be. Our task is, first, to attend to the reasons for that silence and, second, to end it. Another task is to be aware of the system of valuation implicit in the definition of art and to resist it.[5] Art created by and for common people, "folk art," and that created by those who are considered "outsiders" to mainstream culture (whose work for one reason or another is alien to what Fanon called "Mediterranean values"), has not been seen as worthy of the accolades "masterpiece" or "classic."

Whatever its origin, art has always been made against the odds. For artists of proletarian origin, the odds against them have been greater. Not only economic, but also social and racial oppression have added weight to the silence.[6] Despite the odds, American proletarians—Colorado miners, Pittsburgh steelworkers, New York "Jews without money" —did make art. Some of it is unjustly neglected.[7] And, what is probably true with respect to any given current or undercurrent in art, much of it does not bear sustained attention.[8]

The movement for proletarian poetry in the thirties was a political as well as a literary movement.[9] Its partisans were not limited to those of strictly proletarian origin or to those who earned their living in literary vineyards. Despite the publication of manifestos, petitions, and calls for writers' congresses, there was never a cohesive or organized group called "proletarian poets" or anything like one. The partisans of the movement were not all communists, fellow travelers, sympathizers with the American or Russian Communist parties, with the Comintern, or with other organized groups for political action. Few writers of the time ever were, being writers. About as far as many went was to join one of the John Reed Clubs, an early (and very loose) effort by the American Communist party to organize writers. By nature, writers are great signers of petitions and open letters but not great actors on the stage of history.

The battles for proletarian poetry and the barricades that were set up against it for the most part took the form of debates and publications. Just as communism and fascism were the great ideas of the decade, posed in dialectical opposition, there were similarly opposed doctrines in poetry. Proletarian poets took their places on the left, with "art as a weapon" as their slogan. On the right were the fighters for "art for art's sake."

I take the *Partisan Review* of 1934 to 1936 to be the most vocal exemplar of the right wing "art for art's sake" position, although many may differ with my opinion; such a choice only shows how narrow was the spectrum of opinion. It was originally founded as the literary organ of the New York City John Reed Club and its editors (William Phillips and Philip Rahv) were Trotskyists. Ostensibly "left," it supported such fundamentally bourgeois tenets as the individualism of the artist and the uniqueness of the artist of genius. But those who believed in "art for art's sake" were essentially anarchist at heart. They believed that art has its own imperatives which must be respected; that artists can subscribe to no given line or position but must remain individualist, solitary, and free; that art transcends the dictates of party, organization, government, and nation. At one time or another its partisans included some Southern agrarians, certain New Critics, and, most important, the modernist faction whose names (Pound, Eliot, Williams, Stevens, Moore, Crane) have become icons.

On the left were the revolutionary proletarian poets who saw "art as a weapon." They believed that literature above all else is communication, and that communication from one ivory tower to another is as valuable as that kind of law which "forbids the rich as well as the poor from sleeping under bridges." Far from existing in a world apart, literature for them was part of the forward motion of history; they saw the literary transmutation of ideas into art as part and parcel of that historical context.[10] Since a Marxist view of history foretold the collapse of capitalism and the eventual triumph of the working class, they believed that the purpose of art must be to raise and sharpen the consciousness of that class which alone could make, or remake, history. They strove to make of the working class a class not "of itself" but "for itself" so as to hasten the revolution which was inevitable anyway. Accordingly, they tried to write not for the intellectuals but for the people. If they were not themselves of proletarian origin they tried to write for proletarians, to make their silence articulate. They wanted to address the basic concerns of ordinary people in language and forms that would be accessible and intelligible to them. For if once the people awakened and united moved, the earth would be moved also and history transformed.

If the substance of this debate (which I have only outlined, so that it lacks texture) sounds naive or simplistic to modern readers, I must point out that any epoch, but particularly the thirties, must be understood in its own context.

Let us think for a moment about the year 1932.

After the stock market crash in 1929, the twenties had come to a precipitous end. The Jazz Age, the heyday of the flapper and bootleg liquor, the "new woman" amidst the bohemianism of Greenwich Village, the energy and spirit of the Harlem Renaissance—all must have seemed as irrevocable as one's youth. The policies of Hoover had been declared bankrupt and Roosevelt was elected for the first time that year. It was the depth of the Depression, and by the end of the year fifteen million Americans were out of work.[11] National income had dropped from $81 billion in 1929 to $42 billion, and bank "holidays" had become epidemic. That summer thousands of Bonus Marchers (veterans of World War I who had petitioned the government for immediate payment of their army bonuses) had been driven from Washington, D.C., by General (then Captain) MacArthur's troops. Evicted and jobless people camped out in "Hoovervilles" and many took to the roads and trains in a vast migration of people seeking work. There was no welfare to speak of, no unemployment insurance, no Social Security pensions (those were the result of later New Deal reforms). Roosevelt's inauguration speech the following spring, in which he declared that "we have nothing to fear but fear itself," must have been brave indeed, since he had hardly a clue as to what policies might augur recovery.

An upheaval in political attitudes had also occurred. Back in 1916, Max Eastman had commented that the word *bourgeoisie* was one "we didn't even know how to spell in America," and another reporter had translated a banner in Petrograd as "Proletarians of every country, join yourselves together!"[12] By now the phrases of radicalism came fluently from many tongues and not exclusively in the accents of the foreign born. Not only the Democratic and Republican but also the Communist, Socialist Labor, and Farm Labor parties were active, while the Prohibition party still lingered. Bloody Harlan County in Kentucky and other areas had become battlegrounds between the forces of capital and labor. Domestic demagogues like Huey Long ("Every man a king") in Louisiana and Father Coughlin of Michigan, a "radio priest," attracted considerable followings. Sacco and Vanzetti had been executed in 1927; the Scottsboro Boys, after a circuslike trial in 1931, would spend years in jail. Lynching of blacks was still a common outrage in the South and would continue into the forties; "Jim Crow," the color line, was still a way of life there. The Klan was both powerful and active and not just in the South; one of its strongholds was red-neck Oregon and Washington.

The forces of progress and reaction battled also on foreign fronts. After the Reichstag fire, Hitler came to power in Germany. The anti-Semitic attitudes of his Brown Shirts were already well known and Jews were emigrating or being expelled from Germany; Einstein among others came to the United States the following year. Mussolini had been in power in Italy for years and would invade Ethiopia within a few more. Léon Blum, who with Britain and the United States would pursue a rigid "noninterventionist" policy with regard to Spain after Franco's coup there in 1936, headed the government of France. The single word Spain would thereafter become the catalyst for a generation. In Asia, the Chinese Communists had been betrayed and massacred by Chiang Kaishek and the Kuomintang in 1926–27, and the two groups were engaged in a bloody civil war in the midst of invasion, for imperialist Japanese forces had invaded Manchuria in 1931 and occupied Shanghai in 1932. In Latin America, Cuba and Haiti were both under brutal dictatorships. The Mexican Revolution, which had been vividly reported by John Reed, was long dead, and U.S. Marines would shortly put the Somozas in power in Nicaragua.

In the view of many in the United States it seemed that capitalism was on the point of self-destruction and the American "way of life" had lost its promise. Many eyes turned to the Soviet Union, where Stalin was at the helm. He had already murdered millions of peasants in the drive for collectivization and purges were well under way, but much of this was not yet widely known. The show trials were yet to come (1936 to 1938), followed by secret ones, to be followed by later and fuller accounts of atrocities and the camps. What American intellectuals knew was that the Russian Revolution of 1917 had been the only successful Marxist revolution in history and that the Soviet Union was the only existing socialist state. To be sure, there was famine in Russia in

1932 and widespread poverty and illiteracy, but it was felt that hardships were shared equally; the country was on a crash program of modernization. While many objected to the lack of freedom of speech and other fundamental democratic rights in the Soviet Union, others were satisfied that these were temporary necessities in a country which was still very much in the process of defending the revolution and building socialism. But most important, *everyone in the Soviet Union was employed.* At a time when having any kind of job, not a "good" job but any kind at all, literally meant survival, this seemed the economic equivalent of nirvana.

Moreover, many American intellectuals were aware of and admired the new Russian art. Experiments in Constructivism and Futurism were indicated if not yet clearly delineated. The work of Meyerhold in theater, Eisenstein and others in films, was known and admired. Mayakovsky, Pasternak, Pilnyak, and Babel had been translated into English; there were various anthologies of Russian revolutionary writing in circulation, and enthusiastic criticism of it was written by various hands. To many on American shores (and not just ideologues), the contrast between the apparent forward mobility of the Soviet Union and the obvious decline of the United States led to a striking conclusion. In Arthur Koestler's words: "They are the future—we, the past."[13]

Proletarian literature, its forms, language, and attitude, was largely imported to this country from another; partly for that reason, it never gained a strong hold on American literary minds. And political disillusion came fast, so the proletarian movement in American literature was a short one. But it was revived again in the sixties, under different conditions, with new young faces (many more of them black and female), and with a new style. And again it was eclipsed. But it remains true today that many more of us are poor than rich, many more are shut out than let in, and for these among other reasons I expect it to come round again.

Although their political attitudes and publication dates vary, the writers I have chosen to discuss—Carl Sandburg, Langston Hughes, Meridel LeSueur—were part of the proletarian movement in literature in the thirties.[14] Their sympathy for and identification with the common people was basic to their work, coupled with an expressed desire for radical change in the interests of greater equality and justice.

Carl Sandburg, Roughneck Singer

Carl Sandburg is almost unread today, when he is not a laughingstock, among those who still read poetry. The charges against him are severe, and of many of them his poetry stands convicted. Yet there are many other poets, poets who *are* read (or at least taught) and whose reputations are higher, who are equally guilty. During his lifetime, Sandburg's work was taken seriously by many whose business it is to take poetry seriously. And—what is not true of others—Sandburg was one of the most genuinely popular American poets of this century.

In some ways it is difficult to write about Sandburg without sounding an apologia. It may be true that his intellectual capacity was slight and his capacity for sentimentality great. His imagery is jejune, his philosophizing worse. His poetry is far too dependent on nouns and adjectives and not enough on verbs. It contains copious description and yet little imagery. His lyrics are not lovely, his narratives have no dramatic tension, his meditations lack depth. His longer poems are almost entirely shapeless, and he has a tin ear.

All this and more is readily conceded. But it was Whitman who wrote, "The words of my book nothing, the drift of it everything." However much he liked to affect the lingo of a bumpkin, Sandburg was not ignorant of the rules. He broke them deliberately in the interests of a larger intention, something poets have done since poetry was named. For Sandburg, this most Whit/manic of poets, the drift was everything. It carried him far.

But where? Toward the creation of an American myth. Stubborn as a Swede (and he was fond of ethnic characterizations), Sandburg had one subject: America, meaning the United States, and one politic: radical democracy. Beyond that, his policy like Lincoln's was "not to have a policy." Accordingly, he took everything that came in his line of vision or experience—a great grab bag of people, ideas, objects, landscapes—and tried to make of it a mythic expression of America and its people.

Myth is an expression of "primitive" people, people in the process of making what we call civilization, and its purpose is to explain and support them against the darkness. Sandburg took the long view, saw the country as young, its people still in the process of forging an identity, of testing and examining the possibilities of who they might become. The time in his poetry is therefore the present—and the future. Even in his historical poems he does not dwell on the past but uses it as an exploration of what might come next.

Myth is also a counter against mortality in a world in which life is "solitary, nasty, poor, brutish, and short." Death is a constant presence in Sandburg's poems, and this is significant in a poet who has been read as an optimist. Nor does he emphasize only human frailty on an individual scale, but also constant is the consciousness of death of whole peoples, nations, civilizations. Sandburg's emphasis on the solitude, brevity, and transitoriness of all things human is almost Greek in its proportions.

Myths are also composed—if they are "composed" and not built by accretion, like deltas—by anonymous authors. It would never occur to us to wonder, for example, who wrote the one about Demeter and Persephone. Nobody wrote it. Everybody did. It doesn't matter.

And herein we begin to define the difference between Whitman and Sandburg. A century apart, each chose the same subjects and many of the same attitudes and methods—traveled the same ground, as it were. It was even the same act of optimism or faith for each to publish his major work when he did. *Leaves of Grass* first appeared in 1855, when the country was rushing toward civil war and possible dissolution. Sandburg brought out *The People, Yes* in 1936, when it was by no means clear that the country would survive as an economic or political entity. An American myth—yes. Democracy—yes.

But the voice through which Whitman's oracle spoke was not anonymous, unknowable, terrifying, like the oracle at Delphi. *Leaves of Grass* had a distinctive voice, highly idiosyncratic and personal (difficult and contradictory as that was), and it was Whitman's own. Its hero was The Poet, the visionary and seer who could prophesy the promised land. Sandburg's voice is altogether different from this; it strives to melt into the anonymous voices of the people; its ideal is not the particular but the general—or the universal, if you will. Lincoln was Sandburg's personal hero, but Sandburg's poetry is distinguished largely by Lincoln's absence. The hero of Sandburg's work is not Lincoln but the people, "democracy en masse." Hence, it lacks the concern, so striking in Whitman, for the self, the I, the ego, the personality. In this sense, at least, Sandburg's voice was more essentially mythic than Whitman's. Thus, Sandburg is not a later and weaker clone of Whitman.

Rather, he is more like Allen Ginsberg—a new hybrid grafted from the original tree.

In general, Sandburg's best poems are also his best-known poems: "Chicago," "Slabs of the Sunburnt West," "Good Morning America," and "The People, Yes."[15] All are long versions of incantations, invocations, and chants (primitive prayers) written in favor of ancient verities and sometimes flung into the void of an indifferent universe. Their language is a peculiar mix of the slangy lingo of a low-down cuss combined with the intonation of a preacher or priest; half of it is reminiscent of the speech of "Waiting for Lefty" while the other half is derived from ancient texts like the Bible. Choosing at random a few lines from a Sandburg poem, the first half might look like this: "Go to it" and "independent as a hog on ice." An example of the second half is this: "Remember this city" and "fished from its depths" and "a text." Combined as Sandburg wrote them in "The Windy City," the lines are these:

> Go to it and remember this city fished from its
> depths a text: "independent as a hog on ice."[16]

The poems are constructed like ancient religious rituals: slow, deliberately repetitious, the main chant-line changing slightly each time it is brought around again, sparks from the bonfire shooting occasionally into the circle of celebrants, the climax building, reached, then released in a final coda. The whole appears loose enough to permit spontaneity and also varying lengths, depending on the needs of each performance (though on the page the poems are presented in full).

I have no doubt that Sandburg consciously strove to recall and reclaim *in an utterly American context* both the lyric and epic voices of the ancient Greeks. "Good Morning, America" is an example.[17] It is crammed with American folk tales, tall tales, and legends, from Paul Bunyan to Sleepy Hollow, used in various versions, with proverbs, aphorisms, epigrams, and fables, commercials, slogans, pamphleteering, huckstering, folk songs, and hymns. It utilizes almost everything that Sandburg can find or think of which can be placed or identified as in some way American. Yet its central trope plays on the theme of mutability and its closing section is a kind of hymn to the earth.[18]

A myth is not made by a single voice but by a chorus of voices over time; it also requires a community, a system of shared values which we as Americans may not have. It may also be the product of a more finite world than the one in which we live. Or Sandburg's failure, truth be told, may simply be the result of his own shortcomings as a poet.

But his popularity in his lifetime seems to me indicative of something—that Sandburg, like Will Rogers, Charlie Chaplin, and a few others, touched a deep and responsive chord in common people, in common American people, to whom all his work was dedicated. Sandburg tried to speak to them and for them in their own various and anonymous voices, for he believed that art as well as American politics was a radical experiment in democracy. His poetry was intended as a modest contribution to that experiment.

Langston Hughes, Comrade Singer

As a young poet, Langston Hughes was influenced by the poetry of Sandburg for reasons which go beyond the fact that both grew up in the Midwest.[19] Through Sandburg, Hughes first began to study the art of unrhymed free verse; through Paul Laurence Dunbar, Negro dialect poems. But Hughes shortly went beyond both, and in one of his first major poems, "The Negro Speaks of Rivers,"[20] found his true subject from which his politics developed. This was negritude, or soul.

Hughes is called "the poet laureate of the Negro people" and as such his work has not been neglected. But his work is generally discussed in the context of something called "folk poetry," a term I confess I fail to understand.

Almost all poetry I can think of was originally derived from an oral tradition of chants, songs, and storytelling—from a folk tradition based on a kind of collective or racial memory; that is, it was preliterate. It seems immaterial to me whether the particular "folk" involved were Homeric or Scottish as opposed to African, Caribbean, or Asian. What they made was poetry. And everything we are now accustomed to call poetry was once, in an earlier incarnation, folk poetry.

The fact that a literate tradition (written as opposed to oral literature, and literature based on other literature) later developed in the West, and that this *kind* of literature became the sum of what we know and recognize *as* literature, is to me a historical development which is most relevant.[21] For in the course of that development certain unspoken judgments were made. Folk art was not only differentiated from other kinds of art, it was also differentiated in terms of what was seen as its quality. Not only the artifacts of a particular culture but also whole cultures came to be stratified in terms of "high" and "low," "advanced" and "backward."[22] The evaluation of literature became similarly stratified: literature itself was defined as that which was within the literate tradition (the *Western* literate tradition at that), and this kind of literature was seen as worthy of the attention of educated, that is, "civilized," people. Literature based on an oral or folk tradition was acknowledged as something, but not-quite-yet literature, not deemed worthy of serious or extended critical attention. It was reserved for "primitive" or "developing" peoples, and folk poetry was relegated to a subgenre.

Since I do not subscribe to those kinds of critical judgments I do not distinguish between folk poetry and other kinds of poetry. Distinctions must continue to be made in terms of the epoch or cultural milieu in which a particular work was produced—poems must be read in their own context. A poem produced by a black American slave in the year 1619 (if we knew one) would certainly be different from a sonnet composed by Shakespeare in the same year. But I am not willing to say that one is poetry and the other is not, or that one is better poetry than the other. Who is to do the saying? The kind of reader who would choose Shakespeare is one who is trained to appreciate Shakespeare; that is, is familiar with Spenser or Petrarch or—again—a certain literary tradition. The community in which that slave lived might feel that he is the Shakespeare of *his* tradition.

So I am willing to acknowledge Langston Hughes as the Shakespeare or master of his tradition, because black readers (who ought to know) believe him to be one,[23] but I am not so willing to categorize him as a "folk poet," because the category itself is fraught with difficulty. To be sure, his poetry is infused with jazz, blues, spirituals (forms of black music which are also outside the canonical tradition), and the argot of the urban ghetto. Those things are elements of black culture, and if he hadn't drawn on that culture for his poetry, I would like to know what culture we would have expected him to draw on, or what he might have written. I feel sure that he would not have become a poet laureate of anything in particular. He would have been a poet in exile from his sources, in limbo; being himself, he might have made great poetry out of *that*, but it would have been poetry of an altered kind. To call Langston Hughes the "poet laureate of the Negro people" in nearly the same breath as calling him a "folk poet" seems to me to equate black culture with primitive culture, and this is misleading, to say the least.

If Langston Hughes is a folk poet, it means only that he wrote out of a certain time and place from the perspective of a minority people,[24] much as Wordsworth did when he wrote "Michael," or Allen Ginsberg when he wrote "Kaddish." Which is not to suggest an argument for the so-called universality of poetry, for I do not believe in one. The *particular* time and place, the *particular* people, are facts not to be ignored or glossed over in the interests of an easy identification by those who are different, who live by different assumptions. Adrienne Rich's "Twenty-one Love Poems," written by a woman to a woman, are violated by heterosexual lovers who read them aloud to each other, gazing with liquid eyes.[25] Rather, the reader must do the additional work necessary to identify the particular time and place, the particular perspective, from which the poems came, to become familiar with their context, and therby begin to understand the poems on their own terms.

The identification of Hughes as a folk poet obscures the fact that he is a brilliant poet of ideas, and radical ideas at that. The concepts of negritude and soul, the politics of Black Power, the psychology of black rage, are so familiar to children of the sixties that it comes almost as a shock to realize that Hughes was presenting articulate and concrete images of them in his poetry in the twenties and thirties. While these ideas did not originate with him,[26] he embodied them in verse of such fluency and power that it seems undated half a century later. Moreover, he consistently combined them with the basic premises of revolutionary socialism,[27] and this sympathy is evident—hard to miss—in his work not only of the thirties but to the end of his life.

"The Negro Speaks of Rivers,"[28] then, is only the beginning of a long chain of poems by Hughes which confront, distill, extend, and transform the historical experience of black people into an art both limpid and programmatic. As in all of Hughes' hallmark poems, its distillation is as extreme as any in Issa's haiku. The "I" of the poem is not that of "a" Negro but "the" Negro, suggesting the whole of the people and their history. Most of the consonants—*d*'s, *n*'s, *l*'s, *s*'s—are soft, and of the vowels, long *o*'s reoccur, contributing by sound the effect of an ancient voice. The tone of the repeated declarative sentences is muted, lulling. Every element of the poem combines to suggest that when the Negro speaks of rivers it is with the accumulated wisdom of a sage. The function of a sage is to impart the sometimes secret but long accumulated history of a people to its younger members so that they might make the lessons of the past active in the future. This impartation occurs in the central stanza of the poem:

> I bathed in the Euphrates when dawns were young.
> I built my hut near the Congo and it lulled me to sleep.
> I looked upon the Nile and raised the pyramids above it.
> I heard the singing of the Mississippi when Abe Lincoln
>   went down to New Orleans, and I've seen its muddy
>   bosom turn all golden in the sunset.

Moving by suggestion, by naming particular rivers and particular activities performed nearby, the poem implicates the whole history of African and American slavery without ever articulating the word. "I bathed in the Euphrates" and "I built my hut near the Congo" are the normal activities of natural man performed in his natural habitat. That may be an unnecessarily anthropological way of putting it, but the lines are the equivalent of the speaker having said, "I made my life undisturbed in the place where I lived." The shift—and the lesson— occurs in the next two lines. Raising the pyramids above the Nile was the act of slaves, and if ever "Abe Lincoln went down to New Orleans,"[29] it would have been in the context of American slavery and the Civil War. Implicit in the history of a people who had first been free and then enslaved is the vision of freedom regained, and therein lies the program. The final line of the poem, "My soul has grown deep like the rivers," suggests wisdom in the word "deep." The wisdom imparted by the poem, beyond the memory of the suffering of slavery, includes a more deeply embedded memory of freedom. This is perhaps the more powerful memory, or the more sustaining one, and even if deferred,[30] will reemerge in one form or another.

But now I will skim over Hughes' other great poems of soul, which are well known, in order to concentrate on his less well known poems of political action. The two themes are inextricably twined in his work, but the specific radical content of the latter has often been ignored.

While Hughes was never a member of the Communist party,[31] he was more sympathetic with its ideals than is usually acknowledged.[32] Reading him solely as a folk poet or making him into a kind of (passive) black saint is an error partly because it obscures or diminishes the very important part played by political activisim in his work.

"Good Morning, Revolution"[33] is one of the most emblematic poems of Hughes' radical work. Significantly, it is not included in Hughes' *Selected Poems*.[34] Its opening greetings sets the tone:

> Good morning, Revolution:
>> You're the very best friend
>> I ever had.

Never a friend of organized Christianity, which Hughes saw as an agent of oppression, contributing to the ignorance and passivity of the people,[35] the "great day in the morning" for Hughes was not the Second Coming but the coming of the revolution.

> Listen, Revolution,
>> We're buddies, see—
> Together,
> We can make everything. . . .

The poem makes it crystal clear that worker "buddies" will wrest "all the tools of production" from "the boss" who has "got all he needs, certainly. . . ."

> And turn 'em over to the people who work.
> Rule and run 'em for us people who work.

As always for Hughes, whose vision is consistently international, intercultural, and interracial,[36] whose poems always begin with the familiar gritty texture of home but expand therefrom into wider realms, the revolution will spread around the world:

> Greetings to the Socialist Soviet Republics
> Hey you rising workers everywhere greetings
>> And we'll sign it: Germany
>> Sign it: China
>> Sign it: Africa
>> Sign it: Poland
>> Sign it: Italy

> Sign it: America
> On that day when no one will be hungry, cold, oppressed,
> Anywhere in the world again.
>
>   That's our job!
>   .   .   .   .   .
>   Let's go, Revolution!

When it is quoted in pieces, as I have been forced to quote it for reasons of space, the poem gives the impression of agitprop. But anyone who reads it in full, especially if he is familiar with the leaden lines of some political poetry, will greet the poem as a breath of light, stunning air. Hughes uses blueslike repetitions and, in the partial last stanza I have quoted above, the call-and-response pattern of gospel preaching and song to inject energy into emblematic lines. This poem, as in Hughes' most characteristic political work, distills complex ideas into images which are powerful in themselves and at the same time comprehensible to ordinary, "unlettered" people, those who are "just folks." To anyone who has tried to put statement into poetry, the apparent ease of Hughes' achievement is extraordinary.

Hughes' political party is successful as poetry because, in this as in his other work, he retained his own poetic voice and his individual political integrity. When he wrote poems in defense of the African, Chinese, Cuban, Russian, or Spanish peoples, as he did at various crucial historical moments, he continued to write in the voice of your average "Joe" or "Simple" which could nevertheless reach eloquence.[37] His integrity is also evident where, in his political poems, he frankly refuses to endorse the orthodox or "correct" political line. In "Good Morning, Revolution" he acknowledges the fact that, in "democratic" America and despite its own origins, the country at large (including perhaps much of his audience) did not view revolution as a friend:

> He wrote a long letter to the papers about you:
> Said you was a trouble maker, a alien-enemy,
> In other words a son-of-a-bitch. . . .[38]

In "Final Call," a call for heroes in a time of trouble, some of the heroes called upon would in certain circles be considered outrageous choices. These include Jesus *and* Robespierre, Lenin *and* Trotsky, Malcolm X *and* Adam Powell.[39] In "Black Panther" Hughes sees that revolutionary group as righteously mistaken.[40] While he wrote much topical poetry on minor and major political issues, Hughes retained his integrity by remembering who he was and by keeping his personal priorities straight.

It seems to me significant that Hughes' radical influence has been largely ignored in this country while it has been great abroad, especially in the Third World.[41] Poets take what they need from wherever they find it, without regard to conventional critical categories or interpretations. The poets of Africa and Latin America have long recognized Hughes as a master of political poetry and used his voice as a model for their own.[42] It is past time for us in the United States to repair a myopic critical vision and, perhaps for the first time, read the work of Langston Hughes whole.

Meridel LeSueur, Mother Singer

The work of Meridel LeSueur is worse than neglected; it is part of that great body of work by women which has been "hidden from history." In the thirties she was part of a group of radical writers which included Tillie Olsen, Agnes Smedley, Grace Lumpkin, Tess Slesinger, Genevieve Taggard, Josephine Herbst, and Margery Latimer; most of this work is still largely unknown or only recently rediscovered. "Every woman who writes is a survivor," Tillie Olsen has said, and LeSueur added, "Survival is a form of resistance." As survivor and resister, LeSueur has turned out to be one of the hardiest of all.[43]

LeSueur was born in Murray, Iowa, in 1900, and throughout a life of "migrations" (a key word for her) has remained a creature of the Midwest. Her father was the first socialist mayor of Minot, North Dakota, and her mother overcame shyness and the most straitlaced of small town backgrounds to become an activist on behalf of women's and workers' rights. LeSueur grew up in a home steeped in political radicalism, and it remained a commitment which shaped all her work. By her own account she joined the Communist party as early as 1924; lived in various communes in New York and the Midwest; participated in numerous political actions, including the Minneapolis truckers' strike in 1934 through the Poor People's March on Washington in 1968; was blacklisted in the forties and fifties and rediscovered with the reemergence of the women's movement in the sixties and seventies. Her life has been marked by rootlessness, poverty, and struggle, and her work, especially of the thirties, reflects these experiences to an agonizing degree. But she considers that her life has been a long "ripening" and her recently published work, especially her poetry, constitutes an affirmation of life that only the most visionary poetry achieves.[44]

Unlike Sandburg's optimistic vision, LeSueur's America is a scene of a civilization dead and dying. The words and images which reoccur in LeSueur's writing of the thirties are of devastation, ruin, wreckage, violence and ravishment, suffering, desperation, and terror. "When you look at the unemployed women and girls you think instantly that there must be some kind of war,"[45] and she thought the Depression was "worse than a war." Her fiction and reportage of the time is an extended investigation into the causes and effects of that destruction, destruction which extended to all strata of society and culture. In her work, LeSueur shows how the mechanisms of developing capitalism had destroyed the dignity of human labor;[46] its cyclical failures destroyed any possibility of "upward mobility" for working people;[47] its requirements for wider markets meant abuse of the land as a means of production;[48] and in the process the people who created value were destroyed, denied, abused.[49] If LeSueur's work of this time were limited to a detailed catalog of such destruction it would be almost too painful to read and might have value as journalism or history but not as art.

That is not the case, however, because LeSueur's work is informed at the same time with a call for reconstruction, restoration, recreation, and rebirth.

> Capitalism is a world of ruins really, junk piles of machines, men, women, bowls of dust, floods, erosions, masks to cover rapacity and in this sling and wound the people carry their young, in the shades of their grief, in the thin shadow of their hunger, hope and crops in their hands, in the dark of the machine, only they have the future in their hands.
> Only they.[50]

The Communist critic in the thirties who called the emphasis on human suffering in LeSueur's work "defeatist" and symptomatic of a "nonrevolutionary spirit" missed the point.[51] LeSueur was anything but defeatist in her emphasis on a vision of the future based on what she called "communal solidarity."[52] For only when people were linked fully and consciously together across the divisions of sex, class, and generation would reconstruction be possible.

LeSueur's vision of recreation and rebirth amid the ruins may also have been missed or misunderstood because she so often expressed it in terms of women and the earth. These above all were the mnemonic sources of her generative re-vision, and she returns to them again and again. Women had historically been identified with the earth as givers and nurturers of life, and LeSueur returned to this ancient and mystical identification as a means through which a new culture could be created.

Of her contemporaries, LeSueur was a pioneer in her exploration of women as a central subject for her work, and specifically of what has been called the "biological reality" of women.[53] Few others made the subject so central an inspiration or approached it in a similar way. LeSueur's closest peers in this regard would have been Gabriela Mistral, the Chilean poet, and Georgia O'Keeffe, the American painter. Waldo Frank, writing in *The Nation*, called Mistral "the bard of mothers and children" and "the laureate of her vast American earth,"[54] and by the thirties she was almost revered as a kind of Latin American Demeter. Her influence during those years was very great, culminating in the award of the Nobel Prize for Literature in 1945, but her reputation has since declined. While Mistral's work was not translated into English until 1957, it is likely that LeSueur was aware at least of its basic themes. There is no doubt that she knew O'Keeffe's; the two women were friends, and LeSueur later said that she could not have written without O'Keeffe's encouragement and example.[55] She pronounced O'Keeffe "probably nearer to the inner dream of women who want to see as women. . . ."[56] "At last, a woman on paper!" is what Stieglitz is supposed to have said on first looking into a sheaf of O'Keeffe's drawings.[57] Indeed, O'Keeffe's imagery, particularly of pubiclike mounds, breastlike hills, flowers blooming in skulls, and many of the Native American motifs of her later work, is similar to the imagery used in LeSueur's poems.

It is in her poems, published as a group only late in her life, that LeSueur's generative re-vision of women and earth begins to come clear. "I returned to the haven of woman, land, the great beloved woman of my country," LeSueur had written,[58] and her poems take up this theme with mystical intensity. In her eighties, LeSueur said, "I think I am daring to write as crazily excessive abundant absolutely in extremity . . . on the far edge of the circle."[59] The poems are written with that intensity, almost seeming to emerge out of the earth's surface like lava under pressure, out of a generations-long conflict of struggle and suffering. They are written not in an individual or private voice, but in the voice of LeSueur's own "continuous woman": "the woman linked to other generations of women both biologically, through the body, and historically and spiritually, through the reality of struggle and survival."[60]

Most of the poems in LeSueur's book *Rites of Ancient Ripening*[61] draw on Native American sources for their imagery and symbolism. These are used to express LeSueur's Demeter-like identification with the natural cycle of birth/death/rebirth, that repetition which has no beginning or end. In the title poem an old woman faces her death, which is envisioned as an ultimate reopening into new life. As in the mystical poems of Saint John of the Cross or of Sor Juana Inés de la Cruz, death is longed for, not (as in their poetry) as a deliverance unto God, but (in LeSueur's) as a union with earth. As in their poetry also, the language is heavily oxymoronic.

> I am luminous with age
> In my lap I hold the valley.
>
> .   .   .   .
>
> The corn kernels cry to me in the fields
>   Take us home.
>
>   .   .   .   .
>
> I fall and burst beneath the sacred human tree.
> Release my seed and let me fall.
> Toward the shadow of the great earth
>   let me fall.
>
>   .   .   .   .
>
> Pound me death
>   stretch and tan me death
> Hang me up, ancestral shield
>   against the dark.

Burn and bright and take me quick.
Pod and light me into dark.
. . . .
The little seeds of my children
                    with faces of mothers and fathers
Fold in my flesh
                    in future summers.
. . . .
All was ground in the bodies bowl
            corn died to bread
                    woman to child
                            deer to the hunters.
. . . .
The rites of ancient ripening
Make my flesh plume
And summer winds stir in my smoked bowl.
Do not look for me till I return
                    rot of greater summers
Struck from fire and dark,
Mother struck to future child.
Unbud me now
Unfurl me now
Flesh and fire
            burn
                    requicken
                            Death. [62]

The dying woman is not faded with age but luminous as a ripening bud. Her death is not the end of her life but a merging with past and future generations of human life, with the entire life cycle both natural and human, and this is not a terrifying event but one both solemn and ecstatic. As in Keats' "Autumn" ode, the end of the life cycle is not a weakening fade into oblivion but a culmination of great richness and beauty.

And of course it is a culmination drenched in sensuality. In this respect, LeSueur's poems draw less on Native American sensibility than on the tradition of ecstatic mystical poetry already mentioned and on her own constant reworking of the Demeter-Persephone myth. "Green Unfurl Me," "Lost Mother Lode," "I Light Your Streets," and others are poems in which the Persephone figure cries out her violation; "I Hear You Singing in the Barley Ripe," "Behold This and Always Love It," and "Budded with Child" are written in the voice of the Demeter figure.[63] In these poems LeSueur uses mythic figures to suggest a primal connection, beginning with mother and daughter but extending to all generations of women, between women *as* women, and to make what she called "a great song" rising out of their suffering. LeSueur acknowledged D. H. Lawrence as the writer who first freed her into sensuality in her writing,[64] and one of the limitations of that influence is that heterosexuality is emphasized but homosexuality is largely unacknowledged. Some of the influence of Sappho might be beneficial here. But it has always been a characteristic of LeSueur's work, in fiction as well as poetry, to delineate a knifelike edge of violence in male sexuality, and this often appears prominently in the midst of mutual heterosexual passion.[65]

In LeSueur's poetry generations of women are drawn together across boundaries of nation, culture, class to form in a single stream one "continuous woman." In "*Corridos* of Love,"[66] a hemisphere-to-hemisphere dialogue takes place between a white North American woman and a brown woman "below the border." The brown woman speaks first of her suffering and in an accusatory voice asks the other, "Didn't you hear my crying? . . . / Didn't you hear me plowing with my fingernails? / Or the sound of the spades of a million small graves? / Did our pain rise above the border you stole? / Was your sky darkened with our darkness? / Did you pay duty at the border of pain? / Have you a visa to permit you to feel it?"[67] The white woman replies by acknowledging the other's suffering, then describes her own, at every point emphasizing the similarity of oppression between the two women, and ends by seeking alliance with the other.

> Amidst lamentations, wounds, separations and lesions,
> continuously and massively bruised under the hooves of
> 　conquerors,
> we have loomed our lives,
> with the same passion as high corn,
> for the velocity of pollen spreading to all days.
> As an ally I take you to my village.
> In the diurnal green
> the leaves forgive the root and raise the fruit!

> I'm seeking you among the ancient stone!
> In the dusty faces,
> In the raised fist,
> In the resurrected heart![68]

The hope of the poem is in solidarity based on shared suffering, shared understanding of the ways in which history has dealt with them similarly (while recognizing genuine difference), shared life dependent on each other and on the earth, and, finally, shared action ("in the raised fist") to achieve resurrection of the human heart. The poem is Job-like in its voices but not at all in its resolution. This is also true of "Dòan Kêt," a long poem addressed to Vietnamese women (the title means "solidarity" in Vietnamese), which expresses the mutuality of suffering between women, a prescient sense of ecology and the interdependence of peoples on earth, and which also ends with a guerrilla fighter's song of love and cry for action.[69]

So, in her recent poetry as well as in her fiction and reportage of the thirties, LeSueur begins to close the circle at the point where she commenced: with frankly radical political work based on the shared consciousness of women as women. The portrait she has drawn is of the "continuous woman" rooted in the continuous earth. She began with a vision of civilization dead and dying from which she developed a vision of recreation and rebirth.

Conclusion

Carl Sandburg, Langston Hughes, and Meridel LeSueur were all radicals who lived in an epoch distinguished even more than most by physical suffering and human terror. It cannot be surprising if some of their solutions were radical or if their responses during the thirties now seem to us naive, narrow, or arcane. They were honest writers who did honest work, and all of them did a great deal of it. They shared an activist view of their art, one which is now out of fashion. They tried to address the pressing issues of their time in ways which most people would understand and appreciate. They wrote their poetry "from the bottom up," simply enough, because the world as we know it was made the same way. Their work may have been neglected outright, misinterpreted, or put to uses they would never have intended or approved, but it should not be ignored.

Notes

The title is taken from historian Jesse Lemisch, who called for "a revolution in historiographical attitudes, a rejection of elite history: a history 'from the bottom up' will be more nearly objectively valid than has been the attempt to understand the past through the eyes of the few at the top." Quoted by Barton J. Bernstein, ed., in his introduction to *Towards a New Past: Dissenting Essays in American History* (New York: Random House, 1968), pp. xi–xii. The poets I will discuss tried to write from this point of view, and I believe their work, and poetry in general, should be written and read in this way.

This essay is dedicated to Amy Kesselman, who first introduced me to radical history, and, for her sustained love and work, to Ruth Gundle.

1. See, e.g., Samuel Hynes, *The Auden Generation: Literature and Politics in England in the 1930's* (New York: Viking, 1977).
2. Radical reportage in the thirties was somewhat different from mainstream journalism and was more or less a precursor of the "New Journalism" of the sixties. Writers injected fictional elements and personal narrative into their accounts in an effort to bring the reader more fully into the action. One source for this method was probably John Reed, and Mencken may also have been an influence.
3. Two useful anthologies are the following: Granville Hicks et al., eds., *Proletarian Literature in the United States* (New York: International Pub., 1935), and Joseph North, ed., *New Masses: An Anthology of the Rebel Thirties* (New York: International Pub., 1969). My list is obviously partial. Such luminaries as Fitzgerald and Hemingway have been omitted because they believed that living well, as opposed to doing much, is the best revenge.
4. Quoted by Daniel Aaron in *Writers on the Left* (New York: Avon, 1961), p. 34; this book is a valuable guide to the entire period. Haywood's was a Wobbly view and characteristically appealing and romantic; Communist party views were more rigid and doctrinaire.
5. The work of my friend Barbara Herrnstein Smith is instructive on the point. See "Contingencies of Value," in *Critical Inquiry* 10, no. 1 (September 1983).
6. On the silence of women writers, see Tillie Olsen, *Silences* (New York: Delacorte, 1978); the difficulties of black writers are amply documented in C. W. E. Bigsby, ed., *The Black American Writer, Vol. I: Fiction, Vol. II: Drama and Poetry* (Baltimore, Md.: Penguin, 1969).
7. For example, see the poetry of Kenneth Fearing in *Proletarian Literature in the United States;* see also Dan Tannacito, "Poetry of the Colorado Miners: 1903–1906," followed by an anthology, and Paul Lauter, "Working Class Women's Literature—An Introduction to Study," followed by a bibliography in *The Radical Teacher* 15 (December 1979).

8. A phenomenon which appears to be peculiar to poetry, as opposed to the other literary arts, is that many are attracted to it who would be better off elsewhere. The poetry of Mike Gold is a case in point. He was a kid from the New York slums who grew up to be a skilled organizer, a sensitive reporter, and a fiery polemicist (although in 1930 he did manage to lose a debate with that famous orator Georgia O'Keeffe). But he was not a poet. "A Strange Funeral in Braddock," reprinted in *Proletarian Literature in the United States*, p. 158, must be one of the slowest dirges ever written.

9. For the sketchy account that follows I rely heavily on *Writers on the Left*; see also Daniel Aaron and Robert Bendiner, eds., *The Strenuous Decade: A Social and Intellectual Record of the 1930's* (New York: Anchor, 1970); Christopher Lasch, *The New Radicalism in America 1889–1963: The Intellectual as a Social Type* (New York: Knopf, 1965); Wilson Record, *Race and Radicalism, the NAACP and the Communist Party in Conflict* (Ithaca, N.Y.: Cornell, 1964); William L. O'Neill, *Everyone Was Brave, a History of Feminism in America* (Chicago: Quadrangle, 1969). Numerous memoirs of the period, many of them well known, have been intuitively relied on but are not cited here.

10. Carl Sandburg saw that the consequences of an "ivory tower" view of art would be the writer's silence on living issues, and that "a writer's silence on living issues can in itself constitute a *propaganda of conduct* leading toward the deterioration or death of freedom" (emphasis added). From "Notes for a Preface," in *The Complete Poems of Carl Sandburg, Revised and Expanded Edition* (New York: Harcourt, Brace, 1969), p. xxvi.

11. The population reported in the 1930 census was 122,775,046. Much of this account is drawn from Irving S. Kull and Nell M. Kull, *A Chronological Encyclopedia of American History* (New York: Popular Library, 1952).

12. Quoted in *Writers on the Left*, p. 60.

13. From *Arrow in the Blue*, quoted in *Writers on the Left*, p. 169.

14. Other poets who were at one time or another part of the movement included Muriel Rukeyser, Kenneth Patchen, Horace Gregory, Archibald MacLeish, Claude McKay, James Agee, Stanley Burnshaw—all of whom came to be widely known in other contexts or admired for other kinds of work.

15. From *The Complete Poems of Carl Sandburg*, found respectively at pp. 3, 307, 320, 439. This list is meant to be more indicative than definitive. "Fog," while well known, is omitted from the list. It is one of Sandburg's better lyrics, principally because he resisted the temptation to add what would have been a more characteristic last line, something like "So the fog comes." In general, I think Sandburg's better poems are the longer ones.

16. From *The Complete Poems of Carl Sandburg*, p. 271.

17. Ibid., p. 320.

18. "The People, Yes" is omitted from this discussion because it is a book-length poem and I cannot hope to do justice to it here. The points I would make about it parallel those I have made about "Good Morning, America," and I note that its ending, almost in recognition of the myth-making process, is open. (ibid., p. 617)

In the darkness with a great bundle of grief
the people march.
In the night, and overhead a shovel of stars
for keeps, the people march:
"Where to? What Next?"

19. Langston Hughes, *The Big Sea, an Autobiography* (New York: Hill and Wang, 1940), p. 28. His second autobiographical volume was *I Wonder as I Wander.*
20. From Langston Hughes, *Selected Poems* (New York: Knopf, 1959), p. 4.
21. See B. H. Smith, "Contingencies of Value."
22. I see this stratification as a consequence of white and patriarchal cultural hegemony and the whole course of it connected with the eventual development of capitalism. But this is an essay, not a history of the world.
23. I put the sentence this way because I believe that when a white reader (like myself) reads the work of a black poet (when a woman like myself reads the work of a man, and so on), she or he must be conscious of performing an act of translation. As in any translation, much is lost, and much of which the reader might not even be aware.
24. People of color, of course, are hardly "a minority" in the world at large. I speak of them as a minority in terms of the perspective of the United States, and also as makers of minority cultures, as seen from the perspective of the prismatic Western tradition which I have been criticizing.
25. See my essay, "Disloyal to Civilization: The Twenty-one Love Poems," in Jane Roberta Cooper, ed., *Reading Adrienne Rich: Reviews and Re-Visions 1951– 1981* (Ann Arbor: University of Michigan Press, 1984).
26. The themes of rebellion and revolt and black solidarity and pride had been an integral part of black history and literature from the beginning of the colonialist era. Hughes was intimately familiar with this history and much of his work constitutes the teaching of it. Also, the thirties in Africa was a pivotal decade in the development of negritude and I am sure its influence on Hughes was great. "A new era, combining modern scholarship, militancy, and the authentic voice of African humanism, began in the 1930's. This was a most productive period, culminating in 1938 with the publication of Jomo Kenyatta's *Facing Mount Kenya*. During the previous year Nnamdi Azikiwe brought out his *Renascent Africa*, and Leon G. Damas's *Pigments* appeared in Paris. The following year Aime Cesaire's *Cahier d'un retour au pays natal* and Senghor's 'Ce que l'homme noir apporte' were published. These were the years when négritude was discovered in Paris by French-speaking African students, led by Senghor of Senegal, Cesaire of Martinique, and Damas of French Guiana." Mercer Cook, "African Voices of Protest," in Mercer Cook and Stephen E. Henderson, *The Militant Black Writer in Africa and the United States* (Madison: University of Wisconsin Press, 1969), p. 11. Hughes knew French, was widely traveled in both Europe and Africa, and would have been moved by these currents.
27. A valuable (but out of print) collection which makes this point indisputably is Langston Hughes, *Good Morning, Revolution: Uncollected Writings of Social*

Protest, ed. Faith Berry (New York and Westport, Conn.: Lawrence Hill and Co., 1973).

28. From *Selected Poems*, p. 4. The poem, if the author's account is to be credited, was written before Hughes was out of high school. See *The Big Sea*, pp. 55–56.

29. I cannot confirm that Lincoln ever made such a trip, and I doubt it. But the uses of the idea as metaphor are obvious: the Great Emancipator of the slaves sailing past Cairo, Memphis, Vicksburg, and Port Hudson, battlefields all, to one of the commercial and political strongholds of the Confederacy is a powerful image.

30. I am thinking of course of "Harlem," which begins, "What happens to a dream deferred?" See *Selected Poems*, p. 268.

31. While Richard Wright, Claude McKay, and others were. But for various reasons they have been excluded from this discussion.

32. It is probably fair to describe Hughes as a fellow traveler of the party until the Nazi-Soviet Pact in 1939. While this was a point of massive defection from the party, in the context of the thirties it is rather late. It is true that Hughes differed with many important policies of both the American and Russian Communist parties and said so. He never followed the American party's call for a separate black "nation" to be carved out in the South; he objected publicly (though not, I think, while he was there) to the limitations on freedom of speech of writers and others in the Soviet Union. However, he was extremely active in Communist and (what McCarthyites would call) Communist-front activities for many years. To wit: (a) He went to the Soviet Union in 1932 as part of a group of black Americans who were engaged to work with the Russians on a film called *Black and White*. When the film project fell apart, most of the others in his group returned to the United States; Hughes stayed for a year and wrote numerous articles and poems in support of the revolution and the regime. (b) He was a U.S. delegate to the Second International Writers Congress, held in Paris in 1937. (c) Also in 1937 he spent six months in Spain as a correspondent for *The Afro-American Newspapers*; during that time he wrote numerous articles and poems in support of the Loyalist cause. (d) He was elected a vice-president of the League of American Writers in 1937 and remained one of its most active supporters until it was dissolved in 1942. (e) In 1949 and later he wrote a number of articles and poems in support of the Chinese Revolution. (f) He gave militant speeches at two of the four American Writers Congresses in 1935 and 1939. (g) In the late forties and early fifties some of his books were banned by certain agencies of the U.S. government and he was blacklisted in some quarters. He was called before (McCarthy's) Senate Committee on Government Operations in March 1953, and his statement to that group is a model of skillful evasion; it is neither apologetics nor lies. All this is described and documented in *Good Morning, Revolution*.

33. From *Good Morning, Revolution*, p. 3; first printed in *New Masses*, September 1932.

34. The accounts of Saunders Redding and Faith Berry in *Good Morning, Revolution* make clear that Hughes was often reluctant to read publicly or allow to be widely printed (in anthologies) his most radical work. He had been wounded by

right-wing attacks on his work, notably a campaign that had been conducted against "Goodbye, Christ." Berry attributes Hughes' nervousness not to any change in his political commitments but to the fundamentals of bread and butter: Hughes made his living by giving readings and lectures and by writing books. It is not hard to imagine what Hughes' circumstances might have become if such poems as the "Ode to Lenin" or "Roar China!" were more widely known.

35. See "To Certain 'Brothers,'" "God to Hungry Child," "A Christian Country," "Goodbye, Christ," pp. 35–36, and "Concerning 'Goodbye, Christ,'" pp. 133–135, in *Good Morning, Revolution*; cf. James A. Emanuel, "Christ in Alabama: Religion in the Poetry of Langston Hughes," in Donald B. Gibson, ed., *Modern Black Poets, A Collection of Critical Essays* (Englewood Cliffs, N.J.: Prentice-Hall, 1973), p. 57.

36. *And* anti-anti-Semitic *and* anti-sexist.

37. Simple is the hilariously wise antihero of several Hughes stories: *Simple Speaks His Mind, Simple Takes a Wife, Simple Stakes a Claim*.

38. From *Good Morning, Revolution*, p. 4.

39. From Langston Hughes, *The Panther and the Lash, Poems of Our Times* (New York: Knopf, 1967), p. 20.

40. From *The Panther and the Lash*, p. 19.

41. With the crucial exception of American *black* radical poets, especially those of the sixties (Baraka, Lee, Sanchez, Giovanni, and others). They have themselves been largely ignored by the establishment.

42. See *The Militant Black Writer in Africa and the United States*, pp. 12, 102–103. Hughes edited a volume, *Poems from Black Africa*, and translated the work of Gabriela Mistral, Nicolás Guillén, and others; such attention was repaid.

43. Of the writers under discussion, she is the only one still living.

44. The biographical information here is taken from Elaine Hedges' introduction to Meridel LeSueur, *Ripening: Selected Work, 1927–1980* (Old Westbury, N.Y.: Feminist Press, 1982), edited by Hedges.

45. From "Women Are Hungry," in *Ripening*, p. 44.

46. See "Harvest," in Meridel LeSueur, *Harvest* (Cambridge, Mass.: West End Press, 1977), p. 29, a story in which a farm wife resists her husband's "lust" for a threshing machine.

47. See "The Return of Lazarus," in Meridel LeSueur, *Song for My Time* (Cambridge, Mass.: West End Press, 1977), p. 59, a story in which an old man's refrain, "the mortgage, the mortgage," becomes a lament for a needlessly wasted life.

48. See "Eroded Woman," in *Song for My Time*, p. 19, a story about a struggling family in an abandoned mining town, "a wasteland of ruined earth and human refuse."

49. See "Annunciation," in *Ripening*, p. 124, a story in which a young husband tries to talk his wife into ending her pregnancy because he cannot afford another mouth to feed. These examples are used by way of shorthand illustration only and can be multiplied throughout LeSueur's work.

50. From "The Dark of the Time," in *Ripening*, p. 239.

51. Quoted by Hedges in *Ripening*, p. 11.

52. From "The Fetish of Being Outside," quoted by Hedges in *Ripening*, p. 15. What LeSueur meant is dramatized in her famous story "I Was Marching," in *Ripening*, p. 158.

53. The phrase is taken out of context from Robert Duncan, *The H. D. Book*, quoted in Jerome Rothenberg and George Quasha, eds., *America a Prophecy, a New Reading of American Poetry from Pre-Columbian Times to the Present* (New York: Vintage, 1973), p. 543. In my view, H. D. was too much a disciple of Pound and Freud to have had a very articulate vision of the "communal sensibility" of women, although there are striking glimpses of it in her work.

54. Quoted on the jacket of *The Selected Poems of Gabriela Mistral*, trans. Langston Hughes (Bloomington: Indiana University Press, 1957).

55. See Laurie Lisle, *Portrait of an Artist: A Biography of Georgia O'Keeffe* (New York: Seaview Books, 1980), pp. 164–165.

56. Ibid., p. 430.

57. Ibid., p. 85.

58. From "The Dark of the Time," in *Ripening*, p. 232.

59. Quoted by Hedges in *Ripening*, pp. 18–19.

60. See Hedges in *Ripening*, p. 19.

61. Meridel LeSueur, *Rites of Ancient Ripening* (Minneapolis, Minn.: Vanilla Press, 1975).

62. From *Rites of Ancient Ripening*, pp. 24–27.

63. Ibid., pp. 12, 8, 4, 35, 22, 20.

64. See Hedges, in *Ripening*, p. 6.

65. See, e.g., "O Prairie Girl, Be Lonely," in *Ripening*, p. 175; "Summer Idyl, 1949," in *Song for My Time*, p. 26; "Fudge," in *Harvest*, p. 40; "Autumnal Village," in *Harvest*, p. 52; in the poems, see "Lost Mother Lode," in *Rites of Ancient Ripening*, p. 8; "Green Unfurl Me," p. 12; "Corridos of Love," p. 47.

66. From *Rites of Ancient Ripening*, p. 47.

67. Ibid., p. 48.

68. Ibid., pp. 49–50.

69. Ibid., p. 51.

Annette Kolodny

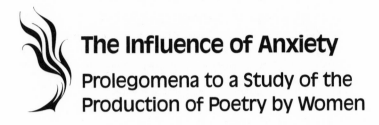

The Influence of Anxiety
Prolegomena to a Study of the Production of Poetry by Women

A sister's hand may wrest a female pen,
From the bold outrage of imperious men.

Mercy Otis Warren, "To Mrs. Montague" (1790)

In 1973, in *The Anxiety of Influence: A Theory of Poetry,* Yale critic Harold Bloom first propounded his theory that those whom he termed "strong poets"—like Blake, Keats, and Wordsworth—were successful combatants in a defensive battle for psychic survival. Compounded from various sources, including Freud, the books of the Kabbalah, Vico, and Valéry, Bloom's thesis rests on the central assumption that there exists in every poet's creative imagination a constellation of beings within which he reenacts a psychological drama not unlike that which Freud attributed to the biological nuclear family. Before a rich and overwhelming tradition in which prior poets—or precursors—appear to have exhausted the very resources which the aspiring poet would claim for himself, Bloom's poet-ephebe becomes "not so much a man speaking to men as a man rebelling against being spoken to by a dead man (the precursor) outrageously more alive than himself."[1] Seeking to overcome "the dread that there will be not enough for oneself . . . the fear of there not being enough left to do"[2] (which Bloom terms an anxious sense of "belatedness"), the would-be poet attempts to rewrite, correct, or even appropriate a precursor's poetic vision as his own. As Bloom explained in *A Map of Misreading* (1975), in order "to live, the poet must *misinterpret* the father, by the crucial act of misprision, which is the re-writing of the father" (AMOM, p. 19). If the poet-ephebe is successful in this he emerges as a "strong poet," having performed an imaginative act of displacement that closely approximates the Freudian schema of the son doing battle with the father who had sired him. Blake thus confronts Milton as did Oedipus and Laius at the crossroads.

The result is a theory of poetic influence which does away with our more usual notions of generic evolution or creative borrowings. Instead, Bloom posits a dialectical poetic history which *"always proceeds by a misreading of the prior poet, an act of creative correction that is actually and necessarily a misinterpretation."*[3] For Harold Bloom, in other words, "mis-reading or misinterpretation" constitutes "the commonal or normal mode of poetic history."[4]

To be sure, Bloom has repeatedly insisted that it was never his aim "so to apply Freud (or even revise Freud) as to arrive at an Oedipal interpretation of poetic history."[5] Bloom's version of the family drama places "the emphasis less upon phallic fatherhood, and more upon *priority*" (TAOI, p. 56), and his notion of the precursor/father is flexible enough to incorporate the possibility of several personages compounded and experienced as one or, theoretically, all of poetic history itself (though his examples tend toward individual precursor figures) (TAOI, p. 11). Even so, Bloom's iteration of "intra-poetic relationships as parallels of family romance" (TAOI, p. 8) did not long remain in the realm of parallels or extravagant models. Less than two years after the appearance of *The Anxiety of Influence*, Bloom laid claim to "latent principles, principles that can be uncovered and then taught systematically."[6] The new language clearly imputes cognitive import, tacitly signalling Bloom's belief that his revisionist family romance, to use Paul Ricoeur's phrasing, "suggests, reveals, unconceals . . . the deep structures of reality."[7] And, in fact, repeated through five books and innumerable articles, Bloom's metaphoric psychodrama so galvanized attention and so focused the shape of subsequent inquiry that it ceased to serve as merely analogue or parallel and became, instead, a cognitive solution to the question of poetic influence.

"Ironically," then, noted the *New York Times* book reviewer, when a major new study of women's intrapoetic relationships appeared in 1979, it too found itself "indebted to that most patriarchal of critics,

Harold Bloom"[8] The irony, of course, lay in the fact that a feminist analysis had accepted as its inspiriting authority a male critic who, with only the rarest exceptions, ignores the fact of women's poetic production and accepted as its paradigmatic model a version of literary history in which the female symbolizes only threat or harlotry. For, in Bloom's version of the family romance, Lilith (Adam's first wife and "the Adversary Female of Kabbalah") reminds the poet of his belatedness (FOCI, pp. 264–267), while the more conventional Muse "is mother and harlot at once" (TAOI, p. 63)—incestuously embracing her lover/son so that he may beget himself upon her (TAOI, p. 37) but reminding him always that she has "whored with many before him" (TAOI, p. 61). Not only are the images of the female here decidedly unappealing, but nowhere does Bloom consider how the psychology of the flesh-and-blood woman might participate in this particular dynamic of literary engendering.

The irony notwithstanding, it was precisely to answer this last question—and to compensate for Bloom's omissions—that Sandra Gilbert and Susan Gubar attempted their 1979 construction of a feminist poetics. As they explained in the preface to *The Madwoman in the Attic: The Woman Writer and the Nineteenth-Century Literary Imagination*, their aim—as that of so many other feminist critics—was to "recover not only a major (and neglected) female literature but a whole (neglected) female history."[9] In this, they followed Joanne Feit-Diehl, who had argued in an earlier article that "any theory of influence must" take into account the sex of the poet because, inescapably, "the constellation of the 'family romance' alters when the poet is a woman."[10] Concurring with Feit-Diehl in "the Bloomian premise that literary history consists of strong action and inevitable reaction" (MA, p. xiii) and accepting as well Bloom's version of literary history as male, Gilbert and Gubar—like Feit-Diehl before them—sought to understand "the dynamics of female literary response to male literary assertion and coercion" (MA, p. xii). They took seriously, in short (as Bloom never does), the peculiar dilemma of the woman poet who must acknowledge, along with Adrienne Rich, "that my style was formed first by male poets."[11]

Gilbert and Gubar's study of the stratagems by which (mainly) nineteenth-century English women novelists struggled both with male literary priority and with male literary versions of the female may have yielded what another feminist critic termed only "a schematized and essentialist view of the relation between women and writing."[12] But that is beside the point. For, in addition to exhilarating readings of individual texts, *The Madwoman in the Attic* initiated two vital swerves in current critical thinking. First, it opened what had been Bloom's controlling metaphor to discussion and dissection. And, second, it insisted that Bloom's (and others') relative silence concerning poetry by women could not be accepted as tacit evidence that would-be women poets had failed to successfully overcome some father/ precursor. Instead, Gilbert and Gubar offered the humbling notion that, in our ignorance of the processes governing the production of poetry by women, we may stand—along with Bloom—simply and sadly unable to recognize a strong woman when we read her.

When to her lute Corinna sings
neither words nor music are her own . . .

Adrienne Rich, "Snapshots of a Daughter-in-Law" (1963)

In a strikingly compassionate passage in *Figures of Capable Imagination* (1976), Bloom sympathizes with the Jewish poets of his generation as he considers what it meant for them, as in a Charles Reznikoff poem, to have "'married the speech of strangers'" (FOCI, p. 252). Never, however, does Bloom contemplate any analogous "peculiarly internalized disadvantage" (FOCI, p. 156) for women poets who, in their own way, might also be said to have been forced to marry the speech of strangers. That Bloom did not make this connection is surprising in light of the fact that, just a year earlier, in *A Map of Misreading*, he had at least hinted at the possibility that Homer might have sired daughters as well as sons: "Everyone who now reads and writes in the West, of whatever racial background, sex or ideological camp, is still a son or daughter of Homer" (AMOM, p. 33). But in keeping with his model of male competition, the emphasis Bloom derives from this passage is on Homer as the primary father/precursor for all subsequent male poets. In Bloom's schema, Sappho enjoys no similar priority. (She simply does not exist.) Nor do Homer's potential daughters—whether as readers or as writers—attract more than this passing notice. Unfailingly, Bloom inscribes the gendered assumptions of what Tillie

Olsen has called the sheer "saturation—the never-ceasing, life-long saturation" of "The poet: he (his). The writer: he (his)."[13]

To consider for a change *The poet: she (hers)* is to question whether that sense of "belatedness," which Bloom asserts as "probably the largest component in the anxiety-of-influence" (FOCI, p. xi), encompasses the same meaning for the daughters of Homer as he says it does for the sons. After all, given Bloom's view of literary history as overwhelmingly male, a woman's perception of her late-coming may have little to do with any fear that a rich tradition of gifted precursors had exhausted her potential resources and materials. Rather, as Emma Lazarus suggests in "Echoes" (1880), a woman's sense of belatedness may derive from the anxiety that *her* unique resources have yet to find a place in poetic discourse:

> Late-born and woman-souled I dare not hope
> The freshness of the elder lays, the might
> Of manly, modern passion shall alight
> Upon my Muse's lips, nor may I cope
> (Who veiled and screened by womanhood must grope)
> With the world's strong-armed warriors and recite
> The dangers, wounds, and triumphs of the fight;
> Twanging the full-stringed lyre through all its scope.

Taking her cue from the misfortunes of the nymph whose name titles the sonnet,[14] Lazarus poses in the opening octave the problem of being deprived of authentic expression. The speaker's late-coming onto the stage of poetic history deprives her of the ability to sing with "the freshness of the elder lays." But—and this is given the greater emphasis—the fact of her being "woman-souled" deprives her of access to the very drama and subject matter that appear to constitute the "scope" of that history.

The "act of creative correction that is actually and necessarily a misinterpretation," to which Bloom attributes the dialectical continuity of "the main tradition of Western poetry since the Renaissance" (TAOI, p. 30), is unavailable to the speaking voice of "Echoes." "Veiled and screened by womanhood," she can neither experience directly "the might / of manly, modern passion" nor "cope . . . With the world's strong-armed warriors" to "recite / The dangers, wounds, and triumphs" to which such passions give rise. Deprived thus by both chronology and sex from direct and authentic participation in the wellsprings of that tradition, unable ever to twang "the full-stringed lyre through all its scope," let alone contribute her own corrective refrain, she resolves the problem by resigning herself to the only possibility that remains: an echoing retreat.

> But if thou ever in some lake-floored cave
> O'erbrowed by rocks, a wild voice wooed and heard,
> Answering at once from heaven and earth and wave,
> Lending elf-music to thy harshest word,
> Misprize thou not these echoes that belong
> To one in love with solitude and song.[15]

Given the generic options within which Lazarus places her speaker's dilemma, the conventional alternative to the epic of martial strife is the lyric (or song) of pastoral solitude. Here, though, the significance of the song that issues from that solitude is rendered ambiguous by its clear association with the plight of Echo. Able to plead her love for Narcissus only by repeating fragments from his speech and failing in her attempt to woo him, it is variously reported that Echo pined away, leaving merely her voice behind, or, as in Ovid, that she was changed into a stone which still retained the power of echoing human speech. The voice in the poem appears caught between the continuing attempt to engage the very tradition which has excluded her and, at the same time, the acknowledgment that, at best, she can respond to it only with what are to be the "misprized" and muted echoes of its "harshest word." Wanting to be "wooed and heard," she is nonetheless incapable of independent action or expression; and even if her voice be that of nature itself, it is no more than passively responsive, "*Answering* at once from heaven and earth and wave."

Echo's story thus provides Emma Lazarus the poignant paradigm for the recurrent dilemma of the woman seeking to create poetry within the Western literary tradition as Bloom describes it; that is, the woman for whom Homer figures as the inevitable and inescapable precursor. The speaking voice's inability either to share in or to disavow "the elder lays"—as Echo could neither consummate nor evade her love for Narcissus—accounts for the juxtaposition of the octave's frustrated yearning to twang "the full-stringed lyre" with the sestet's resignation to total dispossession. The sonnet's profferred consolation in pastoral withdrawal is undercut by the fact that the songs produced are only the fleeting echoes of "elf-music" contrasts, and the "solitude," for Echo, is not so much chosen as imposed. At best, to use Bloom's terminology, the speaker may woo the "strong-armed warrior"/precursors by forever echoing back to them fragments of their own songs; but, even so, whether "veiled and screened" or "o'erbrowed by rocks," she will still remain hidden and unseen where the act of making (or simply repeating) poetry is concerned.

In composing this chilling study of women's accommodation to their exclusion from the main tradition of Western poetry, Lazarus succeeded not only in exposing that tradition's inherently self-regarding narcissism but, as well, she tacitly invoked a precursor other than Homer. In this sense, the poem is itself a solution to the dilemma it poses. The speaker's preference for "solitude and song," articulated within a sonnet, aligns the work not with celebrations of "the world's strong-armed warriors"—whose reciters, after all, "misprize" the speaker—but rather with the singers of lyric, said to trace *their* lineage from Sappho. If that reading is permitted, then to refuse Echo's invisibility, to assert a voice that is more than echo, means that a woman need not (to use Bloom's phrase) creatively rewrite the father/ precursors. Instead, she must refuse that heritage altogether, and with it the dialectic that is for Bloom the history of poetic influence.

In its most familiar rendering, the refusal takes a defensive or an apologetic posture—or some combination of the two. Antedating Lazarus by two hundred years, Anne Bradstreet obviously felt some need to explain the absence in her work "of wars, of captains, and of kings, / Of cities founded, commonwealths begun." Composed as a formal prologue to the first major body of English poetry written by a woman in America (1650), Bradstreet's lines adapt the conventional "apologia" in such a way as to anticipate both those who would say "my hand a needle better fits" and, as well, those who would find in her *lack* of martial and epic sweep evidence of a "foolish, broken, blemished Muse." Her tack was to charm her potential adversaries into silence by using their arguments against her as a protective shield. Insisting that she will attempt only what she can, "according to my skill," she wonders why any tongue should carp when her admittedly limited lines must surely serve, by comparison, to reflect back the superior worth of more established traditions:

> And oh ye high flown quills that soar the skies,
> And ever with your prey still catch your praise,
> If e'er you deign these lowly lines your eyes,
> Give thyme or parsley wreath, I ask no bays;
> This mean and unrefined ore of mine
> Will make your glist'ring gold but more to shine. [16]

It is a stratagem that many a woman poet has been forced to employ, in one form or another, at some time during her career in order to be able to assert for herself her right to a craft which had, since Homer, been expropriated from *human*kind to *man*kind. (Sappho, we recall, comes down to us only in fragments.)

In the process of taking up that challenge, it appears that most women writers experience some aspect of Echo's plight. For the strong woman poet (by which I intend the poet who will essay an authentic voice despite the absence of audible or available female precursors and in the presence of a dominant male tradition in which she is either silenced or excluded), for *this* poet, at some point in her development, there comes the recognition that, as Tillie Olsen put it, she had previously been "writing in dominant male forms, style, although what seeks to be expressed might ask otherwise."[17] The characteristic response is a shocked, angry, bitter, or even ironic outcry against oneself for having so loved Narcissus as to falsify one's art. Almost confessional, asking forgiveness for the fraud, but newly empowered by "memory" that gives access to the authentic event which her adherence to formulae from the male literary tradition had obscured, Muriel Rukeyser's "The Poem as Mask" (1960) marks precisely this turning point:

> When I wrote of the women in their dances and wildness, it was
>   a mask
> on their mountain, god-hunting, singing, in orgy,
> it was a mask, when I wrote of the god,
> fragmented, exiled from himself, his life, the love gone down
>   with song,
> it was myself, split open, unable to speak, in exile from myself.
>
> There is no mountain, there is no god, there is memory
> of my torn life, myself split open in sleep, the rescued child
> beside me among the doctors, and a word
> of rescue from the great eyes.

Punning on the multiple meanings of *mask* and *masque*, the first stanza owns up to the fact that, in an earlier work (her long poem, "Orpheus" [1949], which was itself composed as a masque), the poet had employed forms of disguise, masking both experience and identity, and had thereby diminished true Orphic power. The disguise, in short, produced only an elaborate entertainment, akin to the ornate but essentially trivial court masques of the seventeenth century. The maenads tearing Orpheus to pieces is a physical sensation *she* knows through childbirth; but what she successfully rescued from death, through her own body, was a child rather than a lover. The storehouse of symbolic structures which we call our literary heritage, however, offered neither models nor validation for the importance of *that* kind of tearing and rescue; only "memory" had preserved the masked truth of the event intact.

Quite literally, then, the first stanza becomes itself a mask, at once exposing the earlier poem's *masque*rade and, with that, serving as prelude to the significant action which is to follow; that is, the second stanza's fuller explanation of the deception and the consequent revelation of the poet's (painful) ecstasy in childbirth. The myth's assertion of the Orphic power that comes only through the ecstasy of dying is here displaced by Rukeyser's assertion of the ecstasy of bringing forth life. And, as the closing lines indicate, this ecstasy, this "aggressive act of truth-telling,"[18] also renders Orphic power, as life replaces death and fragments become whole:

> No more masks! No more mythologies!
>
> Now, for the first time, the god lifts his hand,
> the fragments join in me and with their own music.[19]

Repossessing the significance of the "memory / of my torn life," Rukeyser is liberated from a sense of "exile from myself." No longer "unable to speak," capable now of renewed—but also different—music, Echo is returned to speech.

> "Mother, I'm pregnant with a baby girl and. . . She
> wants to know who else is coming."
>   "Tell her Mother Margaret is coming, Mother Louisa is
> coming, Mother Emily is coming, Mother Rosa is coming,
> Mother Doris is coming, Mother Charlotte. . ."
>   "Then she has many friends."

> Esther Broner, *Her Mothers* (1975)

In many ways, Amy Lowell anticipated the recent feminist critique of Bloomian poetics when, in 1925, she applied his question "For why do men write poems?" (TAOI, p. 22) to "we women who write poetry":

> Taking us by and large, we're a queer lot
> We women who write poetry. And when you think
> How few of us there've been, it's queerer still.
> I wonder what it is that makes us do it.

She explains why there have been so few women poets by noting that women are "mother-creatures, double-bearing, / With matrices in body and in brain." "There is just the reason" for their relative scarcity, she avers, for in the societal trappings of female procreativity, "The strength of forty thousand Atlases / Is needed for our every-day concerns." As to "what . . . makes us do it," in spite of all, she consults a precursor/sisterhood that includes Sappho, Elizabeth Barrett Browning, and Emily Dickinson. What she discovers, to her dismay, is "how extraordinarily unlike / Each is to me." "For older sisters are very sobering things," to be sure, but they cannot tell Lowell "which way shall I go" or answer for her "What it is that makes us do it." What her imagined afternoon visit to "these my spiritual relations" offers instead is both a recognition of just how little of that tradition begun by Sappho remains to "tell / The reasons, as she possibly conceived them" and, as a result, a heightened experience of participating in "a strange, isolated little family": "For we are such a little family / Of singing sisters."

The frailty which such an image conjures up denies the need for any Bloomian battle for "breathing space" (KC, p. 84) because, clearly, the speaking voice here—presumably Lowell herself—does not regard Sappho, Browning, or Dickinson as having usurped her poetic possibilities by their priority. And so, in place of the Bloomian combat for psychic survival she can assert a sisterly intimacy:

> I understand you all, for in myself—
> Is that presumption? Yet indeed it's true—
> We are one family.

At the same time, she accepts the inadequacy of that sisterhood to provide either solace or direction:

> Good-bye, my sisters, all of you are great,
> And all of you are marvellously strange,
> And none of you has any word for me.[20]

By thus invoking a female literary history modelled on sisterhood, Lowell not only does away with the Freudian romance of murderous competition; she also renders misprision—that is, the rewriting of the precursor—unnecessary to a dynamic of literary influence. The poem *is* composed, after all, though it corrects nothing that her precursor/sisters have written. On the darker side of Lowell's constellation, however, stands the tacit admission that sisters, unlike parent/progenitors, are somehow inadequate or insufficient: "And none of you has any word for me." The fact of their priority has helped Lowell ward off her anxious sense of isolation and aberrance, but she credits it neither with nurturing nor engendering her own poetic efforts. And, in the end, the imagined afternoon visit has still failed to answer for her "what it is that makes us do it."

At least in part, "what it is that makes us do it," and what it is women often do when they write, is precisely what Lowell's "The Sisters" is all about; that is, the woman poet's repeated need to assert for herself some validating female tradition and to repossess its voices for her own needs. In the continental United States, at least, this is the stance with which women's poetry begins. In the eighteenth century, Annis Boudinot Stockton (1736–1801) nominated herself "a sister muse" to the Philadelphia poet Elizabeth Graeme Fergusson (1737–1801), declaring that Fergusson's work had

> ". . . rais'd ambition in my breast," but
> Not such as envious souls possess,
> Who hate another's praise.[21]

Judith Sargent Murray (1751–1820) looked to the English playwright

Hannah Cowley to celebrate a woman writer whose work "inspires, / Wraps my glad soul, and all my fancy fires,"[22] while Mercy Otis Warren (1728–1814) felt that she could "take my stand by fam'd Parnassus' side, / And for the moment feel a poet's pride" if only the English critic of Shakespeare, Elizabeth Robinson Montague, might "across the Atlantic stretch her eye" and cast an approving glance on Warren's work.[23] When a sisterhood of contemporaneous writers on both sides of the Atlantic would not suffice, the earliest women poets of America turned to the originating precursor they recognized as their own. Invoking inspiration from her Muse in 1725, Jane Colman Turell (1708–1735) pleaded, "O let me burn with Sappho's noble fire."[24]

Misogynist pundits like the anonymous author of "To a Poeticall Lady" in the *Boston Weekly Magazine* for March 2, 1743, might try to discourage—"Yet still, to rule her house aright / Would better far become her, / Then to surpass the noblest flight / In Milton or in Homer"[25]—but such verses fell wide of the mark. The women privileged to have the education and the leisure to compose poetry in eighteenth-century America continued to publish, to dedicate their work to one another, and to circulate their manuscripts among themselves. Milton and Homer, moreover, were not the only models to whom they looked. (And Lowell's "little family / Of singing sisters" was larger than she knew.)

But the very fact that in 1925 Amy Lowell could read Sappho only in fragments and find only bowdlerized and highly selected editions of Emily Dickinson and that she seemed unaware, as well, of two prior centuries of women's poetry on this continent denotes not so much absence (as Lowell implied) but loss. There *was* a history, after all, but it had never *carried over*, so to speak. In the first major attempt to compose a literary history of early America, for example, only two women received recognition. Moses Coit Tyler's two-volume *A History of American Literature, 1607–1765* (1878) offers a respectful discussion of Anne Bradstreet, while Jane Colman Turell merits merely brief mention and a footnote as a "verse-writer."[26] Relatively prolific poets like Phillis Wheatley, Mercy Otis Warren, Ann Eliza Bleecker, or the scores of women whose poetry peppered the pages of eighteenth-century magazines find no mention in Tyler's literary history. Indeed, so little of what eighteenth-century women had accomplished remained available to their nineteenth-century daughters that

women themselves began to internalize that loss as absence and restriction. In consequence, as early as 1829 Sarah Josepha Hale (who
later became editor of the influential *Godey's Lady's Book*) predicted
precisely the problem with which Emma Lazarus would grapple at the
end of the century. As Hale told readers of the *Ladies' Magazine*, "the
path of poetry, like every other path in life, is to the tread of woman,
exceedingly circumscribed. She may not revel in the luxuriance of
fancies, images and thoughts, or indulge in the license of choosing
themes at will, like the Lords of creation."[27]

Despite such prescriptions, the nineteenth century—like the eighteenth—saw an outpouring of creative and experimental poetry by
women as diverse as Margaret Fuller in New England and sisters Alice
and Phoebe Cary in the Ohio Valley. But these, again, did not *carry
over.* And so, harking back to the only validating precursor upon whom
they might securely call, nineteenth-century American women began
to articulate the anxiety which now beset them, the anxiety that despite
present popularity and critical acclaim their voices would soon enough
be lost.

At mid-century, Mary E. Hewitt covertly inscribed in "Sappho to
the Sibyl" (1853) her fear that, like Sappho's, her work too would go
unheard or even disappear from literary history. Casting herself in the
voice "of a popular poet whose lover has perhaps never listened to her
song," Hewitt's irony, as critic Emily Stipes Watts has noted, was palpa-
ble.[28] For, in the face of the growing circulation of a number of
women poets and despite her own critical success among the New York
literati in the 1840s and 1850s, Hewitt nonetheless announced in
"Sappho to the Sibyl" not the power of women's poetry but rather its
powerlessness before a recalcitrant male audience:

> Beyond the hills, where flows the Egean wave,
>   I sweep the lyre amid the applauding throng—
> Tell me, dread sibyl of this mountain cave,
>   Has he I lov'd e'er listened to my song?[29]

Following what was then the common misconception that Sappho had
exhausted both her life and her talent in unrequited love, the poem's
concluding stanzas strongly hint that the answer to the speaker's question will continue to be *no.* Thus, in the nineteenth century, the historic Sappho took on some of the characteristics of the mythic Echo.
And, as a precursor, Sappho came to stand not only as a figure of

validating priority but as an emblem of women's literary history, past and present.

Hewitt's poem was prophetic. Along with all but one of her female contemporaries—Emily Dickinson—her work was forgotten soon after her death and thereby denied the status of "influence that extends past one generation." She could not, in other words, participate in that "carrying-over of influence" that for Harold Bloom constitutes the essence of an ongoing "tradition" (AMOM, p. 32). The only tradition Bloom recognizes, however, is that in which "the covert subject of most poetry . . . has been the anxiety of influence, each poet's fear that no proper work remains for him to perform" (TAOI, p. 148). But the poetry of women like Hewitt suggests another "covert subject" altogether: the fear that, like Sappho, her works will be lost or, like Echo, her words go unheeded. This hardly suggests any Bloomian anxiety of influence but, rather, *the influence of anxiety*. It is women poets' peculiar anxiety, as Muriel Rukeyser framed it in our own century, lest they join the ranks of "the wasted ones, lost as surely as soldiers . . . / gone down under centuries / Of the starved spirit."[30]

> I want to remember this season in layers
>   of colors   the year I was ten
>   and discovered pointillism
>   red blue green gold silver
> spreading slow hot points
>   on the tree
>   because my mother started up in us this urge
>   for more
>
> Kathleen Fraser, "Dear Laura, in December" (1978)

Joanne Feit-Diehl, in her essay " 'Come Slowly—Eden': An Exploration of Women Poets and Their Muse," and Sandra Gilbert and Susan Gubar, in *The Madwoman in the Attic*, concluded that Bloom's adaptation of the Freudian family romance must undergo nothing less than radical revision if it is ever to account for the pathways of literary influence affecting women. Any theory of poetic influence which claims completeness, they argue, would have to begin by distinguishing between the male poet's need to make a place for himself in a tradition already overcrowded with (male) greatness and the female's discovery of her exclusion from or veiled presence within that same tradition. Their emphasis, therefore, is on a psychodrama for women that emerges amid a pantheon of precursors which, from Homer on, offered narcissistic fathers/lovers but precious few nurturing mothers or audible precursor/sisters.

Following Bloom's family model rather closely but altering his basic question so as to ask "how . . . women poets perceive their relation to a male-dominated tradition," Joanne Feit-Diehl discovered in the work of Elizabeth Barrett Browning, Christina Rossetti, and Emily Dickinson an essential and dramatic engagement with a variety of male persona and, in Emily Dickinson's work especially, "overwhelming proof of the taut balance she strives to maintain between independence and the power of the Precursor/father."[31] Similarly, in examining women's responses "to male literary assertion and coercion," Gilbert and Gubar revealed their authors' strategies for subverting male-made forms and image patterns to female use. Redefining Bloom's notions of "revision" and "misprision," Gilbert and Gubar insists that the strong woman writer's "battle . . . is not against her (male) precursor's reading of the world but against his reading of *her.*" As a result, their theoretical chapters survey the means by which eighteenth- and nineteenth-century women were able to conceive "fictional worlds in which patriarchal images and conventions were severely, radically revised" while their readings of specific texts and authors examine women's special "concern with assaulting and revising, deconstructing and reconstructing those images of women inherited from male literature" (MA, pp. 49, 44, 76).

Taken together, these studies declare that the would-be woman writer inevitably and irrevocably enters literary history subdued, intimidated, and alienated. Her work invokes a mythology of madwomen and fractured psyches, the daughters relentlessly given over to the fathers' imperatives. After all, the law that declares that "culture is by definition both patriarchal and phallocentric" must, as Sandra Gilbert acknowledged, always and only "transmit the empty pack of disinheritance to every daughter."[32] Compelling as their readings are, it may be that these critics err in acceding too easily to the "essentially male literary history Bloom describes" (MA, p. 48). "No song or poem will bear my mother's name," writes Alice Walker, "yet so many of the stories that I write . . . are my mother's stories."[33] For pathways of literary influence such as this, Bloom's controlling metaphor leaves no room. Thus cognitively fixing the limits of discourse, he prevents us from seeing whether, side by side with a poetics forged in the face of female absence and male priority, women writers have been enabled by another, alternative linkage: a poetics that rescues female priority.

In pursuit of this possibility, Bloom's "radical analogue between human and poetic birth" and, with that, "between biological and creative anxiety" (TAOI, p. 58) leads to a renewed appreciation of Virginia Woolf's insight in *A Room of One's Own* (1929): "we think back through our mothers if we are women."[34] "If not to have conceived oneself" stands as the burden which translates, for the strong male poet, into that "more hidden burden: not to have brought oneself forth" (and thereby initiates the ephebe's anxiety of influence [AMOM, pp. 15–17]), it is hardly a burden generated by the psychodynamics of women's relationships in the world. Although, as in Bloom's paradigm, men "must enter by force, drawn back like Jonah / into their fleshy mothers," Anne Sexton discerned that "A woman *is* her mother. / That's the main thing."[35] Nowhere are the creative implications of that more clear than in the career of the second Elizabeth Stuart Phelps.

Written when she was in her fifties, Phelps' autobiography *Chapters from a Life* (1896) opens by recounting the writing talents and successes of the pious New England ministers who were her forebears. Distinguishing writers from other sorts of people by their greater tendency to be "either rebels to, or subjects of, their ancestry," she locates the beginning of her vocation "a good while before" her birth and announces herself "one whose literary abilities all belong to one's ancestors."[36] It is a matter of wonder for her to consider "the beautiful and terrible law by which the dead man and women whose blood bounds in our being control our destinies" (CFAL, p. 4). Her autobiography thus opens with a statement of both biological and creative belatedness. But as it progresses, the story swerves from engagement with male ancestors and reveals instead the daughter's lifelong impulse "to extend, reveal, and elaborate her mother's . . . thwarted talents." As Rachel Blau DuPlessis has phrased it, "the younger artist's future project as a creator lies" not in competing with but "in completing the fragmentary and potential work of the mother."[37]

Having touted the publishing successes and the longevity of her grandfathers and great-grandfathers, Phelps leaves off the men, turns abruptly to her most obvious progenitor, her successful writer-mother, the elder Elizabeth Stuart Phelps, and introduces, first thing, the fact "of her death . . . at the first blossom of her very positive and widely-promising success" (CFAL, pp. 12–13). Whether intended or not, the contrast between the male ancestors' longevity and the mother's early death is obvious and pointed—as obvious and pointed as the young girl's decision then to take on her mother's name and craft. Only eight years old at the time of her mother's death, she admits in her auto-biography to a lifelong inability to clearly "distinguish between the effect produced upon me by her literary success as I have since understood it, and that left by her own truly extraordinary personality upon the annals of the nursery" (CFAL, p. 11). What does emerge—perhaps because of this very confusion—is the daughter's early awareness of the price exacted by her mother's "difficult reconciliation between genius and domestic life" (CFAL, p. 12). Not until her mid-thirties had her mother begun to find time for her writing, but even then, as the daughter recalled, there was never "one hour in which her children needed her and did not find her" (CFAL, p. 13). Her energies exhausted by domestic toil and loving obligations, her precious free hours "torn by the civil war of the dual nature which can be given to women only" (CFAL, p. 12), the mother came to personify for her daughter the woman caught between her duty to her family and her duty to her own talents and interests, a conflict depicted in the mother's finest short story, "The Angel over the Right Shoulder." Themes from that story, in fact, resonate throughout the daughter's cameo of her mother:

> Now she sits correcting proof-sheets, and now she is painting apostles for the baby's first Bible lesson. Now she is writing her new book, and now she is dyeing things canary-yellow in the white-oak dye—for the professor's salary is small, and a crushing economy was [required]. . . . Now she is a popular writer, incredulous of her first success, with her future flashing before her; and now she is a tired, tender mother, crooning to a sick child while the MS. lies unprinted on the table. . . . (CFAL, p. 14)

Repeatedly, as she dredges up these memories, the mature woman lashes out at the cause of her mother's death: "Her last book and her last baby came together, and killed her." And, again, three pages later: "The struggle killed her" (CFAL, pp. 12, 15).

"Impossible to be her daughter and not to write," she concludes (CFAL, p. 15), her pages hinting all the while that the daughter of the woman who had composed the phenomenally successful *The Sunny Side; or, The Country Minister's Wife*[38] might, in her own time, deal instead with the shadows. The rest of her life essentially given over to answering "what would have been the fate . . . of my mother, had she lived to work her power to its bloom" (CFAL, p. 133), Elizabeth Stuart Phelps began to write in earnest at an early age, first finding her way into print at thirteen (with a short story in *The Youth's Companion*). Confirmed in her chosen vocation by reading Elizabeth Barrett Browning's *Aurora Leigh* at age sixteen (CFAL, pp. 65–66), comforted, perhaps, by discovering there the story of another poet who, as a girl, had longed to recover the memory of her own dead mother, Phelps toiled diligently for the next few years at the moral and moralizing juvenile fiction which she called her "safe and respectable . . . dozen Sunday-school books" (CFAL, p. 106). But she nonetheless found herself, by 1864, at age twenty, ominously repeating her mother's struggle: resentful of her household chores, called to attend an increasingly invalided father, and unable, amid the playful noise of the children of his third marriage, to secure the peace and quite required for her writing, she set about, in spite of all, on what she "distinctly" understood to be "a venture totally dissimilar" to anything she'd done before (CFAL, p. 106). Wrapping herself in an old fur cape of her mother's, she resorted, when she could, to her unheated bedroom or to the attic and that year began *The Gates Ajar*,[39] the novel which was to bring her immediate acclaim and, a little later, the funds with which to refurbish as her own the summer house which had once served as her mother's study (CFAL, pp. 114–115). Published in 1868, *The Gates Ajar* "became the century's second best-selling book by a female author." As Christine Stansell reminds us, "only *Uncle Tom's Cabin* surpassed it in fame and sales."[40]

"Impossible to remember how or when the idea of the book first visited me," Phelps would later write of *The Gates Ajar:* "The angel said unto me 'Write!' and I wrote" (CFAL, p. 95). Though surely never consciously intended as such, the statement links this, her first serious literary effort, with her mother's short story "The Angel over the Right

Shoulder" (1852). In that story, a dream sequence records a kind of internal debate between two competing obligations in a woman's mind: while the angel over the right shoulder keeps track of Mrs. James' devotion to maternal duties and household chores, the fearsome angel over her left shoulder enters into God's Ledger Book every moment withheld from the children for herself, every fragment of time given over (however guiltily) to the cultivation of her own mind and heart. By the end of the dream, the angel over the right shoulder has taken precedence, and the best that Mrs. James can hope for, as she croons over her infant daughter's cradle, is that she may pass on to her child a life "all mended by her own experience. It would have been a comfort to have felt that, in fighting the battle, she had fought for both."[41] We may speculate from her autobiography that when the younger Elizabeth Stuart Phelps embarked upon *The Gates Ajar*, she did so—at least in part—in order to enter the debate posed by her mother's story. Only *her* purpose was to give the fearsome angel its due, as her mother and her mother's protagonist could not.

To give the angel its due, she had to reckon with her mother's major literary legacy, the best-selling quasiautobiographical novel about the domestic life of a country minister's wife. Filled with graphic details about the daily round of activities such a woman would take on, even in the face of hardship and poverty, *The Sunny Side; or, The Country Minister's Wife* not only utilized its author's experiences as the wife of the Andover, Massachusetts, professor of theology, Austin Phelps, but, as well, served as a memorial to the older Phelps' mother, Abigail Clark Stuart, who had herself raised seven children while shouldering the burdens of a country minister's wife. Little wonder that Elizabeth Stuart Phelps the daughter said of *The Gates Ajar* that it "grew so naturally, it was . . . inevitable" (CFAL, p. 95). It had been inevitable for three generations. It was the opening salvo in what Carol Farley Kessler has called the "daughter's quarrel with the world on her mother's behalf"[42]—just as *The Sunny Side* had been, in its way, a muted protest against the self-effacement required in the life of the elder Elizabeth Stuart Phelps and in that of her mother's before her. But where the elder Phelps tried to show a heroine capable of sustaining the superhuman demands upon her, her daughter would identify the only appropriate realm for such domestic fantasies.

Long dismissed for its lachrymose sentimentality and for its covert tendency toward "spiritualism," repeatedly relegated to the sorry status of "the apotheosis of the consolation literature of the day,"[43] *The Gates Ajar* has too often been treated merely as a vision of heaven which provided ready consolation to the bereaved mothers, widows, and sisters of the Civil War dead. Indeed, "so far as I can remember having had any 'object' at all in its creation," Phelps recorded in her autobiography, "I wished to say something that would comfort some few . . . of the women whose misery crowded the land" (CFAL, p. 96). And the novel does, in fact, revolve around conflicting attempts, by friends and relatives, to offer solace to young Mary, whose brother Roy has been lost in the war.

Until the recent rereadings by Christine Stansell and Carol Farley Kessler, however, what had generally escaped critical notice was the fact that the novel derives its power from depicting heaven as a comfortably middle-class order of existence in which the domesticity that, in real life, brought only drudgery and self-denial could, in fact, offer women peace of mind, affection, and leisure—even time to play the piano. In Carol Farley Kessler's words, the novel transmitted "a view of Heaven as compensation for earthly ills."[44] Mary's aunt's vaunted vision of heaven, moreover, closely resembles in its details the fictionalized township of Weston in *The Sunny Side*. It is what Bloom would call "misprision" of a high order—but with a difference. For, in thus restoring her mother's fictionalized Weston as her own fictionalized heaven, Phelps rewrote or, better still, elaborated her mother's muted protest by displacing the blissful elements in the elder Phelps' domestic scene to what the daughter regarded as its proper domain: the imaginative and, in this world, unattainable. In so doing, she tacitly commented upon her mother's fictionalized and overly optimistic delusions while, at the same time, she made of heaven not so much "a consolation prize," as Ann Douglas put it,[45] but an acceptably pious emotional abstraction, granted sufficiently graphic visual detail, so as to bear critical witness to the deficiencies and unfulfilled promises of a disappointing present reality.

The success of *The Gates Ajar* empowered the young author to assert a voice of her own. Rejecting Austin Phelps' adamant (and, later, published) opposition to women's suffrage, his daughter declared "that she should forthwith approve and further the enfranchisement and elevation of her own sex" (CFAL, p. 250). To that end, in a variety of subsequent sketches and novels—including two sequels to *The Gates Ajar* (*Beyond the Gates,* published in 1883, and *The Gates Between,* published in 1887)—Phelps continued to explore the full implications of women's frustrating struggle to lead fulfilling lives in the face of an impoverished set of life choices. Rescuing in that process her mother's muted voice and name in the wide circulation of her own uncompromising protests, the adult Elizabeth Stuart Phelps was at last consoled for the eight-year-old's loss. And in *The Story of Avis,* undoubtedly her strongest novel, her mother's failed blooming was at last made good as the daughter anatomized her own hard-won understanding of the struggle that had destroyed her parent.

If the elder Elizabeth Stuart Phelps had intended *The Sunny Side* both as fictionalized autobiography and as a memorial to her own mother, so too may her daughter have intended *The Story of Avis* (1877). Avis Dobell, the central character in that novel, reads Elizabeth Barrett Browning's "Aurora Leigh" when she is sixteen—as had Elizabeth Stuart Phelps—and for the same reasons. Like the author, Avis Dobell has lost her mother at an early age. A father who does not encourage his daughter's early strivings (as Austin Phelps had never nurtured *his* daughter's abilities) causes the girl to long for maternal support, hoping for "a soul which loved her so, that it could not *help* believing in her."[46] Again, like Phelps, Avis' mother had also been an aspiring artist (an actress) but had been forced to waste her energies in domestic duties.

These autobiographical resonances notwithstanding, other elements in the novel point back toward the author's mother as the model for Avis. The fact that Avis is an artist of some talent suggests Phelps' belated homage to her mother's potential in that area. As an adult remembering her mother's illustrations for the stories she wrote for her children, Phelps judged her "gift" as "original" and surmised that "had she not been a writer she must have achieved something as an artist" (CFAL, p. 13). Beyond this is the fact that the structure of *The Story of Avis* takes up the debate which was at the heart of the mother's story "The Angel over the Right Shoulder." And crucial elements from that story echo within the lines of *Avis.*

Countering the habit of popular romantic novels and stage comedies to end with the marriage of the heroine, Phelps makes it the major concern of her novel's second half. She examines what happens to the

talented young painter Avis Dobell when she "surrenders" to the urg-
ings of the man who loves her and permits her engagement to become
a marriage. The change brings with it neither obvious bondage nor
even, at first, the harsh cruelties of a demanding husband; instead, it
entangles her by love. The result is a recapitulation of Phelps' mother's
dilemma as the novel offers a heartbreakingly detailed study of the
impossibility of reconciling artistic aspirations with a woman's domestic duties. Although the text does not end with the physical death of
the would-be artist, it does nonetheless signal an analogous failure of
talent to come to fruition:

> The year ran fleetly. Van [her young son] was ailing a great
> deal that spring; and in the summer her father was ill. Thus, in
> the old, sad, subtle ways, Avis was exiled from the studio. She
> could not abandon herself to it without a feminine sense of
> guilt. . . . She was stunned to find how her aspiration had ema-
> ciated during her married life. Household care had fed upon it
> like a disease. . . . She wished, with all the wild, hot protest of
> her nature, that the spirit of this gift with which God had cre-
> ated her—in a mood of awful infinite irony, it seemed—would
> return to Him who gave it, that the dust of her days might
> descend to the dust in peace. She wished she were like other
> women,—content to stitch and sing, to sweep and smile. She
> bowed her face on the soft hair of her children; but she could
> not forget that they had been bought with a great price. She
> thought of the husband whose love she had mislaid, and count-
> ed the cost of her marriage in the blood of her soul.

In the elder Phelps' short story, the angel over the right shoulder—
the angel who records the woman's conventional domestic respon-
sibilities—proves victor in Mrs. James' psychomachy. Even so, the author's sympathies—and ours, as readers—remain with Mrs. James'
thwarted attempts to preserve some space for herself amid the daily
grind of household chores. In compensation for what has been given
up, the story closes with Mrs. James hoping to pass on to her infant
daughter a life "all mended by her own experience." In fact, the story
offers no tangible evidence that Mrs. James' efforts have in any way
altered the limitations on women that her daughter, too, will ultimately inherit. And so the story ends on an ambiguous note with the
conditional "it would have been" signaling a consuming doubt: "It

would have been a comfort to have felt that, in fighting the battle, she had fought for both." The assurance of that comfort, though, is grammatically withheld.

What the elder Phelps could not prophesy the daughter would. In the closing pages of *The Story of Avis*, Avis reflects, "It would be easier for her daughter to be alive, and be a woman, than it had been for her; so much as this, she understood." The grammatical assurance withheld by the writer-mother is offered by the daughter. But so too does the second Elizabeth Stuart Phelps repeat her mother's consuming doubts.

Visiting with her friend Coy in the neighboring parsonage (Coy is married to a minister), Avis questions how Coy "'seem[s] to keep pretty well, . . . with all your care.'" Coy answers with a catalog of family trials and domestic tribulations, only to conclude with a single complaint: "'There is one thing I must admit: I do *not* like to ask John for money. There! But that is all, Avis.'" "Was it all indeed!" wonders Avis, deciding to herself that "it was a peaceful, pleasant story." The suggestion, of course, is of amelioration—not truth—in this "pleasant story." Just a few paragraphs later, as the novel closes, we are confronted again with a story that teases assent. It is the tale of Galahad's successful quest for the grail following upon the failure of his father, Lancelot. Avis' little daughter has asked her mother to read it to her. In the view of Rachel Blau DuPlessis, this ending symbolizes "generational displacement": "The mother reads her child the story of the Quest for the Holy Grail, and we understand that while the first generation (Sir Lancelot) failed, the second, purer generation of seekers will achieve the quest."[47] The child, in other words, will accomplish what the mother could not. But with Coy's "pleasant story" still fresh in the reader's mind, it may be that a different kind of displacement is occurring: Avis' earlier certainty that "it would be easier for her daughter to be alive, and be a woman" has now been identified with yet another amelioration. Like Coy's obfuscations, the stories of the Round Table are indeed pleasant, but they are also full of romantic delusions. The ending is, at best, ambiguous. In the finest of her works, then, Elizabeth Stuart Phelps engaged the central theme of her mother's life and work. Not in the Bloomian sense to rewrite either, but to write both again.

Rather than any "fear that no proper work remains," Phelps' fiction thus reveals the daughter's painful perception of just how much her mother—as both precursor and Muse—had left unsaid and, as well, her perception of how much of what her mother *had* said needed to be said again. Baptized Mary Gray Phelps and later married to Herbert Dickinson Ward, Elizabeth Stuart Phelps early took on her mother's name and continued to publish under it for the rest of her life. Attempting thereby to resurrect her mother's unused talents, the daughter devoted her entire career to keeping at bay her anxiety that not only would her own talents go unused but that they would go unused as had her mother's before her. This hardly constitutes the murderous engagement of Laius and Oedipus at the crossroads.

It may be objected here that I have altered the terms of the argument by switching from poetry to prose, using for my example only a second-rate novelist and, with that, made of Bloom's "radical analogue" a case history. To which I answer: Bloom himself does not intend "by 'poet' . . . only verse-writer," including, as he does, Emerson, Nietzsche, and Freud under that rubric.[48] Further, it is Bloom's failure to investigate the pathways of literary influence for women which forces me to seek out, wherever I can discover it, the illuminating case history that comes from life *as women know it*. It is, moreover, a case history whose resonances are to be found throughout women's poetry, beginning perhaps with Sarah Wentworth Morton in the United States. When preparing *My Mind and Its Thoughts* (Boston: 1823) for the printer, she incorporated her mother's name (Sarah Wentworth) into her own on the title page and for the first time signed her name to her published work.[49] Such instances recommend the potential applicability of the mother-daughter relationship as both descriptive model and interpretive paradigm. And finally, as we learn better how to read an author like Elizabeth Stuart Phelps we may discover that she is not, after all, anything less than the strong woman writer whom Bloom and others simply could not properly value.

And no one comes to cradle cold Narcissus. . .

Maxine Kumin, "Nightmare" (ca. 1958)

In our own time, as feminist scholars excavate a rich history of "singing sisters," the singular mother/daughter relationship of the two Elizabeth Stuart Phelpses is fast being replaced by generations of women poets who can remember their nonbiological mother/progenitors. "And when I think of them," declared Alice Walker at a college convocation in 1972, "I understand that each woman is capable of truly bringing another into the world." When women do it, that harking back to literary forebears entails neither psychic competition nor any antiquarian dwelling on the past for its own sake. Rather, what women redeem from the past is a renewed capacity to know and thereby express their present selves because of the secure context offered by a rich and ongoing cultural accretion. For the would-be white woman poet as for the black, as Alice Walker put it, "there is not simply a new world to be gained, there is an old world that must be reclaimed. There are countless vanished and forgotten women who are nonetheless eager to speak" to the woman who would take up the pen today.[50]

In thus reconstituting what Adrienne Rich has termed "an interconnectedness which . . . would give me back myself,"[51] however, lies both the promise and the threat of what women writers now attempt. Consider: In the process of "becoming her own midwife, creating herself anew"[52] and enacting thereby the successful female analogue to Bloom's frustrated poet/son who would (but cannot) be self-begotten, the woman poet is essentially declaring her independence of male poetry and masculinist poetic theory alike. With Adrienne Rich, she advances "a whole new poetry beginning here."[53] And she follows Alice Walker's "sisterly advice" to "be nobody's darling":

> Make a merry gathering
> On the bank
> Where thousands perished
> For brave hurt words
> They said.

> Be nobody's darling;
> Be an outcast.
> Qualified to live
> Among your dead.[54]

Precisely these declarations of poetic independence may explain the peculiar anxiety that permeates the work of a critic like Harold Bloom. Delcaring the "Muses, nymphs who *know*, . . . are now departing," Bloom ominously prophesies that "the first true break with literary continuity will be brought about in generations to come, if the burgeoning religion of Liberated Women spreads from its clusters of enthusiasts to dominate the West. Homer will cease to be the inevitable precursor, and the rhetoric and forms of our literature then may break at last from tradition" (AMOM, p. 33). To be fair to him, Bloom acknowledges some ambivalence about The Great Western Literary Tradition—an ambivalence stemming from his preference for "the morality of the Hebrew Bible to that of Homer" (AMOM, p. 33). But the possibility that the "burgeoning religion of Liberated Women" might free him from the strictures of that tradition seems only a threat, never a promise, to Bloom.

Given the psychology of his theory of literary influence, his anxiety is understandable. If "all men are belated in their stance towards all woman," as Bloom asserts (FOCI, p. 273), and then, as ephebe, the poet also knows himself cuckolded by a whoring mother/Muse, it would be psychological suicide for him to face as well the power of a real flesh-and-blood female poetic precursor. As Bloom reads Freud, in other words, the male poet-ephebe could not survive meeting Jocasta at the crossroads.

It is not clear, however, that even if it emerges "a whole new poetry" by women would necessarily entail the total break with "the rhetoric and forms of our literature" that Bloom predicts. For, as Gilbert and Gubar have demonstrated, what eighteenth- and nineteenth-century women bequeathed their twentieth-century successors were increasingly more effective defensive strategies by which to resist Homer's priority; and insofar as twentieth-century women utilize and elaborate those strategies, then their poetry, too, must inevitably betray its origins in the forms of that resistance. Thus, Bloom's prophecy will have to be modified: still trained by mostly male teachers to read mostly male texts, forced, in effect, from a very early age to "marry the speech of strangers," even those women who would seek to locate themselves in an exclusively female tradition will necessarily turn to precursors who, in part, learned their own evasions by resisting male texts. In the face of an educational establishment that continues to accord women and women's creations only second-class citizenship, and in the face of the irremediable loss of a coherent history of women's writing commencing with Sappho, even the increased access to the last three hundred years of women's poetry will not soon displace Homer as an inevitable precursor; but, as Bloom surmises, it may help to render him eventually no longer *the* inevitable precursor.

That said, Bloom's anxiety is not unjustified. The Muses *are* departing—at least from *his* version of literary history. Women's poetry today announces, as it never has before, that women "can no longer be primarily mothers and muses for men." Discovering, with Adrienne Rich, that "we have our own work cut out for us,"[55] women now call back the Muses as their own, revel in their shared misprisions and revisions of the whole of poetic history, and, like choruses of Echoes all declaring their independence, attempt the restitution of so much that our literary tradition had previously misprized, discarded, or ignored:

> I have written so many words
> wanting to live inside you
> to be of use to you
> Now I must write for myself   for this blind
> woman scratching the pavement   with her wand of thought
> this slippered crone   inching on icy streets
> reaching into wire trashbaskets   pulling out
> what was thrown away   and infinitely precious[56]

No, "the nymphs who *know*" are not "departing" altogether. But until such time as male poets and otherwise sensitive and astute critics like Harold Bloom will look up from their reflecting pools, they will fail to understand that the nymphs have become crones who will no longer woo Narcissus.

Notes

1. Harold Bloom, A *Map of Misreading* (New York: Oxford University Press, 1975), p. 19; henceforth cited in the text as AMOM.
2. Harold Bloom, *Figures of Capable Imagination* (New York: Seabury Press, 1976), p. xi; henceforth cited in the text as FOCI.
3. Harold Bloom, *The Anxiety of Influence: A Theory of Poetry* (New York: Oxford University Press, 1973), p. 30; henceforth cited in the text as TAOI.
4. Harold Bloom, *Kabbalah and Criticism* (New York: Seabury Press, 1975), p. 107; henceforth cited in the text as KC.
5. Harold Bloom, "Poetry, Revisionism, Repression," *Critical Inquiry* 2, no. 2 (Winter 1975): 250; see also his *Poetry and Repression: Revisionism from Blake to Stevens* (New Haven: Yale University Press, 1976), p. 25.
6. Ibid.

7. Paul Ricoeur, "The Metaphorical Process as Cognition, Imagination, and Feeling," *Critical Inquiry* 5, no. 1 (Autumn 1978): 153.

8. Le Anne Schreiber, "I'm Nobody. Who Are You?" *The New York Times Book Review*, December 9, 1979, p. 11.

9. Sandra M. Gilbert and Susan Gubar, *The Madwoman in the Attic: The Woman Writer and the Nineteenth-Century Literary Imagination* (New Haven: Yale University Press, 1979), p. xii; henceforth cited in the text as MA.

10. Joanne Feit-Diehl, " 'Come Slowly—Eden': An Exploration of Women Poets and Their Muse," *Signs* 3, no. 3 (Spring 1978): 586.

11. Adrienne Rich, "When We Dead Awaken: Writing as Re-Vision" (1972), repr. in *Adrienne Rich's Poetry*, ed. Barbara Charlesworth Gelpi and Albert Gelpi (New York: W. W. Norton, 1975), p. 94.

12. Mary Jacobus, review of *The Madwoman in the Attic*, *Signs* 6. no. 3 (Spring 1981): 521.

13. Tillie Olsen, *Silences* (New York: Delacorte Press/Seymour Lawrence, 1978), p. 239.

14. According to Ovid's *Metamorphosis*, Hera, angered that Echo's chatter prevented her from detecting Zeus' illicit liaisons, deprived the nymph of normal speech, allowing her the power only to repeat what others had said. When Echo later fell in love with Narcissus, she could woo him only by repeating fragments from his own (self-adoring) speech.

15. Emma Lazarus, "Echoes," a manuscript sonnet dated October 10, 1880, but unpublished until the posthumous collection edited by her sisters, *The Poems of Emma Lazarus*, 2 vols. (Boston: Houghton, Mifflin and Co., 1889), vol. 1, p. 201. See Dan Vogel, *Emma Lazarus* (Boston: Twayne Publishers, G. K. Hall, 1980), p. 95.

16. Anne Bradstreet, prologue to *The Tenth Muse Lately Sprung Up in America* (London: 1650), pp. 3–4.

17. Olsen, *Silences*, p. 250.

18. See Rachel Blau DuPlessis, "The Critique of Consciousness and Myth in Levertov, Rich, and Rukeyser," *Feminist Studies* 3, nos. 1–2 (Fall 1975): 203.

19. Muriel Rukeyser, "The Poem as Mask," in *The Speed of Darkness* (New York: Random House, 1960; repr. 1968), p. 3.

20. Amy Lowell, "The Sisters" (1925), repr. in *No More Masks! An Anthology of Poems by Women*, ed. Florence Howe and Ellen Bass (Garden City, N.Y.: Anchor/Doubleday, 1973), pp. 40–44.

21. Annis Boudinot Stockton, "To Laura," in Pattie Cowell, *Women Poets in Pre-Revolutionary America, 1650–1775: An Anthology* (Troy, N.Y.: Whitston, 1981), pp. 95–96.

22. Judith Sargent Murray, "Valedictory Epilogue to 'Who's the Dupe,' a Farce which Is the Production of the Elegant Pen of Mrs. Cowley. . . Written by Constantia, in the Spring of 1790, and Spoken by Mr. Allen," in Cowell, *Women Poets*, pp. 131–133.

23. Mercy Otis Warren, "To Mrs. Montague, Author of 'Observations on the Genius and Writings of Shakespeare' " (1790), in Cowell, *Women Poets*, p. 86.

24. Jane Colman Turell, "To My Muse, December 29, 1725," in Cowell, *Women Poets,* pp. 48–49.
25. Quoted in Cowell, *Women Poets,* p. 9.
26. See Moses Coit Tyler, *A History of American Literature, 1607–1765,* 2 vols. (New York: G. P. Putnam's Sons, 1878), vol. 1, pp. 277–292 and vol. 2, p. 133, n. 1.
27. Quoted in Susan Phinney Conrad, *Perish the Thought: Intellectual Women in Romantic America, 1830–1860* (New York: Oxford University Press, 1976), p. 47.
28. Emily Stipes Watts, *The Poetry of American Women from 1632 to 1943* (Austin: University of Texas Press, 1977), p. 81.
29. Mary E. Hewitt, "Sappho to the Sibyl" (1853), quoted in Watts, *Poetry of American Women,* p. 81.
30. Muriel Rukeyser, "Letters to the Front," from *Beast in View* (Garden City, N.Y.: Doubleday, Doran and Co., 1944), p. 37.
31. Feit-Diehl, "'Come Slowly—Eden,'" pp. 573, 586.
32. Sandra M. Gilbert, "Life's Empty Pack: Notes toward a Literary Daughteronomy," *Critical Inquiry* 11, no. 3 (March 1985): 358.
33. Alice Walker, "In Search of Our Mothers' Gardens" (1974), in *In Search of Our Mothers' Gardens: Womanist Prose* (New York: Harvest/Harcourt Brace Jovanovich, 1984), p. 240.
34. Virginia Woolf, *A Room of One's Own* (1929) (repr. Middlesex, England: Penguin, 1945, 1972), p. 76.
35. Anne Sexton, "Housewife," in *All My Pretty Ones* (Boston: Houghton Mifflin, 1961), p. 48.
36. Elizabeth Stuart Phelps, *Chapters from a Life* (Cambridge, Mass.: Riverside Press/Houghton Mifflin, 1896), pp. 3–4; henceforth cited in the text as CFAL.
37. Rachel Blau DuPlessis, *Writing beyond the Ending: Narrative Strategies of Twentieth-Century Women Writers* (Bloomington: Indiana University Press, 1985), pp. 93–94.
38. H. Trusta [Elizabeth Stuart Phelps], *The Sunny Side; or, The Country Minister's Wife* (Philadelphia: American Sunday-School Union, 1851).
39. Elizabeth Stuart Phelps, *The Gates Ajar* (Cambridge, Mass.: Riverside Press/Houghton Mifflin, 1868).
40. Christine Stansell, "Elizabeth Stuart Phelps: A Study in Female Rebellion," *The Massachusetts Review* 13, nos. 1–2 (Winter–Spring 1972): 239, n. 1.
41. Elizabeth Stuart Phelps, *The Angel over the Right Shoulder; or, The Beginning of a New Year* (Andover, Mass.: Draper, 1852).
42. Carol Farley Kessler, "A Literary Legacy," *Frontiers* 5, no. 3 (1981): 29.
43. See Ann Douglas, *The Feminization of American Culture* (New York: Alfred A. Knopf, 1977), p. 224.
44. Carol Farley Kessler, "The Heavenly Utopia of Elizabeth Stuart Phelps," in *Women and Utopia: Critical Interpretations,* ed. Marleen Barr and Nicholas D. Smith (Lanham, Md.: University Press of America, 1983), p. 89.

45. Douglas, *Feminization*, p. 224.
46. Elizabeth Stuart Phelps, *The Story of Avis* (1877), ed. Carol Farley Kessler (New Brunswick, N.J.: Rutgers University Press, 1985). All quotations from the novel are from this reissue.
47. DuPlessis, *Writing beyond the Ending*, p. 90.
48. See Bloom, *Poetry and Repression*, p. 2.
49. See Cowell, *Women Poets*, p. 181.
50. Walker, "A Talk: Convocation 1972," in *In Search of Our Mothers' Gardens*, pp. 39, 36.
51. Rich, "When We Dead Awaken," p. 97.
52. Ibid., p. 98.
53. Adrienne Rich, "Transcendental Etude" (1977), in *The Dream of a Common Language: Poems 1974–1977* (New York: W. W. Norton, 1978), p. 76.
54. Walker, "Be Nobody's Darling," in *In Search of Our Mothers' Gardens*, pp. 39–40.
55. Rich, "When We Dead Awaken," p. 98.
56. Rich, "Upper Broadway" (1975), in *The Dream of a Common Language*, p. 41.

What's Happening in Black Poetry?

"We are almost a nation of dancers, musicians, and poets," declares Olaudah Equiano in *The Interesting Narrative of the Life of Olaudah Equiano, or Gustavus Vassa, the African*, first published in London in 1789. "Thus every great event [in Igbo life] . . . such as a triumphant return from battle or other cause of public rejoicing is celebrated in public dances, which are accompanied with songs and music suited to the occasion." Almost two centuries later, assessing "What Black Writers Owe to Music," the *New York Times* of October 4, 1985, announced that "spirituals, jazz and the blues have influenced the style and content of Black writers from Langston Hughes to Alice Walker."

The *Times* article, occasioned by the Broadway production of August Wilson's *Ma Rainey's Black Bottom*, a play concerning blues singer Gertrude ("Ma") Rainey (1886–1939), identifies a number of contemporary black playwrights, novelists, and poets—Ralph Ellison, Amiri Baraka, Charles Fuller, and Michael S. Harper, among others—whose work reflects the influence of Afro-American music. Significantly, what the article suggests is how consistently the New World descendants of Olaudah Equiano have worked within a tradition, an Afro-American literary tradition rooted in Africa but growing from the first utterances of African slaves on American shores through their songs and shouts, their stories, their patterns of expression, to become a recognizable, formal literary tradition by the middle of the eighteenth century, as seen in the writings of slave poets Phillis Wheatley, Jupiter Hammon, and, later, George Moses Horton and Frances Ellen Harper.

To understand what is happening in black poetry today, one must first consider the literary tradition out of which black poets write, a tradition in which music plays an important part along with a number of other distinguishing elements—a tradition that allows for a continuity rich in variety and promise.

Former University of Grenoble professor of American Studies Jean Wagner (1919–1984), in his *Black Poets of the United States*,[1] published in English in 1973 and hailed as the first full-length study of black poetry, develops the central thesis that two interdependent themes exist in Afro-American poetry—the racial and the religious, both resulting from the Afro-American experience with the contradictions of slavery in a Christian society. For example, Wagner identifies Harlem Renaissance poets like James Weldon Johnson, Langston Hughes, and Sterling A. Brown as poets in whose work the racial theme predominates. These poets, for the most part, rejected Christianity and took their poetic inspiration from the race, the folk tradition: its folk sermons, work and prison songs, ballads, blues, and jazz. Wagner identifies Harlem Renaissance poets like Claude McKay, Jean Toomer, and Countee Cullen as "spiritualists" in their emphasis on religious (Christian) themes. Afro-American poets prior to the 1920s (poets from Phillis Wheatley to Paul Laurence Dunbar), Wagner argues, concentrated on religious themes, Dunbar being a transitional poet who moved Afro-American poetry away from the spiritual realm into the secular with his use of dialect and his depiction of the folk aspects of plantation life.

Wagner's study stops short of a discussion of poets like Gwendolyn Brooks, Margaret Walker, Robert Hayden, Owen Dodson, and those who began publishing in the 1960s and makes too sharp a distinction between the racial and the spiritual, the folk and the literary, as Professor Eugene B. Redmond points out in *Drumvoices*,[2] his critical history of Afro-American poetry, but Wagner does perform an important service in identifying race and religion as two important themes in Afro-American poetry, and he approaches his subject with an absence of condescension still rare in the criticism of black poetry by scholars who are not black.

Stephen Henderson's *Understanding the New Black Poetry*,[3] in contrast to Wagner's work, is an anthology with an extended introduction that focuses on poetry written in the 1960s by poets most of whom are still writing today: Amiri Baraka, James Emanuel, Gerald Barrax, Mari Evans, Sonia Sanchez, Audre Lorde, Jay Wright, Etheridge Knight, Haki Madhubuti (Don L. Lee), Michael S. Harper, Eugene B. Redmond, Dudley Randall, Ted Joans, Carolyn Rogers, Nikki Giovanni, and others, as well as Margaret Walker and Gwendolyn Brooks—poets of what Professor Henderson terms "The New Black Consciousness," a consciousness that "shifted from Civil Rights to Black Power to Black Nationalism to Revolutionary Pan-Africanism." On the basis of his investigations, Professor Henderson concludes that there are two overlapping and intersecting traditions in black poetry, the folk and the formal, and that there exist clusters of themes around the idea of Liberation/Freedom—an idea which, he says, is energized by the oral tradition, where one finds "the dogged determination of the work songs, the tough-minded power of the blues, the inventive energy of jazz, and the transcendent vision of God in the spirituals and sermons." Professor Henderson, who is director of the Institute for Arts and Humanities at Howard University, observes that the best poets of the 1960s, although influenced by those of the Harlem Renaissance, moved beyond them in challenging their community to view itself "in the larger political and spiritual context of Blackness." Much better informed about their African heritage and no longer interested in writing protest poetry or proving their humanity through their performance in the arts, the poets of the 1960s attempted to speak directly, if not exclusively, *"to* Black people *about themselves* in order to move them toward self-knowledge and collective freedom." This concern of black poets for the welfare of the community is, Professor Henderson implies, an essential feature of the Afro-American literary tradition.

Crucial to an understanding of this new black poetry, Henderson points out, is an appreciation of the importance of black speech and black music as "poetic references." In black speech Henderson finds "a complex and rich and powerful and subtle linguistic heritage whose resources have scarcely been touched that [black poets] draw upon." This "black linguistic elegance," as he terms it, can be seen in naming and enumerating techniques; "jazzy rhythmic effects" (often lost unless the poem is read aloud by the poet); hyperbolic imagery common to black vernacular speech and church sermons; understatement; compressed and cryptic imagery; and "worrying the line," an expression for "changes in word order, repetitions of phrases within the line itself, and the wordless blues cries that often punctuate the performances of . . . songs" (as defined by poet Sherley A. Williams in her essay "The Blues Roots of Contemporary Afro-American Poetry").[4] Henderson also sees in black poetry a typical bluntness of language and the use of "mascons," words containing "a massive concentration of Black experiential energy"—what Sherley A. Williams refers to as "Afro-American archetypes." All of these techniques and concepts can be found in the folk forms—street rhymes, church sermons, toasts and boasts, the blues, jazz, and spirituals.

Henderson locates instances of the use of music as a poetic reference in the frequent selection by black poets of musicians and songs as subjects for poems; the inclusion of song titles and lines from songs in poems; the use of musical forms such as the blues, spirituals, gospel, and jazz; the treatment of the written poem as a performance score or chart—a technique applied with notable success in the poetry of Askia Muhammad Toure, the late Larry Neal, the ensemble presentations of The Last Poets and the performance poetry of Nikki Giovanni, Sonia Sanchez, Jayne Cortez, Ntozake Shange, and Amiri Baraka, whose poem "Reggae or Not" is subtitled "A Piece to be read with Reggae accompaniment." These poets "play the air like a drum," as poet Camille Yarborough describes the technique in her manuscript on the spiritual.

Stephen Henderson emphasizes what he sees as the political commitment of poets of "the New Black Consciousness" and takes the position that black people are best qualified to judge black poetry because only they understand its ethnic roots. Nevertheless, *Understanding the New Black Poetry*, through its development of a vocabulary and a context (although it overlooks important poets like Ed Roberson, Isaac J. Black, and Primus St. John), serves to move the discussion of poetry by black writers beyond the limits of psychological or sociological analysis.

A more recent contribution to an understanding of what is happening in black poetry today is a group of essays, *Black Literature and Literary Theory*, edited by Cornell University professor Henry Louis Gates, Jr.[5] Concerned with the question of the formal relation between black literatures and Western literatures, these scholars attempt to consider how applicable is contemporary literary theory—"Anglo-American and French structuralist, feminist and post-structuralist criticism"—to the reading of the African, Caribbean, and Afro-American literary traditions by analyzing significant black literary works.

In his provocative introduction, which is followed by essays from writers and scholars such as Wole Soyinka, Robert Stepto, Mary Helen Washington, and Houston C. Baker, Gates argues that every great work in the black literary tradition, which consists of interrelated formal and vernacular traditions, is "double-voiced"—possessed of what W. E. B. DuBois in *The Souls of Black Folk* identifies as "double consciousness," the consciousness of being both American and black. Gates also asserts that there exists in the black literary tradition identifiable "black" uses of figurative language. "Black people," he says, "have always been masters of the figurative: saying one thing to mean something quite other has been basic to black survival in oppressive Western cultures."

Professor James A. Snead, in his essay "Repetition as a Figure of Black Culture," discusses the relationship between the uses of repetition and improvisation and offers insights essential to a full appreciation of contemporary Afro-American performance poetry. Identifying what he sees as African-derived patterns of repetition and recurrence, which "find their most characteristic shape in performance: rhythm in music, dance and language," the Yale scholar notes that "without an organizing principle of repetition, true improvisation [a major feature of black creative expression, found notably in jazz and the blues] would be impossible."

Professor Barbara E. Bowen of Wellesley College gives additional insight into the blues form through her "Untroubled Voice: Call and Response in *Cane*," an analysis of Jean Toomer's classic. She writes: "The statement-variation-response sequence which is the essence of the blues is a development of the call-and-response pattern of collective work-songs and spirituals. For the blues singer, the importance of the call-and-response pattern is its continual affirmation of collective voice." This "affirmation of collective voice" is no doubt what Walt Whitman had in mind when he said, "To have great poets there must be great audiences too."

Clearly at odds with the exclusively black critical orientation of Henderson's *Understanding the New Black Poetry* and more concerned with literary theory and the close reading of black texts than Wagner's *Black Poets of the United States*, Gates' *Black Literature and Literary Theory* presents useful models for discussing the work of Afro-American, African, and Caribbean poets—perhaps one day permitting us to see them as part of a single, broad tradition.

What I have tried to suggest by identifying these three approaches to black poetry is that not only are its features being thoughtfully defined—and one has only to read journals such as *Callaloo, Obsidian, Black American Literature Forum, Black Scholar,* and old issues of *Black World* and become familiar with the work of poet-scholars Sherley A. Williams, Eugene B. Redmond, Melvin Dixon, and Lorenzo Thomas to see the wealth of discussion that exists—but that certain features identifying a black poetic tradition can be observed in what poets are writing today. A few of these features are: (1) an extensive use of black music and speech as poetic references; (2) an interplay of the folk (vernacular) and formal traditions; (3) an impulse toward racial and spiritual themes; (4) a double-consciousness operating in structure and language; and (5) a social and political awareness that relates to a sense of community responsibility.

The rich variety that an Afro-American poetic tradition allows is nowhere more strikingly illustrated than in the uses contemporary poets make of the blues, with its classic three-line stanza (the first line making a statement; the second line repeating it, with or without variation; and the third line providing a rhymed response or resolution, often in strict iambic pentameter), its attitude of stoicism, its tough humor, its themes of love, work, travel, pain, death, and transcendence. From Ma Rainey's "Countin' the Blues":[6]

> Layin' in my bed with my face turned to the wall,
> Lord, layin' in my bed with my face turned to the wall,
> Tryin' to count these blues so I could sing them all

through Langston Hughes' "Midwinter Blues":[7]

> I'm gonna buy me a rose bud
> An' plant it at my back door,
> Buy me a rose bud,
> Plant it at my back door,
> So when I'm dead they won't need
> No flowers from the store

and "The Backlash Blues":[8]

> Mister Backlash, Mister Backlash,
> Just who do you think I am?
> Tell me, Mister Backlash,
> Who do you think I am?
> You raise my taxes, freeze my wages,
> Send my son to Vietnam

and Sterling A. Brown's "Tin Roof Blues":[9]

> I'm goin' where de Southern crosses top de C. & O.
> I'm goin' where de Southern crosses top de C. & O.
> I'm goin' down de country cause I can't stay here no mo'

contemporary poets have received an inheritance to which they frequently turn.

Mari Evans, in her "Cellblock Blues,"[10] uses the classic blues structure and traditional subject matter while exploiting the orthographic possibilities of words to effectively convey the class and emotional condition of the speaker, "Layen" and "Layin" providing a fine example of the repetition/improvisation feature associated with the blues:

> Layen in the joint wonderin
> when ah mona raise
> Layin in the joint wonderin
> when ah mona raise
> Doin black/time by the hour
> don eeeven be about no days

In "Transformation,"[11] Quincy Troupe abandons the classic structure to address the ironic mingling of joy and pain found in the blues, its transformational capabilities, its oral ("rap") qualities, the poem echoing Ralph Ellison's definition in *Shadow and Act*:[12] "The blues is an impulse to keep the painful details and episodes of a brutal experience alive in one's aching consciousness, to finger its jagged grain, and to transcend it, not by the consolation of philosophy, but by squeezing from it a near-tragic, near-comic lyricism." Quincy Troupe writes:

> catch the blues song
> of wind in your bleeding
> black hand, (w)rap it around
> your strong bony fingers
> then turn it into a soft-nosed pen

> & sit down & write the love
> poem of your life

Contemporary poets working within the blues tradition seem to draw more frequently upon the subject matter than upon the classic form. Nevertheless, simply to call a poem a "blues"—a "mascon" word of tremendous power—can place it and the tradition in resonant relationship. Sonia Sanchez's "Blues" presents a nightmare:[13]

> i see walls dripping screams up
> and down the halls
>   won't someone open
> the door for me? won't some
> one schedule my sleep

from which the speaker finds release remembering a moment of sexual fulfillment, the emotion's objective correlative represented by images in a Bessie Smith song:

> Yeah, bessie he put in the bacon
> and overflowed the pot.

Al Young's "What Is the Blues?"[14] gives a hard, direct look at the human condition. Its three stanzas play against the three-line stanza of the classic blues and capture the style and attitude of the quintessential blues singer who, though drowning in the blues, keeps

>   coming up for air: my
> tiny fair share of cool fulfillment.
>
> And to vanish wouldn't be so bad.
> Look at the visible, behold it slowly
> and closely with unreddened eyes.
> Without the stirrings of the heart
> swimming in borrowed light, what could
> we ever possibly lie down and see?

Calvin Hernton's "D Blues"[15] answers Al Young's question by stripping the language to its essentials, the idea to its concrete representation, undercutting the agony of utter loneliness with the language of the minstrel show:

> De blues
> What you woke up wit
> Dhis mourning

What you toss and turn
All night in your bed wit

From a sharecropper's battle with floods and boll weevils to John Henry's legendary confrontation with a steam drill, conflicts with nature and machines have always provided materials for blues poets. Where man is the measure of all things earthly, technology (even The Bomb) comes under wry scrutiny. Raymond R. Patterson's "Computer Blues" complains:[16]

> I put my troubles in the computer
> To find out what's troubling me.
> I say I put my troubles in the computer
> To see what's the matter with me.
> My card had so many holes,
> Holes was all that I could see.

The pain of the blues, unrelieved by humor but transformed through craft, is captured in Michael S. Harper's "Village Blues."[17] The poem transplants the "strange fruit" of Billie Holiday's American South (perhaps to South America) to render a monstrous image (suicide or lynching?) familiar by virtue of the poem's double consciousness and its ironic allusions not only to Christian ideas of resurrection but also to black texts such as "Christ in Alabama" by Langston Hughes:

> The birds flit
> in the blue palms,
> the cane workers wait.
> the man hangs
> twenty feet above;
> he must come down;
> they wait for the priest.
> The flies ride on the carcass

Great female blues singers Ma Rainey, Bessie Smith, Big Mama Thornton, Billie Holiday, and Dinah Washington, along with their songs of lost love and abuse at the hands of some "no-good man," also sang of assertive women who celebrate their strength and independence. Two contemporary blues poems in that tradition are Mariah Britton's "reports"[18] and Lucille Clifton's "Miss Rosie."[19] Landlords, store owners, and racism, not lovers, are the source of trouble for Mariah

Britton's "woman / with a mountain / of stones / she didn't / throw. . . . lately though," she says, "i hear / reports of / broken glass." In Lucille Clifton's poem, the strength of women who survive the ravages of time and circumstance is evoked through the archetypal Miss Rosie. "When I watch you," the poet declares, "I stand up / through your destruction / I stand up."

Contemporary black poets writing out of an Afro-American literary tradition have not limited themselves to lyric poems but have produced examples of epic poetry deserving attention. A connection between contemporary Afro-American epic poetry and traditional African epic poetry awaits explication, but African epic features no doubt survived in the narratives of early slave poets, those "black and unknown bards of long ago" immortalized by James Weldon Johnson. The Afro-American literary epic, however, finds its earliest formal expression in the nineteenth century in Albery A. Whitman's *The Rape of Florida* (concerning the Seminole Indian Wars) and *Not a Man and Yet a Man* (chronicling an individual's quest for freedom). Nevertheless, characteristics of the genre can be seen in the poetry of Phillis Wheatley, and certainly the twentieth century contains fine examples in Melvin B. Tolson's *Libretto for the Republic of Liberia* and *Harlem Gallery*, Calvin Hernton's *The Coming of Chronos to the House of Nightsong*, and *Black Anima* by N. J. Loftis. If one thinks of the urge to write the epic as an urge to establish a sense of community, to delineate an ethos, it is not surprising that black poets move in that direction. Twentieth-century contributions to the poetic sequence, in its various modes including the epic, are numerous and can be seen in the work of Jean Toomer, James Weldon Johnson, Countee Cullen, Langston Hughes, Robert Hayden, and Gwendolyn Brooks and in the work of younger poets such as Michael S. Harper, Sonia Sanchez, Ishmael Reed, June Jordan, Ai, Sherley A. Williams, and Caribbean poets Edward Brathwaite, Derek Walcott, and Wilfred Cartey.

Two recent attempts at the epic by black poets are *The Double Invention of Komo*[20] by Jay Wright and *Iwilla/Soil* by Yvonne.[21] *The Double Invention of Komo*, the author tells us in his afterword, is a poem of initiation given shape by a study of African, Mexican, and South American cosmologies with elements of Western culture, using the rituals of the Bambara Komo initiation rite to open an exploration of history as a way toward self-knowledge. The poem's voices are African, European, and American. In the poet's words, the poem seeks to redeem and to discover social, historical cultural, intellectual, and emotional dimensions now obscure in the African and Afro-American worlds and to make these dimensions available for creative use in the necessary transformation of an enhanced world of intransigent act.

Ambitious and complex, the poem owes allegiance to a variety of literary ancestors and does not readily reveal itself through excerpts; however, one theme, that of double consciousness operating in structure, language, and idea, is unmistakably sounded as only a true son of Olaudah Equiano would:

> I know my double exile in song,
> and the way the heel comes down,
>   remembering a dance,
> on unfamiliar ground.

Yvonne's *Iwilla/Soil*, a poetic sequence of epic sweep, combines African, Native American, and Judeo-Christian ritual in a New World setting. Book 1 of a projected trilogy, it is structured as an arrangement of voices telling the story of Iwilla, "the first American Mother of my family," and the daughters who came from her. Aunt Ida (1881–1971) operates a hair-dressing parlor. This fragment of her life captures the sad eloquence of the blues:

> Radiant
> glorified
> effervescent
> they scatter from beneath Aunt Ida's hands
> the Negro women of this shambling town
> a shattering of raven wings
> chatoyant
> falling stars

The long and well-established tradition of social and political awareness in Afro-American poetry extends back to the earliest recorded poem by an Afro-American, "Bars Fight" by Lucy Terry, which concerns an Indian attack in Deerfield, Massachusetts, in 1746. Phillis Wheatley's lines to Britain's Lord Dartmouth[22]—"Should you, my lord, while you peruse my song, / Wonder from whence my love of Freedom sprung"—are also of that tradition, as are the slave spirituals, the abolitionist verse of the nineteenth century, the protest poetry of the early decades of the twentieth century, and the revolutionary poetry of the 1960s and 1970s. Such poems continue to be written by black poets. Jayne Cortez reminds us in the opening lines of "For the Brave Young Students in Soweto":[23]

> Soweto
> when i hear your name
> i think of you
> like the fifth ward in Houston Texas
> one roof of crushed oil drums on the other
> two black hunters in buckets of blood
> walking into the fire of Sharpeville
> into the sweat and stink of gold mines
> into your children's eyes suffer from malnutrition
> while pellets of uranium are loaded into boats
> headed for France for Israel for Japan
> away from the river so full of skulls
> and Robben Island so swollen with warriors
> and the townships that used to overflow
> with such apathy and dreams

And so it would appear that many black poets today work out of a tradition that can best be understood as distinctly Afro-American, the African element proclaimed long ago by Olaudah Equiano; the American element only partially understood by Stephen Vincent Benét in 1928, when in *John Brown's Body*[24] he envisioned the yet unwritten "black-skinned epic, epic with the black spear," with its "Deep mellow of the husky, golden voice / Crying dark heaven through the spirituals, / Soft mellow of the levee roustabouts, / Singing at night against the banjo-moon"—Afro-American poetry is all of that, yet much more.

Notes

1. Champaign: University of Illinois Press, 1973.
2. Anchor Press, 1976.
3. New York: William Morrow and Co., 1973.
4. *Massachusetts Review* (Autumn 1977).
5. New York: Methuen, 1984.
6. In *Woke Up This Morning* (New York: Bantam, 1973).
7. In *Selected Poems* (New York: Alfred A. Knopf, 1975).

8. In *The Panther and the Lash* (New York: Alfred A. Knopf, 1967).
9. In *The Collected Poems* (New York: Harper and Row, 1980).
10. In *Nightstar* (Los Angeles: UCLA Publications, 1981).
11. In *Snake-Back Solos* (Danbury, N.H.: Reed Books, 1978).
12. New York: Random House, 1964.
13. In *I've Been a Woman* (Black Scholar Press, 1978).
14. *Hambone* 2 (Fall 1982).
15. In *Medicine Man* (New York: Reed, Cannon and Johnson, 1976).
16. In *Elemental Blues* (New York: Cross-Cultural Communications, 1983).
17. In *Images of Kin* (Champaign: University of Illinois Press, 1977).
18. In *With Fire* (New York: Meta Press, 1982).
19. In *Good Times* (New York: Random House, 1969).
20. Austin: University of Texas Press, 1980.
21. New York: Chameleon Productions, 1985.
22. In *The Poems and Letters of Phillis Wheatley* (Mnemosyne Publishing, 1969).
23. In *Coagulations: New and Selected Poems* (Thunder's Mouth Press, 1984).
24. New York: Holt, Rinehart and Winston, 1928.

Notes toward a New Multicultural Criticism
Three Works by Women of Color

I wish to examine works of three women poets from distinct cultural traditions—Joy Harjo, Creek Indian; Lorna Dee Cervantes, Chicana; and Janice Mirikitani, Japanese American. Harjo and Cervantes were born in the early 1950s, Mirikitani near the end of the Second World War. Each represents a broader culture—American Indian, Hispanic, Asian American—which has produced a significant new literature within the author's lifetime. In sections to follow I will treat the specific project of each of these writers; here I wish to examine what they have in common.

All three are members of oppressed minorities in the United States. The ancestors of present-day American Indians were subdued by military conquest by their Euro-American invaders and placed on reservations. The Southwestern ancestors of the Chicanos, themselves descendants of Hispanic and indigenous peoples, were subjugated politically and sometimes militarily by the same Euro-Americans. They were followed to the United States by waves of poor Mexican immigrants, especially after the Mexican Revolution. The immigrants from Japan, China, and the Philippines came seeking employment and were subjected to systematic legal repression governing their entry, the nature of their employment, and their segregation from the dominant society. In addition, Japanese Americans like Mirikitani suffered internment in military prison camps during the Second World War as suspected agents of a hostile foreign power. Members of all these groups have also been subject to acts of racial prejudice (including racial murders and lynchings) and have been punished economically, in the job market, and by restriction of access to homes and other material benefits. This may be said to be stating the obvious. But it is important to realize that the women poets represented here are emergent writers who have struggled to gain a new voice, not simply "multiethnic" writers exercising the privilege of self-expression in an American "melting pot."

All three writers have witnessed and participated in the increasing politicization in their cultures in the decades since the Second World War. The contrast between the boom period enjoyed by the white majority population in the 1960s and the situation on the reservations and in the barrios and ghettos gave oppressed peoples substantial cause for organized defiance and revolt. In the case of Native American tribes, earlier attempts by the U.S. government to terminate some and relocate others into city slums led to political and cultural resistance. The young "City Indians" of the 1960s and 1970s sought to fight ghetto conditions and at the same time to reconnect with their tribal pasts. Chicanos, politically active since the end of World War II, paid special heed in the 1950s and 1960s to the condition of migratory farm workers in California; many other people in the nation supported them in this effort. Asian Americans developed a keen sense of community organizing in such cities as San Francisco and New York while undertaking a close study of their past. They concluded that the dominant culture in America, working "under legislative racism and euphemized white racist love," had "left today's Asian Americans in a state of self-contempt, self-rejection, and disintegration,"[1] and they banded together to fight these conditions.

The Modern Language Association took note of the emerging literatures of these groups in the 1970s. Its Commission on Minority Groups and the Study of Language and Literature sponsored a national symposium on minority literature in New York in 1976, some of the proceedings of which were published the following year.[2] The literature of American Indians, Chicanos, and Asian Americans was specifically treated in another volume, *Three American Literatures*, gathered in the 1970s and published in 1982.[3] Perhaps the most significant result of the MLA project was an anthology, *The Third Woman: Minority Women Writers of the United States*, edited by Dexter Fisher in her capacity as director of English Programs for the MLA and published in 1980.[4] Copiously documented, annotated, and footnoted, it provided essential texts of American Indian, black, Chicana, and Asian American women writers of the 1960s and 1970s for later editors to follow.[5] Harjo, Cervantes, and Mirikitani were all included in this volume.

Perhaps half a dozen major works of scholarship have been written or compiled in the three literatures up to the present time. Of these, three major works have been produced by women scholars: *Studies in American Indian Literature*, an MLA critical reader and handbook edited by Paula Gunn Allen; *Contemporary Chicana Poetry*, a critical study by Marta Ester Sanchez; and *Asian American Literature* by Elaine H. Kim. I will make use of these works in the pages to follow.[6] I will rely first on the testimony of critics before me (especially women within each poet's own culture), then give close textual readings based on the standard methods of current criticism, and argue finally for the consideration of these works as part of a revised canon of American literature.[7]

She Had Some Horses by Joy Harjo

> The ceremonies as they had been performed were enough for the way the world was then . . . elements in this world began to shift, and it became necessary to create new ceremonies.
>
> Leslie Marmon Silko, *Ceremony*[8]

The essential focus of modern-day American Indian literature from the time of its emergence after World War II has been survival. The survival of many peoples under material and spiritual attack has been the theme of its great novels, from N. Scott Momaday's *House Made of Dawn* (1969) to Leslie Marmon Silko's *Ceremony* (1977) to Louise Erdrich's *Love Medicine* (1984). The use of ceremonial devices in the stories to suggest or promote psychological or social healing (they are the whole subject of Silko's *Ceremony*) has generated critical interest.[9] What has not been so often remarked is that the theme of survival and the techniques of ceremony have also permeated the poetry, most apparently in the women poets such as Wendy Rose, Leslie Marmon Silko, and Joy Harjo.

Paula Gunn Allen has remarked that American Indian literature calls for a "functional" definition of genre into "ceremonial and popular, as opposed to the Western prose and poetry distinction."[10] Ceremonial literature "includes all literature that is accompanied by ritual actions and music and that produces mythic (metaphysical) states of consciousness and/or conditions" and thus is invested with "an intangible but very real power or force." Using "language of its own," it may include "songs for many occasions," such as healing, harvesting, blessing new undertakings, personal power songs, and vision seeking. "Each serves to hold the society together, create harmony . . . [and] ensure prosperity and unity."[11] Allen takes pains to distinguish sacred Indian ceremony, which is wholly or partly secret to the tribe, from the literary use of ceremonial devices. But it is clear that aspects of ceremonial understanding have entered literature. These include ritual elements such as opening and closing prayers, references to and actual use of "old stories," uses of natural symbolism and symbolic persons, and certain narrative devices such as telling a story on several levels and alluding to things forbidden to be spoken.

Indian symbols are never counters for other things which they are not; they are natural entities subject to transformation through ritual. Allen describes this use of "magic":

> The tribal person perceives things, not as inert, but as viable and alive, and he or she knows that living things are subject to processes of growth and change as a necessary component of their aliveness. Since all that exists is alive, and since all that is alive must grow and change, all existence can be manipulated under certain conditions and according to certain laws.[12]

The inseparability of symbols and the world of which they are a part, and their availability for interpretation, are movingly described by Lame Deer, quoted by Allen:

> We Indians live in a world of symbols and images where the spiritual and the commonplace are one. To you, symbols are just words, spoken or written in a book. To us they are a part of nature, part of ourselves, even little insects like ants and grasshoppers. We try to understand them not with the head but

with the heart, and we need no more than a hint to give us meaning. [13]

Can we speak of the "role of the poet" in American Indian culture? Only in guarded and qualified ways. What we seem to find are writers privileged to take on poetic roles as witnesses to the dangers of the time. These writers are to be seen as representative members of a social group, all of whom enjoy a personal relationship with nature. But if the writer is both an observer and a manipulator of symbols, the work is likely to be polysemous in "story lines," with literal and symbolic levels of interpretation. Allen has remarked of writers such as Momaday and Silko that they share an "achronicity":

> These people can actually think four stories at the same time. And they can do it simultaneously in their brain, which is analogous to the sort of universe the [modern] physicists are describing. That's one of the marks of an Indian person. They do it automatically. [14]

One reason for the complication of the stories is that one level at least—the most occult kind of knowledge—is only alluded to. This may be the level of witchery or of other ceremonial secrets. Often this level awaits the unraveling of the other levels of the story in order to be fully understood. Such would appear to be the case with *She Had Some Horses* by Joy Harjo.

In her early writing, Joy Harjo already addressed themes of land and people, fear and healing. Speaking of her native landscape, she remarked:

> What is breathing here is some sort of dangerous anger that rises up out of the Oklahoma landscape. The earth is alive with emotions, and will take action on what is being felt. This way of seeing is characteristic of most native poets and writers of Oklahoma. That which has happened to the earth, has happened to all of us as part of the earth. . . .
>
> What Oklahoma becomes, in a sense, is a dream, an alive and real dream that takes place inside and outside of the writer. . . . Our words begin inside of the dream and become a way of revealing ourselves within this landscape that is called Oklahoma. Language becomes all of the people that we are. Living voices surround us and speak from the diverse and many

histories we have been, the ones we have become, and most of
all, how we will continue. There are those voices among us who
will assume the cadence of an ancient and living chant.[15]

Nothing in Harjo's early work quite prepares the reader for the overall
arrangement—a plot structure operating on several levels—of *She Had
Some Horses,* her third book, published in 1983.[16] The book begins by
confessing the poet's fear. It then describes the fate of other "survivors"
like herself who have had to deal with such fear. It introduces intermediary
figures—human and symbolic—who negotiate between the poet
and her fear. It tells a story of the breakup of the poet's relationship with a
man and her discovery of the love of a woman. It ends with the freeing of
the horses, who are the symbols of her frightened spirit, and the freeing
of the poet from old, repressive images to live her own life. The end is a
ritual prayer, closing off the matter begun with the first poem.

The first poem, "Call It Fear," introduces most of the thematic material
in the book.

> There is this edge where shadows
> and bones of some of us walk
>   backwards.
> Talk backwards. There is this edge
> call it an ocean of fear of the dark. Or
> name it with other songs. Under our ribs
> our hearts are bloody stars. Shine on
> shine on, and horses in their galloping flight
> strike the curve of ribs.
>
> . . . .
>
> There is this edge within me
>   I saw it once
> an August Sunday morning when the heat hadn't
> left this earth. And Goodluck
> sat sleeping next to me in the truck.
> We had never broken through the edge of the
> singing at four a.m.
>
> . . . .
>
>   And there was this edge—
> not the drop of sandy rock cliff
> bones of volcanic earth into
>   Albuquerque.

Not that,
        but a string of shadow horses kicking
and pulling me out of my belly,
        not into the Rio Grande but into the music
barely coming through
            Sunday church singing
from the radio. Battery worn-down but the voices
talking backwards.

The "edge" of fear is the subject of the book. The fear is protean, taking many shapes: notably the backwards-talking Holy Rollers on the radio and the nightmare of the horses pulling the poet's entrails out of her belly ("Or name it with other songs"). The people of Harjo's acquaintance sit by the volcanic cliffs outside Albuquerque trying to propitiate this fear ritually by talking and singing and "walking backwards." Still it persists ("Under our ribs / our hearts are bloody stars"). Someone who might stand as an intermediary between the poet and her fear, Goodluck, her friend and a symbolic figure, has been unable like her to "[break] through the edge of the singing at four a.m."

Succeeding poems speak of those who survive even in a hostile environment. The poet quickly establishes her sense of identity with people of color in America in her poem to Audre Lorde, "Anchorage":

And I think of the 6th Avenue jail, of mostly Native
and Black men, where Henry told about being shot at
eight times outside a liquor store in L.A., but when
the car sped away he was surprised he was alive,
no bullet holes, man, and eight cartridges strewn
on the sidewalk
        all around him.

Everyone laughed at the impossibility of it,
but also the truth. Because who would believe
the fantastic and terrible story of all of our survival
those who were never meant
           to survive?

The survivors take many forms, but perhaps the most stirring image in these poems is the relationship of women to the earth. It begins in the poem "For Alva Benson, and for Those Who Have Learned to Speak":

And the ground spoke when she was born.
Her mother heard it. In Navajo she answered
as she squatted down against the earth
to give birth. It was now when it happened,
now giving birth to itself again and again
between the legs of women.

The image is heightened in a later stanza, the action of which makes a completed circle, with Mt. St. Helens the governing symbol:

The child now hears names in her sleep.
They change into other names, and into others.
It is the ground murmuring, and Mt. St. Helens
erupts as the harmonic motion of a child turning
inside her mother's belly waiting to be born
to begin another time.

Contrasting to this woman-image of cyclic restoration is the tragic image of the man, drinking and out of control, which repeats itself in several poems. In "Night Out" it is a man in a barroom on New Year's Eve:

Your voice screamed out from somewhere in the
darkness
another shot, anything to celebrate this deadly
thing called living. And Joe John called out to bring
another round, to have another smoke, to dance dance it good
because tomorrow night is another year—
in your voice.
I have heard you in my ownself.
And have seen you in my own past vision.

The poet takes pains to universalize and understand the figure:

It doesn't end
For you are multiplied by drinkers, by tables, by jukeboxes
by bars.
You fight to get out of the sharpest valleys cut down into
the history of living bone.
And you fight to get in.
You are the circle of lost ones
our relatives.

> You have paid the cover charge thousands of times over
> with your lives
>   and now you are afraid
>
>   you can never get out.

These poems show separate ways of knowing: a man's way, harsh and fatalistic, of meaningless rebellion, or a woman's way, embracing the history of the whole earth of which one is a part. It is the second way the poet will choose to follow as the book develops.

The figure of Noni Daylight appears in three poems near the end of the first section. Old and shrunken, the mother of many children by as many fathers, she is first cited as the woman who stayed where she was to raise her family:

> Because she knew
> that each star rang with separate
> colored hue, as bands of horses
> and wild
>   like the spirit in her
> that flew, at each train whistle.
>   ("Kansas City")

In the next poem where she is mentioned, Noni is afraid of familiar voices.

> She talks softly
>   softly
> To the voice on the radio. All night she drives.

Finally she perceives how she will free herself.

> It is not the moon, or the pistol in her lap
> but a fierce anger
>   that will free her.
>   ("Heartbeat")

In the third poem in which she appears, Noni reveals her true character to the poet and proposes the key to the poet's rescue.

> "We are closer than
> blood," Noni Daylight
> tells her. "It isn't
> Oklahoma or the tribal

> blood but something more
> that we speak."

She speaks directly to the poet of her "cure" and reveals herself as a spiritual intermediary.

> "Should I dream you afraid
> so that you are forced to save
> yourself?
>
> Or should you ride colored horses
> into the cutting edge of the sky
> to know
>
> that we're alive
> we are alive."
> ("She Remembers the Future")

The poet must now seize the initiative.

The second section, "What I Should Have Said," focuses on the poet's changing of her relationship from a man to a woman lover and the confusion, disruption, and difficulty she has in "commuting" (literally from Albuquerque to Santa Fe and back again) to teach, care for her children, and be with her new lover. The moon becomes the symbol of her new consciousness, but also her new fate:

> She is moon.
> Her eyes slit and yellow she is the last
> one out of a dingy bar in Albuquerque—
> Fourth Street, or from similar avenues
> in Hong Kong. Where someone else has also
> awakened, the night thrown back and asked,
> "Where is the moon, my lover?"
> And from here I always answer in my dreaming,
> "The last time I saw her was in the arms
> of another sky."
> ("Moonlight")

In her acceptance of the promiscuity of the moon, the poet affirms a new existence, one which Noni Daylight unlocked when she told her she must "know / that we're alive / we are alive." In a new poem, written while driving between her lover and home, the poet begins to explore the meaning of this.

Alive. This music rocks
me. I drive the interstate,
watch faces come and go on either
side. I am free to be sung to;
I am free to sing. This woman
can cross any line.

                    ("Alive")

The horses which figured in the first poem in the book return in the third section, bursting forth in a terrible and wonderful emergence.

The title poem of the section "She Had Some Horses" is an extended catalog of "horses"—personal traits, poetic images, manifestations of fear and anxiety or danger from external forces—known to the poet. She writes it with bare logical connection, in the manner of Christopher Smart's "For I Will Consider My Cat Jeffrey." The ending of the poem gives some of its most important elements, threats from within and without and what they actually have amounted to.

She had horses who whispered in the dark, who were afraid to
    speak.
She had horses who screamed out of fear of the silence, who
carried knives to protect themselves from ghosts.
She had horses who waited for destruction.
She had horses who waited for resurrection.

She had some horses.

She had horses who got down on their knees for any saviour.
She had horses who thought their high price had saved them.
She had horses who tried to save her, who climbed in her
bed at night and prayed as they raped her.

She had some horses.

She had some horses she loved.
She had some horses she hated.

These were the same horses.

Several more poems treat horses in their different aspects. In the fifth poem, the remarkable "Explosion," all the horses are set free—those belonging to others and to the poet herself.

The explosion—on a highway—takes place in the poet's home country. (We may recall what Harjo saw elsewhere as "some sort of

dangerous anger that rises up out of the Oklahoma landscape.") She
first tries to associate it with an apocalyptic future event of significance
to her people. Finally she sees what has happened.

> But maybe the explosion was horses,
>> bursting out of the crazy earth
> near Okemah. They were a violent birth,
> flew from the ground into trees
>> to wait for evening night
> mares to come after them . . .
>
> . . . .
> Some will not see them.
>
> But some will see the horses with their hearts of sleeping
>> volcanoes
> and will be rocked awake
>> past their bodies
>>> to see who they have become.

It is important to view the horse poems not as simply a hodgepodge
of loosely related material but as ceremonial shapes, from the naming
of the horses to their freeing, which make it possible for the poet and
others who believe her to look to the future with hope and to "see who
they have become" (the "they" of the last line is, I believe, purposely
ambiguous). This freeing is the climax of the book, leading to the
concluding poem, which echoes the beginning.

"I Give You Back" works at many levels. The first level is the ritual
release of the fear that was expressed in the beginning.

> I release you, my beautiful and terrible
> fear. I release you. You were my beloved
> and hated twin, but now, I don't know you
> as myself. . . .
>
> You are not my blood anymore.

Also released are paralyzing memories of genocide and the poet's sus-
ceptibility to future harm at the hands of the oppressor.

> I give you back to the white soldiers
> who burned down my home, beheaded my children,
> raped and sodomized my brothers and sisters.
>
> . . . .

> I release you, fear, so that you can no longer
> keep me naked and frozen in the winter,
> or smothered under blankets in the summer.

There follows a sequence in ritual repetition, first declaring simply, "I release you" and then itemizing what the poet is "not afraid to be." Then the poet admits her own past complicity in her fear:

> Oh, you have choked me, but I gave you the leash.
> You have gutted me but I gave you the knife.
> You have devoured me, but I laid myself across the fire.
> You held my mother down and raped her,
>   but I gave you the heated thing.

After another sequence announcing her separation from her fear, the poet ends with a passionate inversion, showing the formerly weak element to now be the strong and the strong the weak. It is a note of triumph and even of compassion for the enemy.

> But come here, fear
> I am alive and you are so afraid
>   of dying.

Harjo's indebtedness to traditional storytelling devices, such as her use of ceremonial elements at the beginning and end of the poem, her use of symbols like the horses, the moon, and the spiritual guide Noni Daylight, and her use of multilevel narrative are integral to the structure of the poem: they establish the naming of the fear at the beginning, the intervention of Noni Daylight in the middle, and the freeing of the horses at the end. Two levels of the narrative are literal: the story of the author's changes in lovers and the historical thread running through the book, reminding the reader of the history of white oppression. In both these cases it is important to notice the author's point of view. When she says, "You have gutted me but I gave you the knife," she is making a point both personal and political. Both she and her people, as she has come to understand them, are learning not to be victims.

Optimism is conveyed at the end of *She Had Some Horses* through the notion brought first by Noni Daylight, "We are alive." The poet pronounces this for herself in the course of the discovery of her new love while driving between Alburquerque and Santa Fe one day. Armed with the knowledge, she banishes fear: "I am alive and you are so afraid / of dying." We should recall again what Paula Gunn Allen describes as the "magic" involved in the enactment of ceremony. "Since all that exists is alive and since all that is alive must grow and change, all existence can be manipulated . . . according to certain laws." We may conclude that the method and content of Harjo's book are the same.

Emplumada by Lorna Dee Cervantes

Although Chicano literature has emerged only since the 1960s, it has a remarkable consciousness of its own origins. An early textbook, *Literatura chicana: Texto y contexto* (1972), could already state that it was "composed with the Chicano reader in mind" and trace a cultural heritage including "antecedent Mexican texts [and] pre-Hispanic selections."[17] By 1980, the critic Bruce-Novoa had proposed a paradigm of Chicano poetry as a response to the overall problematic of Chicano history. Such a poetry contained

> a nostalgia for a prior unity, either lost, forgotten, or in the process of disappearing; a lamenting of alienating oppression in the present, a situation which must be corrected lest Chicano culture disappear; and a hope for a future regrouping in a home-land (Aztlan) reclaimed from the United States, and around cultural/historical traditions—a recuperation of the lost unity.[18]

Bruce-Novoa's critical work *Chicano Poetry* (1982) treats eleven men and one woman. In the decade since 1975, however, women have emerged as major voices, a "second generation" of poets marked by different concerns from their male counterparts. Marta Ester Sanchez, in her book *Contemporary Chicana Poetry* (1985), has typified these concerns as ones of gender and ethnic identification, joined by common identity as a poet, and sees the major distinctions among women writers to come from which element of this "triad" they emphasize.[19] Naomi Quiñonez, Los Angeles poet and teacher, has been perhaps more helpful in this connection by viewing the emergence of the Chicana in a concrete perspective:

> In the process of writing, for the Third World woman, several things are happening. The connection with a past, with a

culture, is the motivating force; so you see many women who will bring back the images of our ancestral past, give them new light, put them in a new context, recreating symbols and images that have been given to us effectively from our own culture. Also, we are redefining the images and symbols that have been given to us by the dominant society, putting those in a new context. Finally, we are creating new symbols, new images, and synthesizing all those aspects into new myths sometimes, using a combination of what our past is and what has been imposed on us, giving us something relevant to really be a part of. [20]

Born in 1954 in San Jose, California, Lorna Dee Cervantes is an inheritor of the Chicano tradition that was being thematically established as she was growing up. She had access as a beginning writer to the works of the "first generation" of politically active, primarily male Chicano writers. She began writing the poems that would make up her book *Emplumada* in 1974 and spent seven years arranging the manuscript. While she herself speaks of the "different styles" and "poems dealing with different issues" in the book, she also makes it clear that the arrangement of materials is deliberate: "The book is meant to be read in one sitting. It's meant to be read from beginning to end."[21]

The particular challenge that Naomi Quiñonez sees confronting the first generation Chicana artist is that of combining the materials she found in books with the experience of her own life to produce new poems. There is in this a strong sense of historical process. The *Chicanismo* of the first generation of male poets, especially their search for the "lost unity" of Aztlan, is a gender-influenced myth of heroic discovery.[22] The emergence of *La Chicana* as poet, on the other hand, brings other "images of our ancestral past"—the figures of the grandmother and the mother as nurturing and sustaining forces, the home as the center of the world, and the artist as the synthesizer "using a combination of what our past is and what has been imposed on us, giving us something relevant to really be a part of." According to this view, Cervantes is not so much the seat of conflicting impulses as she is the synthesis of two generations of poetic effort.[23]

Bruce-Novoa observed, in his work *Chicano Poetry*, that Chicano poets in their work follow "basic antimonies of thought" such as those found in the structures of myth. "A system of primitive irreconcilable tensions struggling for resolution, they are manifested in a text in the form of binary oppositions such as life vs. death, individual vs. group, freedom vs. necessity."[24] Cervantes, in *Emplumada*, divides the work according to pairings of binary opposition, in which each new stage of dialectical development leads to new propositions awaiting similar testing in the future.

Cervantes is a great definer of terms. At the very beginning of *Emplumada*, she devotes a whole page to defining her title, according to a binary opposition.

> *em-plu-ma-do* [adj.] m., feathered; in plumage, as in after
> molting
> *plu-ma-da* n.f., pen flourish[25]

My reading of this pairing is that the act of writing has to do with coming into one's own, being empowered for flight (the colorful image of plumage is linked to the Chicano heritage).

The book is divided into three sections. Each has a headnote or short title. Each of these consists of two terms, either stated or understood. The headnote of the first section is ominous: "Consider the power of wrestling your ally. His will is to kill you. He has nothing against you." The pairing around the image of "ally" introduces the contradiction of malign will versus moral indifference. The second section, with the headnote "This world understands nothing but words and you have come into it with almost none," concerns the acquisition of a language necessary to survive in the world. Language has now become the ally with which one must wrestle in order to succeed. The third section is titled simply "Emplumada," referring us back to the pairing "feathered; in plumage" and "pen flourish." This would appear to speak of some synthesis, where the dangers of the world are confronted by a language appropriate to their expression, resulting in the freeing of the writer for an as yet unspecified task.

As the binary terms of each section of *Emplumada* suggest, the book is always in a state of development. The first section, governed by the image of "wrestling your ally," treats the poet growing up in her single-parent household of mother and grandmother, mediating images of "hardness" and "softness" to understand how she will confront the world. The image of the "Ally," along with other imagery of initiation, is borrowed from Carlos Castaneda's *The Teachings of Don Juan;*[26] much of the incidental lore of the first section treats drugs and intimates of the art of the *bruja* or sorcerer. The second section, governed by the problem of language, shows the poet cast out into the world, unable to recover her Mexican heritage and seriously challenged by the harsh world of the Anglo dominant culture. The third section attempts a reconciliation of tradition and modernity. The persona of the poet develops in each case. In the first section a myth of the past is brought into place, showing formative influences on the girl growing up in the barrio. The second section shows the poet in transaction with Mexican and Anglo culture. In the third section she speaks in her own voice. The identity of the poet Lorna Dee Cervantes and the persona of the book become more marked as the book progresses.

In the first poem, "Uncle's First Rabbit," the persona's uncle encounters the world and finds it full of dangerous knowledge. The uncle, while still a boy, kills a rabbit, thinking it a part of his initiation into manhood. Immediately after the killing the boy dreams of escape.

> He was a good boy
> making his way through
> the Santa Barbara pines,
> sighting the blast of fluff
> as he leveled the rifle,
> and the terrible singing began.
> He was ten years old,
> hunting my grandpa's supper.
> He had dreamed of running,
> shouldering the rifle to town,
> selling it, and taking the next
> train out.

The "terrible singing" is his memory of the crying of his baby sister, "pushed . . . into birth" by "his father's drunken kicking," her voice "going faint at its end"—a sound that blends with the cry of the rabbit he bludgeons to death. But killing the rabbit has not only brought the terrible memory back to life, it has passed the crime of the father onto the son. Instead of leaving his brutal and abusive father behind, the boy becomes him. When a young man he goes off to war; he returns to brutalize his own wife; and, as the poem moves to the present, is seen waiting in empty triumph for her to die, still hearing the accusatory singing in his head. The poem ends with the uncle's childhood fantasy still haunting him:

> . . . how he'd
> take the new pickup to town, sell it,
> and get the next train out.

The next poem is also full of hard knowledge, but of another type. In "Cannery Town in August" the poet describes the numbing effects of factory labor.

> . . . Women
> who smell of whiskey and tomatoes,
> peach fuzz reddening their lips and eyes—
> I imagine them not speaking, dumbed
> by the can's clamor and drop
> to the trucks that wait, grunting
> in their headlights below.
> They spotlight those who walk
> like a dream, with no one
> waiting in the shadows
> to palm them back to living.

It appears that in these first two poems the "ally," whose "will is to kill you" though "he has nothing against you," has conquered.

But in the poem actually titled "The Ally," the first of two linked rape poems, Cervantes uses the symbol of "wrestling with your ally" to a different end. While the rapist of this poem is real enough and the stage is set for total defeat and subjugation, the very danger of the event provokes the girl's heroic attempt at defiance.

> But it was the glint
> of steel at her throat
> that cut through
> to her voice.
> She would not be
> silent and still.
> She would live,
> arrogantly,
> having wrestled
> her death
> and won.

The role of this "ally" in bringing the girl to voice is reemphasized, in more bitter detail, in the second poem in the series.

I picked myself up   ignoring
whoever I was   slowly
noticing for the first time my body's stench
I made a list in my head
of all the names who could help me
and then   meticulously   I scratched
each one
                    they won't hear me burning
                    inside of myself
my used skin glistened
my first diamond

                                        ("Herself")

In a subsequent poem, "Meeting Mescalito at Oak Hill Cemetery," the poet intermingles themes of "hard" and "soft" while keeping to the subject matter of initiation. She is sixteen, sitting "crooked with drug" in the cemetery. The gravestones appear "soft and harmless." Here, in a safe world, the drug has triumphed.

I knelt to a lizard with my hands
on the earth, lifted him and held him
in my palm—Mescalito
was a true god.

At night, although "nothing had changed" (Mama sleeps on the sofa and the poet locks her bedroom door "against the stepfather"), as she goes to sleep she sucks "the last of the sweet fruit" and thinks "nothing of death."

("Meeting Mescalito at Oak Hill Cemetery" is a deceptively simple poem. The iconography of much that is within it—"Mescalito," the lizard—comes from *The Teachings of Don Juan*. Lizards are an aid to divination; "Mescalito" (which is Don Juan's favorite name for the peyote plant) is a strenuous endeavor requiring courage on the part of the taker. Perhaps most interestingly in this poem, the apricot pits which the poet sucks while thinking "nothing of death" contain deadly cyanide. It would appear that the poet is gaining in both innocence and experience at the same time and has come closer to death than the surface of the poem makes clear.[27])

Cervantes traces the themes of "hard" and "soft" with delicacy and irony in "Beneath the Shadow of the Freeway" and subsequent poems in the first section. The trusting little girl of that poem ("But Mama, if you're good to them / they'll be good to you back") is echoed in some of the characters she meets in succeeding poems. "For Edward Long" is a poem to an itinerant ditchdigger who "stayed / long enough to give me my voice" and "knew a key so secret / they locked it away." The gentleness of this Anglo man most strikes the poet:

> Pardner, Doctor, crazy
> mathematician and sometimes
> wizard to the child I still am,
> I still believe you.

The last poem in this section tests the poet-persona's "softness" in the same way. Her friend the "Caribou Girl" is the neighborhood character who claims to receive poems and lovenotes from the crows and dances with a peculiar arch of her back, spinning down the street. This figure "spoke the cadence / of her own mythology" and is beloved for this by the poet. But in a final scene, Caribou Girl is seen in a dreamstate slipping from the rocks above into the water, "a thin crazed girl / . . . / and I know she will drown." The author descends a little way with her, but preserves her own safety:

> . . . I'm going
> to leave her
> for another breath
> before I plunge
> with her again.

This section transforms the images of disaster in the opening poems into images of resistance to adversity, finally coming to a clarity about how far one may go in weaving a personal mythology with which to meet the world. Praising the mad girl but not drowning with her, the poet/persona has learned something about survival. But at the same time the transactions described in this section have taken place only at the level of the poet's own protected world of childhood in the barrio. She has yet to confront the dominant culture.

The beginning quotation of the second section, "This world understands nothing but words and you have come into it with almost none," may be confusing at first; surely this poet has already found a voice, and a measure of confidence, in the world described by the poems in the first section. But the new poems of the second section disturb that confidence and threaten to still that voice. Their message is that we are helpless before imponderables. The four-sectioned poem "Four Portraits of Fire" begins with an abstract vision of fire in the mountains; passes to the death of baby birds, fallen from their nest; then relates the tale of a Chicano family burned to death at Christmas while trying to stay warm with a heater improvised from a cannister of oil. Taking in these events, the poet concludes that she can find no charm or magic in her repertoire to provide comfort or security in such cases:

> I am away from the knowledge
> of animal mystics,
> brujas and sorcerers
> or the nudging chants
> of a Tlingit Kachina.
> I am frightened by regions
> with wills of their own,
> but when my people
> die in the snow
> I wonder
> did the depths billow up
> to reach them?

Some of Cervantes' most artful lyrics are in this section. "Starfish" and "Spiders," for instance, bring the poet/persona to consider the transcendence of form over death (in the case of the starfish) and over ugliness (in the case of the spiders) in terms which challenge human comprehension. But that is exactly the problem. The poet's peculiar frustration—at having to discard her poetic language in order to deal with situations it cannot control—surfaces in a poem relating the world of nature to the world of man.

> We watch seabirds flock the tour boat.
> They feed from the tourist hand.
>
> We who have learned the language
> they speak as they beg
>
> understand what they really say
> as they lower and bite.
> ("From Where We Sit:
> Corpus Christi")

In this literal picture of tourists feeding birds in the Texas gulf, a plainer language is being spoken than before—the language of the oppressed. It is used again in the ironically titled "Poem for a Young Man Who Asked Me How I, an Intelligent Well Read Person, Could Believe in the War between Races." From its beginning, this poem offers a contrasting duality—the poet's "land" of wished-for harmony versus the real world where "there is war." The poet angrily confesses that the land of her fantasy is impossible. It is described in terms of an unrealizable future:

> In my land there are no distinctions.
> The barbed wire politics of oppression
> have been torn down long ago.

Or it is depicted in childish terms, easily seen through and even mocked by the poet:

> In my land
> people write poems about love,
> full of nothing but contented childlike syllables.
> Everyone reads Russian short stories and weeps.

The poet stands between this fantasy creation and the real world pressing in on her. She personally embraces the contradiction:

> I am not a revolutionary.
> I don't even like political poems.
>
> . . . .
>
> I believe in revolution
> because everywhere the crosses are burning.

In this poem, Cervantes adds important information to the emerging portrayal of her search for a new language with which to deal with oppression. The forces of the dominant culture have damaged her ability to express herself—in effect, stolen her language.

> Let me show you my wounds: my stumbling mind, my
> "excuse me" tongue, and this
> nagging preoccupation
> with the feeling of not being good enough.

In subsequent poems, Cervantes addresses—as have other Chicano and Chicana poets—the problem of being separated from one's original culture and language.

> Mama raised me without language.
> I'm orphaned from my Spanish name.
> The words are foreign, stumbling
> on my tongue. I see in the mirror
> my reflection; bronzed skin, black hair.
>
> I feel I am a captive
> aboard the refugee ship.
> The ship that will never dock.
> *El barco que nunca atraca.*
> ("Refugee Ship")

In another poem, a vacation in Mexico does not provide a sense of cultural recovery but only further realization of the distance the poet has traveled:

> Mexico,
> I look for you all day in the streets of Oaxaca.
> The children run to me, laughing,
> spinning me blind and silly.
> They call to me in words of another language.
> ("Oaxaca, 1974")

It is only possible for this poet to reconcile her relationship to the two cultures and the two languages when she is faced again with the raw edge of the contradiction between them: oppression. This confrontation takes place in the last poem of the section, "Visions of Mexico while at a Writing Symposium in Port Townsend, Washington."

In the first part of the poem "Mexico," the poet again confronts her own awkwardness in Spanish and concludes something about the Chicano heritage: the culture runs far deeper than language alone.

> I don't want to pretend I know more
> and can speak all the names. I can't.
> My sense of this land can only ripple through my veins
> like the chant of an epic corrido.
> I come from a long line of eloquent illiterates
> whose history reveals what words don't say.
> Our anger is our way of speaking,
> the gesture is an utterance more pure than word.

Back "home," at a writer's conference at the Northwestern corner of the United States, Cervantes observes in a tavern a particularly racist tableau depicting Mexicans "drooling in a caricature of machismo" and responds to it by repeating her thoughts, this time determining to act upon them:

> there are songs in my head I could sing you
> songs that could drone away
> all the Mariachi bands you thought you ever heard
> songs that could tell you what I know
> or have learned from my people
> but for that   I need words
> simple black nymphs between white sheets of paper
> obedient words   obligating words   words I steal
> in the dark when no one can hear me

The poet has come to a realization. Stripped of the language of power by the dominant culture, she has come to see that she must steal it back, fashioning her own power out of the words she can recapture. She has returned to the United States precisely to recover her culture:

> as pain sends seabirds south from the cold
> I come north
> to gather my feathers
> for quills.

The double meaning of the book's title is reinforced in the last two lines. The time is ripe for empowerment.

The third section begins at once, almost comically, with the poet's awakening to the possibility of a new language. She dreams she sees "a hundred robins" on her lawn, "telling it their way." She concludes,

> I am driven from this world, alive
> I come to this world, in dreams.
>   ("This Morning")

The action of the final section of the book is quite different from that of the first two. Poems in the first two sections tend to be narrative and descriptive, about dilemmas faced by the poet/persona, pointing often to partial resolutions which in turn open up further dilemmas. But these final poems are either love poems set in the present, which also may define aspects of the poet's self, or what I call "process" poems, which describe the act of becoming what one will be.

Much of the love poetry in this section contains self-description.

Whether speaking in a corrective spirit to an intended lover or in the language of love itself to the man to whom she has dedicated this book, Cervantes (hardly distinguishable now from her persona) is at pains to describe herself:

> I'm an ugly woman, weedlike,
> elbowing my way through the perfect
> grass. The best of what I am
> is in the gravel behind the train yard
> where obsidian chips lodge
> in the rocks like beetles.
> I burrow and glow.
>
> ("Beetles")

The last two poems of the book are perhaps the author's final statement on the maturation of her art. "Oranges" pictures an old woman "crossing herself, / her eyes burning winter oranges," and compares this to a painting the poet/persona remembers in her grandmother's room depicting a miracle. Just as two children in the painting are about to be swept away in a flood, a guardian angel appears to save them. So now, in the action of the old woman passing by, the poet and her lover "are guided out / of falling." By transmuting a small, mundane event into a miracle, the poem accumulates some of the uncanny power caught in the lyrics of John Donne.

In the final, title poem, the message is a simple one—ripeness is all. The poet sees this in "flowers / . . . born when the weather was good" and again in "two hummingbirds" seeking "what is / given them to find." She concludes,

> . . . These are warriors
> distancing themselves from history.
> They find peace
> in the way they contain the wind
> and are gone.
>
> ("Emplumada")

Following Quiñonez' observation that Chicana poets are "creating new symbols, new images, and synthesizing all of those aspects into new myths," I would take *Emplumada* as a fabulous narrative of development in which we see simultaneously the autobiographical figure of the young poet, the spiritual figure of the artist taking flight, and the social figure of the Chicana struggling to find a language appropriate to deal with reality. After the crafted "family" poems in the first section come more social pieces where the lessons of the world are treated in a vivid way that still allows for a certain didacticism (you must learn to survive in a place full of danger). The increasingly lyrical and personal poems of the last section appear to announce the poet's emergence in her own voice, no longer looking back to family mythology or the "stage" she has passed through of learning how to deal with the world. Cervantes is portraying her own development in the form of a "portrait of the artist as Chicana." Of necessity, she will return to her origins and her social concerns in subsequent writings, with different strategies and seeking different results in the poetry.[28]

Awake in the River by Janice Mirikitani

In the 1970s, encouraged in particular by the black editors of Yardbird Publishing Company in San Francisco, a group of young male Asian American scholars embarked on heroic undertakings. Frank Chin, Jeffrey Paul Chan, Lawson Fusao Inada, and Shawn Hsu Wong put together a ground-breaking anthology, *Aiiieeeee! An Anthology of Asian-American Writers,* which was published by Howard University Press in 1974. This collection restored to print major works of Asian American literature of earlier decades by writers such as Carlos Bulosan, John Okada, Louis Chu, and Tosuio Mori while also publishing current writers, including Chin and Wong. The same scholars were instrumental in forming the Combined Asian Resources Project which, working through several sympathetic university publishers, published or republished editions by Bulosan, Okada, Chu, Mori, and others, including Ben Santos and Monica Sone.[29]

At the same time, the editors of *Aiiieeeee!*—three Chinese American men and one Japanese American man—took a controversial position regarding the roles of Chinese American women as writers in the early immigrant literature. Noting that the novels of Jade Snow Wong, Pardee Lowe, Virginia Lee, and Betty Lee Sung all had tended to reinforce the stereotypes of the dominant culture in the United States, the editors concluded:

> The white stereotype of the acceptable and unacceptable
> Asian is utterly without manhood. Good or bad, the ster-
> eotypical Asian is nothing as a man. At worst, the Asian-Ameri-
> can is contemptible because he is womanly, effeminate, devoid
> of all the traditional masculine qualities of originality, daring,
> physical courage, and creativity. The mere fact that four out of
> five American-born Chinese-American writers [of the period] are
> women reinforces this aspect of the stereotype. [30]

The implication was left to be drawn that Asian American women
writers should step aside until the male writers recovered their literary
"manhood." Echoes of this pronouncement have persisted in the literary community over the years, and partly as a result Asian American
women have had to struggle for an equal voice in the literature of this
movement.

Other organizing efforts touching the Asian American community
in the same period were conceived to unite people around common
goals. The project started by the San Francisco–based group Third
World Communications brought men and women from all the oppressed communities together to produce literary collections and public performances in solidarity against oppression at home and the Vietnam War overseas. Janice Mirikitani was one of the organizers of Third
World Communications. Through the work of its Women's Collective, the anthology *Third World Women* was produced in 1972.
Mirikitani co-edited another project for Third World Communications, an anthology of Third World men and women writers called
Time to Greez! in 1975. She then assumed the role of editor for the
Japanese American Anthology Committee of *Ayumi: A Japanese American Anthology* in 1980. The "blurb" on the back cover of *Time to
Greez!* speaks for the principle of unity in struggle at the heart of these
collections.

> The Editors of *Time to Greez!* have come together from the
> respective Third World cultures/races represented in this an-
> thology. We feel it is a many-sided mirror of our lives, reflecting
> the colors, shapes and sounds, tastes, smells, touch of our
> homes, the rhythms of our music, the music of our food, the
> food of our lives. Share in the feast with us, TIME TO
> GREEZ! [31]

Janice Mirikitani is a Sansei (third-generation American) who was incarcerated as a small child in a U.S. detention center in Rohwer, Arkansas. Too young at the time of her internment to recall it clearly, Mirikitani has reconstructed it in her poetry and prose, collected in the volume *Awake in the River.* [32]

The camp experience has been the central trauma of Japanese American history. As literary historian Elaine Kim says, it "propelled to crisis dimensions the conflicts and tensions already existing in the Japanese American family and community."[33] It also provided a way of conceiving history from within one's own racial and cultural perspective. Japanese American writing reached its maturity in the camps: writers such as Toshio Mori, Hisaye Yanamoto, and Mine Okubo worked there, publishing in the camp magazines, and the great novel of the Nisei (second generation Japanese), *No-No Boy* by John Okada, grew out of camp experience.[34] At the same time, the particular sense of history which was a result of camp life—a history of subjugation within the country of one's residence—provided a backdrop against which to see other events in the world: the bombing of Hiroshima and Nagasaki, U.S. imperialism in Southeast Asia, and the effects of the dominant ideology in the United States on people of color globally. Mirikitani—raised in this place of shame and exile—absorbed these painful experiences and turned her sense of history into a weapon which she has used in all her creative work.

In Mirikitani's work I am concerned with the relationship between two ways she conceives events: diachronically ("horizontally," in terms of temporal succession) and synchronically ("vertically," in terms of simultaneous and systematically organized elements). Mirikitani's poetry is dominated by certain vivid and terrible memories, such as the internment camps, Hiroshima, and Vietnam. The poetry plays itself out in time, encountering the recurrent images and responding to their onslaught. The resolutions are, as in the case of Cervantes, dialectical. But events in history—especially the culturally shared atrocities—rule these poems more absolutely than they do in the work of the other two poets I have considered.

Although *Awake in the River* does not organize itself as a whole book to the degree of *She Had Some Horses* or *Emplumada* (it is not, taken from beginning to end, a ceremony of recovery or a symbolic seizing of images to bring the writer to power), its opening poem sets forth many of the problems, conditions, and dominant imagery of the rest of the author's work. "For My Father" presents contradictory images of one man and suggests that the reasons for the contradictions lie in history. We see first a heroic image:

> He came over the ocean
> carrying Mt. Fuji
> on his back/Tule Lake on his chest
> hacked through the brush
> of deserts
> and made them grow
> strawberries.

Counterpointed to this image is the humble situation of the children (as in much of what is to follow, the contradictory images are indented from the main body of type in the poem):

> we stole berries
> from the stem
> we could not afford them
> for breakfast

The father reveals a second side to his character as he reacts to the children.

> his eyes held
> nothing
> as he whipped us
> for stealing.
>
> the desert had dried up
> his soul.
>
> wordless
> he sold
> the rich
> full berries
> to hakujines
> whose children
> pointed at our eyes
>
>> they ate fresh
>> strawberries
>> with cream.

The economic need which has made the father deny his own children a simple pleasure in order to sell every piece of fruit to support the family is also a terrible form of cruelty, imposed to be sure on the father but imposed by him in turn on the children. This human face of oppression is not lost on the poet.

> Father,
> I wanted to scream
> at your silence.
> Your strength
> was a stranger
> I could never touch.
> Iron
> in your eyes
> to shield
> the pain
> to shield desert-like wind
> from patches
> of strawberries
> grown
> from
> tears.

This poem powerfully establishes a context and certain images for the rest of the book. The contrast between the white world, the world of the "hakujines," and the world of the Japanese Americans is between wealth and poverty, control and oppression, owners and outcasts. The contrast is formed by the relocation experience of the Second World War and confirmed in the genocide at Hiroshima and Nagasaki. The desert is a powerful image of the place of origin-in-exile for the people of Mirikitani's generation who struggle to emerge from it into a world of human relationships again. Cruelty has a historical origin in oppression and emerges as its bitter fruit, whether it takes shape in the oppressor or the oppressed. The naked self stands in furious but often silent protest at this stream of images and events, struggling to be born but carrying the scars of history which have been imposed without mercy and beyond understanding.

A poem near the beginning of the book, "August 6," opens up the poet's technique of juxtaposing synchronic events within the flow of the narrative. In vivid passages the poet juxtaposes the memory of Hiroshima and the official hypocrisies surrounding it:

> Yesterday
> a thousand cranes
> were flying.
> Hiroshima,
> your children
> are still dying
>
> and they said
>
> it saved many lives

Later, more intensely:

> Yesterday
> a woman
> bore a child
> with fingers
> growing from her neck
> shoulder
> empty
>
> and they said
> the arms race

Mirikitani uses this technique later in the volume with the intent of highlighting materials for our closer study so that we will understand them in their full horror. For example, in "A Certain Kind of Madness" she is watching TV with her daughter:

> When we saw Letelier blown up
> in a car, full screen
> you said he must've done something bad.
>
> I told you
> there are hunters who kill by color.
>   ("A Certain Kind of Madness")

The effect of television—to create a powerful image without a context—is countered by the mother teaching the child the part of the message that is withheld.

Perhaps the most effective use of juxtaposition comes in "Crazy Alice," a poem about "Aunt Alice, who has touched the sun . . . victim of American Concentration Camps." The figure presented is a familiar one in recent Japanese American writing: the sufferer of the humiliations and tortures of American incarceration, still present today amid a generation trying to forget the past and embrace the American present as loyal citizens of the United States.[35] Alice's appearance at the start of the poem signals the discomfiture she will bring the wedding party:

> She came to the
> wedding
> in a tattered coat
> called us all by
> the wrong names
>
> Yukio/Mizume/Kyoko
>
> No, crazy Alice
> we died in the camps

Alice fails to recognize the bride, her own daughter. Lost back in the time "before the war" when "i had a name," Alice by her very presence forces the speaker in the poem, a wedding guest, to remember her fate in the postwar era:

> twenty years ago
> she would come to us
> face blue
> eyes like black walnuts
> and down her nose
> blood flowed like tears
>
> battered by husbands
> and lovers
> for hoarding food
> and love
>
> where has love gone?

When the speaker tries to jolt Alice's attention by pointing to her surviving daughter, about to marry, Alice responds, matter-of-factly:

> my child is dead
> my breasts dried
> during the war

> and she died
> from hunger

And when once again the speaker calls her from her bitter reveries, desperately seeking to have her join the present celebration,

> rejoice
> Crazy Alice/your child
> has a new name

she is met with a chillingly metaphysical rebuke:

> life's so strange
> before the war
> i was my child
> i had a name.

The haunting final remark forcibly recalls the time of her innocence before the events which changed her life forever. Alice's wounds will not be silent.

Another kind of juxtaposition comes where the poet encounters white racist stereotypes. The racist speaker is played off against the judgment inherent in the poem, whether the poet actually responds or not:

> The woman
> did not mean to
> offend me,
>
> her blue eyes
> blinking
> at the glint
> of my blade,
> as I cut
> precisely
> like magic
> the cucumber in
> exact, even,
> quick slices.
>
> Do you orientals
> do everything
> so neatly?
>   ("Salad")

Mirikitani speaks about her own family and the generational differences between grandmother and mother, mother and child, in several poems. The tone is suggested by the overriding intent of the poem
in each case. In "The First Generation," subtitled "Elegy to my grandmother," the tone is respectful and grandmother is remembered in her
beauty and dignity.

> She grew wisteria
> as a temple
> in her garden
> and there kept her private peace
>
> . . . .
>
> Her love wore long
> as my sorrow.
> The withered roots
> have given back beauty to the soil.

In "Desert Flowers," Mirikitani sympathetically remembers her mother,
daydreaming of a handsome savior while incarcerated in a desert relocation center:

> Mama, did you dream about that
> beau who would take you
> away from it all,
> who would show you
> in his '41 ford
> and tell you how soft
> your hands
> like the silk kimono
> you folded for the wedding?
>   ("Desert Flowers")

But the entire construct is a fantasy, as Mirikitani makes plain at the
beginning,

> No flowers grew
> where dust winds blow
> and rain is like
> a dry heave moan.

When Mirikitani remembers her own needs as a child, her judgment
of her mother's acquiescence to the military command becomes harsh.
In a poem mixing historical detail with comment, Mirikitani juxtaposes her mother's "songs" and her own:

Her song:
shikata ga nai
        it can't be helped

. . . .

My song:

Watashi ga kadomo wa matte eru
    I am a child waiting
                waiting

Watashi no nahaga umareta
    for the birth of my mother.
                            ("Lullabye")

This is a book in which knowledge is handed down by generations but not in the traditional sense: it is knowledge of genocide, of pitiful surrender, of betrayal and self-betrayal, or of resistance to the death. Some of the most terrible images have to do with Aunt Alice's life after the war:

        and thinking of
        invasions
        and prison camps
        she opened her legs
        to the white boss man
                ("Crazy Alice")

and the mother's experience riding to the camps:

        She rode on the train
        destined for omission
        with an older cousin

        who died next to her
        gagging when her stomach burned out.

        Who says you only die once?
                            ("Lullabye")

But perhaps the most remarkable creations of all have to do with love-making, juxtaposed against the brutalities of white America intent on war, murder, and atrocity against people of color.

In "Jungle Rot and Open Arms" Mirikitani confesses that her "politically correct" view of Vietnam falls apart when confronted with the anger of a returning veteran, is "nothing / in the wake / of his rage."

The story of love literally torn away from the solider is indented and set apart from the rest of the poem:

>   "Her hair was
>   long and dark—like yours"
>   he said
>   "her eyes held the
>   sixth moon
>   and when she smiled
>   the sky opened
>   and I fell through.
>
>   I would crawl
>   in the tall grasses
>   to her village
>
>   and sleep the war
>   away with her
>   like a child on my thighs
>
>   I did not know
>   of the raid
>   and woke
>
>   with her arm
>   still clasping mine
>
>   I could not find
>   the rest of her
>
>   so I buried her arm
>   and marked my grave."

Another soldier, in "Loving from Vietnam to Zimbabwe," describes American atrocities against the Vietnamese, knowing (the poet tells us) "they looked like me." But the shocking thing about this poem is that it describes the couple's lovemaking, sometimes playfully and sometimes painfully, in stanzas parallel to the story of his incursion into the Vietnam jungle.

>   you plod weighted by
>   days of marching
>   nights of terror
>   holding this patch of ground
>   shaped like a crotch.

my teeth on your
shoulder
hungry to enter your flesh
as you call me strange names.

The poem powerfully combines the images of life and death, love and pain, which are the great themes of the book:

I, in the
heavy hot air
between us,
in the crimson room
that begins to blur
feel you enter
my harbor/kiss the lips
of my soul

Call Me Strange Names

hanoi
bachmai
haiphong

It ends with a rare summation made by the poet in her own voice:

loving in this world
is the silver splinting
edge
is the dare
in the teeth of the tiger
the pain of jungle rot
the horror of flesh unsealed
the danger of surviving.

In the final piece in the volume, "Awake in the River," Mirikitani discusses camp life in the most vivid and literal detail, emphasizing themes of dignity and survival.

The little child of the piece (the author) compares herself to a tortoise "digging her toes in the sand." But unlike the tortoises, "she could not go beyond the barbed wire." A tortoise crawls through the camp and the children try to hem it in "in the garden the men had grown from stones and succulents. Making beauty from adversity." But the women urge that it be set free: "It is wrong to imprison any living thing." The ending of the story/poem fuses the image of the people waiting for the end of the war and the tortoise seeking its freedom.

> The men kept their war inside. Pulling weeds by roots.
> Figures bent, not broken, wind rounding their backs.
> Grandfather wears his wait like a shell. Sleep in the desert,
> he warned.

> Tortoise, empty,
> worn,
> plunges to the deep.
> In the steady
> pounding of the waves,
> offsprings wake.

> Mother steady singing by the crib.

> Sleep in the desert.
> Awake in the river.
> ("Awake in the River")

It would be foolish, and futile, to attempt to reconcile the techniques, images, or use of material in the work of Joy Harjo, Lorna Dee Cervantes, and Janice Mirikitani. The common element of their work, after all, is that it is different from the poetry of the dominant Anglo-American culture which represents the aspirations and interests of the majority of the population of the United States (if we are to count the assimilated white ethnic minorities). All then that we can generalize about is the *difference* of this work, which sees its project in diverse ways as one of rescuing images from the dominant culture, restoring a sense of rightness in a threatened social and personal world, and proposing a means of continuing to exist—and to struggle—in the future. The ceremonial long poem of Joy Harjo, the symbolic journey of Lorna Dee Cervantes, and the political and historical enactment of Janice Mirikitani do embody, however, the strength of a literature that is not subjugated, is not silenced, is not bought off. Those of us who care about both literature and political and cultural survival would do well to attend to this work, both for what generalizations about its "difference" we care to draw and for the specific brilliance, passion, and clarity of each author and her project.

Notes

While the conception of this project was my own, I owe a debt to Professor Naomi Quiñonez of the Department of Spanish, California State University College at Northridge, who joined me as co-presenter in a workshop, "Women of Color: New American Writing (1980's)" at a conference, "Our Hidden Heritage of People's Culture," in Kansas City, Missouri, January 26, 1985. I also wish to thank Professor Patricia Clark Smith, Department of English, University of New Mexico, and Constance Coiner, Departments of English and History, University of California at Los Angeles, for reading the manuscript and offering suggestions. The responsibility for the outcome is wholly my own.

1. Frank Chin, Jeffrey Paul Chan, Lawson Fusao Inada, Shawn Hsu Wong, eds., *Aiiieeeee!: An Anthology of Asian-American Writers* (Washington, D.C.: Howard University Press, 1974), p. viii.
2. Dexter Fisher, ed., *Minority Language and Literature* (New York: Modern Language Association, 1977).
3. Houston A. Baker, ed., *Three American Literatures* (New York: Modern Language Association, 1982).
4. Dexter Fisher, ed., *The Third Woman* (Boston: Houghton Mifflin Co., 1980).
5. See, for example, Cherríe Moraga and Gloria Anzaldúa, eds., *This Bridge Called My Back: Writings by Radical Women of Color* (Watertown, Mass.: Persephone Press, 1981); Beth Brant, ed., *A Gathering of Spirit: Writing and Act by North American Indian Women* (Rockland, Maine: Sinister Wisdom Books, 1984); and Rayna Green, ed., *That's What She Said: Contemporary Poetry and Fiction by Native American Women* (Bloomington: Indiana University Press, 1984).
6. Paula Gunn Allen, ed., *Studies in American Indian Literature: Critical Essays and Course Designs* (New York: Modern Language Association, 1983); Marta Ester Sanchez, *Contemporary Chicana Poetry: A Critical Approach to an Emerging Literature* (Berkeley: University of California Press, 1985); and Elaine H. Kim, *Asian American Literature: An Introduction to the Writings and Their Social Context* (Philadelphia: Temple University Press, 1982).
7. For remarks on the importance of reevaluating the canon of American literature, see Paul Lauter, *Reconstructing American Literature* (Old Westbury: Feminist Press, 1983), pp. xi–xxv; and Wayne Charles Miller, "Toward a New Literary History of the United States," *Melus* 11, no. 1 (1984): 5–26.
8. Leslie Marmon Silko, *Ceremony* (New York: New American Library, 1978), pp. 132–133.
9. Paula Gunn Allen, "The Psychological Landscape of *Ceremony*," *American Indian Quarterly* 5 (February 1979): 13–18.
10. Allen, "The Sacred Hoop: A Contemporary Perspective," in Allen, *Studies*, p. 18.
11. Ibid., p. 19.

12. Ibid., p. 15.
13. Ibid., p. 16.
14. Allen, "A Melus Interview," *Melus* 10, no. 2 (1983): 19.
15. Joy Harjo, "Oklahoma: The Prairie of Words," in Hobson, *The Remembered Earth*, pp. 43–44.
16. Harjo, *She Had Some Horses* (New York: Thunder's Mouth Books, 1983). Subsequent citations from poems in this book are identified by title.
17. Antonia Castañeda Shular, Tomas Ybarr-Frausto, and Joseph Sommers, eds., *Literatura chicana: Texto y contexto* (Chicano Literature: Text and Context) (Englewood Cliffs, N.J.: Prentice-Hall, 1972), p. xxi.
18. Juan Bruce-Novoa, *Chicano Authors: Inquiry by Interview* (Austin: University of Texas Press, 1980), pp. 10–11. Bruce-Novoa returned to treat the poetry in detail in *Chicano Poetry: A Response to Chaos* (1982).
19. Sanchez, *Contemporary Chicana Poetry*, pp. 6–7.
20. From a speech, "Women of Color: New American Writing of the '80's," delivered with John Crawford at "Our Hidden Heritage of People's Culture," a conference held in Kansas City, Missouri, on January 25, 1985. Transcribed with editing from tape.
21. Bernadette Monda, "Interview with Lorna Dee Cervantes," *Third Woman* 2, no. 1 (1984): 104.
22. See Annette Kolodny, *The Lay of the Land* (Chapel Hill: University of North Carolina Press, 1975).
23. On Chicana sense of "traditional values," see Tey Diana Rebolledo, "Abuelitas: Mythology and Integration in Chicana Literature," *Revista Chicano-Riqueña* 11, no. 3–4 (1983): 148–158.
24. Bruce-Novoa, *Chicano Poetry*, pp. 4–5.
25. Lorna Dee Cervantes, *Emplumada* (Pittsburgh: University of Pittsburgh Press, 1981), p. viii. Subsequent citations of poems from this book are identified by title.
26. Carlos Castaneda, *The Teachings of Don Juan: A Yaqui Way of Knowledge* (Berkeley: University of California Press, 1968).
27. I am indebted to Professor Patricia Clark Smith of the University of New Mexico for this interpretation.
28. Cervantes may give a hint of what is to come in a recent interview. "I guess I'm real concerned with presenting certain class issues and I think if I'm going to draw the line, that's where it is because I think it's important to document my history." Monda, "Interview," p. 106.
29. The University of Washington Press published new editions of Bulosan's *America Is in the Heart* (1973), Okada's *No-No Boy* (1976), Chu's *Eat a Bowl of Tea* (1979), Sone's *Nisei Daughter* (1979), and a revised edition of stories by Santos, *Scent of Apples* (1979). The Asian American Studies Center at UCLA published two works by Mori, *The Chauvinist and Other Stories* (1979) and a new edition of *Yokohama, California* (1984). See Kim, *Asian American Literature*, p. 175.
30. Chin et al., *Aiiieeeee!*, p. xxx.

31. *Time to Greez!* (San Francisco: Glide Publications, 1975), back cover.
32. Janice Mirikitani, *Awake in the River* (San Francisco: Isthmus Press, 1978), afterword [p. 83]. Subsequent citations from poems in this book are identified by title.
33. Kim, *Asian American Literature*, p. 148.
34. On camp life and literature, see Kim, *Asian American Literature*, pp. 147–156, and Chin et al., *Aiiieeeee!*, pp. xxxiv–xxxvii.
35. See Kim, *Asian American Literature*, pp. 253–255. She notes that the figure of the "crazy woman" of the older generation also appears in other Asian American literatures.

Survival Comes This Way
Contemporary Native American Poetry

Few myths are as deeply ingrained in American literature and the popular consciousness of this nation as those regarding Native Americans. From before Fenimore Cooper, the American Indian's presence in the writing of non-Indian Americans has usually been as one of two opposed yet complementary incarnations: "the murdering redskin" or "the noble savage." These guises, of course, are two sides of the same coin, a currency unfortunately not yet devalued by overuse. As Michael Castro points out in his study of Native Americans in American poetry, *Interpreting the Indian*, the American Indian was either Caliban or Uncas, each stereotype "serving underlying psychic needs of Western culture." Further, whether bloodthirsty beast or nature's nobleman, the Indian continues to be portrayed as one whose culture and bloodlines, for better or worse, are slowly and surely being eroded away by the uncheckable tide of white civilization.

There are notable exceptions, such as John Neihardt's epic poems about the Sioux. By and large, however, American Indian people have been stereotyped, misrepresented, and used as "exotic" characters (a considerable irony when one considers who inhabited this continent to begin with) in the poems of non-Indian Americans past and present. And inaccuracies abound. Longfellow's *Hiawatha*, which presents a noble Indian hero in a misty never-never land, is the most famous example. The deeds Longfellow attributes to Hiawatha were those performed by Manabozho, the great culture hero of the Chippewa. The real Hiawatha was a statesman and political leader of the Iroquois people, one of the founders of the Great Iroquois League of Peace (on which the structure of the U.S. Constitution appears to have actually been modelled). It is rather like writing a poem about the exploits of Paul Bunyan and calling the main character George Washington. Even America's other "ethnic" writers have fallen prey to stereotyping the Indian. More than two-hundred years ago, black poet Lucy Terry described the Indians as "awful creatures" in her poem "Bars Fight, August 28, 1746" about the Deerfield Massacre.

The still strong tendency on the part of majority American culture and its poets to see the Native American as "the vanishing (or already vanished) redman" can be observed in much of the poetry written about American Indians and "from Indian traditions" by contemporary non-Indian writers. In the *Annual Reports of the Bureau of American Ethnology* such diligent field ethnologists as Natalie Curtis, Frances Densmore, and Washington Matthews published thousands of translations of songs, stories, and oral histories from many American Indian cultures around the turn of the century. Over the past two decades innumerable new translations or "reworkings" have been produced and published by non-Indian writers drawing on those same written sources, usually without ever talking to a real Indian from any tribe. The results are that most of those "reworkings" are painfully inaccurate and much less interesting than the original (and sometimes flawed) translations from which they were lifted. (I am not referring to the work being done with living American Indian people now by a few good ethnologist-poets. Dennis Tedlock, for one, has done such wonderful collaborations with Zuni storytellers as *Finding the Center*, which records living oral traditions.) In some cases, those non-Indian translator-reworker-poets have even set themselves up as being "more Indian" than living Native Americans today whom they seem to see as a scattered people of uncertain ancestry. The only good Indian poet is an illiterate dead one.

In 1979, the Twayne World Authors Series contributed to this misconception by publishing *American Indian Poetry* by Helen Addison Howard. Though dozens of contemporary American Indian poets were writing and publishing their work by then, the book does not contain the name of even one living Native American. Instead, it surveys the work of white ethnologists and a few "interpretive" writers who "made good use of" American Indian oral traditions. "The characteristics of Native American poetry," Howard tells us, "are subjects that are close to the daily lives of a primitive people." Her only reference to the possibility of living American Indian writers is an indirect one: "It is hoped that American poets, including modern Indian ones, will continue to develop this virgin field."

There is no doubt that Native American oral traditions constitute a great literary heritage. If anything, the range and meaning of that heritage has only begun to be appreciated. (One of the better recent publications is Karl Kroeber's *Traditional American Indian Literatures*, published in 1981.) Some aspects of certain Native American oral traditions are, in fact, preserved only in the writings of the ethnologists. However, in many Native American communities today the oral traditions are not only alive but growing. Further, anyone who believes that the transcriptions from past decades of American Indian oral traditions represent the full range of American Indian literature is making a great mistake. There is a new, vitally important generation of contemporary American Indian writers. Drawing on both their Native American cultural heritages and the realities and resources of Western culture, they have remained "Indian" while producing a growing body of significant written literature.

In the last two decades a conscious assault has been made by a growing number of Native Americans from many different tribal traditions on the assumption that the end of the "American Indian race" is inevitable. And their efforts have produced results. One example is Louis Oliver, a Creek poet in his eighties who began writing contemporary verse only within the last decade. His first book of poems, *The Horned Snake*, was published in 1982. When interviewed in his home in Tahlequah, Oklahoma, he said, "We were always taught in the schools that the Indian was doomed to be absorbed into the American melting pot and that all of our old ways were only memories. Before I met some younger American Indian writers I was just like that old ground hog. I had crawled in my hole and just accepted that I was forgotten. Now I know different."

Until mid-century, the common assumption was that the American nation's movement was progressive—tomorrow would be better than today. Today, however, everyone knows that technological miracles have spawned not only the luxuries of electricity and indoor plumbing but also Hiroshima and the nuclear balance of terror, the pollution of air and water, and the seemingly unsolvable social inequities of class and race. Today, as we question Pentagon budgets, drug-ridden class-rooms, the PCB-filled streams, many ask if the secret of surviving might be found not just in the dreams of the future but also in the lessons of the past.

But what is the true American past? How far back does the past go in a "nation of immigrants"? For that answer we might well turn to those "Americans" whose roots are deep as the rocks. As the one group of writers whose ancestors are not recent immigrants, American Indian poets are unusually well equipped to speak of the American past and to draw from it lessons relating to survival.

Their very histories and, in fact, their continued survivals as peoples despite mixed bloodlines, lands sold and stolen, ancient customs out-lawed or made impossible point to the tenacity of what might loosely be called the "Indian Way." That the most recent national census shows a doubling of the numbers of American Indians in only twenty years is an indication of that tenacity. It may also be seen as an indica-tion of a growing pride in affirming one's Indianness. Past censuses may have contained many more Indian people than figures actually showed. "Passing for white" is easily done by many Native American people who have discovered that an Indian, even with a face like Geronimo's, can go unrecognized when he or she dresses and talks like those in the majority culture. "Invisibility" has been a survival tactic for at least four centuries for many Native Americans, including some entire communities.

Survival is one of the major themes in contemporary Native Ameri-can writing—survival of the old ways, survival of Indian nations, per-sonal survival, and, in the long run, the survival of the whole bio-sphere. Acoma Pueblo in New Mexico is the oldest continuously occupied settlement on the North American continent. It is the home-land of Simon Ortiz, whose poem "Survival This Way" exemplifies that theme of continuance as it begins:

> Survival, I know how this way.
> This way, I know.

> It rains.
> Mountains and canyons and plants
> grow.
> We travelled this way,
> gauged our distance by stories
> and loved our children.

Notice how alive that landscape is. Not only the plants but even the mountains and canyons are growing, living presences that respond to the blessing of the rain. His images are rooted in the Southwestern landscape of his childhood and the traditions of his people, yet the message is one which virtually any Native American poet would recognize. I have heard it said, for example, by Iroquois writers from the Northeast that "everything which is, is alive." American Indian people—and their poets—survive through the recognition that they are part of, not apart from, the natural world. The language of the poem is simple, declarative, a bit repetitive in structure—like something from the oral traditions. Yet it is an entirely new poem at the same time that it is a very old one.

When N. Scott Momaday's novel *House Made of Dawn* was published in 1968 and won the Pulitzer Prize in 1969, it opened the eyes of a new generation of Native American writers. They read the novel and heard the deeper message of its powerful writing: a person caught between cultures can, despite the deepest of problems, find a way to survive, a road which circles out of the past, "The House Made of Dawn," and ends in understanding. Hopi/Miwok poet Wendy Rose is one of those in-between people and her work contrasts with that of Simon Ortiz. Her language seems more complex, her themes bleaker. An urban Indian (like a number of other successful contemporary Native American artists), Rose was not raised on or near a reservation but in Berkeley, California. A teacher and anthropologist, some of her poems deal with the dilemma of being a student in a discipline which has treated one's own ancestors as little more than bones to be dug up and labelled. She begins her poem "Indian Anthropologist: Overhanging Sand Dune Story":

> They hope, the professors
> to keep the keyhole locked
> where my mind is pipelined

to my soul; they block it
with the shovel and pick
of the pioneer spirit,
the very energy that made
this western earth turn over
and throw us from her back
bucking and hollering
like stars were whipping her . . .

The language and imagery of the poem are markedly different from Ortiz's. Such non-Indian concepts as "professors," "keyhole," "pipe-lined," "shovel and pick," and "pioneer spirit" show the influence of Western civilization. Yet, as in "Survival This Way," the earth itself is alive and showing her displeasure with the arrogance of human beings who've mistreated her by creating earthquakes. The poem returns to a Native vision, especially in the last lines of the poem when Rose says, ". . . I can go on like this / only if I shut my ears / but keep awake in the eyes."

Lance Henson, a southern Cheyenne who is deeply involved in the traditional ceremonies of his people, entitled one of his poems "co-manche ghost dance   an impression." It begins "we will return to life . . ." and concludes:

there will be no distance between our words and the
banished moon

in all that grows while the winter reaps
we will live again

In just a few lines we feel the closeness of the natural world, even at a time when the moon has been "banished" (presumably by the harsh lights—both electrical and intellectual—of modern civilization). Just as plants survive under the blanket of winter snow, the ghost dancers— who stand for the survival and renewal of the old American Indian values—persist and their song is for the life of all things.

One of my favorite poems of Henson's is called "at chadwick's bar and grill." Here are the first few lines:

tu fu and li po have
forgiven nothing
not waking drunk under any moon

or the incessant calling
of a loon

Henson's evocation of those great T'ang Dynasty poets shows that he
feels a kinship with those writers for their love of life, their clarity of
image, their unsentimental relationship to the natural world. It illustrates how, though frequently focusing on American Indian concerns,
Native American poetry is neither insular nor static. There is a wider
world beyond the poet's individual vision, a world which does not depend upon him for validation, as we see in the last lines of the poem:

the spider catches the fly
at morning
whether i am here
or not

The deliberate lack of punctuation and the use of the lower case "i" is
characteristic of a number of Native American poets. Peter Blue
Cloud, Karoniaktatie (Alex Jacobs), Norman Russell, and Barney Bush
are only a few of those who use this device, viewing capitalization and
punctuation as unnatural barriers between themselves and the living
creation all around them. As Barney Bush, the Seneca-Cayuga writer
put it when I interviewed him, it gives him a feeling of naturalness and
freedom. Responding to critics who said that it made his poems harder
to read, he said, "What you need to do with people like that is take
them out into the country for two or three weeks and get them to take
off their shoes and clothes and just run around naked. Then they begin
to understand."

Language, for the Native American poet, is power. N. Scott Momaday exemplifies the American Indian view of the ability of words to make
things happen in his essay "The Man Made of Words." In his essay he
speaks the name of Ko-sahn, an ancient Kiowa woman he knew when
he was a small child. As soon as he says her name, he tells us, she
appears in front of him, her reality as solid as anything else around him.
Then, as she begins to speak with him, Momaday finds his own identity
defined by looking into the history of his Kiowa people through the
vision of that suddenly materialized, one-eyed old woman. Just as his
words made her appear, her words make him.

Another example of how Momaday (and other Native American
writers) find themselves and a right relationship through the spirit of

words can be seen in these lines from his poem "The Delight Song of Tsoai-Talee." (Tsoai-Talee is Momaday's Kiowa name.)

> You see, I am alive, I am alive
> I stand in good relation to the earth
> I stand in good relation to the gods
> I stand in good relation to all that is beautiful

The shared themes of survival, of the aliveness of all creation, of the necessity for balance, and of the making power of words are some of the concepts which are part of what might be called a "Pan-Indian" consciousness, which might be seen as similar to the Pan-African consciousness that informs so much of the powerful poetry which has come from the African continent in the past five decades. It is also reminiscent of the negritude movement, which proclaimed the beauty of blackness and the richness of the African heritage. The African and Caribbean intellectuals, especially Leopold Sedar Senghor of Senegal, Aimé Césaire of Martinique, and Leon Damas of Guyana, who founded negritude, were schooled in France and still living there when they returned in their poetry to the vitality of ancestral African folkways. Like the negritude poets, American Indian writers are from nations which have been colonized. Like the poets of Africa, Native Americans have, until recently, been taught that their own traditions were, at best, of interest only to ethnologists and secondary to the cultures of those of European origin. Like Damas and Senghor and Césaire, they have been educated in some of the finest schools and lived—in many cases—for a good part of their lives in white cities, yet they have not become "white." Instead, they have come away from their educations with a stronger sense of their ethnic and tribal identities and with the sophisticated knowledge of contemporary literary techniques which enables them to express the enduring values of their Native American identity to both white and Indian alike.

Maurice Kenny is one example. A Mohawk who has lived for decades in New York City, he still speaks of the Akwesasne Reservation along the St. Lawrence River as home. Though he hears the sounds of police sirens out his windows at night, his poems return to the rhythms of Iroquois social dances and old chants. One of his most important works is a book-length cycle of poems called *Black Robe*, which was recently made into an award-winning radio drama. It tells the story of

Isaac Jogues, the Jesuit missionary among the Mohawks, from an Iroquois point of view, pointing out with great precision how Jogues still symbolizes much of the insensitivity and destructiveness which the Native American associates with white civilization.

Louise Erdrich, whose first novel *Love Medicine* won the National Book Critics Circle Award in 1984, is yet another example. Her first book of poems, *Jacklight,* was also published in 1984 while she was living in Concord, New Hampshire, not far from her alma mater, Dartmouth College. She draws pictures of contemporary reservation life which are gritty and powerfully detailed, rich in vision and in a reality different from that of majority culture. We can see this in the following lines from the final poem in that book, "Turtle Mountain Reservation," named for her family's Chippewa homeland in North Dakota:

> Grandpa leans back
> between spoonfuls of canned soup
> and repeats to himself a word
> that belongs to a world
> no one else can remember . . .
>
> He walks from St. Ann's, limp and crazy
> as the loon that calls its children
> across the lake
> in its broke, knowing laughter.
> Hitchhiking home from the Mission, if he sings
> it is a loud rasping wail
> that saws at the spine
> of Ira Comes Last at the wheel . . .

Any list of significant contemporary American Indian poets would have to be a long one. In editing *Songs from This Earth on Turtle's Back*, an anthology of American Indian poetry, in 1983, I ended up with fifty-two writers, most of whom have had at least one book of poetry published. Yet were I to edit that anthology today I can think of at least a dozen more writers I would certainly include. That so many poets should be surfacing from a total Native American population in the United States of less than two million might relate to the fact that a great percentage of Native Americans are artists. Art, whether it is pottery or poetry, seems to come naturally to Native American people, perhaps because the traditionally "permissive" and encouraging methods of child-rearing found among Indian people throughout the continent emphasize self-discovery and leave out corporal punishment. It is quite possible that Native American child-rearing methods do not "kill off" the creative spirit that leads an imaginative child to be an artist as an adult. Whatever the reason, there are too many fine American Indian writers for me to mention them all. In addition to those already mentioned, some of the most important, powerful poets are James Welch, Duane Niatum, Joy Harjo, Ray Young Bear, Roberta Hill Whiteman, and Linda Hogan. From their words, which speak *for* Native American people and *to* us all, we can learn many things—not the least of which is that we may find survival by remembering our place on this living planet.

 Chicano Literature
Beyond Beginnings

The awarding of the *Premio Casa de las Americas* to Rolando Hinojosa in 1976 for a Chicano novel, *Klail City y sus Alrededores*, shook to awakening the U.S. literary world. The *Premio* is to Latin America what the Pulitzer is to the United States, and this international literary award has never been taken lightly by those at the forefront of world literature. Chicano literature, on the other hand, has frequently been taken lightly in the U.S. literary world, and major language associations have hesitated to accept it as an appropriate area for research and attention.

This disregard did not surprise those who had for years alleged that "world literature" classes in U.S. colleges and universities reviewed to excess the literatures of England, France, and Germany while ignoring the rapid succession of innovations in style and thought surging out of Latin America (and the rest of the Third World and U.S. minorities). Curiously enough, this occurred while literary critics in France and Germany were focusing on modern Latin American masterpieces and begging for more. The entire situation taken into account, it was hardly shocking that U.S. critics argued that Chicano literature was not "quality literature" and that they based this finding more on what they heard than on what they read.

The *Premio*-winning *Klail City* (later released in the United States as *Generaciones y Semblanzas*) was not the first Chicano *obra* (work) of its kind. For years, those in Chicano circles had praised the sensitivity of Rivera's *And the Earth Did Not Part* and the character development of the haunting protagonists of *Bless, Me, Ultima*. For years Chicano writers and readers had admired the dramatic texture of Estela Portillo Trambley's *Rain of Scorpions* and the *mestizaje* (blending) of worlds, languages, and concepts in poetry by Alurista, Lalo Delgado, Ricardo Sanchez, and Angela de Hoyos. The unforgettable poetic figures of *La Jefita* and *El Louie* in the work of José Montoya epitomized cultural realities, and the Chicano reader responded with a fervent *"Los conozco"* ("I know these people"). These early favorites reflected and defined the characters of the barrio, and we could all appreciate and *see* the pachuco-turned-solider-turned-pool-hall-hero, "with all the paradoxes *del soldado raso*-heroism and the stockade."

> And on leave, jump boots
> shainadas and ribbons, cocky
> from the war, strutting to
> early mass on Sunday morning.
>
> "Wow, is that ol' Louie?"
>
> "Mire, comadre, ahí va el hijo
> de Lola!"
>
> Afterward he and Fat Richard
> would hock their Bronze stars
> for pisto en el Jardín Canales. . . .[1]

Often for the first time in their literary lives, Chicano readers would recognize characters from *their* cultural context—not stereotyped humble peasants and Hollywood hoods and revolutionaries, but guys from just down the street who were, after all, just *"el hijo de Lola"* ("Lola's son"), hocking their war medals for something to drink, heroic-tragic figures whose lives fell short of what society asked of them and whose dreams far outreached what society could offer them.

There was extensive reason why U.S. society was slow to recognize these writings. They were not only alien to the mainstream culture and laden with images that activated gut biases among those who knew "Meskins" only as a servant class, a lower class, or a problem class, but the early writings were doused generously with direct criticisms of the very institutions that were "carriers of the word" for literary acceptance—centers of formal education. Prose and poetry were replete with images of school policy that put student needs second to building needs, daily mass friskings at junior highs, and other indictments of American society and its schools.

> stupid america, see that chicano
> with a big knife . . .
> . . . .
> he doesn't want to knife you
> he wants to . . .
> . . . carve christ figures
> but you won't let him.
> stupid america, hear that chicano
> shouting curses on the street
> he is a poet
> without paper and pencil
> and since he cannot write
> he will explode.
> stupid america, remember that chicanito
> flunking math and english
> he is the picasso
> of your western states
> but he will die
> with one thousand masterpieces
> hanging only from his mind.[2]

Amidst the ever-present criticism that the mixing of English and Spanish reflected a linguistic deficiency (of "culturally deprived" individuals), linguistic masterpieces continued to be woven from the beauties and strengths of both languages. Doubled possibilities for alliteration and double entendre were found in concentrated mélanges of Spanish, English "Texan," black English, even Mayan and Nahuatl word concepts. Imaginations exploded beyond limits, beyond conventions, beyond even our own beginnings.

Regional chauvinists continued to criticize our "Tex-Mex" and to treat it as a "language deficiency" caused by low educational or intellectual levels. And Chicano writers continued to indulge in "language play" (for example, Nephtalí de León's play *Tequila Mockingbird* and Alurista's *Spik in Glyph?*), an inventive and intriguing challenge for linguistic creativity. What had begun with reflections of our own bilingual reality—my own *"me senté allí en la English class"* and Delgado's "chicotazos of history"—turned into the formulation of totally new grammatical styles. Lexical creations sprang from an awareness of our own dually bilingual existence and from the discovery of new worlds of thought and literature—the Mayan, Aztec, Native American, and so forth. Formerly we would, in our daily lives, hispanicize English realities: "I missed" would resurrect in Spanish as "*mistié*," "I flunked" would expand the traditional lexicon with "*flonquié*," and the "big, old thing" ending "*azo*" would turn a party in an English sentence into a *porazo* in a Spanish conversation. Now, those same traditions of interlanguage play would apply to the newly discovered language heritage. Acutely aware of the sounds of English, we would accent our Spanish to a mock-Anglicized "free holes" (for *frijoles*) and then play the reverse by accenting our English with the sounds of Spanish: *pino borra* for "peanut butter." Now, reading through Aztec accounts of *teotl, mitotl, coatl, tomatl*, we exclaimed, instead of the commonplace "*¡Qué loco!*" ("Crazy!"), "*¡Qué locotl!*" And the new *mestizaje* of language yielded concentrated high-impact packs, like the three-word label of the moon by Victoria Moreno—"vanilla, canela crescent."

The juxtaposition in selection of English, Spanish, or a combination of both adds to the power of each word and to the entire verbal context. Some works are, by necessity, in English, utilizing the compact, businesslike high-powered impact of each short jabbing word. The following poem by Sylvia Chacón is an excellent example of this style of writing and of the visual arrangement of the words. The format, together with the words themselves, seems chopped up like little pieces of spaghetti so that the meaning comes out not only from the context of the language but also from the shape and texture of the poem itself. The author compares herself to tangled spaghetti which was not eaten because she

> refused
> to be knifed
> and forked along
> in your eagerness
> to get
> the
> meat. [3]

The eloquence of Reyes Cárdenas' *Poema Sandino* was deliberately woven in an all-Spanish fabric. The profound personal sentiment, the political intent, the entire Spanish-speaking world's contemporary political context add to what is already one of the most powerful statements ever made in Chicano poetry. An excerpt:

> estas cosas que nos arrastran por el piso
> tenemos que pararlas como un arbol seco de navidad
> tenemos que echarle agua hasta que le salgan hojas
> hasta que podamos hablar otra vez
> hasta que podamos mover al siglo
>
> . . . .
>
> pero nosotros, nosotros tenemos que resistir al tiempo
> levantar la pluma aunque sea con huesos
> tenemos que ofender a los que cierran los ojos
> que hasta páginas vacías ahoguen sus sueños dulces
> que despiertan tosiendo buscando aire.[+]

Translation, in poetry, is a dependent and limited form of expression. But, with apologies for this sacrilege, I offer this translation of the segment quoted:

> these things that drag us across the floor
> we have to stand them up like a dried-up Christmas tree
> we have to sprinkle water on them until they sprout leaves
> until we can speak again
> until we can move the century
>
> . . . .
>
> but we, we have to fight off time
> lift the pen, even if it's with our bones
> we have to offend those who close their eyes
> so that even empty pages drown their sweet dreams
> and they wake up coughing searching for air.

Language mixture is an art as surely as any other manipulation of words, as evidenced in the beautiful flow and rich image-laden texture of the first few lines of *"Mis ojos hinchados"* by Alurista.

> Mis ojos hinchados
>   flooded with lagrimas
> de bronce
> melting on the cheek bones

> of my concern
> > razgos indígenas
> the scars of history on my face
> > and the veins of my body
> that aches
> > vomito sangre
> y lloro libertad . . .[5]

The early stages of Chicano literature were full of identity assertions: "I am Joaquín, lost in a world of confusion," or "I am a Quetzal who wakes up green with wings of gold, and cannot fly," or "I am the Aztec Prince and the Christian Christ," or "I do not ask for freedom—I *am* freedom." But Chicano literature has gone beyond its beginnings. It no longer simply asserts and defines an identity. It now paints its context and carries out its visions. The identities of crazy gypsy, Aztec Angel, Mud Coyote, and Crying Woman of the Night now go beyond their own definitions to live out their lives in the more fully developed mythological and social context of Chicano literature.

The symbols and images have already become familiar—we speak a common mythological language. Critics such as Juan Rodriguez, Max Martinez, and José Flores Peregrino have begun to explain and nourish the literary symbols. Flores Peregrino identifies and substantiates motifs, visions, and symbols such as the mirror (symbol of self-knowledge), the creative serpent (cyclical nature of energy and transformation, rather than a linear definition of progress), *in lak ech* (Mayan principle of behavior) and, of course, the parent earth, *la tierra*, as birther, burier, and healer. With a critical base for study, Chicano literature can no longer be ignored by those unfamiliar with its symbols and settings.

The voice of the Chicana poet and writer, the woman, is a strong one within this stream of expression. The powerful work of Margarita Cota-Cárdenas, Evangelina Vigil, Estela Portillo Trambley, and countless others provides a counterbalancing and whole image of our *entire* culture, not just the male perspective of it. The Chicanas remind us emphatically and eloquently of the healthy duality of indigenous cultures, in which the Creative Spirit is both a Mother God and a Father God, combining these two aspects of its reality in its power and sustaining spirit.

Alma Villanueva reflects this search for wholeness on the personal level, reminding her sons that she has "called on the / girlchild inside of / you—made / you live with / her—with me" and that their journey will struggle to mend them:

> . . . until your
> bodies become pregnant
> with birth—then
> you will really be
> men. Men
> who may love
> the woman outside them, like
> the woman inside them—and
> perhaps each other, the
> earth can't wait forever.[6]

Legendary Mexican figures such as La Llorona, La Virgen de Guadalupe, and La Adelita echo feminine voices of pain, protective power, action, and valor. Real predecessors in Chicana and Mexican history provide strong character bases for modern writers—women soldiers, colonels, and a general in the Mexican Revolution, outspoken female intellectuals and writers, the everyday community roles of women leaders in our barrios who are *curanderas* (healers), political organizers and businesswomen, even our own mothers and grandmothers. These images are reflected in our *obras*.

Yet the writings are not merely covered with roses and adulations. The awareness of sex-role oppression voiced loudly by the poet Sor Juana Inés de la Cruz in the 1600s is carried on by the modern Chicana writer. A strong feminist protest of the treatment of human beings as objects to be bought and sold and owned is evident in the mischievously potent poem *Soliloquio Travieso* (Michievous Soliloquy) by Margarita Cota-Cárdenas, who knowingly epic-izes one woman's life in the not-too-subtle image of a flower.

> mucho trabajo   ser flor
>   a veces
>   solitas
>   y en camino
> concentramos muy fuerte   así
>   arrugamos la frente

```
        para marchitarnos antes
y al llegar al mercado          ji    ji
        no nos pueden vender


it's a lotta work          being a flower
    sometimes
        all alone
            and on the road
we concentrate real hard          like this
    we wrinkle our foreheads
        so we can wither before we get there
and when we get to the marketplace          hee hee
    they can't sell us⁷
```

The unconquerable independence of the statement is but one example of the eloquence and expression of power in Chicana literature.
The question of power is an important one within Chicano writings
and perhaps more crucially within Chicana writings, where oppression
and the theft of personal power seem evident in not only the economic
and social spheres but even on the most intimate and corporal level,
where the ownership of one's body is at question. While numerous
writers handle this concept of La Chingada (the raped or screwed one)
within the poetic confrontation of such issues as rape, disempower-
ment, confinement, battering, and degradation, prose writers have
also woven messages of autonomy and power into their works. A more
expanded personal power is achieved in the victory of the protagonist
of the short story "The Paris Gown" by Estela Portillo. Clotilde is the
older woman who accounts to a granddaughter her own story of her
struggle for freedom and autonomy. As a rebellious young girl, she was
scheduled by her father's decision to marry a rich older gentleman who
her father felt could tame her. Despite her objections, plans proceed,
and she finally agrees to quiet her protests on the condition that she be
bought an elegant Paris gown for the engagement party. The conditions are met, the engagement party begins, and the young Clotilde
makes her stunning entrance down the stairs clothed in nothing at all.

> It was simple after that. My father could not abandon an insane
> daughter, but he knew that my presence meant constant re-
> minder. He let me come to Paris with sufficient funds . . . and
> here I made my home.⁸

A solution as creative as that of Cota-Cárdenas' flower results in the acquisition of the basic freedom—autonomy over one's body and, in Clotilde's case, context. The expressions of power found in Chicana literature are often of this most immediate form. The embodiment of power in Chicana writing does not take the form of power as it is defined in White Male Club circles. It is not the power of possession, domination, or exclusion. It is not the power to control others. It is an internal expression, less exclamation than awareness, less containment than context, and less fact than value. Cota-Cárdenas stripped power to its essence, not as control over others but as control (autonomy) over self. Portillo's character embodies her own most naked power not in the visual possession of her body but in the ultimate possession of it. Other Chicana writers also echo this sentiment; this *"no nos pueden vender"* ("they cannot sell us") is only the beginning of a linked chain of "no"s which claim, obstinately, the full extent of the power which one possesses, even if that power is the bare minimum, cleverly created and resurrected from a situation of total repression, of what "You, for all that you can do, cannot do to me." The poem "19 años" is another statement of stubborn survival and the ultimate message that I am still *"dueña de mis propios sentimientos"* ("owner of my own emotions"), as line after line in the writings state *"no me pueden chingar el corazon"* ("19 años"), and "she was taking off those bandages / she carried over those wounds in her heart . . . her laugh rising up to meet the air—natural-like" ("Let the Good Times Come").[9] It is power in its final, most haunting standing-of-ground, naked power, stripped of all accoutrements, stripped of external respect, stripped of even food, but with the inimitable pride that flows from the essence of our humanness, that pride that is its cleanest and kindest when stripped of its nonhuman coverings, that pride that comes from distant eyes and gnarled hands, not rings or robes, that pride of backs that slowly, threateningly, straighten. The following excerpt from "About Emma Tenayuca and the Pecan Shellers" by Teresa Acosta speaks this powerful unfolding of liberty.

> and enter their fight
> sideways/backways
> not always sure which direction is next
> —yet enter their fight—
> knowing that there is a

cleanness
in a workroom empty
of Seligmann's
BIGGEST LITTLE Texas industry

a cleanness
that is empty of his profits in our hunched backs
backs
which have to be stretched
up and right
upright
all
the
time[10]

While some male critics theorize that Chicana writers are more "tense" because of their mission to portray racism and sexism,[11] these writers could be more clearly interpreted as intense; that is, unafraid to speak emotional realities in raw and concentrated form. This taste for directness is evidenced among other minority women writers as well; black writer Alice Walker commented on the tendency to assess her work as "too direct":

> . . . as I write I have a real consciousness of where we are as a people and as a globe in this age of nuclear action and reaction. I don't think that there's a whole lot of time for subtlety, when directness will serve. So I think I'm always moving toward more and more clarity and directness.[12]

This reflects a pattern perhaps typical of women "who handle too much / shit / to use a dust / rag and furniture / polish on it—shovels work just fine."[13]

There is a directness in Chicana literature, there is too much to be said to waste time on conventionalities, too much that is alien not only to the mainstream culture's literature but also to the literature and experience of men. Alma Villanueva handles rape, motherhood, and inhumanity in very physical, immediate terms, not the ethereal "Rape of the Sabines"–type romanticization typical of some male writers. There is no hint of "bleeding poet" myth—sensitive, frail, searching for the dispossessed and the tragic, searching for that suffering from which to feel and hence write.

"We hid our daughters in cellars—
they raped us all, youngest to
old—laughing, grunting
making us suffer more to
watch and hear our children
scream and cry for
Mama, Mama, Mama—I
do not believe these men
were born of women!"

Dark cries.   Dark whispers.

Dark heaving out.   Dark blood.

Jagged entries.   Forced flesh.

Mute skin slicing tongue.

Bound feet.   Bound hands.   Bound womb.[14]

There is a sense of purpose—one that is right in front of our eyes. To call it "tension" is to trivialize the reality of the surroundings. It is more appropriate to see it as the revolutionary *el pésame* of poet Vangie Vigil—a world hard to survive, but in the face of that, amazingly cool strength and sanity, not a tubercular "tension."

A gap in the growing recognition of Chicano writings occurs in the relative absence of quality criticism of Chicana women's writings. What little analysis has been done has often been from the perspective of and in comparison to either white male literature or Chicano male literature. The result is that Chicana literature has often been deemed to have fallen short merely by being different. Again, the symbols and the contexts are misinterpreted or the entire work is sifted through a "biasing filter" which narrows the literary vision of the critic and his expectations of the writer. Male writers are usually assumed to deal with a full gamut of topics; Chicano males are sometimes victims of a critics' debate on "universalism or regionalism" (if they write in Chicano contexts, they are usually accused of nonuniversalism), but even within these accusations they are usually seen as dealing with a variety of topics. For Chicana women writers, the limitation becomes more extreme. The sexual question is forced. Too frequently, the literary interaction of *any* two characters of different gender is assumed to be a "statement" on the existential relationship of men and women. Two examples of this occur in the critical treatment of the poems "La Mal-inche" and "La Isabela de Guadalupe y el apache Mio Cid." In the former, the poet treats the heroic figure of a noted woman in Mexican history, La Malinche, advisor, interpreter, and lover to Hernan Cortes, from *her* voice, not that of the Spanish conquerors:

> I saw our world
>   And I saw yours
>   And I saw—
>   another.
> No one else could *see!*
>
> . . . .
>
> You cried broken tears the night you saw your destruction.
>
> . . . .
>
> But Chingada I was not. . . .
>   I saw a dream
>   and I *reached* it.
>   *Another world . . .*
>
>   la raza.
>
>   la raaaaaaaa-zaaaaa . . . [15]

One critical analysis of the poem, however, states that "the poem on La Malinche poses the main attitude of feminine complaint and re-bellion against male predominance."[16] In the second poem, the cultural mélange of the *raza* is juxtaposed in two characters of very different social classes, one male, one female, who manage, by the end of the poem, to see the overlap between their worlds, and their selves, and to make love.

> I, as an Indian,
> And you, as a Spaniard,
>   How can we ever make love?
>
> I, by *mecate* tied
>   to a red dirt floor
>   *y una casucha de adobe*
>
> . . . .
>
> Y *tu, . . .*
>   *Rey en España,*
>   *Hacendado en Mexico*
>   *Y Emplumado Emperador entre los Aztecas.*

> *Pero yo NUNCA FUI dese tipo!*
> *En España, gitana*
> *En México, criada*
> *Y hasta entre Aztecas,*
> *yo no fuí Azteca, sino obrera,*
> *cara triste,*
> *y calma.*[17]

By the end of the poem, the identities merge and the female persona becomes the Spanish queen, the Aztec, the Moor, as he becomes the Apache, the Toltec, the Jew, and "Nosotros la gente y / nosotros / la gente / y / Amamos" ("We the people and we the people and we love"). However, once more the critic forces the narrow limitations of theme on the writer and states, "'La Isabela de Guadalupe y el apache Mío Cid' . . . deals with the subject of La Chingada and represents Chicana women as slaves of men."[18] This "relationship between man and woman"[19] becomes, in too many of the critical writings, the sole statement and sole competence of Chicana women writers. While this is a pattern not absent in the traditional treatment of mainstream women writers, it is further exaggerated in the case of Chicana writers by the narrower, often hollow, societal images of them and complicated by the fact that even their symbols and processes are misunderstood within the existing structure. In short, "they have not met creatures of our ilk in the literary field before"[20] and, hence, there is no given formula on which to judge us, short of using a forced fit to the world of Chicano men or white women. The rich symbolism of Chicana writers is lost in the face of this blindness.

This gap in relevant criticism and acceptance has, while slowing down recognition and hence to some degree facility and publication, not slowed the pace of progress within Chicana writing. Chicana poets and prose writers alike have continued to innovate and to polish with a sense of purpose that ignores, without spiting, the structure of literary criticism. This purpose is a collectively felt direction, as in an Aquarian Conspiracy,[21] and evokes an exciting recognition on the part of those few critics who are less concerned with their own status in the accepted structure of critics than with their excitement at quality literature:

> . . . three fresh, exciting poets who represent the best . . . of
> the hundreds of Chicano writers across the country today who

do not make excuses for being a Chicano writer, who do not secretly covet the Lamont Poetry prize, who do not seek tenure. They write with care about and for us, recognizing that beautiful art can only come from caring pens, from the people who give us strength to survive the constant barrage of messages that come to tell us we are indeed not free . . . yet. [22]

Once the initial breaking of accordance with stereotype occurred (Chicana writers were, after all, not living up to their image as silent tortilla-makers, bowing humbly to the man's preeminence), all other barriers and limitations began to be questioned, including those dealing with traditional definitions and analyses of literature. Most of their works speak not only to the oppression of human beings for reasons of gender but also for reasons of color, culture, language, accent, and philosophy. They protest the limitation of human beings' rights to full autonomy and personal development. It is a natural connection, for all forms of oppression, behind the masks and labels, are the same—a limitation of growth, a limitation of life.

Chicano writers, male *and* female, charge forward, building their own structures and realities, unlimited by the truisms of accepted modes or encouraged styles. There is indeed a *concientización* in action in Chicano writing, as noted by such Latin American scholars as Guillermo Hernández, who lists four *tendencias* representative of this Chicano literary epoch: *concientización* ("an artistic front in the struggle for the interests and well-being of the Chicano . . . a call of awakening to a new vision of the surrounding reality"), personalism, aestheticism, and professionalism. [23] The first *tendencia* is epitomized in such mythical and concrete realities as the RCAF—teasingly known in Chicano literary circles as "The Royal Chicano Air Force." This nonaeronautic group of nonmembers began as a community of artists and writers working on a *causa*, while the sign on the door read RCAF (Rebel Chicano Art Front). From the first joking reference to a Royal Chicano Air Force, through the growth of the barrio legend and the subsequent investigation of this supposedly military group by the CIA, the community retained its calm and its commitment to an intangible "air force" of artists struggling to win a victory of human awareness and aesthetic freedom. Artist and writer José Montoya serves as informal leader, although the tone of *concientización* insists that it is the elderly janitor who serves as commanding officer of the group.

A parallel development, although more visibly involved in all four *tendencias,* is evidenced in the dramatic literature of Luis Valdez and the Teatro Campesino, where theatrical works were taken to the people and to the streets and expressed in the language of the barrios, continuing from there to a wider acceptance and recognition by theater and film audiences, most notably in the chef d'oeuvre *Zoot Suit.* This Broadway and film success made no apologies for its barrio language mixing, barrio culture, or dual-reality aesthetics as the main character became not a character in the film but the meaning of the film, involved always in opposites, a reflection of himself and of all the others. The conclusion plays out in one way, then another, then another, engulfing all of the realities of different human beings, incorporating audience as actor and actor as audience. It is altogether a new form of media—it is not just a "movie about an event," it is an experience, a philosophy, and ultimately requires the audience to choose the ending.

Such subsequent recognition as the translation of significant Chicano works into German and French and the awarding of other literary markers—a second *Premio Casa de las Americas* for *Tú Nomás, Honey* to poet Jim Sagel; the *Before Columbus America* Book Award for *Thirty an' Seen a Lot,* a collection of poems by Evangelina Vigil; and the 1985 American Book Award for *Living Up the Street,* a collection of short stories by Gary Soto—validated to still others the worth of this genre. Perhaps most significant of all was the tipping of the hat of the literary establishment to a writer who seemed to break all the rules, who explored and transcended all the limits of poetry from form and line to language and content. The author of *Chicano Territory, Anti-Bicicleta Haiku,* and *Survivors of the Chicano Titanic,* co-author of *Get Your Tortillas Together,* this poet also explored the arena of prose in such outrageous, tongue-in-cheek essays as "The Machismo Manifesto" and "Anti-Carnalismo" (which promised a sequel "In Defense of the Vendido [sellout]") and the novel "Los Pachucos y la Flying Saucer." His more experimental poems, including "Agua Jackets," left many critics hesitant to approach him.

Marxist leanings   ESOS
o lo que dejan   VATOS
los last
amores.

Muevo
mi pata inside
the Gulf of Mexico
con Asor.

Años pasan things change
las cositas
but terror.

Mickey Mouse, your cejas French . . . French . . .
become the tail
de una
yegua that's back again
volando . . . vaseline.

And Italy crumbles
cuando tengo mucho.
Cuando tengo muchas palabras
that never decide like agua jackets.[24]

Among the few who did comment were other innovators such as
Cecilio Garcia-Camarillo, poet-editor-journalist, who also experi-
mented with such forms as "bottle poetry," sound poetry, and trilingual
poetry.

> In *Anti-Bicicleta Haiku* el camarada Reys Cárdenas assaults
> conventional logic in the most outrageous manner since the
> invention of lunacy. Present also . . . is Reyes' flippant parox-
> ysms, his now famous rubberization of time, his sexual calen-
> turas, his surgically precise imagery, and that notoriously
> Chicano gusto for language. For the first time Reyes also messes
> around with a kind of double/parallel stanza for sound effect and
> extension of meaning.[25]

Long neglected because his writings were not "understood," in 1985
Reyes Cárdenas received the Austin Book Award for *I Was Never a
Militant Chicano*, a title hardly descriptive of the soft-spoken, black-
and-white-haired shaman with unsinkable humor and unshaken se-
riousness of purpose. In the title poem of the book, he negates confinement in any of the mythological, literary, or historical categories into
which we are stereotyped and states, with an unvarnished honesty, his
underlying purpose.

I was never like a Louie
and I'm not like Joaquin
* * *
I was never
really a pachuco
but I saw then
what I still
see now—
that we're
getting nowhere
that things
are worse
than they were
in the 40's
and 50's
I was never
the Ché Guevara type
but there's
nothing wrong
with revolution
Everybody says
it can't happen here
but hell
it can happen anywhere
I was never
a militant
Chicano
but only because
I've always wanted
more than a revolution
can provide.[26]

The works which have appeared do not complete the story, they simply lead to new frontiers. The work in progress by Chicano writers at present holds promise for even greater innovation. The sensitivity and depth of Rudolfo Anaya's novel-in-progress *Albuquerque* speaks a layered spirituality which superimposes reality on reality as the GI in Vietnam stalks the old man in the village with all the respect and spiritual awe that he used in the hunt of the deer in the mountains of New Mexico. Both men survive, not only physically but spiritually, as the Indian GI and the Vietnamese old man give their communication, their prayersong, and their life to each other without words and without foreignness. The boundaries between the two worlds have melted and the worlds become one. The ongoing power of the works of poets like José Flores Peregrino and Isidro Ortega and the haunting massiveness of impact of prose works by Max Martínez and Helena María Viramontes are simply steps in an *onda* of artists whose styles have come of age.

Chicano literature is not where it began. Tomás Rivera—the late writer and academician best known perhaps for his novel . . . *y no se lo tragó la tierra/. . . and the earth did not part,* which won the first Premio Quinto Sol, a national Chicano literary award, at a time when Chicanos had to build their own publishing houses, critical structures, and awards for lack of other outlets—identified three stages in Chicano literature: (1) a stage of socioanthropological documentation—the preservation of deeds and people in a manner not incongruous with that of folk and oral literature, (2) one of rebellion and conflict, a statement of protest, and (3) a stage of invention and creation.[27] There is ample evidence that the third stage has come to a precocious maturity. Not only can Chicano writers authentically and effectively utilize non-Chicano personas, but non-Chicano writers can effectively utilize Chicano personas and styles and hence participate in a movement of Chicano literature.[28]

And while many local critics, still heavily imbued with a prejudice against language mixing, regional dialects, and ethnic identifiability in literature (when these apply to things Chicano), argue about the relative worth of Chicano writers according to their "freedom" from Chicano themes or universality, Chicano literature continues, recognizing that that which is most characteristic of a human individual, be it in a Chicano cultural context, a coastal fisherman's, or a Steinbeckian Okie's, is that which is most characteristic of humanness itself and is linked by an undercurrent of emotion and intuition, a collective unconscious, to all forms. Rather than trying to write "like a New Yorker" or imitating the current trend in acclaim, the bulk of Chicano literature is moving as it has in the past—with an unswerving awareness of artistry, of self, and of the community in *desarollo,* the human community.

In short, Chicano literature has gone beyond beginnings in many respects—it has gone beyond a definition of our cultural origins, it has gone beyond the beginning stages of myth creation and symbol kinship, it has gone beyond its own awareness of the literary action itself, and, perhaps most significantly to those who struggled for years to be read and to read, it has gone beyond the beginnings of its acceptance and recognition by the literary world as a whole.

Notes

This article was based on a briefer commentary by the same title published in *Southern Exposure* 9, no. 2 (1981).

1. José Montoya, "El Louie," in *Chicano Literature: Text and Context*, ed. Antonia Castañeda Shular, Tomas Ybarr-Frausto, and Joseph Sommers (Englewood Cliffs, N.J.: Prentice-Hall, 1972), p. 173.
2. Abelardo, "stupid america," in *Chicano: 25 Pieces of Chicano Mind* (El Paso: Barrio Publications, 1972), p. 32.
3. Sylvia Chacón, "I am the jealously entangled," *Tejidos* 3, no. 4 (1976): 7.
4. Reyes Cárdenas, "Poema Sandino," in *Survivors of the Chicano Titanic* (Austin: Place of Herons Press, 1981), p. 44.
5. Alurista, "mis ojos hinchados," in *El Espejo/The Mirror*, ed. Octavio Ignacio Romano and Herminio Rios (Berkeley: Quinto Sol Publications, 1969), p. 268.
6. Alma Villanueva, "La Chingada," in *Five Poets of Aztlán*, ed. Santiago Daydí-Tolson (Binghamton, N.Y.: Bilingual Press/Editorial Bilingue, 1985), pp. 151–153.
7. Margarita Cota-Cárdenas, "Soliloquio Travieso," in *Noches despertando en conciencias* (Tucson, Ariz.: Scorpion Press, 1975), n.p.
8. Estela Portillo Trambley, *Rain of Scorpions* (Berkeley: Tonatiuh International, 1975), p. 8.
9. Carmen Tafolla, "19 años," in *Canto al Pueblo*, ed. Leonardo Carrillo et al. (San Antonio: Penca Books, 1978), pp. 61–62; Teresa Palomo Acosta, "Let the Good Times Come," personal papers, 1984.
10. Teresa Palomo Acosta, "About Emma Tenayuca and the Pecan Shellers," in *Passing Time* (Austin: Chapbook, 1984), p. 7.
11. Santiago Daydí-Tolson, introduction to Daydí-Tolson, *Five Poets of Aztlán*, p. 46.
12. Alice Walker, "Writing to Survive," *Southern Exposure* 9, no. 2 (1981): 15.
13. Carmen Tafolla, "Porfiria," personal papers, 1985.
14. Vallanueva, in Daydí-Tolson, *Five Poets of Aztlán*, p. 157.
15. Tafolla, in Carrillo et al., *Canto al Pueblo*, p. 39.
16. Daydí-Tolson, *Five Poets of Aztlán*, p. 51.
17. Tafolla, in Daydí-Tolson, *Five Poets of Aztlán*, p. 10. Translation: "I, by country rope tied / to a red dirt floor / and a small adobe hut / And you / King in Spain / Big rancher in Mexico / And Plumed Emperor among the Aztecs / But I never

was that type! / In Spain, a gypsy / In Mexico, a maid / And even among Aztecs, / I wasn't an Aztec, but a worker / face sad / and calm."

18. Daydí-Tolson, *Five Poets of Aztlán*, p. 51.
19. Ibid.
20. Martha P. Cotera, personal correspondence, Austin, Texas, December 12, 1981.
21. See Marilyn Ferguson, *The Aquarian Conspiracy: Personal and Social Transformation in the 1980's* (Los Angeles: J. P. Tarcher, 1980), for a discussion of the physical and spiritual transformation of the collective unconscious and the informal network or "conspiracy" of individuals of widely varying views and backgrounds who move educational, political, scientific, and social spheres to a new level of community and self-definitions.
22. Juan Rodriguez, introduction to Mary Sue Galindo, María Limón, and Jesse Johnson, *Merienda Tejana*, ed. Juan Rodríguez and Petra Rodríguez (Austin, Tex.: Relámpago Books Press, 1985), p. vii.
23. Guillermo E. Hernández, "El México de fuera: Notas para su historia cultural," *Cuadernos Americanos* 44, no. 259 (1985): 115–119. Trans. C. Tafolla. From pp. 115–117: "Son cuatro las tendencias que ha seguido la literatura en esta epoca y que denomino respectivamente: concientización, personalismo, esteticismo, y profesionalismo. . . . las corrientes son representativas de la época y por lo tanto no todos sus autores y obras exhiben nítida y exclusavamente estos rasgos. . . . En esta época (concientización) se publican una serie de periódicos y revistas y se celebran festivales poéticos, constituyendo todos estos esfuerzos un frente artístico en la labor en pro do los intereses y bienestar del chicano . . . un llamamiento al despertar a una nueva visión de la realidad circundante."
24. Reyes Cárdenas, "Agua Jackets," in *Anti-Bicicleta Haiku* (Chapbook, 1976).
25. Cecilio Garcia-Camarillo, jacket commentary to *Anti-Bicicleta Haiku*.
26. Reyes Cárdenas, "I Was Never a Militant Chicano," in *I Was Never a Militant Chicano* (Austin: Relámpago Books Press, 1985).
27. Tomás Rivera, "Remembering Discovery and Volition in the Literary Imaginative Process," *Atisbos* (Summer 1975): 66–77.
28. Jim Sagel and Amado Muro are among the non-Chicanos who have convincingly and profoundly perfected works which are, in every respect, part of the body of Chicano literature. "Chistizos" (or the "New Mestizo," half Anglo, half Chicano) are also significantly involved in producing works which reflect this bicultural reality, as evidenced by the effective voices of El Huitlacoche (Gary Keller) and Teresa Anderson—bloodline is irrelevant, but the spirit of a Chicano literary reality is not.

Chicano Poetry
An Overview

Attempts to set a point zero somewhere in history for the beginning of Chicano literature are varied and indecisive. Each opinion reflects aesthetic, regional, and ideological concerns which limited space does not permit me to explain fully here. For the purpose of this essay, I shall repeat my position: Chicano literature is a recent phenomenon that coincides with the civil rights struggle known as the Chicano Movement and the awakening and expression of a cultural consciousness which that movement produced.[1] I also should repeat that for me, Chicanos are all those people of Mexican heritage residing permanently in the United States, call themselves what they may; hence, Chicano poetry is all poetic expression by writers who fit the above definition. However, this does not mean that Chicano literature, and most specifically the poetry, lacks roots predating the Chicano Movement, because there exists a wealth of cultural production upon which it legitimately draws, a precursor body of poetry that is slowly growing with each research project on the communities of Mexicans who lived in the territory of the United States before the contemporary period. To understand Chicano poetry it is necessary at least to review the historical context. Only in this way can one appreciate the poetry of the last decades.

Before beginning permit me to set some parameters. There will be no attempt to list every poet of significance, or every poem or book of merit. Those works and authors discussed here have been chosen for their exemplary value or their essential role in what we now call Chicano poetry. Omissions should not be read as negative critical judgments or as recommendations to readers to exclude a text from their own exploration of the literature; no general essay could claim to accommodate all the writers without becoming a simple enumeration, a bibliography at best.

Background

Considering the strength of the oral tradition in all of the European countries during the period of the discovery and exploration of the Americas, we could speculate that Spanish oral poetry made its appearance in what is now the United States with the very first explorers in the sixteenth century. It should be remembered that those ventures of discovery and exploration ranged far beyond the southwestern region of what is now the United States to encompass the entire coast of what only much later came to be known as New England. And if naming one's surroundings can be considered the most basic act of poetry, then Spanish poetry predates English poetry even on the northeast coast. Recently William Boelhower has speculated about interesting correlations among cartography, cultural identity, and national expansionism.[2] The act of tracing a map and naming zones in relation to one's own center is a rhetorical act of possession often followed by actual incorporation of those zones into the territory of the nation. In this sense the naming of the northeast coast of North America, first by the Spanish and then by the English (not to mention previous Native American namings and other European ones), was rhetorical warfare, a precursor of the very real war between Hispanic and Anglo cultures that ensued and is still with us. Since the earliest colonial period, the history of North America has been one of cross-cultural conflict that included a battle of rhetorics, of words, of images—a true war of and for poetic dominance.

In a more specific literary sense, we know that the Oñate expedition to colonize New Mexico (1598) celebrated its crossing of the Rio Grande with a Catholic Mass and a play in the style of the Spanish Golden Age, and since the drama of the times was almost exclusively in verse it would be more than probable that at least part of this work was poetry. Moreover, accompanying the expedition came one Gaspar Pérez de Villagrá, a poet who chronicled Oñate's efforts in an epic poem published in Spain in 1610.[3] Of course we should not overlook the fact that Native Americans also had forms of poetry and song, although to date no study has explored their possible influence on the roots of Chicano poetry. Yet all of the oral expressions are roots, as valid as the early works by the New England Puritans are for the literature of more recent English-writing U.S. authors. However, those early expressions were not yet products of the synthesis of Mexican and Anglo-American cultures, as Chicano expression is, though they certainly are the record of the Spanish and Native American cultures coping with the geographical space we now consider the home ground of Chicanos, and therefore somehow they are precursors.

If we move forward two centuries we find, in records and studies, that the Hispanic inhabitants of what is now U.S. territory had a varied oral tradition as well as some limited access to printed literature. Spanish verse forms survived—and still do—such as the *villancicos, décimas*, and the Mexican adaptation of the European romance, narrative ballads in Mexico called *corridos*. At the same time this society continued to center itself around the Catholic church, with much of its cultural production tied to rituals and feast days. The Catholic church employed music and song for services as well as theater for didactic instruction and reinforcement. We know from sources like the *Tratado de Pablo Tac* that Native Americans were taught to memorize songs for religious services in the California missions in the 1830s.[4] From the same source we also learn that these indigenous mission dwellers maintained their traditional songs and dances and that at least one type resembled what Pablo Tac called the Spanish style of dance. Most likely cross-culturalization was taking place at a popular-culture level that went unrecorded, having come down to us only as oral tradition and music. Prestigious Mexican writers like Sor Juana Inés de la Cruz and Sigüenza y Góngora had introduced indigenous elements into the level of high-culture writings in the seventeenth century. We can assume that some form of this process began to occur all along the cultural borderland in communities throughout the areas Chicanos now inhabit.

Written materials had to be imported into the region during the colonial period and were scarce. The printing press was absent until

1834, when the territories we are concerned with had become part of the newly independent Mexican nation. The first press opened for business in Santa Fe, New Mexico, with a second following shortly after in Monterey, California. [5] But with more pressing needs—political, religious, and social—to occupy the printers, no books of poetry were among their first products.

The first book in Spanish published in the Southwest, *Cuaderno de ortografía* (Santa Fe: 1834), can serve, however, to illustrate a significant characteristic of one predominant trend in Chicano poetry; namely, its didactic purpose. In section 2 of the *Cuaderno*, within a discussion of capital letters, the anonymous author—thought to have been Father Martínez, the Catholic patriarch of New Mexico—resorts to verse for emphasis:

> La doctrina que te doy
> Para que correcto escribas,
> Como atento la percivas
> A tu honor; y fama estoy
>
> .   .   .   .
> atiende á las letras,
> y escrituras de los hombres que
> cuerdo congeturas.

> The doctrine that I give you
> So that you might write correctly
> If you perceive it carefully
> Will honor and fame serve you.
>
> .   .   .   .
> pay attention to the letters,
> and writings of those men whom
> you imagine reasonable.

This venerable method of teaching children their first lessons can be found in any culture which retains some vestiges of oral tradition. The point is that just as New Mexicans utilized poetry to teach in this first Spanish text printed in the Mexican Northern Territories, those same people, trapped in the U.S. Southwest by the shifting border in 1848, as well as the later immigrants and much later the Chicanos, continued to use poetry for didactic purposes.

With the Treaty of Guadalupe-Hidalgo (1848), the United States annexed its present Southwestern states. The influx of foreigners that had begun twenty years earlier steadily increased after the treaty until the Hispanics were outnumbered. In the case of Texas, Mexicans were at a four-to-one disadvantage already before its independence in 1836. The discovery of gold deluged California with newcomers in 1848. During this period Anglo-Mexican interculturization began intensely, with results varying depending on the regional composition of the population. Ironically, while literature could not avoid documenting the process, it also became a means of preserving a Hispanic culture; this dual character prefigures that of Chicano literature.

Since the U.S. occupation of the Southwest, the Hispanic communities have never stopped producing both oral and written poetry. In California, poems and songs chronicled the exploits of the resistance fighter Joaquín Murrieta, although recently Luis Leal has discovered that the poem most often quoted as the original version of the Murrieta story was an adaptation of a *corrido* from Mexico, casting doubt on all of the assumptions of historical reliability claimed for the *corridos*. Américo Paredes' classic study of the *corrido* form demonstrated the workings of the oral process in full strength, its ability to document the story of communal heroes.[6] Yet the Leal discovery reminds us that ballads, like the epic itself, are not concerned as much with historical accuracy as with creating, within traditionally dictated patterns, entertaining narratives. This lesson should not be lost on readers of contemporary Chicano poetry who at times read a poem as a prose statement of fact instead of a fictive creation of literary reality.

As for written poetry, Doris Meyer's studies of New Mexican newspapers from 1880 to 1900 reveal that popular verses were being printed.[7] Predictably, content was usually political; form, narrative. Yet one author, who signed only XXX, published Spanish translations of Byron, Shelley, and Bryant. Thus, in Spanish-language publications at the turn of the century there was already, if not the cross-fertilization of oral and written material and Spanish and English sources, at least the juxtaposition of these texts in the printed matter considered source material for the Chicano community.

Recent research on two major newspapers, *La Prensa* in San Antonio, Texas, and *La Opinión* in Los Angeles, California, initiated during the Mexican Revolution, has found more significant facts. Both publications provided Chicano readers with a steady diet of the best

Latin American poetry. Leading poets from Mexico and other Latin American countries were published almost daily. The ramifications of this discovery are not yet clear, but it indicates necessary revision of scholarship on the backgrounds of Chicano literature. Most likely we will not uncover a great wealth of Chicano poetry from this period written in Spanish according to Latin American models. A more significant question arises, however: why were/are Chicano writers not more influenced by Spanish-language poets? What we can state without reservation is that this poetry was available in the major Chicano communities in a format readily accessible to the average public.

In "Chicano Poetry: Roots and Writers," Philip Ortego gave examples of Mexican American poetry published in the first half of this century.[8] In 1916 Vicente Bernal's *Las primicias* appeared, a collection of banal love poetry in standard English. From the *LULAC News*, 1939, Ortego cites Robert Felix Salazar's "The Other Pioneers," a poem designed to remind both Mexican Americans and Anglos that the first Europeans in the Southwest had Spanish names, as their descendants, now U.S. citizens, still do. The outstanding poet of this period, however, was Fray Angélico Chávez. His *Eleven Lady-Lyrics and Other Poems* (1945) are well-written lyric prayers of praise to Mary the Mother of God in her many forms. The language is standard English; the form and content are universal. Although a native New Mexican who has explored his Hispanic heritage in several publications, in his poetry Chávez seems to be the epitome of the assimilated writer. However, one must recognize that his poetry represents as well a considerable portion of the Chicano community which is still conservative, Catholic, and open to assimilation. To deny this, as was often done in the 1960s and 1970s, is to indulge in utopian fantasies about ourselves.

In the same period that Chávez was writing, however, another New Mexican, Arturo Campa, university professor and eminent folklorist, was interviewing old storytellers and singers of *corridos*, recording the traditional voice of the people. Campa found, for example, Arculiano Barela, who in 1914—two years before *Las primicias*—had composed "El estraique de 1910" (The 1910 Strike) about the Ludlow massacre of unionized miners in southern Colorado.[9] The Barela poem is significant for several reasons. First, it proves that while some writers were moving toward an Americanized form of expression, the oral tradition was alive and well among the people. Also, it documents that later Chicano poems about unionism and strikes are continuations of a tradition of expression of solidarity with the working class. Moreover, the title demonstrates that interlingualism, the combining of two or more languages to form a new synthesis, is not an innovation by contemporary Chicano poets, as some people claim, but that it was already an accepted practice as early as 1914. Finally, Campa's research, his preservation of the oral tradition, prefigures the preoccupation with the oral tradition that marks the study of Chicano literature as well as so much of the poetry itself, where the oral tradition is a theme as much, if not more so, than a process of creation.

In summary, by the time the Chicano Movement took place, producing interest, outlets, and audiences for more intensified literary activity, there existed a poetic process, both oral and written, in the Chicano community. The features of that poetry were a tendency toward didactic purpose and the use of narrative form; an acceptance of both folk-oral and written forms but with a clear preference for the former as a more authentic community expression; a minority of writers seeking to develop a poetry more in tune with the written models of either Mexican, Spanish, or Anglo poets; close links between writing and political activism; the use of poetry to rescue communal history and heroes from oblivion.

Chicano Movement

As the 1960s Civil Rights movement stirred interest in non-black minority groups, Chicanos also organized around a number of regional projects. Each locally based organization utilized print media to propagandize its cause. Tomás Ybarra-Frausto has documented that the major political groups from that early period produced publications in which poetry was included.[10] While the United Farm Workers had *El Malcriado*, Reies López Tijerina's Alianza Federal de Mercedes (Federal Alliance of Land Grants) in New Mexico had *El Grito del Norte*. Both published traditional popular poetry, closer to oral verse than to written forms and almost exclusively propagandistic. These publications allowed the unheard voices of agrarian workers to enter the printed realm. This invasion of the print media by the oral tradition on behalf of the silent, marginal peoples of the United States is one of the principal concerns and themes of Chicano writing present from the start. We must, however, observe that these early publications are the highwater mark of the availability of the unmediated worker's voice. Since then the expression is less from workers and more about workers (albeit poetry written by writers who once shared the workers' background or whose parents belong to that class), yet they have often moved beyond that status. This does not make the poetry of the latter writers better or worse per se, just less a direct expression of those groups usually excluded from print.

If those two political groups preferred a newspaper format open to participation by many writers, the other two major political centers were headed by individuals who also wrote poetry. José Angel Gutiér-rez, leader of La Raza Unida, a third-party political movement in South Texas, wrote an autobiographical narrative in verse about his disillusionment with the assimilationist ideal so prevalent in Texas. "22 Miles" is a good example of a mediocre poem from the start of the Chicano Movement much anthologized in the early 1970s, selected more because of the author's political importance than for its value as a poem.[11] However, it does represent much of the expression of those first years, as well as the type of political doggerel that editors from the mainstream wanted to find among minority writers: it is prosaic, simplistic, cliché ridden, predictable. As José Montoya, the master Chicano poet, has said about this period, there were a lot of bad songs.

The poetic production that emerged from the other center of political action, the Denver-based Crusade for Justice, on the other hand, is far from mediocre. Rodolfe Corky Gonzales' poem *I Am Joaquin* (1967)[12] may be simple, but it is not simplistic; it may depend on popular-culture clichés, but it uses them to their and the poem's advantage as in-group signs and historical symbols; it may create a narrative line based on Mexican-Chicano history, but it also utilizes the proven techniques of oral poetry. While "22 Miles" is a personal confession of assimilation and disillusionment, *I Am Joaquin* is the voice of the community rejecting assimilation in favor of its vast history of struggle. Finally, while "22 Miles" is mediocre as a literary creation, *I Am Joaquin* is, within its own limits and goals, an exceptionally well realized piece of writing. Of the two, only the latter survives today as a poem.

I Am Joaquin probably would have had good distribution and been anthologized strictly because of Gonzales' position as a political leader even had its merits as a poem been poor, but its success, its enormous appeal for Chicanos from the start, and the admiration it provokes from non-Chicanos stem from its intrinsic power as a synthesis of political manifesto and well-planned, carefully structured poem. In fact, it probably has become more important among Chicanos than the author. Enthusiasm for political involvement has ebbed in recent years, but Gonzales' poem is still the best-known and most-read piece of Chicano poetry. More than merely summarizing a historical quest and an identity for Chicanos, *I Am Joaquin* created a way of seeing the present through our history to be able to then move forward, united, toward a common goal. That the actual praxis of goal-achievement never has lived up to the poem's promise is a political problem. Yet at the point when the Chicano Movement reached its zenith this poem best defined it. For that reason we should give it close attention.

Joaquin, the Chicano Everyman, finds himself in a cultural diaspora, besieged by an alien world that threatens to tear him to pieces. So many Chicano works begin in this fashion that *I Am Joaquin* can be seen as the prototype. Joaquin's retreat from society back into his community and its history are also prototypical. Joaquin reviews history from the protection of his communal circle; with the peace which this circle provides him, Joaquin can study the past, formulate a logical version of history (a usable past), and discover why and how he has come to be almost destroyed. His review of Mexican history, from pre-Columbian times to the Mexican Revolution, reveals a process of miscegenation based on bloodletting by and of both master and slave. Equality, in spite of social injustice, sprang from common land ownership, religious ideals of equality before God, and a mutual sharing of death. This evocation of a lost golden age, when Chicanos or their ancestors lived in harmony or peace or balance or whatever, is also common to most Chicano poetry of the early period. Joaquin's review of history on the U.S. side of the border reveals that the Anglo-American has refused to enter into any mixture of blood despite the opportunities offered by Chicanos; hence, the Anglo-American has excluded his group from participation in the human history of the region. Chicanos cannot expect to mix with Anglos and so they must accept that their blood has reached definition and is now "pure"; that is, all the blending of different bloods has produced the Chicano and no more admixture will be tolerated. Armed with a historical perspective and a group identity, the people can now rise up and reclaim their rights—land and a separate nationhood. This appeal to land rights and nationalism, with variations, was also common to many early poems.

I Am Joaquin's style is oral—it functions more with cliché and metonymy than with original tropes and metaphors. Its uncomplicated, short verses flow well with the natural voice and breath. Yet, in spite of its glorification of *corridos* as the source of Chicano history, the poem does not employ the *corrido* form of versification and rhyme but rather a typically American English style of free verse. This is cultural synthesis at work—again, a contradiction of the poem's explicit rejection of any miscegenation with the Anglo-American. Yet this synthesis of cultural sources is, too, a Chicano trait, reappearing in work after work.

Political ideology aside, *I Am Joaquin* is well structured. Framed between two images of opposing giants (the menacing one of Anglo progress and the newly evoked one of the Chicano Movement), a series of historical resumés provide a catalog of facts and images as well as a dynamic process that expands with each venture into the past. Inversely, each resumé can be shorter because previous ones have built up knowledge in the reader which can now be recalled as a vital context for the new material. The poem accelerates as it reaches the final explosion back out from the circle and into the battle with the enemy. This emergence is marked by the prophecy of a future for the pluralistic but unitary Chicano race—a utopian declaration found in many Chicano works. This skillful writing makes the poem an admirable work of art if not always politically or ideologically pleasing.

While it is important that Chicano poetry has often been linked to political groups, it is equally significant to note that most of it has been published by small presses independent from specific political organizations. Abelardo Delgado has been publishing his own work since 1969 through his Barrio Publications—often mimeographed or xeroxed pamphlets.[13] Ricardo Sánchez founded Mictla Publications to print his poetry.[14] Both poets expressed the belief that the necessary social transformation of U.S. society would be achieved, in part, through a takeover of the printed word by Chicanos. In "Chicano Manifesto" Abelardo seemed to think that both Anglos and Chicanos were anxiously thirsting for his words. His "Stupid America" centers the Chicano poet as the future artist of the Americas, the synthesis of all Hispanic tradition from the New Mexican *santeros* to internationally acclaimed Picasso. To this poet falls the obligation of saving the United States from racial warfare. Abelardo metaphorically speaks of the Chicano community itself, but, as is typical of many Chicano poets, he exalts the role of the poet and the printed word in the struggle for equality. In "Homing" Sánchez claims for his press the ability to change stereotypes and free Chicanos from oppression.[15] This faith is explicit in the title of his first book, *Canto y grito mi liberación*: poetry achieves liberation. Many Chicano poets expressed these ideals, but now, far from the heady enthusiasms of the early movement, they seem naive and hyperbolic. Clearly literature's power to transform reality was overestimated, as was poetry's appeal to audiences more conditioned to mass media than to the recitation of verse. Yet at the time the faith and its expression were sincere.

All of the early works were regionally based, even *I Am Joaquin*. This reflected the political movements of the period, which were never firmly united. What appeared on the scene to bring a semblance of unity at an interstate level, if not a national scale, was the student movement in 1968–69. And it, too, had poetry.

At first the activity related to learning centers came from Chicano academics at Berkeley who came together to publish *El Grito* (1969), a journal, and later *El Espejo/The Mirror* (1969), the first anthology of Chicano literature.[16] *El Grito* introduced to a wide reading public poets such as Alurista and José Montoya.

The students began their own movement in 1968 by walking out of schools—first the high schools, later the universities—in protest against the lack of sensitivity of Chicano culture. They demanded Chicano courses; they founded school newspapers and magazines. Thus, on two fronts they opened doors for literary expression. The creation of Chicano literature classes produced consumers for which materials were needed, thus providing a market for Chicano presses. The school publications became an outlet for Chicano poets as well as a training ground for those who aspired to the title. While the school publications have been decimated by economic recession and the rising apathy among Chicano students during the last decade and a half, we can still safely say that the academic audience, although itself dwindling, still accounts for most of the sales of Chicano poetry.

One poet more than any other personified the student spirit: Alurista. He was the first major poet to arise from the student ranks and perhaps for that reason expressed more closely their concerns, and he did so in their language. Yet he was far from a simple barrio poet. We would be better served by thinking of a Bob Dylan figure, a combination of popular forms with highly intellectualized material. His *Floricanto en Aztlán* drew from academic sources such as pre-Columbian mythology and Existentialism and from pop-culture fads like Carlos Castaneda, as well as barrio-life images.[17] His mixture of Spanish and English and a variety of sublanguages like black and Chicano slangs reflected the way students, especially in California, spoke. But his most significant accomplishment was the promulgation of the concept of Aztlán. Alurista is credited with inventing the Chicano version of a homeland myth: Aztlán was the original homeland of the Aztecs. Accordingly, Chicanos were transformed into the heirs of the glorious Aztec tradition and became the seekers of a lost homeland, located by Alurista and others in the Southwest of the United States. However, Alurista was never a cultural nationalist in the limited sense of Rodolfo Gonzales; he always favored a third-worldist vision of the future in pluralistic terms, each race and each ethnic group retaining its uniqueness within a social blending of free choice. This egalitarian pluralism helps explain Alurista's anticapitalism and the subsequent radicalization of his Marxist leanings. His ideal order cannot exist in a society divided into classes. He must call for the radical decapitalization of the state and a return to communal values and traditions. Alurista was in close harmony with the student movements of the 1960s, although perhaps we can now say that those students who actually held sophisticated ideological views were the extreme minority.

The other major poet to emerge from *El Grito* was neither young nor a student but an older teacher—José Montoya. Although a tireless writer, his publications seem few: poems scattered in magazines and one book, *El sol y los de abajo*.[18] His fame, however, rests on even less, one poem: "El Louie." This masterpiece is the epitome of the Chicano literary enterprise, a true prototype. Its language is interlingual, as is much of Alurista's, but with the difference that in

Montoya the languages flow so smoothly that they seem to blend instead of clash.

> Hoy enterraron al Louie
> And San Pedro o sanpinche
> are in for it. And those
> times of the forties
> and early fifties
> lost un vato de atolle.
>
> . . . .
> 48 Fleetline, two-tone—
> buenas garras and always
> rucas—como la Mary y
> la Helen . . . siempre con
> liras bien afinadas. [19]

The theme of the poem is the loss of a cultural signifier for group cohesion, in this case the leader of a pachuco gang. This loss threatens to deprive the poem's persona's group of its life. The poem recalls the figure in its context, thus restoring structure and significance to the world. It is the poem itself which, in the final analysis, becomes the space of signification as well as the protagonist of the signifying act, replacing the dead pachuco as the centralizing cultural force. This process, which I first discussed in "The Space of Chicano Literature,"[20] is the basis for the first book on Chicano poetry: *Chicano Poetry: A Response to Chaos.*[21]

Louie, a pachuco leader, dies. The poem recalls his image, which in turn brings his extended family, the immediate society, and their relationship to the world in ever-expanding circles. At the end of the poem, when the persona is forced to face the fact of the death of Louie, the poem has its own presence, an alternative body to replace Louie's buried one, and thus can ensure the stability of the threatened cultural unit. Chaos is forestalled, cosmos affirmed through the poetic substitution of poem for dead leader. This process is, of course, similar to—if not the same as—that of religious sacred rituals that call a divine but distant presence back from the beyond to commune with the faithful, who would fall into despair without some means of touching the signifying center of their cosmos. We should not overlook the presence of this sense of poetry as sacred act which is strong among some Chicanos. It is this that links them, even more than subject matter, to the Native American tradition.

Following the same pattern, Raul Salinas did for the barrio what Montoya did for pachucos. In "Trip through the Mind Jail,"[22] Salinas resists chaos by restoring to the world the images of his destroyed barrio. The signifying space becomes the setting for the recalled history of the persona's peer group, from street urchins to school mates to pachuco gang members to prison immates. In the end the barrio has been re-called from oblivion, given a new space in that which the poem opens in the world. The poem itself is the new barrio, the space of life-giving significance. Its existence grants the author and his readers a sense of orientation in life, a place in the world. The poem creates cosmos out of menacing chaos.

The poems of Montoya, Salinas, Gonzales, and Alurista spawned countless imitators. Student and community publications were full of sincere but forgettable parodies of major works. Most of them spoke in the fad interlingual patterns, repeating the new images of Chicanismo until they became dull clichés. And when the models themselves used techniques and images often bordering dangerously on cliché, then the imitators were on the shakiest of ground. The Chicano doggerel writers were highly visible because they provided the facile political slogans utilized by the movement. But what the imitators failed to capture was the art of these writers. The models make careful use of detail and selected use of traditional symbols and place them within a harmonious structure, leaving the reader with a sense of totality, of the necessity of each part in the whole. Most important, the model poems, even when utilizing popular clichés, make the images emerge from a logic essential to the poem; the imitations betray the arbitrariness of usage, the sense of superfluousness, of empty repetition. From the start Chicano poetry has been plagued with well-meaning formula writ-ers—but then most poetic movements have the same problem. Time usually filters them out.

Montoya and Salinas are also interesting as examples of the syn-thesis of Mexican and U.S. sources that characterizes Chicanos. Like the pachucos they write about, these poets come from a Mexican en-vironment; it is in their language and images. Both, however, are well aware of U.S. poetry, especially that of the Beat poets. Neither employs the traditional verse and rhyme forms of Mexican popular verse. They create narrative-style poetry more like U.S. models, free of set meter, leery of simple rhyme. Both play with U.S. popular and even pop lore such as movies, cars, music, or junk food. Alurista is similar, adding to this mixture a delight in classical and rock music. Montoya and Alurista both draw on philosophical concepts from academic readings. All three are within the Whitmanesque tradition. Yet this should not surprise us. It is the space of Chicano culture, the intercultural free play of influences open to experimentation. Chicano authors draw eclectically from Mexican and U.S. sources, which in turn open to them a wealth of further international references. Authors can pick and choose, but the essential situation of creating from at least two major cultural sources is a defining characteristic of Chicano literature.

Examples of varying blends can be found in other major poets. Tino Villanueva is a prime example.[23] He writes sonnets in English or Spanish. He pays tribute to Dylan Thomas and creates intertextual references to Borges and Octavio Paz. Yet he also produces interlingual poems about farm workers, pachucos, and political ideology. In his critical writing he insists that Chicanos have "bisensibility," meaning that they experience the world from two points of reference, one Chicano, the other Anglo-American. Theory aside, Villanueva demonstrates in his poetry an ability to slide along the spectrum of interlingualism from standard English to standard Spanish, a remarkable range of tones and registers that few poets can match.

Most Chicano poets definitely favor one or the other pole of reference. Ricardo García, for example, stays much closer to the U.S.-inspired style, with a strong dose of surrealism.[24] Sergio Elizondo swings us back to the Mexican popular tradition in his language and imagery.[25] For him the Anglo-American pole of society is a negative catalyst for Chicano action, a source of Chicano action leading to self-destruction. Elizondo locates his work in the Mexican tradition as a political and cultural statement of resistance to assimilation. Miguel Méndez creates difficult poetry of highly cultured language and intricate symbolism. His long poems develop through permutating images and leitmotifs—he is the expert at mixed metaphors. *Los criaderos humanos (épica de los desamparados) y sahuaros* is a devastating satirical allegory of capitalism and at once an *ars poetica* of commitment to cultural revival through literature. [26] All of these poets, so different in styles, language, and content, share the search for original expression, for a poetic voice. They represent the evolution of that group of writers who sought to create a written tradition of poetry for the Chicano people, in spite of the fact that each of them expresses a concern for the loss of oral culture. Apparently, they believe that the content of oral tradition can only be preserved through written media.

Coexisting with the written poetry, there are oral tradition–style pieces. The authors attempt to publish works modeled on performance poetry. These usually remain at the level of cliché, simple rhyme, blatant expository statement, and trite emotionalism. Their best moments are when they indulge in humor, especially ethnic humor, which produces in audiences a sense of unity. This poetry must be experienced to understand its closeness to ritual. The message is less important than its function as shared act, as communion. The master of this style is José Antonio Burciaga, although others indulge in it at times. [27] Alurista's latest word-play poetry falls somewhat into this category. This poetry is unlikely to please the reader of modern poetry because it indulges in banal prose and lacks original expression. Yet it can be very successful with audiences who have no training in academic poetry.

Recent Trends

A decade after the publication of *I Am Joaquin* the vitality of the early poetry was wearing thin. Readers were tiring of the same clichés. As the political movement lost impetus, the committed poetry lost its contextual support. In 1976 Alurista's third book, *Timespace Huracán*, [28] and Ricardo Sánchez's second, *HechizoSpells*, appeared. Both books are notable in that they disappointed readers. They had the feeling of a spent wave. Alurista was beginning his drift into esoteric and somewhat superficial word games, a tendency he later would intensify in *Spik in Gylph*. [29] Sánchez managed to give us his masterpiece, "Homing," but this poem, which ranks with "El Louie" and "Trip through the Mind Jail," got lost in the shuffle of page after page of circumstantial chatter. The oversized manuscript could have easily been cut to the best pieces and remained a respectable volume. Both poets could have used a good editor at that point. Their plight reflected well the general tendency among minor poets who were bogging down in clichés and incestual inreading (sic). Luckily, something else was beginning to happen.

The first, and perhaps the most significant change, was that women began to publish book-length works. Not that Chicanas had not been writing earlier, they had. However, their manuscripts had not been received well by Chicano presses. The major anthologies of Chicano literature, most of which were published before 1976, were edited by men who seemed to be unaware of women writers or not pleased by what they knew about them.[30] Chicanas were often forced to publish their own books, just as Chicanos had published theirs, the difference being that Chicanas felt excluded by the same Chicanos who had engaged in the rhetoric of liberation just a few years earlier. In 1975 Margarita Cota-Cárdenas (*Noches despertando inconciencias*),[31] Angela de Hoyos (*Arise, Chicano* and *Chicano Poems for the Barrio*),[32] and Dorinda Moreno (*La mujer es la tierra*)[33] published significant books. They confirmed what readers of magazines had suspected all along: Chicana writers had a wealth of material just waiting for publishers to discover. Also, it was immediately obvious that the women's self-image was not the same as the one men had imposed on them. From this moment on Chicanas have enriched the space of Chicano literature in ways that would have been impossible for Chicanos alone to achieve.

Bernice Zamora's *Restless Serpents* appeared a year later.[34] It put her among the leading figures in Chicano literature. No one could ignore the tight control of language, the panoramic knowledge of poetic techniques and forms, the uninhibited intertextual plays with major poets, the carefully planned structure of the book. And all of this to convey a Chicano message with a definitely feminist bent. At the heart of the text were two inseparable themes: first, the characteristic Chicano concern for recovering traditions that have centered the Chicano community, once again the response to the threat of chaos, and second, the insistence on women's right to share equally in the exercise of any and all cultural rituals, a mirroring of Chicanos' demand with respect to Anglo-American society. That same year Miriam Bornstein-Somoza published *Bajo cubierta*, a fine collection in Spanish.[35] Not as ambitious as Zamora's book, it is nonetheless remarkable for its craft and the skill at Spanish language usage. Together they demonstrated that even when individual poets are not openly interlingual, the space itself of Chicano poetry is—these two poets co-exist, and their dialogue creates that space. Obviously they also co-exist with the larger group of Chicano poets, and it is with them that the women forced a dialogue that opened that space to an ignored minority. If Chicano poetry had begun with a focus on the man's responsibility to regenerate his culture while the woman stood faithfully and lovingly and silently by, a passive witness and storehouse of tradition, within ten years woman had come to demand a vocal and active role in the creation of whatever Chicano culture was to become. This demand and its poetic expression changed Chicano poetry, marking profoundly its recent products and reshaping its configuration.

Another sign of renewal appeared in the mid 1970s with the publication of texts by poets who openly declared the need for better craftsmanship. First among them was the above-mentioned Bernice Zamora. *Restless Serpents* arises and never drifts far from identifiable Chicano concerns and social reality, but it is anything but trite or careless. Zamora's years of dedication to the manuscript and the study of poetry show in the polished product. Second, a group of young poets began publishing small magazines with a markedly different tone. On the east coast, Orlando Ramírez and José Saldívar collaborated on *Cambios/Phideo*. Ramírez would go on to win the Irvine Prize for poetry in 1979 with *Speedway;*[36] Saldívar has become one of the most promising young literary critics in the new generation of Chicano academics. *Mango*'s editor was Lorna Dee Cervantes, who would go on to win a Pittsburgh Press Award for her first book of verse, *Emplumada.*[37] The three of them came together in the late 1970s to work at *Mango* along with Gary Soto, whose *The Elements of San Joaquin* preceded Cervantes as a Pittsburgh Award winner by several years.[38] These young poets worked with some of the established writers of the earlier generation to produce a series of publications that for the most part demanded craft before message. The magazine and its chapbook series did not ignore social poetry or limit itself to any one style of writing, but with few exceptions the material published displayed attention to technique. And in the context of the first ten years of movement poetry this change was significant.

The case of Gary Soto has attracted much attention. From the very start his success at publishing in mainstream, prestigious magazines like *The New Yorker* and winning the United States Award of the International Poetry Forum (1976) with *The Elements of San Joaquin* provoked mixed reactions. Some saw him as the awaited breakthrough author, capable of communicating with Anglo-American readers in the language of contemporary U.S. poetry. Others saw him as the feared assimilationist, the Chicano who won awards because he wrote the way the mainstream demanded and without ethnic concerns. No one could deny his craft—he composes tight poems based more on image and metaphor than on narrative anecdote. There is no superfluous verbiage or ethnic clichés. He has published a series of books at the rate of about one a year and continues to garner praise from mainstream critics. Yet slowly Chicanos have come to recognize his work as one more facet of their cultural production. Of course, in his subsequent publications his Chicano culture has shown through in more obvious fashion. Perhaps audience and writer have drawn each other to a middle ground. Whatever may be thought of his handling of ethnic content (personally I read him as Chicano from the very essence),[39] the quality of his work has set a standard that continues to serve others as a benchmark.

Craftsmanship, quality, and dedication to a personal vision, however, are not limited to Soto or to those who follow the mainstream line. In 1978 Leo Romero published *During the Growing Season*.[40] He attracted none of the national attention that Soto received, but then he had not studied with a major mainstream poet (Philip Levine) as Soto had, so prestigious reviewers were not alerted. Also, the context and region that Romero transposes into poetry, New Mexico, are far from the more familiar backroads of Soto's California. Romero is more in tune with the narrative style of most Chicano writers and, thus, further from the mainstream techniques which most critics favor. Yet in his series of books he too displays a dedication to craft and an avoidance of the facile Chicano cliché. His world is that of the oral tradition, full of magic and folktales conveyed often through the persona of Celso, an aged Chicano free spirit. Alberto Ríos, whose *Whispering to Fool the Wind* won the Walt Whitman Award in 1981, is another young craftsman with a similar obsession for the magical nuances lying just beneath the surface of rural life, this time in Arizona.[41] Then there is Lorna Dee Cervantes, mentioned above, who works her poems over and over until each word fits perfectly. She too falls comfortably into the narrative anecdote, although within that context she displays some brilliant images. Her *Emplumada* (1980) is a purposefully structured voyage of the developing artist from child to commited writer to master poet, an eloquent personal statement among the best in Chicano literature. 1980 also brought us *Palabras de mediodía / Noon Words,* an excellent first book in Spanish by Lucha Corpi, published bilingually in facing translations.[42] Once again the interlingual space renewed itself. And the list could go on and on.

It would be misleading to leave the impression that the poets from the early years have disappeared or receded en masse into mediocrity. First, we must admit that, in most academic courses on the subject of Chicano poetry, it is still the early period that is taught. Therefore, for Chicano students the early poets and works are experienced as the main corpus of our poetry. The best endures while the doggerel assumes the character of historical document, in need of ever more external support for its justification. Second, some of those poets have produced recently some notable additions to their bibliography. Omar Salinas, known for his much anthologized "Aztec Angel" from his now collectors-item book *Crazy Gypsy* (1970),[43] returned to the scene to win the Stanley Kunitz Poetry Prize a full decade later with *Afternoons of the Unreal.*[44] A section of new poems by Alurista in *Return* (1983) shows signs of renewal, especially along the lines of a personal, more intimate voice.[45] Tino Villanueva's long awaited second book finally appeared in 1984, appropriately titled *Shaking Off the Dark.*[46] Villanueva has lost none of his precision; the poems are both personally moving and communally relevant. Villanueva at the same time has initiated a quality international poetry journal, *Imagine,* to serve as a format for Chicano poets to dialogue with their counterparts from all cultures. In 1980 he had edited *Chicanos: antología histórica y literaria,* the best collection of recent poetry by Chicanos, in which the established writers are presented through new poems instead of the standard, well-worn pieces.[47] And the old master, José Montoya, has combined his writing talents with music to collaborate in the long play album *Casindio, Chicano Music All Day.*[48] The older generation is by no means stagnant.

Since the mid 1970s there has been an explosion of poetry by both men and women. The problem for the critic with respect to any ethnic group is trying to define what makes it ethnic. In the first years of contemporary Chicano poetry it was not that difficult, but now the scene is radically different. Chicano poets are less concerned with ideology and more with craft; they explore the personal voice in any register and through any technique. Most still reflect a regional social context and strong ties to their community, notable particularly through the use of regional speech, the details of landscape, and a fascination for popular lore. While many of them still feel the need to rescue a Chicano past from marginal status and to instruct their community about themselves and the world, they no longer feel the need to speak as political prophets. During the 1970s we came to accept what should have been apparent from the beginning, that the Chicano community is far from homogeneous. We cannot expect its poets to speak a monolithic language when there is no monolith to speak for; we cannot expect writers to voice one political ideology when their community has not yet forged that ideological unity and in many cases seems to have rejected the militancy of the 1960s. This makes the recent poetry much harder to study and categorize, much harder to reduce for the sake of students and dabblers from other cultural milieu—but for that very reason much more dynamic, healthy, and interesting.

Notes

1. Bruce-Novoa, *Chicano Authors, Inquiry by Interview* (Austin: University of Texas Press, 1980), pp. 2–10.
2. William Boelhower, *Through a Glass Darkly: Ethnic Semiosic in American Literature* (Venezia: Edizioni Helvetia, 1984).
3. Gaspar Pérez de Villagrá, *Historia de la Nueva México* (Alcalá, 1610).
4. José de Onís, *Las misiones españolas en los Estados Unidos* (New York: 1958).
5. Bruce-Novoa, "*El Crepúsculo* and *Cuaderno*, Oldest Newspaper and Book in the Southwest," *La Luz* (October 1973): 12–14.
6. Américo Paredes, *With His Pistol in His Hand: A Border Ballad and Its Hero* (Austin: University of Texas Press, 1958).
7. Doris Meyer, "Anonymous Poetry in Spanish-Language New Mexico Newspapers (1880–1900)," *Bilingual Review* 2, no. 3 (1975): 259–275.
8. Philip Ortego, "Chicano Poetry: Roots and Writers," *Southwestern American Literature* 2, no. 1 (Spring 1972): 8–24.
9. Arthur L. Campa, "Spanish Folksongs in Metropolitan Denver," *Southern Folklore Quarterly* 24, no. 3 (September 1960): 185.

10. Tomás Ybarra-Frausto, "The Chicano Movement and the Emergence of a Chicano Poetic Consciousness," *New Scholar* 7 (1977): 81–109.
11. In *Aztlán: An Anthology of Mexican American Literature*, ed. Stan Steiner and Luis Valdez (New York: Random House, 1972), pp. 328–330.
12. Rodolfo Gonzales, *I Am Joaquín/Yo soy Joaquín* (New York: Bantam, 1972).
13. Abelardo Delgado, *Chicano: 25 Pieces of a Chicano Mind* (Denver: Barrio Publications, 1969).
14. Ricardo Sánchez, *Canto y grito mi liberación* (El Paso: Mictla Publications, 1971).
15. Ricardo Sánchez, *HechizoSpells* (Los Angeles: Chicano Studies Center, UCLA, 1976), pp. 144–148.
16. *El espejo/The Mirror*, ed. Octavio Romano (Berkeley: Quinto Sol, 1969).
17. Alurista, *Floricanto en Aztlán* (Los Angeles: Chicano Studies Center, UCLA, 1971).
18. José Montoya, *El sol y los de abajo* (San Francisco: Ediciones Pocho-Che, 1972).
19. José Montoya, "El Louie," in *Aztlán*, p. 333.
20. Bruce-Novoa, "The Space of Chicano Literature," *De Colores* 1, no. 4 (1975): 22–42.
21. Bruce-Novoa, *Chicano Poetry: A Response to Chaos* (Austin: University of Texas Press, 1982).
22. José Montoya, "Trip through the Mind Jail," in *Aztlán*, pp. 339–344.
23. Tino Villaneuva, ed., *Hay otra voz Poems* (Staten Island: Editorial Mensaje, 1972).
24. Ricardo García, *Selected Poetry* (Berkeley: Quinto Sol, 1973).
25. Sergio Elizondo, *Perros y antiperros* (Berkeley: Quinto Sol, 1972).
26. Miguel Méndez, *Los criaderos humanos (épica de los desamparados) y Sahuaros* (Tucscon: Peregrinos, 1975).
27. José Antonio Burciaga, *Restless Serpents* (Menlo Park: Diseños Literarios, 1976).
28. Alurista, *Timespace Huracán* (Albuquerque: Pajarito, 1976).
29. Alurista, *Spik in Gylph* (Houston: Arte Público Press, 1981).
30. Miriam Bornstein-Somoza, "The Voice of the Chicana," *Denver Quarterly* 16, no. 3 (Fall 1981): 32–33.
31. Margarita Cota-Cárdenas, *Noches despertando inconciencias* (Tucson: Scorpion Press, 1975).
32. Angela de Hoyos, *Arise, Chicano* (Bloomington Books, 1975) and *Chicano Poems for the Barrio* (Bloomington Books, 1975).
33. Dorinda Moreno, *La mujer es la tierra* (Berkeley: Casa Editorial, 1975).
34. Bernice Zamora, *Restless Serpents* (Menlo Park: Diseños Literarios, 1976).
35. Miriam Bornstein-Somoza, *Bajo cubierta* (Tucson: Scorpion Press, 1976).
36. Orlando Ramírez, *Speedway* (San Jose: Mango úress, 1979).
37. Lorna Dee Cervantes, *Emplumada* (Pittsburgh: Pittsburgh Press, 1980).
38. Gary Soto, *The Elements of San Joaquin* (Pittsburgh: Pittsburgh Press, 1977).
39. Bruce-Novoa, *Chicano Poetry*, pp. 185–211.
40. Leo Romero, *During the Growing Season* (Tucson: Maguey Press, 1978).

41. Alberto Ríos, *Whispering to Fool the Wind* (New York: Sheep Meadow Press, 1982).
42. Lucha Corpi, *Palabras de mediodía/Noon Words* (Berkeley: El Fuego de Aztlán, 1980).
43. Luis Omar Salinas, *Crazy Gypsy* (Fresno: Orígenes Publications, 1970).
44. Luis Omar Salinas, *Afternoons of the Unreal* (Fresno: Abramas Publications, 1980).
45. Alurista, *Return* (Epsilanti: Bilingual Press, 1983).
46. Tino Villanueva, *Shaking Off the Dark* (Houston: Arte Público, 1984).
47. Tino Villanueva, ed., *Chicanos: Antología histórica y literaria* (Mexico City: Fondo de Cultura Económica, 1980).
48. José Montoya, Esteban Villa, and R. Carrillo, *Casindio, Chicano Music All Day* (Sacramento: Centro de Artistas Chicanos, 1985).

Ayumi
"To Sing Our Connections"

While the influence of Japanese poetry has had a profound impact upon American poetry in this century (witness the work of Pound, Rexroth, and Snyder), Japanese American poetry has gained little critical recognition or acceptance into the American canon. This is not so surprising when one considers that with the exception of Lawson Fusao Inada, whose volume *Before the War*[1] was the first book of poems published by a Japanese American, no Japanese American poets have had books published by major publishing houses. And in fact, Inada's book was ignored or attacked by critics such as Allen Beekman, reviewer for the *Pacific Citizen*, who called it "outhouse poetry." When *Yokohama, California*, the short story collection by Toshio Mori, was published in 1949, William Saroyan took time out from his introduction to chastize Mori's "bad grammar." Until recently, then, writing by Japanese Americans has either been ignored or been found wanting by critics who judged it not on its own terms but according to the conventions of standard English.

But as the editors of *Aiiieeeee! An Anthology of Asian American Writers* observe in their introduction, "The universality of the belief that correct English is the only language of American truth has made language an instrument of cultural imperialism. The minority experience does not yield itself to accurate or complete expression in the white man's language." Instead, the task of the Asian American writer is "to legitimize the language of his people's experience, to codify the experiences common to his people into symbols, clichés, linguistic mannerisms, and a sense of humor that emerges from an organic familiarity with the experience."[2]

A literary tradition has long existed in our community, but the work of our writers has largely been confined to the world of small presses, community newspapers, and, most recently, Asian American publications. Despite this general neglect by mainstream publishing, poets Ronald Tanaka, Mitsui Yamada, Garrett Hongo, Geraldine Kudaka, and James Mitsui have all had volumes produced by university or small presses.

Edited by the Anthology Committee, *Ayumi* (Journey) is perhaps the most comprehensive collection of Japanese American writing to date, spanning four generations of Nikkei (Americans of Japanese ancestry) in this country: Issei, Nisei, Sansei, and Yonsei. As its introduction states, "Ayumi is the ongoing journey . . . to sing our connections." By bringing together some of the finest, most important voices in Japanese American literature, this anthology represents a bold challenge to the institutional racism of mainstream publishing as well as a lasting contribution to the multicultural literature of this country.

Most of the Issei (first generation Japanese American) selections are written in the form of journal entries or autobiographical reminiscences and are rather brief in length. In view of their hardships, one has to assume that most Issei had little time to write at all. Of the poetry by the Issei, the senryu and tanka are most effective, making precise, compact use of words: "hay spread for / movie viewing / beneath spring stars" (Hokko) and "thorns of the iron fence / pointed inward / toward camp" (Kyokusui). While the first poem takes nature as its theme with a wry modern twist, the second conveys well the pain and confinement of the camp experience in which 110,000 Japanese Americans were imprisoned in ten American concentration camps during World War II. What distinguishes the senryu and tanka is their stringent economy of expression. Although a variety of themes reoccur in many poems (the shock of internment, observations of daily camp life, remembrances of Japan, expressions of loneliness, isolation, and exile, of conflicted loyalties, and Buddhist perception of transience), these themes are rendered with an economy and precision that make them affecting.

A poem from "Japanese Poems on Angel Island Detention Station," translated by Kiyohi Hama (Karl G. Yoneda), turns upon the irony of a name: "Angel Island—what a beautiful name / But there was no angel here / Only nameless prisoners of immigration." In San Francisco Bay, Angel Island served as an entry station for Japanese and Chinese immigrants at the turn of the century. One of the poems carved into the walls of the barracks where the immigrants were detained, it is an anonymous message to the world recording the mistreatment of newly arrived Asian immigrants with the truth and immediacy of one who experienced it.

Yoshio Yao's "A Pilgrimage to Tule Lake, May 25, 1974" evokes the harsh conditions under which the internees were forced to live with a close attention to detail: "Vast and withered fields, / a dried lake bottom, / where I was once evacuated / and lived for the duration," and "Like dirty crows, / we were forced to live under low roofs."

Finally, Yoshihiko Tomari's poem gives the reader a sense of the daily costs and hazards the Japanese American immigrant faced in order to survive in this country: "After his funeral / I found out he had used a false name / to enter the country." These poems gain their quiet strength through simple, direct statement and clarity of image.

> Through the thirties and forties Japanese-American writers produced their own literary magazines. Even in the internment period, Japanese American literary journals sprang up in the relocation centers . . . The question of Japanese-American identity, the conflicts between Issei and Nisei, yellow and white relations, black, white, and yellow relations, and the war were all examined and re-examined in camp newspapers, literary magazines, diaries, and journals . . . The Japanese-Americans did write of the camp experience, but were not published outside the confines.[3]

The Nisei (second generation Japanese American) section features some of the most consistently realized work in the collection. Born and raised in the United States, the Nisei were bilingual American citizens, a fact that the federal government chose to ignore when it imprisoned them in the camps. But in some ironic sense they had more opportunity to create an authentic Japanese American literature. In this section we see more poems and stories and fewer autobiographical selections.

Hiroshi Kashiwagi's poem "Haircut" deals with familial emotions in a minimalist style:

        papa
        you used to
        cut my hair
        rice bowl style
        carving
        big ears for
        juicy spitball
        targets.

The poet recalls suffering through the private but commonplace ritual
(I, too, can recall being given such a haircut) while feeling a quiet
pride for his Issei father when he chases away a white *Sacramento Bee*
reporter.

Mitsuye Yamada's "In the Outhouse" is extraordinarily powerful ex-
pressing disgust and revulsion for the camp experience:

        I have this place to hide
        the excreta and
        the blood which
        do not flush down
        nor seep away. They pile up
        fill the earth. I am drowning.

After exploiting their labor in agriculture and other fields, the American government exiled the Nikkei to areas of barren desert. Yamada
captures well the sense of unbearable shame and humiliation of that
time. Poets Kashiwagi and Yamada both use spare, stripped-down language and short lines to produce a voice taut with irony and anger.

Yasuo Sasaki's "Spoilage" expresses strong antiwar sentiments with
biblical allusions:

        There is spoilage
        in God's granary,
        for warfare
        takes its toll
        even in wheatfields—
        where chaff remains chaff,
        and injured grains
        are gathered.

James Masao Mitsui's "Nisei: Second Generation Japanese American" possesses the precise but impressionistic quality of Japanese landscape painting:

> Farmers in Kyushu are caught by the floating clouds,
> caught square in the middle of their fields,
> squinting to see who it is
> standing there on the dirt bank, the mud
> in the soft rain, soft as the leading edge of a cloud.

His "Destination: Tule Lake Relocation Center May 20, 1942" is a photographically exact portrait of an Issei woman waiting on a train to leave for the relocation center:

> The fingers of her left
> hand
> worried two strings
> attached
> to a baggage tag flapping
> from her
> lapel.

Mitsui's poem reminded me of Dorothea Lange's photographs of the evacuation, that sense of loss and apprehension at what was to come.

Poet Iwao Kawakami uses the stylistic technique of the camera eye popularized by John Dos Passos as a method of distancing while at the same time recording an event in our buried history. "The Paper" is based upon an incident in which an Issei man was attempting to retrieve a wind-blown paper along the barbed-wire fence in Topaz and was shot and killed by a guard.

Poetry predominates over either fiction or autobiography in the Sansei and Yonsei (third and fourth generation Japanese American) section, perhaps because most Sansei and Yonsei writers find the form of poetry more usable as a way of "saying something" than either fictional narrative or the autobiographical essay.

Jonny Kyoko Sullivan's "Obasan" (Grandmother) is a precise, controlled, sharply imaged poem in five sections. Clearly, it is one of the finest in the anthology, containing vivid, memorable images which convey both remembrances of growing up in Japan and the awkward, tentative experience of returning "home" years later: "My bones are wild herons / trapped in your kimonos" and "And when I kissed your cheek, / the smooth dark jars of your eyes / broke into astonished fragments." Sullivan's "Sagimusume: The White Heron" is also exceptional.

While Sullivan uses sharp, particular images to evoke her "Obasan," the narrator of Momoko Iko's "1963: Obasan Makes Peace" has a tough, street-wise voice. Momoko Iko shares this emotional toughness with Nisei writers Mitsuye Yamada and Hiroshi Kashiwagi.

Janice Mirikitani's "For My Father" is an unsparing portrait: "word-less / he sold / the rich, / full berries / to / hakujin / whose children / pointed at our eyes" and later, "Father, / i wanted to scream / at your silence." As much an indictment of white racism as of her father's un-communicative behavior, Mirikitani's poem is among the most polit-ical in the anthology.

Lonny Kaneko's "Renewal: Algona, Washington" and Lawson Fusao Inada's "My Father and Myself Facing the Sun" delineate relationships between the poets and their Nisei parents in a gentle, devotional tone. Kaneko evokes his mother's life on a farm in the Pacific Northwest with evidences of decay and urban blight, not "renewal," everywhere: "Be-hind us, the ribs of the barn / bowed by rains and dry rot, invite air." But still, she speaks of her own hardship and the need to retain one's identity:

> And when we cross parking lots sparkling with rain,
> my mother's aging face rises out of the darkness.
> She says to her grandchildren,
> "Look for your own faces.
> They rise out of the past like old wounds."

Inada conjures a sublime landscape with the figures of the poet's fa-ther, the poet himself, and his children alongside a lake:

> He is much the smooth, grass-brown slopes
> reaching knee-high around you as you walk;
> I am the cracks of cliffs and gulleys,
> pieces of secret deep in the back of the eye.

While Inada's poem shares a representational quality with James Masao Mitsui's "Nisei," Inada uses the "I," placing the poet firmly in his landscape and thus personalizing the poem.

Karen Tei Yamashita's "Maceio Maceio" gracefully describes her fa-ther fishing in the ocean: "Waves grapple at his knees and / spume his majestic cape, / sputtering behind." This action works as a counter-point to the brutally exact description of an urubu, "a tailless black turkey," feeding upon the poisonous baiacu: "Together they encircle her, / flapping black shadows / poke at the fixed eyes, / pierce the bloated throat." The poet's fascination with this ritual dance and her use of the feminine pronoun suggest an identification with the baiacu: "Drunken salary men in Tokyo / dip her raw pieces / in shoyu and play / fugu roulette. There are expensive ways / to die." By shifting between the twin poles of grace and violence, "Maceio Maceio" is a dark, complex poem which casts a cold eye upon death.

Tillie Olsen has described Mitsuye Yamada's work as "hard wrung poetry." This stringent quality is also present in Momoko Iko's "Obasan." Kyoko Sullivan's poems suggest the binds and constraints inherent in Japanese women's sex roles, while Janice Mirikitani dramatizes sexist and racist stereotypes. And Karen Yamashita's poem seems to identify with the violence of nature to an unusual degree. Japanese American women poets, then, are depicting and challenging traditional gender-defined roles or simply exploding them with taut expressions of rage. Thus, this instinctive concern with women's experience and oppression often bridges generational barriers between Nisei and Sansei women poets.

As a Sansei writer, I believe this anthology is continuing proof of the Japanese American literary tradition. Work by the Issei offers glimpses and illuminations of what those of my grandparents' generation felt and thought in their own language, a language that most Sansei have little command of. Thus, their work brings me closer to those unvoiced histories of our grandmothers and grandfathers.

Some of our best, most prolific writers are Nisei and some continue to write even now. While growing up in New York City, I sensed the effects of the internment on my parents as a weary silence, of speech withheld, of emotions so hurtful that they must be held within at all costs. Nisei poets Mitsuye Yamada and Hiroshi Kashiwagi give passionate voice to those emotions which makes the impact of their poems cleansing—an art that redeems us.

The Sansei and Yonsei poets I admire affect me in other ways, for their poetry indicates possible directions as to where my own writing may lead. Many Sansei and Yonsei find themselves in the predicament of being thoroughly Americanized yet desiring to reclaim their cultural past, however distant and elusive it might be. In Jonny Kyoko Sullivan's work, her exploration of the complexities of identity merged with an extraordinary gift for the image makes her poems doubly exciting to me. But more specifically, I think her work, its tone and sensibility, is indisputably Japanese American.

Finally, the history of Nikkei in the United States from the immigrant experience to the Asian American movement of the present moment can be found in *Ayumi*. Because our history was not told in textbooks and our writers were not even mentioned in literature classes, for a long time I felt that my own experience was outside history. This anthology further dispels the myth that Japanese Americans have not contributed to the multicultural literature of this country.

While some Issei poets worked in traditional Japanese poetic forms and some Nisei and Sansei poets might have been influenced by the Imagist Movement, I would hesitate to place those poets in either tradition. They belong to, and extend, the tradition that is their own. In his "Tribute to Toshio," Lawson Inada says, "Does one merely 'admire' whom one is descended from? There is an abiding love involved, a pride in where the elder has been, what he has done, and from there do we reach out to the world."

Notes

1. Lawson Fusao Inada, *Before the War* (New York: William Morrow and Co., 1971).
2. Frank Chin, Jeffery Chan, Lawson Inada, and Shawn Wong, eds., *Aiiieeeee! An Anthology of Asian American Writers* (Garden City, N.Y.: Anchor Press/ Doubleday, 1975).
3. Ibid.

Documentaries and Declamadores
Puerto Rican Poetry in the United States

If only they
had kept their eyes open
at the funeral of their fellow employees
who came to this country to make a fortune
and were buried without underwears[1]

With this startling image from his long poem *Puerto Rican Obituary*, Pedro Pietri documents the life of his community at the same time that he seeks to raise awareness—to open the eyes of his "fellow employees"—in that very community. This is a dual responsibility frequently accepted by Puerto Rican poetry in the United States, a unique, neglected poetry reflecting the life of its community rather than the life of an educated elite, the focus of so much "mainstream" poetry.

The presence of Puerto Rican poets in the United States can be traced back to the 1860s, according to Efraín Barradas, critic and professor of Spanish at the University of Massachusetts-Boston. The first major figure to emerge, however, was Clemente Soto Vélez, who by the 1950s was no longer writing solely for an audience in Puerto Rico but also for what Barradas calls "a future reader." Soto Vélez, a leader of the independence movement in Puerto Rico who spent eight years in federal prison as a result of his fierce advocacy, a visionary who invented his own phonetic Spanish alphabet, published several books from his exile in New York, including the landmark *Caballo de Palo*

(The Broomstick Stallion) in 1959. Still writing and speaking today in his eighties, Soto Vélez has been instrumental as well in providing guidance and support to many younger writers in the Puerto Rican community.

The most important context for contemporary Puerto Rican poetry in the United States remains the great migration from the island in the 1950s and 1960s, a migration so massive that approximately one-third of the population left Puerto Rico during this time.[2] Roberto Márquez, Caribbean scholar at the University of Virginia and former editor of the influential journal *Caliban*, sees this migration as "class homogeneous: a group of displaced labor was coming here," pushed off the island by the political machinations and economic failures of Operation Bootstrap, the industrialization of Puerto Rico which ultimately benefited North American corporations far more than the majority of Puerto Ricans. From this group of displaced labor emerged the first two poets of the migration: Víctor Hernández Cruz and Pedro Pietri. The poetry of Hernández Cruz, surreal, insistently musical, and bilingual, gained the poet considerable attention by the age of twenty, when his book *Snaps* was published by Random House. Pietri, whose *Puerto Rican Obituary* is probably the best-known and certainly one of the most powerful poetic works to arise from the Puerto Rican community, according to Roberto Márquez "represented the first generation, beginning to write literature out of that experience." Blending humor and rage with genuine verbal inventiveness, a true "street" poet, Pietri's natural eloquence concerning conditions in his community and the reaffirmation of that community won him an enormous following.

By the early 1970s, the self-proclaimed "Nuyorican" literary movement had developed. Originally a derogatory term used against New York Puerto Ricans by Puerto Ricans on the island (that is, neo-Rican, or not really Puerto Rican at all), "Nuyorican," when applied to poetry, came to mean a combination of English and Spanish, frequently in a street idiom, aimed at a bilingual/bicultural audience and reflecting the language as well as the experience of that audience. Some proponents of the poetry such as Miguel Algarín even claimed that a "new language" was being invented; and indeed, says Roberto Márquez, "we'd done something to the language which was not there before." Said Algarín in his introduction to the anthology he co-edited with Miguel Piñero, *Nuyorican Poetry*, published in 1975: "Nuyorican is at its birth. English nouns function as verbs. Spanish verbs function as adjectives . . . Raw life needs raw verbs and raw nouns to express the action and to name the experience."[3] As poetry, the language was clear, direct, and concrete, usually meant to be read aloud, even chanted. The bilingual nature of the poetry encouraged agile wordplay across languages. Witness the Víctor Hernández Cruz pun:

> There will be a Sun
> Risa
> on your lips[4]

The poet blends the Spanish words *risa* (laughter) and *sonrisa* (smile) with the English word "sunrise," a feat which can be appreciated only by an audience familiar with both languages.

The poet and the audience in the Puerto Rican community were, and still are, closely linked. This linkage has deep philosophical roots. In the words of Louis Reyes Rivera, a well-respected New York poet and publisher of Shamal Books, "there is no distinction between the reader and the writer. Without someone to clean streets and sew garments, there would not be someone with time to write poetry." The language used by the poet, maintains Rivera, "reflects what the people themselves have done with language in their everyday use."

The English which has increasingly replaced Spanish as the dominant mode of communication for Puerto Rican poets in this country is often non-standard English and as such owes a considerable debt to the black community. Roberto Márquez provides the context: "El Barrio [in New York] is called Spanish Harlem for a reason. It shares a lot of space with the black community." Sandra María Esteves, another leading Nuyorican poet and director of the African-Caribbean Poetry Theatre, adds: "the Puerto Rican community has merged with the black community in terms of how we are treated by the dominant society . . . The black community here has been dealing with language issues for a long time. That provides a focus for us to deal with the English language."

Black words and music have their strongest influence on the rhythm of Puerto Rican poetry. Louis Reyes Rivera: "In non-standard English, there's more attention to rhythm than meter. One syllable lines can be complete. A series of one syllable lines can be a cutting edge, staccato-like. We end up taking a series of natural sounds—guttural sounds—

and 'spleeeeeing' our way through it. It's a record of what we call hypertension: the paranoia, the pain cutting loose."

Puerto Rican poetry has an oral tradition which antedates its contact with the black community in the United States, though that contact clearly strengthened the tradition of poetry as spoken word. The *declamador*, a dramatic public performer of memorized verse, has held forth in Latin American plazas for centuries, Puerto Rico included. In New York, the oral tradition ranges from Jorge Brandon, an old-style declamador nearing eighty who still recites on street corners, to Georgie Lopez, who, at the age of nine had his oral poems transcribed for the *Nuyorican Poetry* anthology because, according to editor Algarin, he could neither read nor write:

> georgie lopez will be the DDT against
> the rats[5]

Two other factors involved in the development of the oral tradition are the speech patterns and music of the Puerto Rican community itself. Efraín Barradas: "It comes from the community. People sit on stoops, or stick their heads out the window, and talk." Salsa, the hybrid Afro-Caribbean music which fully evolved in New York, is also credited by many with having an impact on Puerto Rican poetry as sound. In fact, the music, in all its variations, is often referred to in the poetry by Hernández Cruz ("The Cha Cha Cha at Salt Lake City Bus Terminal") and numerous others.

The themes of which the poets speak again reflect the migration experience and the many complexities that experience entails. There is, first of all, the theme of Puerto Rico. Barradas defines this as "the [literary] myth of Puerto Rico as paradise." Roberto Márquez sees the myth as "an unavoidable necessity . . . It's comparative. That's paradise compared to here. That's where I belong because I obviously don't belong here." Waves of migrants have "transmitted their sense of return to their offspring." In the poetry, the myth of Puerto Rico as paradise surfaces in imagery of the island's natural world: the mountains, the rivers and the sea, the warm climate, the vegetation. This tendency is found, for example, in the work of Hernández Cruz, who has written dreamlike poems about green bananas falling from the sky onto an urban landscape, or people popping out of mangoes. These images acquire a transcendent power when set off against the harsh conditions faced by Puerto Ricans in the United States. Hernández Cruz, trapped in a cold tenement, remembers an uncle

> Who never left his hometown
> We'd picture him sitting around
> cooling himself with a fan
> in that imaginary place
> called Puerto Rico.[6]

By referring to Puerto Rico as "imaginary," the poet doubts the myth at the same time he revels in it. And indeed, sometimes the myth is contradicted, as with Miguel Algarín's "A Mongo Affair":

> Don't fill me full of vain
> disturbing love for an island
> filled with Burger Kings[7]

Just as Puerto Rico is a major theme in the poetry, so too is the subject of the Puerto Rican. The Puerto Rican cultural character is seen as essentially good; this perspective clearly acts as a reinforcement of the Puerto Rican identity, threatened on the mainland by Anglo stereotyping in the media, schools, the workplace, and elsewhere, as well as the dilution or loss of Spanish and other cultural characteristics. According to Sandra María Esteves, "who is a Puerto Rican and what is a Puerto Rican" are ongoing concerns for the poet on the mainland. When that question is answered, the response is often based on the "reality of Puerto Rican culture, a mixture of Indian, white, and black, even within one family." Thus, continues Esteves, "diversity, and the need for respect among cultures" becomes a recurring subtheme in the poetry. Esteves addresses both the identity crisis of the mainland Puerto Rican and her own African cultural roots in the poem "Puerto Rico, I," where she speaks to the island directly, like a person:

> How can you say I am not your child?
> You are my black mother who teaches
> Me to see in the darkness where
> there exists only music[8]

In poems such as this, Esteves and Louis Reyes Rivera have assured that the black aspects of the Puerto Rican self are recognized.

Most often, the poetry returns to the sense of self held by the poet and the audience, their shared identity affirmed. Pedro Pietri, in "Love Poem for My People," writes:

> if you want
> to feel very rich
> look at your hands
> that is where
> the definition of magic
> is located at[9]

Perhaps the most striking characteristic of Puerto Rican poetry in the United States is its element of protest. At times, this protest manifests itself merely by description of surroundings: when Pedro Pietri writes of funeral parlors and liquor stores proliferating in his neighborhood, that and similar observations based on simply looking out the window may be interpreted as political. The daily enemies of the community are depicted in turn: the landlord, the boss, the police, the pusher, the cold, and even the city itself, be it in the form of bad public hospitals and welfare systems or the apparent soullessness of the metropolis. Exploitation on the job and its debilitating effects on the spirit draw Pietri's ire in the now-classic "Puerto Rican Obituary":

> They worked
> They were always on time
> They never spoke back
> when they were insulted
> They worked
> They never took days off
> that were not on the calendar
> They never went on strike
> without permission
> They worked
> ten days a week
> and were only paid for five
> They worked
> They worked
> They worked
> and they died[10]

Narrative poetry is frequently employed to document, and protest, incidents which would otherwise be left undocumented, as with

Rivera's "Burning Embers," about a police killing, or Esteves' "Lil' Pito," about a child who fell from a broken window. "Lil' Pito" is replete with the precise, authentic details which characterize the use of poetry as documentary:

> I got to the hospital to see
> Rosa standing with a piece of
> Rotten window gate in hand[11]

Thus, the awareness of the audience/community is raised with respect to a particular event, from the perspective of that community, so unlike the point of view reflected in the media, if indeed the media were to cover these events at all. In this way, the traditional role of poet as community historian is perpetuated in the barrio.

According to Rivera, "all mores, sexual, religious, political, moral, are questioned and re-questioned" in the poetry. He comments that the poetry is "sometimes left-leaning, but not consistently enough to be of the left." However, certain poets with a more developed political awareness, such as Rivera, Esteves, Algarín, José Angel Figueroa (in poems such as "Cowboynomics"), and others have produced a definite anticolonial strain in their work, a natural outgrowth of the history and political status of Puerto Rico. Rivera writes in "Grito de Lares" of "enemy soldiers romping" through Puerto Rico:

> in the name of
>   someone else's right
>   to juicy slabs of stolen produce[12]

The poet is tying together centuries of colonial occupation, first under Spain and later under the United States, recalling an earlier rebellion—the "Grito de Lares"—and hoping for another. This kind of anticolonial statement represents Puerto Rican poetry at its most politically universal. In a logical extension of the anticolonial position, a variety of Puerto Rican poets have written about Central America and South Africa as well.

Women's issues have also been addressed by Puerto Rican poets in the United States. Contemporary poets are inspired by the example of Julia de Burgos, who lived in New York during the 1940s and 1950s, leaving behind such well-known poems as "A Julia de Burgos":

You are only the prim ladylike lady;
not I; I am life, strength, woman . . .

You curl your hair and paint your face; not I;
My hair is curled by the wind, my face is painted
by the sun[13]

Today, the work of Sandra María Esteves ranges from a depiction of woman as life-giver in "A Celebration of Home Birth" to the defiant rejection of female servility in "From the Common Wealth." Rosario Morales and Luz María Umpierre write from a consistently feminist perspective. Umpierre's "Rubbish" succinctly states her position:

I b-e-g yul paldon, escuismi
am sorri pero yo soy latina
y no sopolto su RUBBISH.[14]

Not coincidentally, Puerto Rican poetry in the United States has been almost completely excluded from the mainstream. This is nowhere more evident than in the area of publishing. Only one Puerto Rican poet in this country has ever had a book published by a major commercial press: the previously mentioned Víctor Hernández Cruz with Random House. Many accomplished poets—Rivera, Esteves, and Susana Cabanas among them—must self-publish their books. Awards and grants have also been difficult to come by, though Esteves has twice been awarded grants through the New York State Council on the Arts, while Miguel Algarín and Tato Laviera have each received the Before Columbus Foundation American Book Award. Many reasons are offered for the near-total absence of the Puerto Rican poet from the broader community of poets in the United States. Roberto Márquez: "in historical terms, the Puerto Rican just got here . . . Where are the Nuyorican Paul Robesons, Richard Wrights? They're just beginning to form." Says Sandra María Esteves, "It's a manifestation of the colonial mind. Hispanics get excluded from the mainstream at every level: in the job market, in educational institutions, everywhere Puerto Ricans are not allowed to participate as equals." Louis Reyes Rivera sums it up simply by saying that "nobody wants to be reminded that they're wreaking havoc on others." But Efraín Barradas believes that "it's good that the poetry has been excluded. It's provided the possibility of development. It would have otherwise been completely absorbed, assimilated . . . You wouldn't have a corpus called Nuyorican poetry."

There is a consensus among those involved that the Puerto Rican community must develop its own literary institutions. Several small or university presses currently emphasize Puerto Rican poetry. Foremost among them is Arte Publico Press, based at the University of Houston and headed by a Puerto Rican, Nicolás Kanellos. Other presses, such as the Bilingual Press, Waterfront Press, and Ediciones del Norte, though not Puerto Rican–run, have published a good deal of Puerto Rican writing. Where the Puerto Rican community has been quite active is in the area of organizing and supporting reading series. In New York alone, readings have been sponsored by the Museo del Barrio, Grupo Moriviví, the African-Caribbean Poetry Theatre, and the Nuyorican Poets' Cafe.

Yet Puerto Rican poetry in the United States has grown beyond the borders of New York City. The presence of Rosario Morales in Cambridge, Juan Sáez-Burgos in Boston, Naomi Ayala in New Haven, David Hernández in Chicago, and Víctor Hernández Cruz in San Francisco testify to the sweep of the Puerto Rican diaspora and the persistence of its voice.

The prognosis for Puerto Rican poetry in the United States is mixed. Undoubtedly, the fate of the poets is intertwined with that of the Puerto Rican community itself, and they may continue to be excluded from the mainstream as a consequence of identifying with that powerless and resource-poor community. On the other hand, according to Kal Wagenheim, editor and publisher of the Puerto Rican–oriented Waterfront Press, there is cause for optimism: "I certainly do think there's a future. The potential is out there. It's up to the writers and publishers to figure out a way to reach a young and growing community . . . a dispersed community, with its own needs." Louis Reyes Rivera considers it the writer's responsibility to assure that "the literature is there and you yourself made sure it didn't go away." However, the future is probably best summarized by three lines from a poem called "News from the Front," by Sandra María Esteves, which personify the humor and toughness of the people she w ites for and about:

> We lost graffiti battle no. #3
> but reinforcements are on the way
> from lexington avenue.[15]

Notes

Quoted comments from Efraín Barradas, Sandra María Esteves, Roberto Márquez, Louis Reyes Rivera, and Kal Wagenheim were taken from interviews conducted by Martín Espada in November and December 1985.

1. Pedro Pietri, *Puerto Rican Obituary* (New York: Monthly Review Press, 1973), p. 10.
2. Ann Nelson, *Murder under Two Flags* (New York: Ticknor and Fields, 1986), p. 98.
3. Miguel Algarín and Miguel Piñero, eds., *Nuyorican Poetry: An Anthology of Puerto Rican Words and Feelings* (New York: William Morrow and Co., 1975), p. 19.
4. Julio Marzán, ed., *Inventing a Word: An Anthology of Twentieth-Century Puerto Rican Poetry* (New York: Columbia University Press, 1980), p. 169.
5. Algarín and Piñero, *Nuyorican Poetry*, p. 42.
6. Víctor Hernández Cruz, *Tropicalization* (New York: Reed, Cannon, and Johnson, 1976), p. 62.
7. Algarín and Piñero, *Nuyorican Poetry*, p. 55.
8. Sandra María Esteves, *Tropical Rains: A Bilingual Downpour* (New York: African-Caribbean Poetry Theatre, 1984), p. 25.
9. Pietri, *Puerto Rican Obituary*, p. 78.
10. Ibid., p. 1.
11. Esteves, *Tropical Rains*, p. 30.
12. Efraín Barradas and Rafael Rodríguez, eds., *Herejes y mitificadores: Muestra de poesía puertorriqueña en los Estados Unidos* (Rio Piedras: Ediciones Huracán, 1980), p. 74.
13. Angel Flores and Kate Flores, eds., *The Defiant Muse: Hispanic Feminist Poems from the Middle Ages to the Present* (New York: Feminist Press, 1986), p. 79.
14. Barradas and Rodríguez, *Herejes y mitificadores*, p. 108. The Spanish in this verse translates into "but I am Latina and do not tolerate your RUBBISH."
15. Sandra María Esteves, *Yerba Buena* (New York: Greenfield Review Press, 1980), p. 82.

In Search of a Muse
The Politics of Gay Poetry

Something unprecedented happend on June 27, 1969. The patrons of the Stonewall Inn—a Greenwich Village gay bar—did not disperse quietly, as the police, after a routine raid, expected them to. One small homosexual population, mostly "Puerto Rican transvestites and young street people," fought back, first with cobblestones, bottles, and coins, and then with an uprooted parking meter which became a battering ram. It managed to trap a number of policemen inside the Stonewall. Flames suddenly appeared in the bar and reinforcements had to be called in—to rescue the police.

Thus began three nights of rioting that have been immortalized—in the hearts and minds of gay and lesbian people around the world, at least—as the Stonewall Rebellion. If Stonewall doesn't constitute the *beginning* of gay liberation (in *Sexual Politics, Sexual Communities* John d'Emilio details the decades of gay and lesbian activism that prepared its way),[1] it certainly precipitated a heating up of organized insurgency in political as well as other arenas. One of those arenas was the cultural.

Gay identities were fleshing themselves out. Just so gay poetry was coming to be. Or was it? In 1982 the *Advocate*, the most widely distributed gay newspaper in the world, wanted to know. Cultural/Associate Editor Mark Thompson commissioned the two essays which follow—Steve Abbott's reflections on West Coast gay poetry and mine on its East Coast complement. They were published together—along with interviews with poets Richard Howard and Paul Mariah and snippets from the work of James Merrill, Edward Field, James Broughton, James Schuyler, Thom Gunn, and Robert Gluck—in a special issue of the *Advocate* which questioned the existence of a "gay muse."[2]

Abbott considers lesbian as well as gay male poets in his survey, which comes equipped with a historical overview. The division I find among East Coast "gay" poets—between politics and art—seems to me paralleled in novelist and cultural commentator Edmund White's antithesis (in *States of Desire: Travels in Gay America*) between gay political radicals and moderates.[3] "Radicals," according to White, "would call for a thorough change of national (and international) institutions and ways of living. The moderates would want gays to swim into the mainstream. Whereas the radical goal is to transform society, the moderate goal is to enter it." And if the question I pose ("What hope is there that the two tiers will become one?") is mirrored in White ("Are the goals incompatible?"), my guarded optimism probably comes from him too. "Yes, of course" the goals are incompatible, he declares, "but at this moment, at least, I see no reason the two groups can't work together." My hope of a cultural reconciliation? Such as it is, it seems to rest with "Lady Day, the woman in us all."

R.K.

East by Rudy Kikel

Three strikes were against me. Was I out? I certainly hadn't got to first base. At least that was how I felt as I began receiving responses to a "gay poetry" questionnaire I had sent to some twenty East Coast gay male poets and critics, some of whom I knew personally and some of whom were slated to read their work at "Glad Fridays," the visiting gay writers' series I organized in Boston at the gay bookstore Glad Day. First off, I had asked my correspondents if they *were* gay poets. And while they were about it, is there an East or West Coast gay poetry? One from New York City, Boston, Washington, D.C., Philadelphia, or the South? What, by the way, did they think of the notion promulgated and defended by *Gay Sunshine* editor Winston Leyland that there has been "especially since Stonewall" a "Gay Cultural Renaissance" that has been "of equal importance to other literary movements (such as the Beat) of the second half of the 20th century"? Other comments?

The first notion to fall was that of my generic word *poet*. Ian Young, the Canadian poet—er, writer—who lives part-time in New York City, didn't like it: "When someone says to me, 'Come and meet so-&-so; he's a poet,' my first reaction is either 'Poor wretch!' or 'Isn't everyone?' 'Poetry' sounds, unfortunately, anachronistic and pompous. Rather like being a marquis or a G-man. I write other things as well and would rather be known as just a writer."

So much for *poet*. Then Edmund White chipped away—working from left to right—at my second term, *gay*: "I think that before one can answer the question is there a gay poetry, one must first ask, are there gay people, a question Michel Foucault has raised again in the last few years. . . . Foucault has argued that *homosexuality* itself is a Victorian term invented by heterosexuals in order to 'medicalize' sexuality in general and homosexuality in particular. Previously, one might have been a doer of homosexual acts, one might have made love *homosexually*, but one was not oneself *a* homosexual (the word was an adverb but not a noun or even an adjective). Have we allowed desire to be quarantined, by medicalizing it?"

My notion of a "Genius of Place" fared little better than "poet" or "gay." It started to crumble—in my own eyes—in the light of poets' deliberate attempts, perhaps in deference to my silly questionnaire, to prop it up. So Tom Meyer allowed that a "sensuality" he saw as his "aesthetic" had been "nourished" in the South (he lives in Highlands, North Carolina)—"though I'm not much clearer than that about its influences." And Chasen Gaver ventured that in Washington, D.C., "more poems are written about interpersonal questions than about 'abstract' ideas" as a "reaction to the abstractions of everyday life in a city that compiles data for the rest of the nation." But poets Meyer and Gaver would probably be the first to agree that "sensuality" and "interpersonality" are not exclusive to their regions.

Some poets, I thought, do what *I* do—entertain fantasies not so much about where I live but about other places, ripe for projection because they are more mysterious. So Ron Schreiber, who doesn't think the work of the Boston poets he knows are gay "could be grouped together in anything but mutual sexual preference," offered this proposition about San Francisco: "Longer hippydom, slower pace, small city—I suppose these and other things (like proximity to big nature) make many S.F. poets different from poets on this coast." What is mysterious can also be ominous; other-place projections can be negative ones. Asked if there were a West Coast poetry, Bostonian Walta Borawski replied, "Yes, but I've never liked it." Sometimes a poet's projection justified staying in place: Meyer feels he needs "an epicurean tension that I can't find possible on that other, laid-back coast."

And as if to balance the ledger, negative West Coast fantasies about the East Coast were *themselves* entertained by an East Coast writer. Asked if there were an East Coast poetry, J. D. McClatchy suggested I "ask a poet—or better yet, a poetoid—who lives in San Francisco. *They've* made up the conspiracy, and the tiresome code words: *academic, elitist, repressive, obscure, smart, crafted.*"

White, the traveloguer of gay America, offered the only full-scale dichotomy and, I thought, a measured one, constituted as it is of two equally desirable ambiences: "East is more formal, more reserved, more given to traditional verse patterns, more indebted to the visionary strain of Emerson and Wallace Stevens, whereas West is more casual, more demotic in its allusions, more given to the William Carlos Williams tradition." But these are "large and rather vague regional differences," White writes—to be qualified, it is to be presumed, in the particular. And after all, when they were asked to list influences on their own East Coast work, poets Schreiber, Jack Anderson, Felice Picano, and David Eberly listed Oriental poetry or Williams among them. "Think of William Carlos Williams as 'West Coast,'" Borawski muses: "Impossible."

How are we to think of *anybody* as anywhere! That's the problem with a poetry of place. Cross-fertilization, first off, obscures the model, as Tim Dlugos argues: "So San Francisco poet Steve Benson is a language-centered artist with as many connections to New York as to the West; Dennis Cooper's own work is heavily influenced by New York, not the traditional Bukowski poetics of his native Los Angeles; Allen Ginsberg," who is often identified with New York City, "invented Beat Poetry while living in San Francisco." Then, what place do we give credit for a poet's achievement, that of his origin, a stop on the way, or his eventual destination? Robert Frost was born in California (Charley Shively reminds me), Frank O'Hara in Worcester, Massachusetts. Finally, even when a poet believes "literature cannot help reflecting the milieu from which it springs," as Anderson does, he is struck by diversity of style in the work of the regional poets with which he is familiar—as Anderson is in the work of O'Hara, John Ashbery, and James Schuyler, "original" members of the so-called New York School. No wonder Jonathan Williams ("O dear o dear, R.K., I fear you have asked the wrong poet"), in response to my questionnaire, cited lines from another poet, Robert Creeley: "There is no such thing as place, except as it exists within a given man."

Of course one way the notion of place survives is when it is qualified, as here by Picano: "I don't think geographical location means much in poetry . . . but *social* location does." And as if to illustrate Picano's point, here is veteran New York poet, librettist, and publisher Kenward Elmslie: "N.Y.C. was great because of the special friendships possible in it—with Frank O'Hara, John Ashbery, et cetera. Jimmy Schuyler too. And certain painters like Alex Katz. And Joe Brainard. Anne Waldman. Vermont is great (half-a-year at a time) because of the extreme isolation and independence this gives me. Not only is there no gay scene involving other poets, there's NO scene—at least none I'm part of."

None of the tags in my questionnaire escaped scrutiny, qualification, or criticism by some poet or critic. Least of all did the combination term *gay poetry*. At least with *East Coast, gay,* and *poetry* (taken singularly) there was little problem of definition. Everyone seems to agree about where the East Coast is! Is poetry "gay" when it's written by a gay man about his "personal life" (as Joe Brainard implies), on gay subjects or themes (Picano), or when it's addressed to a gay audience (critic Robert Martin)? Definitions abounded and often determined a writer's embrace or rejection of the phrase. So Elmslie, who thinks he "would have to write much more about sex" than he does to be considered a gay poet, feels he is a "poet, period." And Anderson "can't help being a gay poet" because a gay man who writes poetry *is* one, in his view, "no matter what themes" he may explore.

The sands kept shifting around me, or self-definitions did. Was some pattern emerging? I noticed this: how often discussion of the subject of "gay poetry" elicited statements of commitment—to something or other. The something was culture. Poet Alfred Corn's responsibility is to "writing," he said, no matter what labels or rubrics others applied to his work; for Corn, furthermore, "if you place constraints of any sort on an artist, you weaken the enspiriting example of self-realization that surely has been at the heart of all liberation movements." The other was politics. Schreiber's calling himself a "gay poet" is a "political statement and an affirmation of [himself] as a member of an oppressed minority," which has the advantage of "freeing a writer not to have to worry about the issue, from pronouns to anything else" in his life.

Two opposing positions seemed to define themselves in the carpet of my correspondence, constituting, I would suggest, that carpet's emerging "figure," which depicted a conflict between politics and art. Concerning the root of the problem, poet critics Shively and McClatchy—one with a Ph.D. from Harvard, the other with one from Yale—are not far apart. (Schreiber: "Be wary of academics with theories, however.") McClatchy thinks a "gay artist is put into an unusual relationship with the English language, whose diction, syntax, and range is heterosexual, like most of our literary heritage." Here is Shively on language's "heterosexual" diction and syntax:

> Grammarians instruct us that every sentence is composed of a subject and a predicate. Basically the subject fucks the object; fucking (the verb of action) is the most important part of the sentence. Everything in the sentence is subordinate to this fucking. Adjectives are considered inconsequential ornaments, and careful (male) writers are warned to use them sparingly if they don't want to appear faggy or effeminate. Likewise, avoid adverbs and anything gaudy. With objects or lesser indirect objects you can do anything you want; the more forceful your thrust the better. "Simple" sentence structure is considered the most manly form in American construction. And you are advised to avoid the passive voice at all costs. Concentrate on the action: Dick runs; Sally is watching; and no dykes or faggots appear. (Puff is actually a drag queen, but that too has been suppressed.)

Thus far, McClatchy and Shively just might find areas of agreement, but they soon diverge. Here is Shively: "To be free, faggots must destroy the very language we speak and write. Because that language (and the culture it embodies) are at the very core oppressive and heterosexual." Where Shively counsels subversion ("linguistic terrorism"), McClatchy sees a creative challenge: "Any poet learns to twist language for expressive purposes; for a gay artist this is a more difficult and exhilarating business." Shively, whose remarks along with much of his poetry are in the counterculture periodical *Fag Rag* (see Fall 1978) and are specifically addressed to a gay audience, is convinced that conventional art encourages racism and sexism and that "we faggots need to avoid traditional forms altogether and keep searching among the avant-garde works for ways out of the linguistic binds." But for McClatchy, whose "Establishment" credentials are impressive, "unless poetry by gays identifies itself with the imagination and with the major traditions of English verse—instead of with a political struggle or soft-core literalism—there is no chance of its surviving, or of revising any reader's sense of what poetry can do and see and feel."

Both of these positions reflect real fears: of being culturally absorbed (Shively), of being historically erased (McClatchy). And both reflect disturbing risks taken. The risk of a political art is that it will no longer *be* art. In his often reprinted 1975 essay on "The Poetry of Male Love," Ian Young is not so much a "linguistic terrorist" as Shively, but he admires the new poets of "gay liberation" for tending to "identify more with the gay community than with the literary community" and for being "in the main more interested" in what Young calls "a life-oriented poetry than in academism, technical 'experimentation' for its own sake, or purely literary concerns." But according to sociologist Peter Berger in *Facing Up to Modernity*,[4] when members of a youth culture, in order not to be complicit in a corrupt "system," become permanent members of a counterculture and forgo "the higher positions in modern society," what results is "downward social mobility" for the dropouts and "room at the top" for someone else. Are some gay poets, too, in the interest of a "correct" politics and a new gay community, deserting the "purely literary" field and forgoing niches in literary history like those a perhaps less politically savvy past generation of poets, our pre-Stonewall poets, have secured for themselves? Martin, for one, thinks that "gay poetry written for gays alone is the stuff of Consciousness Raising—probably very useful but not really art." More poignant still is the vision of gay poets deserting literary fields for a "community" that may not be there! McClatchy tells of recently meeting

> a gay poet from San Francisco. He is frank, sweet, committed. He has publised a book of poems—wistful lyrics, with no capital letters, and line-drawings of demure rimmings and flowered crotches. (In other words, like most gay-identified poetry written today, it smacks of the '40's. Auden had enough sense to compose his "Platonic Blow" in light verse—and then to suppress it!) The poet had also written a play—based, he said, on The Street ("the only true gay community"). When the play was produced,

he offered free tickets to the hustlers on whom he'd based his characters. None showed up—and he is still, sadly, perplexed. That is because he, like too many gay poets, does not recognize his true audience, or confuses it with his "material."

On the other hand, the risk in a "pure" literature is that it will pass over political realities. In his pathbreaking book *The Homosexual Tradition in American Poetry,* Robert Martin claims gay poets "have no longer felt an impetus to establish a connection between their sexuality and their political views" because "being homosexual is no longer likely to make one lose one's job."[5] "While this may have resulted in a loss of political fervor," Martin concludes, "it has also meant an extension of the forms of gay poetry." Literary concerns—an "extension of the forms"—are thus linked to a diminished need for surveillance. But here is McClatchy, putting us on political guard and divorcing us from "purely literary" concerns *again*, perhaps despite himself:

> I taught at Yale, in the English Department, for several years.
> One expects a certain percentage of gays in any English Department—or rather one counts on them: they're usually the best teachers. At Yale, with an English Department of nearly a hundred, there were three gays on its faculty, and I was the only one out. That statistic says something about a hiring (and firing) policy. I know, not just because of the statistic but because I tried to propose a course called "Homosexuality and Literature." Oh, I eventually taught the course, and it was duly listed in the catalogue. . . . it took me *two years* to fight through committee-opposition to get the course approved—and, some years later, after I'd been let go by Yale, I was told by sympathetic insiders, that my being gay (or, in their words, "pushy about it") got me canned. One is glad to be gone from such an atmosphere—*and* glad to know why. I wouldn't want to pretend it isn't tough on all sorts of people, but I'd still insist that it's easier to *be* cruel to gays.

Shively, I would say, is more solicitous of his "gayness" than he is of the full resources of poetry, while McClatchy's defense of poetry might be at the expense of some radical implications—*in his work*—of "gayness." (Unless every break with silence is itself radical!) "I have written gay poems," McClatchy says, "but I am *not* a gay poet. Some poems are 'responsible' to my sexuality, many others are not. All of them, I hope, are responsible to language and form." Of course the phrase *gay poet* is not entirely fissionable: none of my correspondents defend only one and not the other of its constituent terms. Corn, who has reason to believe heterosexual readers find his poems "useful," is "very much in favor of gay liberation," while Eberly, who writes "first for a gay audience," doesn't see that commitment as literarily disruptive: for him the term *gay poetry* is a "political term, not a creative or critical one." Certain questions, however, continue to be answered in opposite ways: Should poetry sacrifice its traditional "universality" for a political commitment? Must poetry not reflect the light to which "gay liberation" has opened our eyes? The confrontation between politics and art, I would argue, is one that Stonewall has only intensified for gay men writing poetry on the East Coast. It may even have occasioned two *separate* poetries, audiences, and lines of access to publication. Ed Hermance, the proprietor of Giovanni's Room, Philadelphia's gay bookstore, writes about his city's "two-tiered" gay poetry scene:

> On top is a goodly group of people who would prefer to be called poets. For whatever reasons they don't like to read for specifically gay audiences, and they prefer that their books appear in the feminist rather than in the lesbian and gay section of our bookstore. They help run *The American Poetry Review*, *The Painted Bride Quarterly*, and the *Philadelphia Poets Newsletter*. They review for the *Philadelphia Inquirer*, *The New York Times*, et cetera. A lot of them are in my opinion very good. They even write gay poetry. . . . The more fundamental tier is formed of the rabble-rousers and movement people.

What hope is there that the two tiers will become one? Not much. Nor is it required. There is, however, a surprising area of agreement. Shively thinks "the introduction and selections of Louise Bernikow's anthology *The World Split Open* should encourage anyone trying to write poetry outside the straitjacket. Bernikow includes selections from Blues singers Ma Rainey, Bessie Smith, Ida Cox & Memphis Minnie." And he adds: "What would John Wieners or Frank O'Hara be without Billie Holiday?" What were the influences on McClatchy's poetry? "Milton, Keats, Crane, Stevens, Merrill, Hollander, Corn. And singers too, like Billie Holiday." Indeed, according to White,

> in self-styled "gay poetry," no matter where it's written in America today, there are striking similarities of tone, design, subject matter. The gay poem is most often a love lyric, addressed to the

beloved—a confession or an avowal or a lament or an elegy.
The most influential models seem to me the early love poems of
Auden and the Rae Dalven translations of Cavafy and the lyrics
of pop songs, especially sad old ballads of the Billie Holiday
variety.

Perhaps that is the place to start, or to keep going: with Lady Day, the
woman in us all. With Billie Holiday and with the dedication and
enthusiasm of Jack Anderson: "It is often difficult to write of gay themes
without sounding mannered, awkward, hesitant, 'dirty,' preachy, or
merely 'camp.' Yet to try to find a vocabulary and to build a gay poetic
tradition can be a very exciting and necessary undertaking. Certainly, if
this derives from a post-Stonewall gay 'Renaissance,' then I am proud to
be even a small part of it."

West by Steve Abbott

"A gay poem is a poem that sleeps with other poems."
Chuckling over this tongue-in-cheek definition by William Barber a
few years ago, I began thinking of the deeper questions it raised. Does
such a thing as "gay poetry" actually exist, and, if so, what is it? To
what extent, if any, have gay poets helped shape the social or imaginative identity of the West Coast gay community?

Over thirty gay poets—young and old, men and women, and repre-
senting a cross section of ethnic backgrounds—responded to these
questions with a great diversity of viewpoints. Harold Norse, termed
"the American Catullus" by an earlier *Advocate* critic, feels gay poetry
definitely does exist and that its role is "to affirm the reality and naturalness of homoerotic love."

Lyn Lonidier, whose first book was entitled *Lesbian Estate*, says, "I
think we must now create a whole new vocabulary that goes beyond
categories such as gay and straight, feminist and sexist." Today Lonidier calls herself an "allsexual." Lesbian poet and publisher Noni
Howard tends to agree: "Most gay writing fails because it doesn't have
the qualities of universal art. With a few exceptions, such as Judy
Grahn, Adrienne Rich, James Broughton, and Robert Duncan, gay
poetry is sectarian and deals only with its own issues."

Responds Robert Gluck: "That's like saying to Isaac Bashevis Singer,

'Isaac, how about some Gentile stories?' Better to start with the experience of our own community. Then, through this experience, we bring in the rest of the world. If there is a universal, that's how good writing gets to it."

Aaron Shurin, one of the founders of gay male poetry in the early 1970s, sees not just one kind of poetry today but many. "Diversity is the key to our evolutionary strength," Shurin says. "I'm part of the gay community, but I'm part of many other communities as well. I think my writing reflects this." But before we can explore the diversity of gay poetry in 1982 or speculate on its future directions, we must first consider its long, rich history.

Few walking past the Sunset library in San Francisco would recognize the name Charles Warren Stoddard carved in its stone facade. Stoddard was a poet protégé of Bret Harte in the 1870s and later a secretary for Mark Twain. One of America's first openly homoerotic writers, Stoddard carried on a lively correspondence with Walt Whitman.

Although Whitman never came west himself, he gave warm encouragement to young avant-garde feminist and homosexual writers who did. Homosexual? Actually, no positive term for same-sex love existed in Whitman's day, so in *Democratic Vistas* he attempted to create one. "Adhesive love," he called it, "that fervid comradeship . . . at least rivaling the amative love hitherto possessing imaginative literature, if not going beyond it."

Though Whitman's vocabulary never caught on (the term *gay* later appeared in a story published in 1926 by lesbian poet Gertrude Stein, born in Oakland), he prophetically realized that those inclined to same-sex love were a nascent community and, as a counterpart to heterosexuals, were necessary for "the spiritual health of America's democracy." Whitman sang the beauties of same-sex love in his own poetry and exerted great influence on later West Coast gay poets such as Duncan, Norse, and Thom Gunn, to name a few.

Elsa Gidlow wrote openly of lesbian love in the 1920s, but even as late as the early 1950s, when lesbian and homosexual poets such as Duncan, Broughton, Madeline Gleason, Jack Spicer, and Robin Blaser wrote openly of their sexuality, there was still no thought of this being "gay poetry." "I remember Robert Duncan wearing eye make-up and jewelry in those days," Broughton recalls, "but 'gay poetry'? We just didn't think in those terms. We were just writing about our lives."

This was after Duncan's controversial essay "The Homosexual in Society" had appeared in the magazine *Politics* in answer to charges that his poetry was somehow "unmanly." Duncan had grown up in Bakersfield, California, attended UC Berkeley, and lived for a time in New York City, where he was part of Anais Nin's circle. He returned to California and became one of the leaders of the San Francisco Renaissance poetry movement.

As always, West Coast poetry was more experimental, bold, and sexually open than that back east. Duncan was the first to use the word *cocksucker* in a poem. In 1955 his play *Faust Foutu* was performed at Gallery Six; the script called for Duncan to strip naked as he delivered lines such as these:

> . . . In the wet hairy pits of sweat I address you, in the meaty, fruity, fish-sopping odours of sex, I adore you. By cunt, by mouth, by cock, by ass-hole I invoke you. Eternal sexual garden. By suck, by lick, by taste, by tongue, by smell, by nose, by sweat, by piss, by spittle, by shit, O eternal Magician of the ages, I invoke you. . . .

Duncan claims that when Allen Ginsberg saw the play he got the idea to strip during readings of his own poem *Howl*, which was first read at Gallery Six a year later.

More than anyone else, perhaps, Ginsberg thrust homosexuality onto the map of public consciousness in America. *Howl* exploded poetry out of small bohemian salons and into court (the first printed edition of the poem was seized by the police for being obscene) and finally into the pages of *Life* magazine. In the mid 1960s, he traveled through India, Europe, and much of America giving poetry readings.

In 1967, as the editor of a campus literary magazine, I invited Ginsberg to the University of Nebraska in Lincoln for a reading. Over five thousand people crammed into the Student Union Ballroom to hear him, many of them fraternity jocks just looking for a reason to stomp this "dope-smoking, antiwar, fag poet." Ginsberg completely won them over.

Never again would I think of poetry as boring or irrelevant. Never again would I equate homosexuality with cowardice. Despite the guilt over his sexuality implied in some of his writing, the image of Ginsberg bravely facing down that crowd of macho thugs with nothing but the sincerity and beauty of his words would later give me the courage to come out publicly myself.

Meanwhile, San Francisco was giving birth to a new movement, the hippies. *Vanguard*, edited by Keith St. Clair in the Haight-Ashbury neighborhood, and *Sebastian Quill*, edited by Jim Mitchell in the Western Addition, appeared briefly to celebrate poems of same-sex love. Then, in 1969, *Manroot* was born, and in 1970 *Gay Sunshine*. Both went on to become internationally famous presses for gay writing.

Following the 1969 Stonewall riots in New York City, self-proclaimed "gay poets" across urban America began working collectively in gay liberation groups. In Wolf Creek, Oregon, *RFD*, a magazine for gay men living in the country, appeared. Lesbian magazines and presses also flourished: *The Ladder, Country Women, Calyx, Sinister Wisdom, The 13th Moon*, Diana Press, and Shameless Hussy Press are just a few.

In San Francisco itself, Paul Mariah became the crusading voice for "gay poetry" in the late 1960s and early 1970s. Tede Matthews and lesbian poet Pat Parker remember Mariah as a significant gay voice in the Bay Area poetry scene. Being more spread out geographically, Los Angeles had no concentrated poetry community in the early 1970s, but Leland Hickman remembers Joseph Hansen, Robert Peters, and George Drury Smith (who had just started Beyond Baroque) as poets who emphasized gay content in their work.

The zenith of West Coast gay male poetry occurred in the mid to late 1970s. On the occasion of his second gay poetry anthology, *Orgasms of Light*, Winston Leyland filled Glide Memorial Church for a Gay Sunshine Benefit. Along with established poets such as Ginsberg and Norse, younger gay poets such as Gluck and Dennis Cooper, who had just started his *Little Caesar* magazine in Los Angeles, riveted the crowd of over one thousand.

Lesbian poets such as Grahn and Susan Griffin, who read separately from men at this time, drew large, enthusiastic crowds of women to their readings. Said Grahn at the Left Write Conference in San Francisco last year: "Left organizations were hopelessly sexist. [We] joined women's consciousness-raising groups, but when discussion of our lesbianism paralyzed our straight sisters, we dropped out and . . . formed, defined, and acted out lesbian separatism. For the first time we had a voice of our own and we used it loud and clear. We were a mixture of races and classes and used separatism as a *tool*, not as a way of life."

San Francisco gay readings in the late 1970s began to include lesbians and gay men on the same lineup, but not without some discussion. Margaret Sloan strongly criticized a "drag" poem read by Matthews at a gay benefit organized during the fight against the Briggs initiative. Duncan and Karen Brodine defended Matthews' poem. A year later, pandemonium broke loose at a gay reading organized by Howard and David Emerson Smith over a poem read by Norse. Norse was accused of being racist and imperialist.

"I'll admit I didn't have a very highly developed feminist consciousness in some of my earlier poetry," Norse says, "but I've never been racist or imperialist." Anyone who knows the whole of his work or has looked carefully at the poem in question would have to agree. Equally disturbing is a recent effort by a group of white socialists in Los Angeles to get Grahn's *Work of a Common Woman* removed from the Los Angeles Public Library on the grounds that the book is racist. Lesbian poets of color have rightfully come to Grahn's defense.

In the early 1970s, the lesbian and gay community found it necessary to confront greater American society with one voice; the militant "gay is good" theme in poetry was perhaps a historic necessity. Now that the gay and lesbian movements have grown more powerful, gay and lesbian writers are exploring and emphasizing greater diversity.

While this is positive, in that it gives poets more leeway to examine what being gay or being human means, it also makes it more difficult for gay writers to reach their audience. A strong network of women's centers and bookstores has kept lesbian poets in touch with their audience, for example, allowing Rich to draw over one thousand people to a recent reading she gave in San Francisco, but many gay male presses and magazines have either folded or have had to cut back on the amount of poetry they publish.

Both younger and older gay poets express concern about this. Says poet-critic Robert Peters: "At one time I thought gays would be attentive to their own culture as a manifestation of superior gifts. But I don't see that that has happened. Few turn up at poetry readings. Books of gay poetry don't sell well—stack sales up against *Meat* and *Flesh*, for example." Peters notes that while there's a vibrant gay student group at UC Irvine, only one or two gay men enrolled in his gay lit course. Most who attended were straight women.

Avotcja, a black lesbian poet whose first book, *Ache*, is forthcoming from Howard's New World Press, feels the main support for her work comes from the Latino and black communities. "I'm not sure I can depend on white gays," Avotcja says. Part of the reason for this is racism, she feels, and part because of "self-hatred on the part of many gays."

Notes Los Angeles poet Peter Cashorali, "My general impression is that nobody reads poetry or is even aware that it's a form that contains life." At the same time Cashorali feels a poem celebrating cruising or gay domestic life should make gays "feel more substantial to read about their private lives." Brodine agrees, adding: "Coming from a rural background, I was in isolation until I discovered there were words for my feelings, and thus my feelings could become real."

Arizona poet/editor Will Inman concurs. "We need to help homosexuals get beyond guilt and low self-esteem," he says, but he fears the "suicide" of gay ghettoization as an equal danger. "I'm afraid I feel there's as much selfishness and narrowness among gays as among any other element in society. Urging emphasis on our differentness more than on our humanity only plays along with our emptiness."

Gay poets have attempted to solve the problem of audience by creating new groupings or audiences within the greater gay community, by connecting to sympathetic nongay audiences, or both.

Cooper, whose first book *Idols* was a poetry best-seller, has brought together a post-Stonewall generation of poets in his magazine *Little Caesar* and his anthology *Coming Attractions*. Publishing younger East Coast poets as well as older, famous, nongay poets whom Cooper likes, *Little Caesar* also features spunky essays on rock music and film. But Cooper still believes gay poets have a duty to build community, and he is thinking of starting a reading series in the hustler section of Hollywood known as Boystown.

Aleida Rodriguez and Jacqueline di Angelis have teamed up to give a voice to lesbian poetry in Los Angeles with their exceptional magazine *rara avis*. Along with Eloise Klein Healy and others, they put on events at the Women's Building in downtown Los Angeles. Paul Monette, Clifton Snider, and Gavin Dillard are among the gay male poets active in the Los Angeles area.

In San Francisco, Matthews and Randy Johnson helped found Mainstream Exiles, a collective of lesbian and gay artists, musicians, and poets. Besides sponsoring readings, art shows, and workshops, they plan to publish a poetry anthology soon. Matthews also runs a reading series at Modern Times Bookstore, which features a large number of lesbian and gay poets.

Eric Allyn recently advertised another gay writers' network in Bay Area gay papers. Over forty people have attended its first four meetings at the Valencia Rose Cafe. Subgroups meet to discuss play writing and fiction as well as poetry; according to Loren Rhoads, about fifteen people attend the poetry subgroup. Some network members have attended workshops that aren't manifestly gay, but "when you have gay theme pieces, it's more comfortable to discuss them in a gay group," Rhoads says. Groups that support lesbian poets include the Feminist Writer's Guild and the Women Writer's Union.

Other gay poets prefer working alone and don't care to center their writing around the subject of sexuality. Ronald Johnson is one such in San Francisco; Robert Crosson another in Los Angeles. "I am cautious," says Crosson. "I distrust politics, any politics. I am suspicious of fashion. Gay rights is imperative. That has nothing to do with poetry. Poetry to me is a private affair."

Gunn would more or less agree. While some of his poetry concerns gay subject matter and he has given several interviews to gay publications, Gunn prefers not to be labeled as "a gay poet for the same reason I don't want to be labeled a nature poet or a city poet. I'm an everything poet."

Whether working alone or in groups, West Coast gay poets are exploring many new forms and directions. "The gay poet is the keeper of mythology and also the theorist of the future," says Jim Washington, who has performed his work to music. "Some poets have the ability to imbue personal symbols with a mysterious perfume projecting new connections."

Some of the new connections are political, and some involve technology and theater. Shurin, Steve Benson, and Richard Irwin have incorporated slides, film, tape recorders, music, spontaneous raps, or theatrical settings to extend their poetry beyond the format of the "traditional reading." Irwin has become an important promotor of performance art in the Bay area.

Bruce Boone, however, thinks the devices of Postmodernism, if "not rooted in the social origins of language" are often ambiguous. "The point is not to speak *for* but *through* one's community," Boone said in a recent interview in *City Arts Monthly*. Boone feels the new project for gay writers is to incorporate "the aspirations and indignations of those with whom [we are] engaged in an ongoing dialogue."

Randy Johnson thinks "lesbian and Third World gay poets will be heard more in the future" and notes "the increasing exploration of eroticism" in lesbian writing. Brodine also foresees "an increased forging of connections" between radical feminists, feminist men, and writers of color. "Only in activism, in a willingness to stand together on the picket line, have our words of courage taken the substantial, real edge. I think it could happen a whole lot more." Peters sees a "vast improvement in poetry by gays. It used to be that much of it sounded like insipid high-school boy turn-on stuff."

Despite the advances gay poetry has made in recent years, homophobia and even censorship from straight critics and editors are still a problem. Almost all lesbian and gay writers I talked to had experienced at least one such incident.

While openly gay writers such as Grahn, Ginsberg, Aleida Rodriguez, and Peter Orlovsky have received NEA grants, most have not. When Bruce Boone queried NEA as to why he was denied a grant, two of the four panelists judging his work alluded to its homosexual content. One comment read: "Very well written story about the breakup of a love affair which we learn halfway through is a homosexual one. Unfortunately, it is at that point the broad appeal a narrative such as this one might have becomes severely limited." The sole criterion for the awarding of grants is supposed to be "the literary quality of the manuscript submitted."

Houghton-Mifflin wanted a manuscript from Leland Hickman, but when they saw more of his work, they decided it was "too sexual" (90 percent of the material was gay, says Hickman). When Hickman's *Great Slave Lake Suite* came out from Momentum Press, it was nominated by the *Los Angeles Times* for a poetry prize in the 1980 Book Prizes. The book later received several homophobic reviews, inspiring Cashorali to comment, "Whenever I hear heterosexuals talking about gays, I have visions of peasants with pitchforks."

David Trinidad has never been physically threatened at a reading, as Hickman has, but he says that once, when he was reading poems on the radio, a woman phoned the radio station and complained his poems were obscene. "As I hadn't used any of the words ordinarily

considered obscene," Trinidad says, "I assume it was the subject matter—in this case gay—that she considered offensive."

But most gay poets refuse to be intimidated by homophobia. Says
Native American Paula Gunn Allen: "I get homophobia and racist
responses and all sorts of crap, but I get even more empowerment and
validation from those audiences/editors who hear me and use my work
in their lives, criticism, and classes." Cooper finds his work "is taken
pretty seriously on its own terms by straights, that the sex in the poems
seems universal"; he adds that he feels "gratified and honored by letters
I've gotten from young gays who've said that *Idols* had a profound effect
on their self-acceptance as gays."

Despite all the difficulties and aesthetic disagreements, gay poets
will no doubt continue to write, and San Francisco and Los Angeles
will no doubt continue to be the major centers of writing and publishing activity for West Coast gay and lesbian poets. In the words of Aaron
Shurin: "Gay poetries will continue as long as the issue of homosexuality remains embattled in the society at large, which will probably be
a long time. After that there will only be poetry. Ultimately we have a
community of souls, or hearts, and the poet's light lights up matters of
deep integrity in living. The free reign of the imagination can only
further unlock all [closet] doors."

Update 1985

Much has happened in Bay Area gay poetry since I wrote this
survey. A number of new gay magazines have surfaced. My own, *Soup*, while
not exclusively gay, has featured interviews, poems, and fiction by numerous
West Coast poets such as Robert Duncan, Robert Gluck, Dennis Cooper,
Karen Brodine, and others. *Soup 3*, a translation issue, brought forward the
work of gay writing pioneers René Crevel (France) and Eric Muhsam (Germany) to an English reading audience for the first time.

In 1983, Bryan Monte began *No Apologies*, which connected new and
older Bay Area gay writers to Vancouver poets formerly of Jack Spicer's circle
(for example, Robin Blaser, George Stanley). Also, the work of lesbian poets
Dodie Bellamy, Judy Grahn, and Marilyn Hacker appeared along with that of
gay male writers.

When Monte won a graduate creative writing fellowship to Brown University and moved his magazine back east, his associate editor Kevin Killian

began *Mirage*. Issue one was a festschrift to John Weiners on the legendary poet's fiftieth birthday and in celebration of his *Collected Poems* (Black Sparrow) edited by Raymond Foye. Dodie Bellamy guest edited an issue on new experimental writing by women.

Sam D'Allessandro is typical of the new, younger gay writers in that he works in both poetry and prose. His narratives have a cinematic rather than lineal or logocentric drive. "I like to see something that seems definite dissolved by a look from a different angle," D'Allessandro says. "I like people to take stands but I don't like it when they put answers on things that don't have answers."

Notes

1. John d'Emilio, *Sexual Politics, Sexual Communities* (Chicago: 1983).
2. *Advocate*, May 13, 1982.
3. Edmund White, *States of Desire: Travels in Gay America* (New York: Dutton, 1980).
4. Peter Berger, *Facing Up to Modernity* (New York: Basic Books, 1977).
5. Robert Martin, *The Homosexual Tradition in American Poetry* (Austin: University of Texas Press, 1979).

Breaking Out with the Pen
Poetry in American Prisons

Few experiences are as jarring as legal incarceration. Stripped by the state of your possessions, isolated from contact with the everyday world, you become one virtually reborn—or at least cast into a place which, like Dante's Purgatory, is halfway between your final death and the memories of your former life. There, removed from the familiar sights and sounds of your former life, those memories may take on a life of their own. Small wonder that the experience of prison throughout history has turned men of action into introspective writers, transforming the soldier Cervantes into the creator of Don Quixote and prompting the violent Thomas Malory to recreate the chivalrous dreams of Arthur and his knights. The relatively modern term "penitentiary," in fact, comes from the Quakers' idea that a person isolated in a cell can consider the deeds of his or her life, repent, and change for the better.

Though the prisons of contemporary America are a far cry from both the dungeons of medieval Europe and that first concept of the penitentiary as a collection of monastic cells, they are still separate realities from the American culture most of us know. Although there is a great deal of truth in the old prison maxim that "Everything you can find on the street—from drugs and booze to sex—can be found in the joint," it is also true that none of those things are quite the same in a prison as they are on the street. Even a good part of the everyday

286

language spoken by men and women behind bars differs from that of the majority society, though that majority society continually is absorbing (in small doses) words and phrases which originate in the constantly changing body of prison slang. While teaching writing workshops in an upstate New York prison in the late 1970s I helped Michael Baynard, one of my inmate students, put together a small dictionary of prison slang. Here are a few entries:

> *Ace*: nickname for a male. Best friend; a first-rate person; one's lover.
> *Ain't got one of somethin' and two of nothin'*: I have no money.
> A *shot (or "A shot at life")*: chance to make parole.
> *Bogart (used as a verb)*: to forcibly take something, to bully, to act in a forceful manner.
> *Booty Bandit*: a man who craves intercourse with boys.
> *Bozo-fro*: an Afro hair-do with a bald spot in the center caused by hair loss.
> *Back up and live*: a profound threat.
> *Box*: carton of cigarettes; food package sent to someone in prison; tape player.
> *San Dusty*: death. (San Dusty Express: instant death.)
> *Sap Rap*: words which sound good but have no real meaning.
> *Short*: a car; a cigarette.
> *Skid bid*: a "short" sentence. (In city jails, a year or less. In state prisons, five years or less.)
> *Slam*: prison.

As those random samples indicate, the world within the walls is a complex and often violent one. It is, especially when one considers the current images of law-breakers which we see each day in the newspapers, in the movies, and on TV, hardly a place where one might expect to find poets.

Poetry, however, sent me to prison, not as an inmate, but as a teacher. A few months after the infamous Attica riot and massacre of September 1971, I began teaching a workshop at Great Meadow Correctional facility. From the start I found men who were incredibly responsive to contemporary poetry, even though most of them had no previous experience with it. (Of the more than one hundred men who were part of the workshop over the period of eighteen months, ninety percent had never completed high school, nearly all of those with diplomas had received them through High School Equivalency examinations, and only three had ever attended a college class on the outside.) Within a few months, those in my first class were not only reading contemporary poems and responding to them with warm intelligence, they were writing poems themselves that were both powerful and publishable. I was impressed but wondered if I was being objective until I brought in as a guest someone who had just finished teaching at the New School. "These guys are better than the average college class!" he said.

Like most workshops which dozens of other American writers (including Carolyn Forche, Richard Shelton, Galway Kinnell, John Cheever, and Carol Muske) have conducted in prisons throughout the country over the past decade, that first class of mine was an interesting cross-section of prison types and prison life. The only things they had in common were that they had volunteered to take the workshop and they had an intense desire to express themselves. Of the twenty men, four were white and the rest black. Martin, one of the white inmates, was a Jewish anti–Vietnam War activist jailed for trying to bomb a bank. (He would later, after his release from prison, publish an article about his time in prison in *Crawdaddy* magazine.) Another of the white students, Chip, was a drug addict and wrote science fiction poems and stories. The best dramatic poet in the class, Stephen, had belonged to the Black Panthers. Kihiem, who specialized in ironic verse, was doing time for the murder of a policeman. Eight of my students had been at Attica during the riot and four were still recovering from the gunshot wounds they received when the state police stormed the prison, shooting both inmates and hostages alike. (I still have the rough manuscript which Henry, an older black inmate, gave me for safe-keeping. It contains his account of the Attica rebellion and insists in its last pages that he and a group of thirty other level-headed and more mature black inmates were about to retake the prison from the hotheads to free the hostages and hand back control to the guards before "somebody got crazy and people got hurt.")

In the decade and a half since that first workshop I have taught and visited writing workshops in prisons from Maine to California and corresponded with many serious, dedicated writers in prison from every state in the Union. I have read, published, and helped place in other books and magazines hundreds of poems by inmate and ex-inmate writers. I've compared notes with other writers who've conducted workshops in correctional facilities and found that all of us discovered certain things to be true about the effect of contemporary poetry on people in our prisons. Poetry often deeply touches their lives as soon as they begin to read it. When they begin to write it, poetry becomes an act of personal liberation and a validation, not just of their creativity but of their essential humanity, a humanity diminished or denied by incarceration. "When I'm writing poetry," one of my first inmate students said to me, "I'm not in prison." For some inmates, in fact, poetry has been a means to change their lives. Although talent—whether in prison or in the outside world—is neither a guarantee of success nor some sort of indication of moral virtue, there does seem to be some positive correlation between involvement in writing workshops while in prison and success in returning to society and staying straight after being released from jail. Reformation and personal virtue aside, some of the most powerful poetry I have seen in the last ten years has come out of prisons and has been written by men and women who had no experience with and no interest in poetry prior to being jailed. It may be that, contrary to the dictum that "poetry makes nothing happen," reading and writing poems is a powerful force for bringing out the hidden creative potential, for transformation and growth.

It is, of course, ironic that poetry should be so popular in our prisons. We live in a time which has been described as "post-literate." Television (which is found in prisons, too) has taken the place of reading. Commercial publishers are generally uninterested in poetry. Thus, it may come as a shock to hear that men and women labelled as dangers to society, people who never completed high school in most cases, are deeply committed to both the reading and the writing of contemporary poetry. But it is true. From 1973 to 1985, my wife, Carol, and I operated a program (supported, until the Reagan Era, by the National Endowment for the Arts) which sent donated literary magazines and books of poetry to prison inmates on request. Every six weeks mailings went to over five hundred inmates all over the country on an ever-changing mailing list. We received back thousands of letters (and poems) from them. Here are a few excerpts from some of the letters in our archive which spoke directly of the effect of poetry on their lives:

> I never knew this world [poetry] existed. May Allah bless you for letting me know about it. (Salaam A., Florida State Prison, 1974)

> The books of poetry you sent me have become a lifeline to sanity. (Michael P., Walla Walla State Prison, 1978)

> I'm beginning to see, through poetry, that there are still people in America who care, who won't see me as an animal or sub-human. (Jose L., Marion Federal Prison, 1980)

Certain forms of poetry, though this may not be generally known, have been present in American prisons for many decades. The most common is the "toast," a storytelling, usually humorous poem. These long, memorized toasts are rhymed and syncopated. They are closely connected to Afro-American oral traditions but were recited by black and white inmates alike throughout the United States (although the toast tradition seems to now be dying out in prisons). In a sense, these poems are a sort of prison oral history. They tell of tricksters (sometimes human, like Shine, sometimes animal, like the Signifying Monkey) who are able to survive by using guile and down-home common sense to deceive those more powerful but less clever. The best-known of America's contemporary poets who began writing while in prison is Etheridge Knight. His first book, *Poems from Prison*, was published in 1968 and praised by Gwendolyn Brooks as "a major announcement." A veteran of the Korean War, he became addicted to drugs as a result of the morphine he was given while recovering from his wounds and eventually ended up in prison. He began writing his poems in jail before the advent of prison writing workshops, and the influence of the toast tradition can be seen in his work. His poem "I Sing of Shine" (anthologized in Dudley Randall's landmark 1971 anthology from Bantam, *The Black Poets*) is a direct tribute to the hero of numerous toasts, Shine, the black man whom folk traditions say survived the sinking of the Titanic by being smart enough to swim. It begins with these lines:

> And, yeah, brothers,
> while white/america sings about the unsink
> able molly brown
> (who was hustling the titanic
> when it went down)

I sing to thee of Shine
the stoker who was hip
enough to flee the fucking ship . . .

At this writing, only one major critical study has been published on contemporary writing from American prisons. First published in 1978, *Prison Literature in America* by H. Bruce Franklin traces inmate writing directly back to the slave narratives. The prison, Franklin says, is just a modern version of the slave ship and the plantation. Michael Hogan, a brilliant ex-inmate poet and critic who began writing in the 1970s in the Arizona State Prison workshops taught by Richard Shelton, disagrees with at least part of Franklin's contention. In his article "Some Further Observations on the Convict as Author," published in *New Letters* in 1979, Hogan points out that Franklin's thesis seems to leave out the large part of the prison population which is not black. Writing from prison, Hogan says, is not just a reaction to slavery. It is more complicated than that. In some ways, prisons are a microcosm of American society. The experiences which shape the perceptions of the inmate poet are not that different from those encountered in majority culture. The inmate poet, though, is more clearly on the cutting edge. What is done today to us in the prisons, Hogan says, may be done tomorrow to those of you who think yourselves to be "free."

While in prison, Hogan edited a superb anthology of poems from the Arizona prisons, *Do Not Go Gentle* (Blue Moon Press, 1977). In his introduction to the book he said:

> Many of these strong and beautiful poems have appeared previously in magazines and chapbooks. But I see these poems primarily as weapons of psychic survival and only incidentally as good literature. Each man represented in these pages fought to preserve his identity, his existential wonder, his joy at being alive in the world, his rage at being imprisoned. In doing so he gave courage to others who might have abandoned the fight, might have succumbed as so many before them had, to the darkness of not seeing, not feeling . . .

The winner, while in prison, of a National Endowment for the Arts Poetry Fellowship, Hogan does not, however, fall into the trap of imagining—as did some of the "revolutionaries" of the 1960s—that all prisoners are noble. One of his closest friends in prison, inmate poet

Charles Schmidt, was murdered by other prisoners who bore him an old grudge. Though his strongest identification is with those locked in, Hogan is still able to see the keepers as human. The following lines from his poem "Spring" show both his clarity of vision and his exact touch with image:

> Ice has been cracking all day
> and small boys on the shore
> pretending it is the booming of artillery
> lie prone clutching imaginary carbines . . .
>
> Old cons shiver in cloth jackets
> as they cross the naked quadrangle.
> They know the inside perimeter is exactly
> two thousand eighty-four steps
> and they can walk it five more times
> before the steam whistle blows for count.
>
> Above them a tower guard dips his rifle
> then raises it again dreamily.
> He imagines a speckled trout
> coming up shining and raging with life.

Two decades ago, before the advent of writing workshops in correctional facilities, most of the published writing from prisons tended to be letters, autobiographies, or novels. Many of those books were written by inmates who wanted to both express themselves and make money. Today, with far more poetry being written in prisons and a good deal of it being published in literary magazines (which usually pay only in copies), the average inmate writer is much less mercenary. In fact (as most poets everywhere know), a major commitment to writing poetry is pretty much a *de facto* statement that you are *not* in it for the money. Unlike the isolated inmate working at night in his cell to hand write a novel (which might end up being confiscated by the warden), many of the prison writers of today are in workshops approved of (if not blessed by) the prison administration and conducted by practicing writers. Interestingly, it appears that the worst prison troublemakers often become the best writers. Further, after entering a workshop, they no longer cause trouble in the prison. In California, where a statistically sound study has proven that arts programs in the prisons are cost-effective because they create a safer and more stable environment in the prison with a consequent decrease in spending for such things as guard overtime, the state department of corrections budgets close to a million dollars a year for arts programs in the prisons. Two years ago, in fact, the warden at San Quentin said something like, "Things are pretty tense down in C Block. Looks like we'd better get a poetry workshop going in there." One result of such prison writing workshops has been to not only channel formerly destructive energy into creative channels, but also to produce writers whose work may sometimes be as polished and professional as that of students in graduate writing programs.

Although many workshops have been terminated or threatened because of funding cuts, there are still long-standing programs continuing in more than a dozen states and new ones being started. In Arizona, workshops in the prisons were begun with state funding and coordinated for years by University of Arizona Professor Richard Shelton, whose own poems sometimes reflect the experiences of teaching in prisons. In Pittsburgh, Pennsylvania, the Academy of Prison Arts was founded by inmate writers, coordinated by a civilian employee of the Western State Penitentiary, and funded through grants from the National Endowment for the Arts. In Maine, workshops were started in the state prison by James Lewisohn, a published poet before his incarceration (he was sent to prison for the shooting of his wife—a death which many facts indicate to have been the result of criminal negligence rather than murder). At Attica Prison in New York State workshops have been offered as part of the college program run within the walls by the Consortium of the Niagara Frontier. Florida, Oklahoma, Texas, South Carolina, Alaska, New Mexico, Connecticut, and Ohio all now have or had in the recent past creative writing workshops in their prisons. Since less than 5 percent of the total U.S. prison population of about half a million are women, the majority of inmate poets who've been published are male. Writing workshops have been made available to women inmates much less frequently than to men, but when such opportunities have arisen women have been quick to respond. Carolyn Baxter, a veteran of Carol Muske's poetry workshops in the Riker's Island Prison, and Diana Bickston, who studied with Pamela Stewart in the workshop in the women's prison in Arizona, both have published books of poetry. Here are a few lines from one of Bickston's poems "For Zorro":

>when I read a poem that i feel
>like a taste or smell, lingering to be tried once more,
>i want to write, as if to answer in mouthfuls
>words i could not say . . .

One of the strongest long-standing workshops in an American prison is called "Bright Fires." Founded by Jean Samuel and Sharon Stricker, it still operates in the California Rehabilitation Center for Women. One of several literary magazines published in American prisons, *Poppy*, is edited and published on a yearly basis from the Bright Fires workshops. (Other inmate-edited literary magazines include *Empire* magazine from the Arthur Kill Correctional Facility on Staten Island and *Sentences* from the New Haven, Connecticut, city jail.)

In March of 1980, a graduate student at the University of Colorado, Emmanuel Diel, completed a master's thesis on writers in prison published by the small press and little magazines. His bibliography listed more than seventy individual published volumes and anthologies of poetry by inmates. Today, six years later, that list would be more than twice as long. Of the sixty inmate writers I included in *The Light from Another Country*, my anthology of poetry from American prisons (published in 1985), all had already published individual poems in magazines or anthologies and more than half had published books. Yet almost most every one of those men and women had not written—or read—poetry before entering prison.

Some continue to view the work of writers in prison as little more than a literary curiosity, despite the fact that much of the current poetry from prisons is moving and highly crafted, despite the fact that a large part of the poetic output of American inmates makes no mention of prison and is being published because of its excellence, not its origin. The only fair way to judge the work produced by that varied community of men and women in our nation who have been legally defined as outcasts is to use the same criteria you use to judge all good writing. You may find, as I have found, that there is a special energy in a surprising percentage of the poetry from prisons, that the poems—even when they focus on the specific and narrow details of prison life—are also about *all of us*. You may come to believe—as I do—that if such a community of letters can spring to life in the blighted atmosphere behind the high concrete walls and razor wire, a profusion of poets as unexpected as flowers in a field of glaciers, then there may be hope for us all.

Literary Reputation and the Thrown Voice

In Kingsley Amis' side-splitter *Lucky Jim*, we find the hapless hero agonizing over the first sentence of his unwritten and long-delayed dissertation. "In considering this strangely neglected topic . . ." he writes, but he can get no further. He chants the phrase over and over as he questions whether he really has a topic and whether its neglect is all that strange. His ill-chosen topic, "The Economic Influence of the Development in Ship Building 1450–1485," makes his loss for words understandable, but part of Jim's discomposure lies in approaching a subject from the angle of its neglect. To use this strategy is to cast oneself in the role of the attentive discoverer—the exceptional one who did not neglect—but the approach may easily backfire by strengthening the associations between one's topic and its neglect, especially in the case of the so-called neglected author whose name might be already too well associated with an insufficiency of reputation. Similarly, attempts to elevate an "underground" artist may prove self-defeating. The mere use of the tag may push him deeper into that vaguely subversive netherworld. The hazards of the "neglect approach" may be reduced by first turning attention to the processes by which literary reputation is created or stifled.

Notions of literary neglect and recognition are nettlesome because they involve so many extraliterary factors. Posterity may be viewed as the final arbiter who confers repute according to the criterion of durability, but the reputation of a writer within his own time is calculated by a more complex set of reckonings. More often than not, a writer achieves contemporary reputation when he finds himself situated at a graph-point where talent, cultural fashion, publishing-world pull, and even image all intersect. The possibility of a purely literary determination of reputation is severely reduced by the sociological, cultural, and economic factors at play. Bitterly aware of these complications, Wordsworth remarked that the original poet must "create the taste by which he is to be enjoyed."

The question of poetic reputation today is vexed by public obliviousness to poetry and by the fact of the media-flooded global village which offers the possibility of a scope of recognition unknown to previous ages. Of course, the concern over writerly fame is an ancient one. One of the conventional subjects treated in medieval religious tracts was "pride of authorship," a literary version of the first deadly sin; but until the nineteenth century artistic renown as we think of it today hardly existed, especially among poets. Whatever reputation poets enjoyed was limited to a coterie of upper-class people who were wealthy enough to buy books and educated enough to read them. Only with mass literacy and the growth of a culturally avaricious middle class in the nineteenth century did the possibility of wider recognition arise. No poet before Byron—who said he awoke one morning to find himself famous—luxuriated in what we would call celebrity status. And since then only Tennyson, laureate and favorite of Queen Victoria, achieved in his own lifetime a broader national fame. If poetry continues to be ignored by the public, perhaps no other poet will ever match Tennyson's contemporary renown. What American poet has been lifted by reputation out of the circle of the literati? One thinks of Ginsberg and his beat flamboyance and of Frost reciting at Kennedy's inauguration, the wind almost blowing the pages out of his old hands. Within our celebrity-obsessed culture the desire for fame can become a psychological disorder, a disease of the ego. Andy Warhol's dry prediction that in the future everyone would be famous for fifteen minutes suggests a dystopia in which the mass media's democratic ideal of "equal time" is married to universal narcissism.

At the center of the issue of poetic reputation is the seeming hegemony of that curious phantom which has no address or phone number, the Poetry Establishment. Like other unincorporated establishments (art's, academia's) poetry's is both everywhere and nowhere. It is not composed of a board of directors (though there are boards and committees and prize-granting groups within it), nor does it have an official membership. The closest one can come to locating the Poetry Establishment is to say it is defined by a canon, a body of acknowledged work. Just as the Church and the academic establishment draw a chalk-circle which embraces canonical texts and excludes apocrypha, so too the authority of the Poetry Establishment seems to rest on a body of "authenticated" poets and their works. [1] The canon, of course, is always changing. Works once considered "heretical" (or more often the case with poetry, ignored) sometimes receive an imprimatur. The reverse occurs but less frequently; canonical works are cast out, their authors "defrocked" and consigned to a state of illegitimacy. No work or author can be sure of a tenured position within the institution— remember that Saint Christopher, patron saint of the dashboard, was himself decanonized—and no work or author outside the canon can ever be certain of being admitted. The canon changes—books and authors entering and exiting through revolving doors—by mysterious processes, but a real canon nonetheless exists. Like the Church, the Poetry Establishment honors some of its dead by conferring a kind of sainthood. Lacking England's Poets' Corner in Westminster Abbey where the Greats are interred, this country maintains a Poetry Hall of Fame, invisible but as tightly controlled as the one in Cooperstown. Robert Frost is American poetry's Babe Ruth.

Neglect by the Poetry Establishment becomes its own kind of reputation, the reputation of a poetry-singer for being himself unsung. Poets may become somewhat well known for *not* being well known. This kind of antireputation is bred and maintained within the hyperactive world of Small-Press-Little-Magazine publication whose growing dimensions are reflected by Len Fulton's burgeoning directory. There are many poets active and well known within this literary demimonde, many poets who could be examined as case studies, but the work and reputation of California-based poet Robert Peters seem particularly exemplary. Author of over twenty books of poetry and several volumes of contemporary criticism, an active public reader (whose readings have become theater) and relentless contributor to small periodicals, Peters has established himself as a general among the rank and file of the small press world, but according to a paradoxical formula it is his stature in this world which keeps him from gaining wider acceptance.

There may be a few specialized and almost self-inflicted reasons why a poet of Peters' talent and output has not been "Nortonized"—surely, the Norton anthologizers comprise the closest thing the Poetry Establishment has to a synod. His salty and outspoken criticism, collected in two volumes of *The Great American Poetry Bake-Off*, has acquired a sort of infamy for its reckless iconoclasm and its off-beat, irreverant voice, a style Peters has called "informal and funky." Here he pulls the tails of sacred cows, dismantling their reputations and offering ready insights into their sexual posturings. As a literary columnist for *Margins* Peters used as a by-line "The Big Bad Wolf"—someone waiting to ambush you on your way to grandmother's house and eat all the poems in your basket.

From an establishment point of view, Peters' career presents other embarrassments. Although his first book of poems, a moving and risky elegy on the death of a son, was shot from the big guns of W. W. Norton, Peters used small presses for most of his subsequent volumes. This is a departure from the hierarchical logic by which one is expected to make only upward moves on the ladder, leaving the small presses behind once one has been knighted by a big house. After all, the mayor doesn't run for dog catcher in the next election. What's worse, Peters has committed the unpardonable sin of self-publication in a volume with the uncloseted title *Love Songs for Robert Mitchum*, a collection of hilarious, kinky homoerotic fantasies. Sure, Emerson did it but Emerson was Emerson. Just because no one wants this dance with you doesn't mean you should get up there and dance with yourself.

Another reason why Peters' work has not garnered a wider reputation is the sheer diversity of his output. His books jump through a range of disparate genres, styles, voices, and forms. Turning from one volume to another, the reader has to readjust his compass to a new direction. Such unclassifiable versatility may frustrate readers who expect a steady predictability in their poets. His early works tend to maintain an autobiographical focus. *Songs for a Son* is the response to his child's death which compelled him to begin writing poetry at the age of forty. *Bronchical Tangle, Heart System*, and many poems in *The Sow's Head* revisit Peters' boyhood on a Wisconsin dirt-farm. Here begins one of Peters' most obsessive themes: the betrayal of creatures by their own mortal guts, a theme spelled out in stark biological or, better, visceral language. In a poem about the butchering of a sow,

We shaved her hair,
spun her around, cut off
her feet and knuckles,
hacked off her head
slashed her belly
from asshole down through
bleached fat throat.
Jewels spilled out
crotches of arteries
fluids danced and ran . . .
The liver, steaming, monochrome,
quivered with eyes.[2]

But later Peters abandons autobiography for the unnerving surrealism of *Holy Cow: Parable Poems*, the comic found-poems of *Pioneers of Modern Poetry*, and the literary parodies and burlesques of *The Poet as Ice-Skater*. This almost playful diversity and experimentalism quiets down only in Peters' more recent poetry at the point where he appears to discover his true form. The final section of *The Poet as Ice-Skater*, "Byron Exhumed," is a series of monologues spoken in reaction to Byron's death by a mixture of real and fictitious characters, including a sensitive Harrow schoolboy, Byron's wife, and the church sexton who tends the burial plot. Here Peters begins his work in the form which was to determine the shape and substance of his four subsequent books, the extended biographical monologue. His exploration of this form, which has extended the frontiers of the monologue genre, amounts to a major contribution to the body of American poetry and points to an enlargement of his poetic reputation, his deserved canonization.

The four full-length books in this monologue form are *The Gift to Be Simple*, spoken in the person of Mother Ann Lee, founder of the Shakers; *Ikagnak, the North Wind*, spoken by Elisha Kent Kane, the Arctic explorer; *Hawker*, whose speaker is Robert Stephen Hawker, an eccentric Cornish vicar; and *Picnic in the Snow*, written from the point of view of King Ludwig of Bavaria, the mad castle-builder and patron of Wagner. Enriched by Peters' research into the life and times of his subjects, each work is a series of poems delivered in the voice of the central character.

The intentions behind the use of this form seem similar to those of Browning, whose name is almost synonymous with the genre. Like other Victorians, Browning was reacting against the mode of personal confession which the Romantics before him had conceived and popularized. Browning's own evasion of Romantic directness involved a double maneuver, a retreat into the past (usually the Italian Renaissance), and a rhetorical displacement of the author by a dramatic speaker. Browning's sympathies and preoccupations are detectable in the monologues (he is fascinated with his aesthetic villains and failed artists), but by avoiding direct address he gains a measure of objectivity. Retelling replaces telling. The other replaces the self.

Peters' work within this genre also reflects a dissatisfaction with the limitations of the confessional style and the weary modern "I" who has long dominated the poetic stage. By now the neo-Romanticism of Lowell, Plath, Merrill, and their followers has pushed self-portraiture to the point of exhaustion and has spawned a mob of self-haunted speakers, hypersensitive gadflies relentlessly present in every line. The substitution of a historical speaker for the poet's self provides an escape from the claustrophobic enclosure of his own ego. This is similar to the relief sought by Yeats and Pound in their adoption of masks and personae and by Eliot, who defined poetry as an escape from personality; but in the dramatic-historical monologue, the speaker is both a tone of voice to which the poet ascribes rhetorical independence and the embodiment of an alien consciousness. Peters' speakers are drawn from the nineteenth century, a kind of historical childhood to moderns, and they imply a disaffection with our own age, a period Peters has dubbed "lower-case times," in which capitalized abstractions no longer carry meaning.

The Victorian monologue is a flow of talk which catches a character at a single dramatic juncture. The assumption here is that each moment in a person's life contains his being; each utterance is like a soil sample. Start someone talking and soon you will know his essence, for life is a continuous act of self-revelation and speech is the entrance to the soul. But Peters' expansion of the genre into a sequence of speeches takes into account growth and change. Browning's characters, forever themselves, never change but only stand more revealed, to paraphrase Charles Olson. Peters' characters move through stages of development like characters in novels. Browning's characters are synchronically frozen, often exposing themselves in their first sentence; in Peters' monologues the process is cumulative and accretive. Each poem displays one facet of the gem of being. Speech touches on narrative, poetic biography, verse history.

The first of these monologue books, *The Gift to Be Simple*, traces the life of Mother Ann Lee, daughter of a Manchester blacksmith and founder of the Shakers, that quasi-mystical departure from Quakerism which espoused celibacy, communal sharing of property, virtual economic self-sufficiency, and the public confession of sins. The poems, most of them uttered in her voice, follow Ann Lee's development from her girlhood through her religious involvement, her subsequent persecution and imprisonment, and her seventy-eight-day crossing to America to establish Shaker communities. The poems bring us into contact with a woman who is simple in her piety, tormented by carnality, and heroic in the fervor and spiritual zeal that led her to believe she was the Female Christ. What makes this contact so direct and evocative is the employment of a language rinsed of modern usage and faithful to the vocabulary and idiom of the times. Many poems have an almost nursery-rhyme simplicity:

> Ann at twilight, Ann
> at dawn, Ann with her
> meager playthings on
> the lawn, a stick doll
> tucked into her pocket
> a polished hen bone for
> a locket, and on another
> string a miniature tin dog
> with a tin ball in his mouth. [3]

There is even a Shaker alphabet book included:

> A is for Apse and Altar and Aisle, as A is for
> Ant, Angel, Apple and Ann . . . [4]

The language becomes more heated and complex as Ann's obsession with God takes hold. Her first sex with her husband is an assault which she sublimates through a religious vision:

> He strokes my back, bites as he pumps
> to a pitch. As he falls, there is a

luminous angel: his feet are curly
and he blows a horn. His hair
is silver, his wings are rainbow-
stained. He loves me! He loves me!
My angel loves me![5]

After four of her children die in infancy she is visited by terrifying visions, one of a choir of people burning,

Their mouths
are eaten through above the
lips, blue gums, their heads
are turtles, chinless, leather
and green[6]

and another of Adam and Eve engaged in animalistic sex, a shocking, anti-Miltonic picture. To exorcise these sinful confabulations she taps wood slivers under her fingernails, binds her breasts with thongs, and seals her vagina with mud and dung, all the while praying, shaking, hallucinating Christ. The book concludes peacefully with Ann's arrival in America and her anticipation of Shaker life there: the "impeccably plain" white houses of the communities, orchards, gardens, and workrooms which will produce buckles, pails, tubs, cheese hoops, oval boxes, hand-crafted furniture, and Shaker inventions such as the straight broom and the washing machine. All of this productivity will be realized in the new Zion.

Peters seems to invade Ann Lee's spirit by an act of possession. The poems were composed near one of the few surviving Shaker communities, and Peters got into the habit of paying regular visits to her grave. There is an otherness to Ann's voice and a fidelity in the language to her historical milieu. But at the same time Peters does infuse these monologuists with his own tensions and obsessions. Perhaps what these works finally present are double characters, half-themselves, half-Peters; in other words, explorations of Peters-Lee, Peters-Kane, Peters-Hawker, Peters-Ludwig. By grafting his feelings onto theirs and throwing his voice into history, Peters performs an eerie act of ventriloquism by which two voices, two consciousnesses, converge and become indistinguishable.

Ikagnak documents Dr. Elisha Kent Kane's doomed voyage to the Arctic, where his ship became imprisoned in ice; he was forced to walk for eighty-four days back to civilization with a handful of survivors. Based on Kane's journals, the poems capture the painful drama of survival in a cryptlike landscape of glacier and ice. Some poems focus on the practical matters of living in this hostile environment: how to control a dog-team, how to defrost a cheek, how to kill a seal, capture a duck, or share an igloo with fourteen sleeping Eskimos. But as the expedition's situation deteriorates, the poems present a saga of hardship in stark, unsentimental language. Crew members die off from gangrene, scurvy, hunger, or mere exposure to this brutal place; the survivors, who are subsisting on boiled bear paws, whale tongues, and the meat of their dogs, sprinkle snow for dust on the graves. Kane, a doctor, performs amputations with a saw ("A foot thuds to the floor. A rush / of dogs: the whips, the whimpering") and describes the guts of his creatures hit by scurvy:

> Hematoma in the
> gastroenemius and
> gluteus muscles. Swollen gums,
> thickened skin-layers. Fatty
> changes in liver, spleen, kidneys
> and heart.[7]

As a historical work, *Ikagnak* resurrects an almost forgotten American explorer-hero whose funeral in 1856 "was second only to Lincoln's in grandeur," and as a tale the book reads like a poetic version of Piers Paul Read's gripping *Alive*.

In *Hawker*, Peters assumes the identity of Robert Stephen Hawker, a Cornish vicar who tended a church on the vertiginous cliffs of England's west coast where shipwrecks were common. Dressed in a "claret cassock, old yellow wool pancho, fisherman's boot and a bright red hat," this odd Victorian would recover the bodies of sailors washed ashore and anoint and bury them in his churchyard. He would invite farm animals to church services, and at night he would play mermaid by festooning himself with seaweed and singing by the shore as he caught moonlight in a mirror. When his wife died he took up opium to assuage his grief; his own decline was punctuated by bouts of hallucination and paranoia.

The Hawker poems begin with the vicar's ruminations on the everyday business of the vicarage, then move into his mystical communings with his patron Saint Morwenna and his obsession with the corpses of sailors, and end with his vividly frightening opium visions. Some of the best poems show Hawker's concern with such matters as the running of his parish school, the hiring of a new verger, diseases of swine, his wife's baking, the ailments of his parishioners, and his friendship with Gyp, a pet pig who followed him everywhere. In precisely paced language, Peters captures the innocent daftness of the vicar, who sees

> An oak-tree branch, snow crammed,
> with a dozen merry elves in a row,
> in German leather pants
> and buttons as large as ox eyes.
> Tasselled mutli-colored caps . . .[8]

as well as his Franciscan love for the creatures of God's world. Hawker combines a rural saintliness with a kind of tender mania. He drops violets and robins' eggs on the grave of a friend and feeds his parishioners cabbages and whortleberries; he is stimulated by erotic visions of angels and tattooed sailors. Like Ann Lee, Hawker is a spiritual over-reacher and a stranger-than-fiction exotic; but behind the quirks and aberrations lies an example of humanity standing on the sheer cliff-edge of a holy madness. The volume ends with a bold rhetorical switch whereby Hawker becomes aware of Peters' presence and addresses him in prose, assessing his book and scolding him for implying that Hawker was homosexual and for being too ornate in his description of Hawker's opium pipe.

Picnic in the Snow, spoken in the voice of King Ludwig II of Bavaria, best expresses Peters' attraction to sexual and artistic eccentricity. Ludwig is famous for his castle building and his sexually ambiguous role as Wagner's friend and patron. His extravagant architectural legacy, now a draw for tourists, consists of a half-dozen castles—some on the scale of Versailles—which blend Gothic, Baroque, Teutonic, and Byzantine styles with Ludwig's own penchant for fantasy, manifested in several elaborate artificial grottoes featuring cast-iron stalactites, waterfalls, mechanical lighting effects, swans, painted scenes from Wagner's operas, and shell-shaped boats in which Ludwig would be rowed by servants as he soaked up the atmosphere. He visited one of the castles only once for a period of ten days.

The monologues are notable for mapping the Bavarian landscape, its mountains and flower-bordered lakes, and for penetrating the king's mind, which was torn between the political pressures of running the country and his compulsive love for the fantasy-land of operatic performance. The poems explore Ludwig's dreams:

> I believe
> the salt of my own blood is a swan's.
> The sweat of my palms has the fragrance of
> feathers. I ruffle the surface of lakes,[9]

and his difficult boyhood in a bizarre family which included an aunt who maintained the belief that she had swallowed a glass piano. Ludwig's subjects grew infuriated over the king's lavish spending, the neglect of his royal duties for aesthetic pursuits, and the cultivation of his own vanity—he noted that "if I didn't have my hair curled every day, I couldn't enjoy my food." Declared insane, he was imprisoned and later died mysteriously, his body found floating in the shallow water of Lake Starnberg.

Taken as a group, these monologues express a fascination with the possibility of pursuing a personal vision to its extreme, whether the grail be purity, heroic adventure, God, or aesthetic opulence. Each character crosses the boundaries of social sanity and moves into an uncharted tundra of the spirit. The poems are reenactments of these characters' wild exertions rather than disengaged commentaries on them. As acts of exhumation, the poems fit these historical characters with flesh and return to them their voices. And while they speak always within their own times and cultures, they speak also out to ours.

The importance of Robert Peters' poetry rests on the fact that it modifies poetic language and breaks new artistic ground. By combining playful rhymes with painfully serious matter, he has returned new tonal possibilities to poetry. By fully exploiting the metaphor of the body, its epidermal shape and vulnerable interior, he has provided a fresh code for the expression of feeling. By historicizing and enlarging the scope of the dramatic monologue, he has revitalized an important genre and implied its almost limitless potential. No doubt others will rush into the fields he is now clearing.

Peters is currently writing a new monologue sequence in the person of Elizabeth Bathory of Hungary, known in her time as the Blood Countess, a madwoman who believed she could preserve her youthfulness by bathing in the blood of virgins. Her victims were locked in a metal cage equipped with inward-pointing spikes, and she would stand naked below showering in their blood. Over six hundred virgins died in the name of her beauty before they walled up Elizabeth in her castle in 1611.[10]

Notes

1. Frank Kermode draws a similar analogy in "Institutional Control of Interpretation," reprinted in *The Pushcard Prize V: The Best of the Small Presses,* 1980–81 edition, pp. 107–123.
2. *The Sow's Head and Other Poems* (Detroit: Wayne State University Press, 1968), p. 86.
3. *The Gift to Be Simple: A Garland for Ann Lee* (New York: Liveright, 1973), p. 3.
4. Ibid., p. 12.
5. Ibid., pp. 22–23.
6. Ibid., p. 43.
7. *Ikagnak, the North Wind: with Dr. Kane in the Arctic* (Pasadena: Kenmore Press, 1978), p. 34.
8. *Hawker* (Greensboro: Unicorn Press, 1984), p. 10.
9. *The Picnic in the Snow: Ludwig of Bavaria* (New Rivers Press, 1982), p. 21.
10. Robert Peters' Selected Poems—*Gauguin's Chair*—was published by the Crossing Press, Trumansburg, N.Y., in 1977. Recent books include *Hawker* and *Kane* (Greensboro, N.C.: Unicorn Press, 1985).

Contemporary Appalachian Poetry

Sources and Directions

At the beginning of 1960, you could have counted the important Appalachian poets on both hands. Since then, over seventy collections of Appalachian poetry have appeared; anthologies and little magazines have featured it; and scholars have written essays about it. This sudden flowering is impressive and, because some of the earlier poets are out of print, may seem miraculous. But it has its roots in work that came before, in individual voices, and in what they expressed for the region as a whole.

Ballad of the Bones, Hounds on the Mountain, Song in the Meadow—the titles of these books of Appalachian poetry from the thirties and forties reveal its origin in closeness to the earth and love of song. These collections by Byron Herbert Reece of north Georgia and James Still and Elizabeth Madox Roberts of Kentucky are rooted in tradition, formally as well as thematically. They contain sonnets, ballads, song cycles, and carefully reined free verse, often with a biblical cadence. While they employ less dialect than Ann Cobb's ground-breaking *Kinfolks: Kentucky Mountain Rhymes* (1922), they show a kinship to those poems, to Roy Helton's *Lonesome Waters* (1930), and to Jesse Stuart's *Man with a Bull-Tongue Plow* (1934) in that they wish to examine and most often to preserve the stories and values that have been islanded within the culture as a whole. As James Still writes in "White Highways":

To the broad highways, and back again I have come
To the creek-bed roads and narrow winding trails
Worn into ruts by hoofs and steady feet;
I have come back to the long way around,
The far between, the slow arrival.
Here is my pleasure most where I have lived
And called my home.[1]

Still's "homing place" is quiet in the world's sense, a cove away from the scream of machines and rapid transit, but it is lapped in music: "The dulcimer sings from fretted maple throat" ("Mountain Dulcimer"). We hear "the mellow banjos of the hounds' throats" and "shrill notes of a sheep's horn billow down the mountain" ("Fox Hunt"). Most importantly, the human songs are handed down and sung, and the *song* comes to symbolize identity, not just personal but cultural, the unbroken strand of life. Byron Herbert Reece not only writes of those singing the ballads, but also casts many of his poems in the ballad mold, emphasizing the timelessness of his themes, the beauty of song, and its power of renewal. "Mountain Fiddler" begins:

I took my fiddle
That sings and cries
To a hill in the middle
Of Paradise.

The fiddler tunes up, prepared to play to the emptiness around him. But, after the first few notes, "a crowd of wings" comes toward him and a voice says:

"Our halls can show
No thing so rude
As your horsehair bow,
Or your fiddlewood;

"And yet can they
So well entrance
If you but play
Then we must dance!"[2]

Song is a loom for weaving together the joys and sorrows of the earth, for shaping the human story. And narrative threads its way through the lyrical work of these poets, as though the ballad has not yet split into written forms of lyric and narrative. Notice how the light dance of rhythms in "When Daniel Was a Blacksmith" by Elizabeth Madox Roberts prepares us for a new look at the story of Daniel Boone and plays against the heaviness of our standard image of him. In form and fable quality the poem is reminiscent of Blake:

> When Daniel was a Blacksmith
>
> .   .   .   .
> He fitted for the dray horse,
> He shod the little wild colt,
> And shod the dappled gray.
>
> .   .   .   .
> And the wild beasts in a thousand hills,
> And in a thousand valley prongs,
> They lifted up their quivering ears
> To hear his anvil songs.[3]

Roberts, best known for her fiction (*The Great Meadow*, 1930), is a central Kentucky native whose work often deals with Appalachian themes and experiences. In "Love in the Harvest" she writes of "a song in the meadow and a song in the mouth."[4] Certainly her fellow poets—Still, Reece, Cobb, Helton, and Stuart—find in nature's song, the "song in the meadow," the impulse for human expression, the "song in the mouth." Jesse Stuart makes this relationship explicit in his introductory poem to *Man with a Bull-Tongue Plow* (1934), a collection which further illustrates the strain of romanticism in Appalachian poetry. If his proclamation seems defensive or willfully provincial, consider that he was launching his poems on the same stream as Hart Crane and T. S. Eliot. A literary world which had seen *The Bridge* (1930) and *Ash Wednesday* (1930) was not likely to praise the "farmer singing at the plow":

> . . . I can sing my lays like singing corn,
> And flute them like a fluting gray corn-bird;
> And I can pipe them like a hunter's horn—
> All of my life these are the songs I've heard.
> And these crude strains no critic can call art,
> Yours very respectively, Jesse Stuart.[5]

Louise McNeill's *Gauley Mountain* (1939) marks a change in this pattern of poets singing the land, for its impulse is more narrative than lyrical and the story of the land emerges through the stories of the people. The relationship between the two is still crucial, but the emphasis has changed. With the focus on story comes a new concern with character, not just of heroes or ballad figures, but of everyday people. Here is an exchange between the Gauley mail rider and a Washington postal clerk, based on a letter that once hung on the wall in a West Virginia post office. The first stanza establishes that the mail carrier has been asked why his mail was three months late during the winter. Note how in his rejoinder the mountaineer's tall-tale humor works to give him the last word:

> Jed Kane
>
> . . .
>
> . . . "Respected Sir,
> You ask the reason and this be her—
> If the gable end blowed out of hell
> Straight into the drifts of a snow that fell
> Last fall on the ram's horn point of Cheat
> It would take till Easter for brimstone heat
> To melt a horsepath. So I remain
> Your obdt. svt., Jedson Kane."[6]

The poem with which *Gauley Mountain* closes brings the human stories, with all their urgency, to rest in the hill's shadow, but there is evidence already of the difference human values are making in the landscape:

> Now they have bridged the canyon of the Gauley
> And built a lock above the Swago shoal
>
> . . . .
>
> Along the shore where passing Mingo warriors
> Built drift-wood fires to parch Ohio maize
> Coke ovens glare red-eyed upon the darkness
> And belch their cinders at the fevered days.
> ("The River")[7]

The uneasiness evidenced in this poem increases as we come closer to our own time, and the relationship between nature and song in Appalachian poetry changes more profoundly. It is not just that the poets are disconnected from the land (though some are, and clearly that is the movement of the culture), it is that the land no longer presents itself as a constant, the hub of the wheel of seasons, of present and past, of birth and death, struggle and fulfillment. Improper road building, damming, and timbering as well as the onslaught of strip mining have changed the land and the lives lived on it dramatically. Lifting up one's eyes unto the hills becomes less comforting when the hills stand in need of help. Folksinger Jean Ritchie chronicles the change in "Black Waters":

> O the quail, she's a pretty bird, she sings a sweet tongue;
> In the roots of the tall timbers she nests with her young.
> But the hillside explodes with the dynamite's roar,
> And the voices of the small birds will sound there no more;
> And the hillsides come a-sliding so awful and grand,
> And the flooding black waters rise over my land.
>
> Sad scenes of destruction on every hand;
> Black waters, black waters run down through the land.[8]

Alongside the exploitation of the land has come an accelerated modernization of life in the mountains. The speed and scale of this change, along with the economic roller-coaster of coal production and increasing industrialization, make for a very unstable way of life. As Mike Clark explains in his foreword to *Voices from the Mountains*, "The real story of Appalachia today is the attempt by mountain people to retain the humanistic elements of the old culture and at the same time to adapt to the pressures and demands of a technological society."[9]

As in James Still's "White Highways," the road is often seen as both a symbol and an agent in this transformation. Billy Edd Wheeler, West Virginia poet, playwright, and songwriter, whose *Song of a Woods Colt* appeared in 1969, gives one version of this in "The Coming of the Roads":

> O look how they've cut all to pieces
> Our ancient poplar and oak
>
> . . . .
>
> We used to curse the bold crewmen
> Who stripped our earth of its ore
> Now you've changed and you've gone over to them
> And you've learned to love what you hated before
>
> Once I thanked God for my treasure
> Now, like rust, it corrodes

And I can't help from blaming
Your going
On the coming
The coming of the roads.[10]

Kentucky poet Lee Pennington captures a more ambivalent attitude, this time toward the railroad, which hauls away the life-product of the Harlan County train watchers and gives only longing in return:

I have seen them down at the crossing,
their eyes dug out with silence,
their mouths hanging caves on faces
and their feet tapping rhythm of train horn blow.
("Train Horn")[11]

The movement of contemporary Appalachian poetry, then, is from a rooted, traditional body of work to a more volatile, politically active, and varied offering. Not that there was not political awareness before, most obviously in Georgia poet Don West's *Clods of Southern Earth* (1946), a collection which exposes the condition of workers in factories, on sharecropped farms, in the mines, and in the steel mills, where West himself worked. But the political considerations which inspired songwriters like Florence Reece had not been a major source of poetry in the mountains. From the mid-sixties on, not only labor movement questions but also the old interest in and involvement with the land demanded more political thinking. It became clear that Granny had to walk uphill just to throw water off the back porch, and, as Jim Wayne Miller, poet, critic, and one of the central voices of the seventies, tells us, possession of a small farm turned into a counter-cultural act:

Sometimes a whole farm family comes awake

.   .   .   .

to find their farm's been rolled up like a rug
with them inside it. . . .

.   .   .   .

It's a ring, a syndicate dismantling farms

.   .   .   .

disposing of them part by stolen part.

Parts of farms turn up in unlikely places:

. . . .
One missing farm was found intact at the head
of a falling creek in a recently published short story.
One farm that disappeared without a clue
has turned up in the colorful folk expressions
of a state university buildings and grounds custodian.
A whole farm was found in the face of Miss Hattie Johnson,
lodged in a Michigan convalescent home.
        ("Small Farms Disappearing in Tennessee—*Headline*")[12]

Given these opposing forces at work in Appalachian life—the long-lived isolation which preserved ignorance along with strong family ties, the volatile coal economy with its exploitation of human and natural resources, the accelerated modernization and the accompanying loss—it is not surprising that its poetry offers varied and often contradictory visions. While one can say that in general it is less traditional in form, less given to the use of dialect, and more diverse in voice and rhythm than the poetry which led up to it, it is difficult to characterize more specifically than that. Two things can safely be said. First, it most often concerns itself with revaluation or reclamation of the past, which includes a strengthening or at least an exploration of the bonds between generations. Second, its strong tie to the land has continued, whether in the pastoral work of poets like Jeff Daniel Marion, Robert Morgan, Fred Chappell, and Maggie Anderson or the more consciously political poems of Jonathan Williams, P. J. Laska, Mary Joan Coleman, and Bob Snyder.

This recognition of the bond between generations (usually the speaker in the poem and someone older), while it may be celebratory, painful, angry, or a combination thereof, is a way of remapping the land, reforesting so that the past does not erode into floods of present isolated ego. We see examples of this in the work of two young West Virginia poets, Bob Henry Baber and Mary Joan Coleman, who were part of the Soupbean Collective, a group of writers at Antioch College/Appalachia in Beckley, West Virginia.[13] A stubborn integrity, a continuity, is handed down in Baber's "Roofing for Aunt Pearl." Her relatives think she is too old to live out in the country by herself. They want her to move to town, but she tells them:

". . . I'm Cold Knob born,
Cold Knob bred,
'n' when I die, by God,
I'm gonna be COLD KNOB dead!"[14]

Exploring one's connections with the past is a kind of self-discovery and definition of wrongs as well as a delineation of what is valuable. This is evident in Mary Joan Coleman's description of her father's relationship with the world in "the man of stones":

my father wrote a poem forty years ago
about laying stones for a wall

. . . .

i knew if my mother would take the hatchet
from the pickled bean shelf in the cellar
and strike his breast the steel
would ring upon solid rock,
i have read his statement of stoning
a hundred times since childhood

. . . .

we seldom speak; but in the vacuum
i often hear the undeniable
crumble and groan
of old stones shifting.[15]

Where Baber's and Coleman's poems have the active quality of film, Tennessee poet and editor Jeff Daniel Marion's work is closer to still life. Contemplative, generally low-toned, his poems approach the past and the joining of generations in a different way from Baber and Coleman, but the poets share many of the same concerns. Marion writes in "Ebbing and Flowing Spring":

Coming back you almost
expect to find the dipper
gourd hung there by the latch.

. . . .

"Dip and drink," [Matilda would] say,
"It's best when the water is rising."

. . . .

You waited while
Matilda's stories flowed back,

seeds & seasons, names & signs,
almanac of all her days.

. . . .
Moons & years & generations
& now Matilda alone.
You listen.

. . . .
. . . before you know it
the water's up & around you
flowing by.

. . . .
This is what you have come for.
Drink.[16]

"This is what you have come for": the past as a source or way to a source of life is accessible in "Ebbing and Flowing Spring" at least in the rhythms of the earth, of the rising water. The speaker is able to carry out the commands of the past because basic facts of the landscape have remained constant and he has kept his life tuned to them. A life tuned to the stripped landscapes of eastern Kentucky or West Virginia is apt to produce more jagged lines. The threat of overburden is constant, as many protest songs tell us. Mike Kline's "Strip Away," based on "Swing Low, Sweet Chariot," is particularly effective:

Strip away, big D-9 Dozer,
Comin' for to bury my home,
I'm a-gettin' madder as you're gettin' closer,
Comin' for to bury my home.[17]

The wedding in this song of an old hymn of hope with a vision of future hopelessness is significant, an effort to graft present powerlessness onto the strength of the past and thus regain power. And some power lies in declaring the truth, whether or not action is possible. This is a recurring message in the poetry of P. J. Laska, West Virginia writer, socialist critic, and editor of *The Unrealist*. His "Follow-up Report from Farmington" deals with the devastation resulting from deep mining, reminding us that the enemy is more subtle than dozers or the enormous power shovel called Big Bertha:

First the high school cracked,
one whole wing separated

. . . .

The basements of the houses
began to crumble

. . . . .

The field on the hillside
behind the cemetery opened up

. . . .

Bethlehem Steel wouldn't pay anything
because those worked out sections
under the town
filled up with water,
and now nobody can go down there
to prove that they pulled out
those pillars of coal
they were supposed to leave standing . . .[18]

The force of this poem is its revelation of a truth that victims know but can do nothing about. The situation is a little more hopeful in Lillie D. Chaffin's "Old-Timer to Grandchild," despite its recognition that to some extent mountain people have signed on the dotted line of their own destruction:

[Our kinfolks] let some Philadelphia lawyers
tell them they could sell the yoke
and keep the egg. . . .
. . . And now the yoke owners
are claiming their gold, and squashing
the shell. . . .
. . . Let folks talk about our
backward ways. . . .
. . . If forward's now,
then I feel sorry for the ones who'll
never know. But you will remember
a little bit. You tell them birds
do fly low before a storm.[19]

The hope here is in the communication of values from one generation to another, as in Marion's and Baber's poems and in the warning of the last two lines.

While it is evident that people cannot "go into backup" on any large scale, at least not unless the economy collapses, they can offer a personal resistance by declaring the truth, as in "Farmington" and "Old-Timer," and by "holding onto their rights, both mineral and otherwise," as Lee Howard says in the dedication of her book *The Last Unmined Vein* (1980). The speaker in the title poem refuses to sell coal from under his farm "to make steel in Ohio / turn on the lights in New York City / and heat houses in Detroit" because he knows the consequences. And he has figured out how to make selling hard for his children, too:

> I done got my marker
> and laid out the lines for my grave
> right smack in the middle
> of that vein
> They gonna have to chip out the coal 6 foot by 6
> and then put her right back on top of me
> and that will be the end of that[20]

The best the speaker (and the poet) can do is "remind them / of what it's gonna cost them," the speaker by his own dead body and the poet by the body of her work.

That the acceleration of change in the mountains is also an acceleration of loss is clear. Why this change and loss should result in a burgeoning of poetry in the last decade is not so obvious. If there are ten names that must be mentioned in discussing Appalachian poetry up to 1960, there are at least thirty of significance since then, most of whom published primarily between 1969 and 1980. There are complex reasons for this. Along with the increased political awareness characteristic of the nation as a whole in the sixties came the growing consciousness of Appalachia as a region, a realization from within that its distinctiveness and importance were being distorted and sold in the "Beverly Hillbillies" market and praised and misunderstood by outreach programs, governmental and religious; that the people, like the land, were being stripped of their ore. From the outside, Appalachia attracted mercenaries and missionaries; from the inside, Appalachians wondered if the War on Poverty were being waged against them, if their lives were both quaint and deplorable, like the little shellacked outhouses sold in Mountain Kraft stores. A cultural crisis resulted, and it is still going on.

Poetry, so often considered impractical, a luxury, is in fact a natural human response in dealing with this loss and distortion of value, because poetry is a valuing process. Through its intense selectivity in imagery, in rhythm, in sound, and in word, poetry imparts value; its light shines on the few things chosen till they become luminous, radiating a truth long locked within. North Carolina poet Robert Morgan, whose books *Zirconia Poems, Red Owl,* and *Groundwork* span the seventies, has many poems which illustrate this process. Language circles, analyzes, polishes, and explores in "Stove":

> The stove is an extra digestive tract,
> a vehicle for translating
> the ancient vegetable
> heat to the present.
>
> . .   .   .
>
> The stove is motor.
> Tobacco juice ferments in the bucket of ashes.
> Later the heat returns and vanishes
> through the coals.
> The campfire dies while the hunters
> are off hunting.
> A sour wet silence pours down the stairwell.[21]

By the sheer act of naming, poetry declares what is lasting and eases the mortality of people and places it is concerned with. By rendering us speechful, poetry incants us, and the incantation both recognizes and bestows value.

The obvious question is, why poetry? Isn't this valuing process part of all literature which is essentially, however desperate, an act of affirmation? Certainly, but poetry is the logical vehicle here for many reasons. To begin with, its intensity matches the feeling of crisis and its immediacy—it is not, after all, as time-consuming as fiction—matches the urgency of the situation. Poetry dresses the wound on the spot rather than waiting for the tests, prep, and major surgery of a novel. Poetry is also a natural development of expression in a song-and story-fed culture.

More importantly, poetry is rooted in paradox, and paradox is as indigenous to Appalachia as the coal: wealth and poverty (personal, cultural, ecological), beauty and ugliness, the stereotype with its wink of truth. The violent good neighbor, loving father who puts a fork in his boy's arm at the dinner table. Steady, wise hill farmer who would like to burn up all the kids in the university before they burn it down themselves. Straightforward corruption—revivalist who saves a new wife every night. People so poor their new baby sleeps in the box of their color TV, people starving to death behind the wheel of a car, people whose lives are up on blocks, gutted, rusted out. All these leaves and seeds of paradox fall down that steep air and rot into rich ground where poetry can take hold, for the energy of poetry lies in language and paradox. The force of metaphor comes from its wedding of like and unlike to make something new without destroying the separate identities of the old. It is easy to see how this approaches the dilemma of Appalachia itself.

Poetry offers, then, some healing, a map of relatedness amid the fragmentation and isolation of modern life and the template sameness that is its deadening connector. Furthermore, its recognition of paradox, its mission work among the irreconcilable forces in our lives, is a form of healing. And to the extent that *to name* and *to tell* are to know and thus to control, poetry gives us a measure of power over those forces.

Notes

This article first appeared in the *Kentucky Review* 2, no. 2 (1981).

1. James Still, *Hounds on the Mountain* (New York: Viking Press, 1937), p. 45.
2. Byron Herbert Reece, *Ballad of the Bones* (New York: E. P. Dutton, 1945), p. 56.
3. Elizabeth Madox Roberts, *Song in the Meadow* (New York: Viking Press, 1940), p. 98.
4. Roberts, *Song in the Meadow*, p. 26.
5. Jesse Stuart, *Man with a Bull-Tongue Plow* (New York: E. P. Dutton, 1934), p. 3.
6. Louise McNeill, *Gauley Mountain* (New York: Harcourt Brace, 1939), p. 40.
7. McNeill, *Gauley Mountain*, p. 98.
8. Jean Ritchie, "Black Waters" (New York: Geordie Music Publishing Co., 1967).
9. Mike Clark, "Appalachia: The Changing Times," foreword to *Voices from the Mountains*, collected and recorded by Guy and Candie Carawan (New York: Knopf, 1975), p. ix.

10. Billy Edd Wheeler, *Song of a Woods Colt* (Anderson, S.C.: Droke House, 1969), p. 106.

11. Lee Pennington, *Scenes from a Southern Road* (Smithtown, N.Y.: JRD Publishing Co., 1969), p. 45.

12. Jim Wayne Miller, "Small Farms Disappearing in Tennessee," in *Voices from the Hills: Selected Readings of Southern Appalachia*, ed. Robert J. Higgs and Ambrose N. Manning (New York: Frederick Ungar Publishing Co., 1975), pp. 350–351.

13. Baber's book, *Assorted Life Savers*, appeared in 1976 and Coleman's *Take One Blood Red Rose* in 1978, but both poets' work had appeared earlier in the Antioch/Appalachia literary magazine *What's a Nice Hillbilly Like You . . . ?* and in works published by the Southern Appalachian Writers Cooperative, which they helped to found. SAWC sought to form a network of writers in the region in order to overcome the problems of isolation, the reluctance of publishers, and the obstacles to truth telling which they all felt. In 1977 they published *Soupbean: An Anthology of Contemporary Appalachian Literature and New Ground*, an anthology co-published with *Mountain Review*, the Appalshop magazine out of Whitesburg, Kentucky. In 1978 SAWC published *Mucked*, a collection of writings and photographs in response to the 1977 flooding of Appalachia.

    While the Soupbean poets are no longer a group, SAWC is still holding on, most recently with the help of the Appalachian Poetry Project, a year-long effort, supported by a grant to the University of Kentucky's Appalachian Center from the Witter Bynner Foundation to encourage poetry in the mountains. To date, the project has held seventeen reading/workshops in a five-state area. Many of these were led by old Soupbean and SAWC poets whose work appears in the most recent SAWC publication, *Strokes: Contemporary Appalachian Poetry* (1980).

14. Robert Henry Baber, *Assorted Life Savers and Poems from the Mountains* (Beckley, W.Va.: Troy Baber, 1976), p. 32.

15. Mary Joan Coleman, *Take One Blood Red Rose* (Cambridge, Mass.: West End Press, 1978), unpaged.

16. Jeff Daniel Marion, *Out in the Country, Back Home* (Winston-Salem, N.C.: Jackpine Press, 1976), p. 65.

17. Mike Kline, "Strip Away," in *Voices from the Mountains*, p. 36.

18. P. J. Laska, *Songs and Dances* (Prince, W.Va.: Unrealist Press, 1977), p. 30.

19. Lillie D. Chaffin, "Old-Timer to Grandchild," in *Mucked*, ed. Bob Henry Baber and Jim Webb (Williamson, W.Va.: Hesperus Press, 1978), unpaged.

20. Lee Howard, "The Last Unmined Vein," in *The Last Unmined Vein* (Washington, D.C.: Anemone Press, 1980), pp. 50–51.

21. Robert Morgan, *Red Owl: Poems* (New York: Norton, 1972), p. 46.

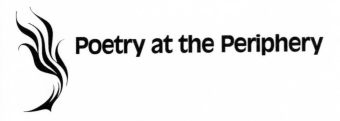

Poetry at the Periphery

There are those for whom Appalachian culture is no more than "a region of the heart." The metaphor here is one of emotion and feeling rather than one of perception of reality. The suggestion is that Appalachian culture is more past than present and more desire than fulfillment, and that therefore it is accessible only as folk culture. I suggest a different approach to Appalachian culture, one that links the folk and heritage concepts to the idea of a living people's culture. What I mean by "people's culture" is significantly different from mass culture and something clearly distinct from the elitist culture of modernism. In Appalachia it includes the surviving part of that native folk culture that once gave a degree of identity and unity to life in these mountains. The important question for my purposes is whether these remnants and the tremendous enthusiasm for them will develop a living value in the present, and whether "the mountain experience" and the "things Appalachian" will encompass reality as well as history. At this juncture I think it is the poets of the region who are pressing this question upon us, and what follows is my attempt to explain the significance of their work.

Side by side with the pursuit of heritage and regional self-consciousness, which has been largely a scholarly, intellectual effort, there has been a virtual explosion of activity on the part of writers and poets of the region. One critic has written recently that "poems are pouring out of the region as if a sensitive nerve had been touched." He wonders whether all this activity will ultimately be classified as a famous literary movement. My own view is that something more basic, more revolutionary than a mere interest in literature is behind this upsurge. The outpouring of poetry in Appalachia in the past decade is part of a larger development which we have begun to see in the cultural life of the country. I would argue that in the past decade Appalachian poets have been at the forefront of a significant change emerging in American cultural life, a change that constitutes a major break with the past and with the cultural hegemony of urban modernism.

To substantiate this rather large assertion I offer the following brief survey, which will probably not convince anyone but may enable me to get a foot in the door. An urban cultural hierarchy has been in place in this country since at least the early fifties, probably since the war period. Politically, it has been decidedly right wing, or very conservative, as has been the dominant politics of the nation. In the early fifties what survived of a left-wing cultural opposition was driven into hiding by a right-wing hysteria that came damn close to elevating another Hitler (some say he later came to power only to be dethroned by newspaper reporters).

This cultural opposition has been slow in its return to public life. The "Beat Movement," which began in the fifties, was not left wing. It was hardly political at all. It was, however, opposed to the formalism and careerism of the established poets clustered around American universities. This urban cultural hierarchy had at the time enough power to reduce any cultural movement that rejected its standards of taste to the status of a *peripheral* phenomenon.

And this is what happened, in spite of the media interest in the Beats. The net effect of nonrecognition and ridicule was a status of cultural pariah for a whole group of writers whose literature and lifestyle flouted the dominant cultural values. Donald Hall's influential anthology of American poets, originally published in 1962, contained only Gary Snyder among the Beats, no blacks, and few women. The upheavals of the sixties brought a change to this picture of the contemporary scene. In the second edition of his *Contemporary American Poetry* (1972), Hall added more poets, including Allen Ginsberg, whom he admits having misjudged. More importantly, though, he included two black poets and was turned down by a third (Amiri Baraka, then Leroi Jones).

This little background survey illustrates what is an obvious truth to many, that social forces are the strength of cultural forces. It is also a truth that is borne out by developments of the seventies. The seventies have seen a continuation of social upheaval in America centered around the family and racial and ethnic identity. Toward the latter part of the seventies there has also appeared a lot of poetry to which the Canadian poet Tom Wayman has given the label "New Realism." In the United States there are an increasing number of little poetry magazines that feature what we could call "new realism" poetry in a broader sense than Wayman's. Some of the ones I have seen are *Quindaro* (Kansas City), *Cultural Correspondence* (Providence, Rhode Island), *Working Cultures* (Washington, D.C.), *West End* and *Nostoc* (Boston), *Main Trend* (New York), and *The Unrealist.* Also, established literary journals like *Minnesota Review, Praxis,* and *Left Curve* all feature poetry which embodies social and historical perspectives.

An anthology of the seventies would also have to take account of the rise of regionalism in American culture. The poetry upsurge in Appalachia is contemporary with a revival of poetry in other regions of the country. Regional markets for poetry are evident all across the country, and these markets are in fact part of the mainstay of the small press publishing business. As a result certain poets have a large following in the area in which they live and publish but are not known or attract little interest outside that area. The "region" can be entirely ersatz in this sense. Away from the urban centers we find poets taking localism more seriously than as a literary game, some to the point of becoming consciously regionalist. It is difficult to imagine the work of Vincent Ferrini apart from the Gloucester's fishermen and the Cape Ann area of Massachusetts. In his latest book, *Know Fish,* Ferrini returns to the Italian-English dialect of his immigrant parents and writes some of his best poems. David Budbill, a regional poet in Northern New England, is another example of a poet who uses dialect. In his book, *The Chain-Saw Dance,* he writes of the people of the northern Appalachian mountains and reproduces some of their speech.

This sort of thing is going on outside the national literary network. California, New Jersey, New York, Washington, D.C., and its suburbs, even Hawaii have all seen anthologies of their poets. In some cases they have more than one. So far, it has been in the heavily populated urban areas of the country that the money has tended to concentrate.

We can look at what is happening in the country culturally from the side of the old, which is breaking up, or from the side of the new, which is just beginning to appear. What is breaking up is the cultural life, its ability by controlling the production of art to define the standards of perception and taste, as well as the modes of enjoyment, in American society. What has appeared on the horizon to replace it is the regional focus of populist cultural developments that threaten to break down the traditional hierarchy in the arts and perhaps create new hierarchies in its place. The bureaucratic scaffolding for such regional hierarchies is already in place in many states. One's reaction to this cultural dialectic is likely determined by whether one's politics are populist or elitist. Those who lament the passing of the old order talk about the seventies as "a decade of dispersal" and argue, for example, that Robert Lowell is the last of the great American poets because of the scattering of cultural focus and the fracturing of the national audience. Daniel Bell, the sociologist who pronounced the end of ideology in the fifties, argues in a recent book that American society is experiencing a crisis of values and that the most pressing problem is the loss of a center. He and others are concerned to reestablish the central clearinghouse concept of culture even if it takes a new ideology to do it. But the reaction of elitists to the breakup of the cultural core cannot be better illustrated than in the flap which saw CCLM (Coordinating Council of Literary Magazines) in an uproar when a grants board of the latter, dominated by elected small magazine editors, voted to disperse their monies in equal amounts to all applicants. With action equal to their conviction, this CCLM grants board refused to sit in judgment of the relative merit of the various diverse literary magazines around the country and thus refused to play the role of Pro-Tem Cultural God that had been allotted to them. For this betrayal of elitist trust and bureaucratic authority, this grants board of CCLM was roundly criticized, castigated, and ridiculed, although many editors of small magazines were delighted.

So the fight is on. The arts are no longer divorced from politics. And although Congress continues to appropriate large funds for the arts without much debate, the day of floor fights may not be far off. In a recent article entitled "Post Post-Art—Where Do We Go from Here?" Douglas Davis described our cultural situation as a problem of perception. We are "tumbling into infinitely complex sub-sets . . . older, tighter structures are decentralizing, spreading . . . [and] we do not clearly perceive the premise behind the action." Davis sees elitist culture as poised at the end of modernism without being able to define what is "post-modern." This is a humbling experience for Davis, who concludes that "small has to be beautiful now." What I find interesting is that Davis takes for granted that the end of modernism means the end of progress. *Après moi, le déluge.* "Each of the great Modernist states," he says, "is breaking into component parts, the reverse of the Global Village metaphor." As though he had looked into an abyss, Davis is engaged in the desperate search for a new metaphor to stem the tide of decentralization "before we're engulfed." Those whose politics are of a populist bent are likely to view what is happening as a positive development which opens up new possibilities. The thought that never seems to occur in these decline-of-the-West discussions is that decentralization brings with it the possibility of genuine people's culture.

The unity of art and life that occurs in folk culture is utopian to modernists (with their conception of art as commodity and museum pieces) and they are unable to take it seriously. Yet from the Appalachian vantage point, in which the remnants of a real folk culture are still immediate, it can be taken seriously. And those who do take it seriously will have a very different attitude to what is happening to modernist culture.

In a wide sense culture is the shared beliefs which inform our work and its shaping of physical existence. Cultural pluralism allows many shapes and elaborations as real. The cultural imperialism of mass culture resulting in a bureaucratically controlled consumption cannot permit any real pluralism because it would mean the end of the mass market in many areas of life. This imperialism has taken its toll on the psyche of the population. The results are evident in the alienation and unreality that people experience and in the proliferating psychological and religious attempts to counter the meaninglessness of everyday life.

The cultural life of a people cannot be successfully controlled or managed unless the power to shape life, *poesis* as the Greeks called it, is taken away from the people. *Poesis* lies at the basis of culture. It is the origin of all art, literature, drama, and even of language and thought itself. Originally, the folk artist only embodied and articulated what was the common creation of the whole people, *their style of life*. The people created the form of life, the artist recorded it.

For the purposes of power what matters is that *poesis* come under the control of an elite. This is an old story. Written language for the few and the illiteracy of masses over the centuries gave us a hieratic ideology which says that the power of *poesis* is the special gift of the few. In modern culture it is known as the gift of genius. What is creative in the culture is supposed to exist in their work. The living culture of the folk, with its union of art and life, is broken up into an elite producing the "high art" of novel experiment on the one hand and a mass culture entertainment industry on the other. Both are virtually empty of any real content.

The elitist "high art" defends itself against the charge of emptiness and irrelevance by the argument of art for art's sake, which says that the value of the work lies in how well it deals with its own challenge and not in any articulation of human meaning and truth. The argument uses the autonomy of art as an ideological defense. It says that the absence of the human dimension is not a permissible criticism. So long as there is something novel in the work to serve as evidence of genius, any reference to human reality is inessential. It sees no struggle between form and content or between reality and unreality because everything takes place on the side of the individual's imagination.

But the dues have to be paid somewhere, and they are paid through loss of meaning. Obscure, meaningless, and trivial works of art come to predominate and art is alienated from the people. The proliferation of novelty in a void is a necessary consequence of the theory and its practice. And since the only judgment of any importance about the merit of these works concerns their intrinsic qualities, we naturally have to have a captain-critic to tell us whether a new work is metal or dross.

It turns out that the problem with modern culture is the *cult*; that is, the hieratic clique. Historically, the tendency has been for the cult to dislodge the spontaneous genius of the people and install its own rules, which had something secret and mysterious about them. Now the opposite appears to be taking place. People's ignorance about the power of *poesis* within themselves and the cultural heritage of fear and self-deprecation that comes with ignorance is giving way everywhere to interest in the arts. Also, in Appalachia the emergence of oral history, folklore, and heritage studies has begun to reclaim some public space and funds for what was once a flourishing people's culture. The decentralization toward regionalism is a positive development, full of possibility for bringing together art and life in the region.

Folk culture and people's culture are not identical in concept, but I think they are closely interrelated. They are on a continuous line and I think it can be shown that what survives of the folk is part of people's culture. Both are populist conceptions of culture that reverse the elitist form. They are not derived from theory or ideology but arise in response to real needs. They develop around the interchange of artists and craftsmen with the people. If Appalachian poetry is seen as inclusive of mountain folk, blues, gospel, and grass songs, as well as the songs of work and protest, then I think we can document this continuous line. It's not something that I could attempt here, but it is something that should be attempted.

There is a tendency in modern poetry and modern criticism to pooh-pooh the song, to downgrade its aesthetic value as poetry. Modern poetry anthologies don't usually include songs that had popularity over the period covered by the anthology. I think this highlights the antilyrical, antipopulist bent of modern poetry. In the days of the oral tradition, prior to the book revolution, song was the main form for the poem to take. I'm not suggesting that the new Appalachian poets should all start writing songs. The song is only one form of poetry, and the limits of the musical form resulting from use of rime and fixed beat make it inappropriate for certain purposes. My point is that *thematically* the early Appalachian poetry, whose form is the song, is closely linked to the new poetry coming out of the hills. The folk themes and the political themes are inseparable because our people's lives have been and are now filled with struggle.

In the past the Appalachian poetry of song was an organic part of a genuine folk culture. The modernist break has been felt as the break *from* the lyric form. This break was progressive in that it opened up new forms for poetic work, but the price was paid in terms of alienation because its avant garde experimentalism tended to downgrade the folk as passé and to set modern poetry apart from people's culture. It remains to be seen whether Appalachian poetry, which is now consciously finding itself, will become an integral part of that collectivity that the folk represents in a way that modern poetry could not. To become part of the life of the people it will have to be a poetry in which the poem responds not merely to the challenge of itself but responds to the felt but perhaps unarticulated needs of the people. What makes poetry valuable to the people is not the novel linguistic inventions but the experience of the people that is articulated.

The *poesis* at the basis of popular culture is both real and repressed. We can think of the removal of this repression as the liberation of poetic power on the part of the people and as the fulfillment of the idea of art. It is an idea that traces its beginnings in the old work songs, whose practical function in one way or another assisted the laborer or assuaged his pain. Think of the prudential advice offered in "The Miner's Lifeguard,"

> Union miners stand together
> Heed no operator's tale
> Keep your hand upon the dollar
> and your eye upon the scale.

Or the humor appropriate to the absurdities of mining low coal as in Turner's "Hignite Blues,"

> Bumps all along to skin your back
> You lay your wire and hang your track.

Or of the surreal quality of the dream in which freedom is symbolized by a sea-gull in "Coal Loadin' Blues,"

> Thought I heard a sea-gull
> Way down in the ground;
> Must've been those miners
> A-turnin' that coal around.

Real freedom—free time and free mind—is the fulfillment of the idea of art. It is a revolutionary break to get poetry away from the cult and back into the life and consciousness of the people. In his last work German philosopher Herbert Marcuse wrote that "the truth of art lies in its power to break the monopoly of established reality . . . to *define* what is *real*." What he seems not to have seen is that art only has this power when it is in the hands of the people.

Appalachian people's culture is a real possibility for our generation. We have now the opportunity to nurture the growth of that organic relation between past and present, between poetry and people.

David Walls' core-periphery model has done much to reshape our thinking about the region. The limitation of the core-periphery model lies in the fact that in the present situation it is economically applicable but rapidly becoming culturally inapplicable. Culturally, the core is disintegrating at the same time that the Appalachian "periphery," along with other regions of the country, is experiencing a cultural renaissance. It is possible for the cultural core of American capitalism to become so weakened that there will no longer be any justification for speaking of Appalachian culture, or that of any of the other regions, as peripheral. Theoretically, then, we should remember that there is no periphery without a core.

Of course, the break-up of the "core" does not imply that a regional people's culture will emerge in its place. Other changes in the cultural superstructure are consistent with the continued functioning of American capitalism, even in its more or less dysfunctional "late" or post-Keynesian stage. One cannot say, for example, that the economics of American capitalism rules out an elitist cultural dispersal. The economic base of capitalism *is* consistent with the development of cultural pluralism under the control of regional elites. The important thing for capitalism is that a bureaucratic society of controlled consumption be preserved.

Is it not understandable, then, that in Appalachia the money flows in the direction of cultural heritage programs and not in the direction of contemporary programs which nourish a living people's culture and that would, in the words of the French philosopher Lefebvre, "create a culture that is not an institution but a style of life." The practical obstacles to people's culture have to do with where the money goes and where it doesn't go. State and private investments have been lavished, even squandered, on the collection and preservation of the remnants of folk culture in museums, libraries, and heritage centers. Heritage is a safe investment so long as it does not materially affect the present. A contemporary people's culture, on the other hand, is risky. Just how risky is stated with the exhortation of a mountain preacher in a recent paper by Cratis Williams when he says that Appalachians are a people "who have risen from our long fast in the mountains, the agony of our neglect and abuse, and the sharp thorns of perfidy that have been our anguish, and are now shaking our hides and flexing our muscles as we reach for the control box that determines our destiny." To the extent that this assessment is true, the "periphery" will turn out to be more like the front lines. Its truth value makes it dangerous to the established order because it identifies the fate of a culture with the *action* of the people. This is an important and far-reaching perception.

Socially and politically, a division takes place when there is serious talk about reaching for the control box. We know that the control box is ultimately outside Appalachia, but a good many in the region who support the folksy heritage concept of culture are tied in with those whose hands are on the controls. The controllers will permit a plurality of ethnic identities, their agents will give grants to assist in their development. What they will ridicule and condemn is the possibility that these identities should have *a living value in the present*, one that possesses real social power such that the people of the region gain control over their destiny.

Our self-consciousness has brought us to a crucial juncture. Now is the time to invest in contemporary work in an unparalleled manner. Heritage and "roots" are not enough for a *living* identity. We need to take another look at folk culture and recognize that the folk are the people of the present, in need of a living culture. Folk culture must extend into the present as people's culture. If it doesn't, we will lose it all.

Bibliography of Publishers, Journals, and Anthologies

The following is a list of presses, magazines, and anthologies in which the work of American poets discussed in the essays can be found. Because some of the work may be difficult to locate through conventional channels, we have included addresses so that material can be ordered directly from the presses. And, since there is no single anthology in which a range of representative work is collected, we have mentioned a number of anthologies and collections by way of a beginning. Some of the titles have been suggested by our contributors, some are our own choices, others have been culled from *The International Directory of Little Magazines and Small Presses*, edited by Len Fulton and Ellen Ferber. (This very useful volume can be ordered directly from Dustbooks, P.O. Box 100, Paradise, CA 95969. It is updated periodically.)

Books mentioned in individual essays are cited only in the essays' endnotes. Small presses that also publish magazines are included in each magazine's entry. Where clarification seemed necessary, we added a brief annotation.

Many university presses emphasize the work of writers within their region. Among them are the University of Arizona Press, the University of New Mexico Press, the University of Indiana Press, the University of Pittsburgh Press, and the Navajo Community College Press. We would advise the reader to examine the university and community college lists for relevant texts. And, of course, bookstores which specialize in poetry can be an invaluable resource.

For the time being, anyone interested in locating the works of the full spectrum of American poets must see the task as a search. We can only hope that the reader will find the process enlightening and the results exciting.

Presses and Journals

A, a journal of contemporary literature. A Publications, Box 42A510, York Station, CA 90042 (Third World publishers with Native American preferences).

Afro-Hispanic Review. 3306 Ross Place N.W., Washington, D.C. 20008.

Akwekon: A National Native American Literature and Arts Journal. Mohawk Nation, Rooseveltown, NY 13683.

Alice James Books, 138 Mt. Auburn St., Cambridge, MA 02138 (emphasis on publishing poetry by women).

American Book Review. P.O. Box 188, Cooper Station, New York, NY 10003 (includes reviews of books from small, regional, Third World, and women's presses).

American Indian Culture and Research Journal. American Indian Studies Center, 3220 Campbell Hall, University of California, Los Angeles, CA 90024.

American Indian Quarterly. American Indian Studies Department, University of California, Berkeley, CA 84127.

Appalachian Consortium Press, University Hall, Appalachian State University, Boone, NC 28607.

Azalea. 306 Lafayette Ave., Brooklyn, NY 11238 (published by and for Third World lesbians).

Aztlán: International Journal of Chicano Studies Research. Chicano Studies Research Center Publications, UCLA, 405 Highland Ave., Los Angeles, CA 90025.

Bilingual Review. Bilingual Press, Office of the Graduate School, SUNY-Binghamton, Binghamton, NY 13091 (Spanish/English, Hispanic culture in the United States).

Black American Literature Forum. Indiana State University, Parsons Hall 237, Terre Haute, IN 47809.

Black Maria. Metis Press, Inc., P.O. Box 25187, Chicago, IL 60625 (material by and about women).

Black Oyster Press, P.O. Box 8550, Chicago, IL 60680 (feminist).

The Black Scholar: Journal of Black Studies and Research. The Black Scholar Press, P.O. Box 7106, San Francisco, CA 94120.

Blue Cloud Quarterly. Blue Cloud Abbey, Box 98, Marvin, SD 57251 (poetry by Native Americans).

Boletín Anglohispano. Bola Publications, 8769 Devon Ave., Hesperia, CA 92345.

Bridge: Asian American Perspectives. 32 E. Broadway, New York, NY 90002.

Café Solo. Café Solo Press, 7975 San Marcos, Atascadero, CA 93422 (includes prison poets, Spanish literature).

Calamus Books, Box 689, Cooper Station, New York, NY 10003 (work by or about lesbians and gay men).

Callaloo. Department of English, University of Kentucky, Lexington, KY 40506 (creative literature by black writers and critical works about black literature).

Calyx: A Journal of Art and Literature by Women. P.O. Box B, Corvallis, OR 97339 (special issue of Native/Latina work, *Bearing Witness/ Sobreviviendo,* published 1984).

Carta Abierta. Relampago Books Press, Center for Mexican-American Studies, Texas Lutheran College, Sequin, TX 78155.

Common Lives/Lesbian Lives. P.O. Box 1553, Iowa City, IA 52244.

Conditions. P.O. Box 56, Van Brunt Station, Brooklyn, NY 11215 (feminist with emphasis on writing by lesbians).

Contact/II: A Bimonthly Poetry Review Magazine. Contact II Publications, P.O. Box 451, Bowling Green Station, New York, NY 10004 (multicultural, special issue—*Asian American: North and South,* vol. 7, no. 38/39/40 [Winter/Spring 1986]).

Crossing Press, 17 W. Main St., Box 640, Trumansburg, NY 14886 (multicultural list).

Exquisite Corpse. 630 Lakeland Drive, Baton Rouge, LA 70802 (eclectic—poetry, articles, reviews, criticism).

Fag Rag. Good Gay Poets Press, Fag Rag Collective, Box 331, Kenmore Station, Boston, MA 02215.

Feminary. 3543 18th St., San Francisco, CA 94110.

The Feminist Press at the City University of New York, 311 East 94 St., New York, NY 10128.

Feminist Studies. c/o Women's Studies Program, University of Maryland, College Park, MD 20742.

Firebrand Books, 141 The Commons, Ithaca, NY 14850 (feminist).

Focus: A Journal for Lesbians. Focus Collective, 1151 Mass. Ave., Cambridge, MA 02138.

Gay Presses of New York, P.O. Box 294, Village Station, New York, NY 10014.

Gay Sunshine Journal. Gay Sunshine Press, P.O. Box 40397, San Francisco, CA 94140.

Greenfield Review. Greenfield Review Press, RD 1, Box 80, Greenfield Center, NY 12833 (the Greenfield Review Press has a multicultural list and runs the Native American Distribution Project as well as publishing the Prison Writing Review).

Hambone. 132 Clinton St., Santa Cruz, CA 95062 (black periodical).

Helicon Nine: The Journal of Women's Arts and Letters. P.O. Box 22412, Kansas City, MO 64113.

Heresies: A Feminist Publication on Art and Politics. Box 766, Canal St. Station, New York, NY 10013.

Ikon. Ikon Press, P.O. Box 1355, Stuyvesant Station, New York, NY 10009 (feminist political, cultural magazine with writing by lesbian, Third World, and working-class women).

Indian Truth. 1505 Race St., Philadelphia, PA 19102.

Inside/Out. Time Capsule Inc., GPO Box 1185, New York, NY 10116 (publishes only incarcerated writers).

Kalliope, A Journal of Women's Art. 3939 Roosevelt Blvd., Florida Jr. College at Jacksonville, Jacksonville, FL 32205.

Kitchen Table: Women of Color Press, Box 2753, New York, NY 10185.

The Laurel Review. West Virginia Wesleyan College, Buckhannon, WV 26201 (encourages writing from Appalachia).

Lector. P.O. Box 4273, Berkeley, CA 94704 (Hispanic-related material).

Long Haul Press, P.O. Box 592, Van Brunt Station, Brooklyn, NY 11215 (feminist).

Lotus Press, Inc., P.O. Box 21607, Detroit, MI 48221 (emphasis on black poets).

Magic Circle Press, 10 Hyde Ridge Rd., Weston, CT 06833 (has done special project on poetry of women in prison).

Melus (The Journal of the Society for the Study of the Multi-Ethnic Literature of the United States). Department of English, University of Southern California, Los Angeles, CA 90007.

Minor Heron Press, P.O. Box 2615, Taos, NM 87571 (emphasis on Southwestern Hispanic and Native American poetry and fiction).

Motheroot Journal. Motheroot Publications, 214 Dewey St., Pittsburgh, PA 15218 (women's press, journal reviews small press books by or about women).

Moving Out: Feminist Literary and Arts Journal. P.O. Box 21249, Detroit, MI 48221.

New Victoria Publishers, 7 Bank St., Lebanon, NH 03766 (women's press).

Obsidian: Black Literature in Review. English Department, Wayne State University, Detroit, MI 48202.

Pacific Bridge. P.O. Box 883903, San Francisco, CA 94188 (gay Asian).

Parnassus: Poetry in Review. 205 West 89th St., New York, NY 10024.

Primavera. 1212 E. 59th St., Chicago, IL 60637 (feminist).

rara avis, Books of a Feather. P.O. Box 3095, Terminal Annex, Los Angeles, CA 90051 (includes women of color, lesbians).

Revista Chicano-Riqueña. Arte Publico Press, University of Houston, University Park, Houston, TX 77004 (Hispanic literature).

Seal Press, Box 13, Seattle, WA 98111 (feminist).

Second Growth: Appalachian Nature and Culture. P.O. Box 24, East Tennessee State University, Johnson City, TN 37619.

Seven Buffaloes Press, Box 249, Big Timber, MT 59011 (publishes *Black Jack*, *Valley Grapevine*, which focus on regional and rural writing).

Sez: A Multi-Racial Journal of Poetry and People's Culture. Shadow Press, P.O. Box 8803, Minneapolis, MN 55408.

Shamal Books, G.P.O. Box 16, New York, NY 10016 (multicultural list).

Shameless Hussy Press, Box 3092, Berkeley, CA 94703.

Signs: Journal of Women in Culture and Society. Center for Research on Women, Serra House, Stanford University, Stanford, CA 94305.

Sing Heavenly Muse!: Women's Poetry and Prose. P.O. Box 14059, Minneapolis, MN 55414.

Sinister Wisdom. P.O. Box 10234, Rockland, ME 04841 (feminist and lesbian writing).

South End Press, 302 Columbus Ave., Boston, MA 02116 (publishes books which aid the day-to-day struggle to control life).

Southern Exposure. Institute for Southern Studies, P.O. Box 531, Durham, NC 27702.

Spawning the Medicine River. Institute of American Indian Arts, Santa Fe, NM 87501.

Spinsters, Ink, 803 De Haro St., San Francisco, CA 94107 (feminist).

Steppingstones: A Literary Anthology toward Liberation. Steppingstones Press, Box 1856, Harlem, NY 10027 (especially Third World and black).

Strawberry Press, P.O. Box 451, Bowling Green Station, New York, NY 10004 (Native American).

Sunbury Press, 22 Catherine St., Basement Workshop, New York, NY 10038 (women, Third World, working class).

Suntracks. English Department, University of Arizona, Tucson, AZ 85721 (Native American).

Third World Press, 7524 So. Cottage Grove Ave., Chicago, IL 60619.

13th Moon. P.O. Box 309, Cathedral Station, New York, NY 10025 (particularly interested in feminist and lesbian work; vol. 7, nos. 1 and 2, is a double issue on working class experience).

Tulsa Studies in Women's Literature. 600 S. College, Tulsa, OK 74104.

The Universal Black Writer. P.O. Box 5, Radio City Station, New York, NY 10101.

Vanguard Books, P.O. Box 3566, Chicago, IL 60654 (literature reflecting current social struggles).

West End Press, P.O. Box 291477, Los Angeles, CA 90029 (politically progressive).

Whetstone. San Pedro Press, 212 Clawson St., Bisbee, AZ 85603 (Native American, Southwest).

Woman Poet. Women-in-Literature, Inc., P.O. Box 60550, Reno, NV 89506.

The Women's Review of Books. Wellesley College, Center for Research on Women, Wellesley, MA 02181.

Women's Studies Quarterly. The Feminist Press, Box 344, Old Westbury, NY 11568.

Wood Ibis. Place of Herons Press, P.O. Box 1952, Austin, TX 78767 (Chicano, Hispanic, Native American, among others).

Anthologies

Algarin, Miguel, and Miguel Piñero, eds. *Nuyorican Poetry: An Anthology of Puerto Rican Words and Feelings*. New York: William Morrow and Co., 1975.

Allen, Terry, ed. *The Whispering Wind, Poetry by Young American Indians*. New York: Doubleday, 1972.

Amburgey, Gail, Mary Joan Coleman, and Pauletta Hansel, eds. *We're Alright but We Ain't Special*. Beckley, W. Va.: Mountain Union Books, 1976.

Astrov, Margot, ed. *American Indian Prose and Poetry*. New York: Capricorn Books, 1946.

Baber, Bob Henry, George Ella Lyon, and Gurney Norman, eds. *Common Ground: Contemporary Appalachian Poetry*. Charleston, W.Va.: Jalamap Press, 1985.

Bambara, Toni Cade, ed. *The Black Woman, An Anthology*. New York: New American Library, 1970.

Baraka, Amiri, and Amina Baraka, eds. *Confirmation: An Anthology of African-American Women*. New York: Quill, 1983.

Barradas, Efraín, and Rafael Rodríguez, eds. *Herejes y mitificadores: Muestra de poesía puertorriqueña en los Estados Unidos*. Puerto Rico: Ediciones Huracán, 1980 (bilingual).

Bernikow, Louise, ed. *The World Split Open: Four Centuries of Women Poets in England and America, 1552–1950*. New York: Vintage, 1974.

Bierhorst, John, ed. *In the Trail of the Wind*. New York: Farrar, Straus and Giroux, 1971.

Bly, Robert, ed. *News of the Universe: Poems of Twofold Consciousness*. San Francisco, Calif.: Sierra Club Books, 1980.

Brant, Beth, ed. *A Gathering of Spirit: Writing and Art by North American Indian Women*. Rockland, Maine: Sinister Wisdom Books, 1984.

Bruchac, Joseph, ed. *Breaking Silence, an Anthology of Contemporary Asian American Poets*. Greenfield Center, N.Y.: Greenfield Review Press, 1983.

_____. *The Light from Another Country: Poetry from American Prisons*. Greenfield Center, N.Y.: Greenfield Review Press, 1984.

_____. *Songs from This Earth on Turtle's Back, Contemporary American Indian Poetry*. Greenfield Center, N.Y.: Greenfield Review Press, 1983.

Bulkin, Elly, and Joan Larkin, eds. *Lesbian Poetry: An Anthology*. Watertown, Mass.: Persephone, 1981 (distributed by Gay Presses of New York).

Chapman, Abraham, ed. *Literature of the American Indians*. New York: Meridian, 1975.

Chiang, Fay et al., eds. *American Born and Foreign*. New York: Sunbury, 1979.

Delgado, Abelardo, ed. *Chicano: 25 Pieces of a Chicano Mind*. Denver: Barrio Publications, 1969.

Epringham, Toni, ed. *Fiesta in Aztlán*. Santa Barbara, Calif.: Capra Press, 1981.

Fisher, Dexter, ed. *The Third Woman: Minority Women Writers of the United States*. Boston, Mass.: Houghton Mifflin, 1980.

Frumkin, Gene and Stanley Noyes, eds. *The Indian Rio Grande: Recent Poems from 3 Cultures*. Albuquerque, N.M.: San Marcos Press, 1977.

Gibson, Donlad B., ed. *Modern Black Poets*. Englewood Cliffs, N.J.: Prentice-Hall, 1973.

Green, Rayna, ed. *That's What She Said, Contemporary Poetry and Fiction by Native American Women*. Bloomington, Ind.: Indiana University Press, 1984.

Henderson, Stephen. *Understanding the New Black Poetry*. New York: William Morrow and Co., 1973.

Hicks, Granville et al., eds. *Proletarian Literature in the United States: An Anthology*. New York: International Publishers, 1935.

Hobson, Geary, ed. *The Remembered Earth, an Anthology of Contemporary Native American Literature*. Albuquerque, N.M.: University of New Mexico Press, 1981.

Howe, Florence, and Ellen Bass, eds. *No More Masks! An Anthology of Poems by Women*. New York: Doubleday Anchor, 1973.

Japanese American Anthology Committee, ed. *Ayumi: A Japanese American Anthology*. P.O. Box 5024, San Francisco, CA, 1980.

Katz, Janet, ed. *I Am the Fire of Time, Writings by Native American Women*. New York: Dutton, 1977.

Keller, Gary, and Francisco Jimenez. *Hispanics in the United States: An An-*

thology of Creative Literature. Tempe, Ariz.: Bilingual Press, Arizona State University, 1980 (vol. 1), 1982 (vol. 2).

Kenny, Maurice, ed. *Wounds Beneath the Flesh, 15 Native American Poets.* Marvin, S. Dak.: Blue Cloud Quarterly Press, 1983.

Kherdian, David, ed. *Settling America: The Ethnic Expression of 14 Contemporary Poets.* New York: Macmillan, 1974.

Leyland, Winston, ed. *Orgasms of Light: The Gay Sunshine Anthology.* San Francisco, Calif.: Gay Sunshine Press, 1977.

Lourie, Dick, ed. *Come to Power: Eleven Contemporary American Indian Poets.* Trumansburg, N.Y.: Crossing Press, 1974.

Lowenfels, Walter, ed. *From the Belly of the Shark.* New York: Vintage, 1973.

Matila, Alfredo, and Iván Silén, eds. *The Puerto Rican Poets.* New York: Bantam, 1972.

Miles, Sara et al., eds. *Ordinary Women, Mujeres Comunes, an Anthology of Poetry by New York City Women.* New York: Ordinary Women, 1978.

Moraga, Cherríe, and Gloria Anzaldúa, eds. *This Bridge Called My Back: Writings by Radical Women of Color.* Watertown, Mass.: Persephone Press, 1981.

Niatum, Duane, ed. *Carriers of the Dream Wheel, Contemporary Native American Poetry.* New York: Harper and Row, 1975.

North, Joseph, ed. *New Masses: An Anthology of the Rebel Thirties.* New York: International Publishers, 1969.

Randall, Dudley, ed. *The Black Poets.* New York: Bantam Books, 1971.

Simon, Myron, ed. *Ethnic Writers in America.* New York: Harcourt Brace Jovanovich, 1972.

Steiner, Stan, and Luis Valdez, eds. *Aztlán: An Anthology of Mexican American Literature.* New York: Random House, 1972.

Stetson, Arlene, ed. *Black Sister: Poetry by Black American Women 1746–1980.* Bloomington: Indiana University Press, 1981.

Troupe, Quincy, and Rainer Schulte, eds. *Giant Talk: An Anthology of Third World Writing.* New York: Random House, 1975.

Young, Ian, ed. *The Male Muse: A Gay Anthology.* Trumansburg, N.Y.: Crossing Press, 1973.

———. *Son of the Male Muse: New Gay Poetry.* Trumansburg, N.Y.: Crossing Press, 1983.

Biographical Notes

Steve Abbott studied poetry with Karl Shapiro and John Berryman and has taught writing at Emory University. He has published three books of poetry and edited *Poetry Flash* from 1979 to 1985 as well as the magazine *Soup* from 1980 to 1985. He has read at the One World Poetry Festival in Amsterdam and the Village Voice Bookstore in Paris. He taught a gay poetry workshop for the James White School in Wisconsin and currently teaches writing at the University of San Francisco.

Kathleen Aguero is the author of a collection of poems, *Thirsty Day* (Alice James Books, 1977), and has a new collection, *The Real Weather*, from Hanging Loose Press. A recipient of a Massachusetts Artists Fellowship in poetry, she has also published reviews. She has taught writing and worked in the Poets-in-Residence Program for many years and is now working as a children's librarian. She lives in Somerville, Massachusetts.

Juan Bruce-Novoa currently teaches in San Antonio, Texas, in the Foreign Languages Department of Trinity University. His books include *Inocencia Porversa/Perverse Innocence* (poetry); *Chicano Authors: Inquiry by Interview; Chicano Poetry: A Response to Chaos*. His articles, reviews, and fiction have been published in major journals in the United States, Latin America, and Europe. He is currently developing an international association of scholars to focus on Latino cultures of the United States.

Joseph Bruchac and his wife are editors and publishers of the multi-cultural literary magazine *The Greenfield Review*. His own books include collections of poetry, novels, and retellings of Native American folk tales. His newest, *Iroquois Stories*, was published in 1986 by the Crossing Press and his bool: of interviews with American Indian poets will be published in 1987 by the University of Arizona Press.

Billy Collins has published two books of poetry: *Pokerface* (Kenmore Press) and *Video Poems* (Applezaba Press). His work has appeared in periodicals such as *Paris Review, Field, Ploughshares, Rolling Stone, Florida Review,* and *Sierra Madre Review.* He teaches at Lehman College in New York.

John F. Crawford has taught at seven U.S. colleges and universities, worked as a journalist and a typesetter, and served as editor and publisher of *West End* magazine (1971 to 1976) and West End Press (1976 to present). His press has published such writers as Meridel LeSueur, Thomas McGrath, Don West, Sharon Doubiago, Wendy Rose, Cherríe Moraga, and Nellie Wong: forty-three volumes in all, of which twenty-five are in print. He is currently lecturer in English at the University of New Mexico.

Martín Espada is the author of *The Immigrant Iceboy's Bolero* (Waterfront Press) and *Trumpets from the Islands of Their Eviction* (Bilingual Press). Espada has been awarded a 1984 Massachusetts Artists' Foundation Fellowship and a 1986 National Endowment for the Arts Creative Writing Fellowship. He notes that "Documentaries and Declamadores" was written, not by a scholar or critic, but from the perspective of a participant-observer in the community of Puerto Rican poets here in the United States.

Marie Harris is the author of two volumes of poetry: *Raw Honey* (Alice James Books, 1975) and *Interstate* (Slow Loris Press, 1980). She works as writer-in-residence for the New Hampshire Council on the Arts and is a partner with her husband, Charter Weeks, in Isinglass Studio, an industrial advertising agency.

Rudy Kikel writes frequently for the gay press—the Los Angeles *Advocate*, Philadelphia's *Gay News*, and Boston's *Bay Windows*—on subjects ranging from gay male poetry to lesbian powerlifting. He's the arts and entertainment editor of *Bay Windows* and one of that newspaper's two poetry editors. His book of poems, *Lasting Relations*, was published in 1984 by Sea Horse Press.

Annette Kolodny, professor of literature at Rensselaer Polytechnic Institute, is the author of *The Lay of the Land: Metaphor as Experience and*

History in American Life and Letters (1975), *The Land before Her: Fantasy and Experience of the American Frontiers, 1620–1860* (1984), and many prize-winning articles on feminist criticism and American women writers.

Lynda Koolish's work has appeared in *Signs, The Women's Review of Books, Feminist Studies, Sinister Wisdom,* and elsewhere. Indiana University Press is publishing a collection of essays by contemporary American women poets which she is editing called *What Moves Me Brings Me to Myself.* She is currently revising a book-length critical study of contemporary American feminist poetry and is at work on a book on the slave narrative tradition in Afro-American women writers from the Harlem Renaissance to the present.

P. J. Laska lives near Seattle. He is working on his second novel.

Paul Lauter directs "Reconstructing American Literature," a project funded by FIPSE, the Lilly Endowment, and the Rockefeller Foundation aimed at changing the teaching of American literature so that it reflects the full range of voices in American culture—women as well as men, minorities as well as whites. He is currently coordinating editor for a new two-volume anthology of American literature to be published by D. C. Heath in 1989. He edited *Reconstructing American Literature,* a collection of syllabi and course materials. He is co-author of "The Impact of Women's Studies on Curriculum and Campus" (NIE, 1980), author of "Race and Gender in the Shaping of the American Literary Canon," *Feminist Studies* (1983), and a theoretical study directed to the marginalization of women and minority American writers.

George Ella Lyon works as a writer and teacher in Lexington, Kentucky. Her publications include *Mountain,* a chapbook (Andrew Mountain Press, 1983), *Father Time and the Day Boxes,* a children's book (Bradbury Press, 1985), and *Common Ground,* an anthology which she co-edited with Gurney Norman and Bob Henry Baber (Jalamap, 1985). Her play, *Braids,* was produced in April 1985 at Transylvania University through the support of the Kentucky Arts Council.

Adrian Oktenberg is currently working on a novel set in the sixties. Her work appears frequently in *The Women's Review of Books* and other feminist publications.

Richard Oyama was coordinator of the Basement Writers Workshop, an Asian American community arts organization in New York, from

1974 to 1978. He co-edited *American Born and Foreign*, an anthology of Asian American poetry, published by Sunbury Press in 1979. His poems, essays, and critiques have appeared in *downbeat, Greenfield Review, Bridge, East Wind, Sunbury, Time Capsule*, and numerous other publications.

Raymond R. Patterson teaches at the City College of the City University of New York. He is the author of two collections of poems, *26 Ways of Looking at a Black Man and Other Poems* and *Elemental Blues*.

Carmen Tafolla is a writer and educator. The former director of the Mexican American Studies Center at Texas Lutheran College, head writer for the bilingual children's TV series *Sonrisas*, and presently associate professor of women's studies at California State University, Fresno, she is currently on leave doing full-time writing on a novel and several collections of poetry in Flagstaff, Arizona. Among her publications are three books of poetry and a book on racism, sexism, and Chicana women entitled *To Split a Human: Mitos, Machos y la Mujer Chicana*.

EP151